SB
Shojo Beat

Demon Love Spell

1

STORY AND
ART BY
**MAYU
SHINJO**

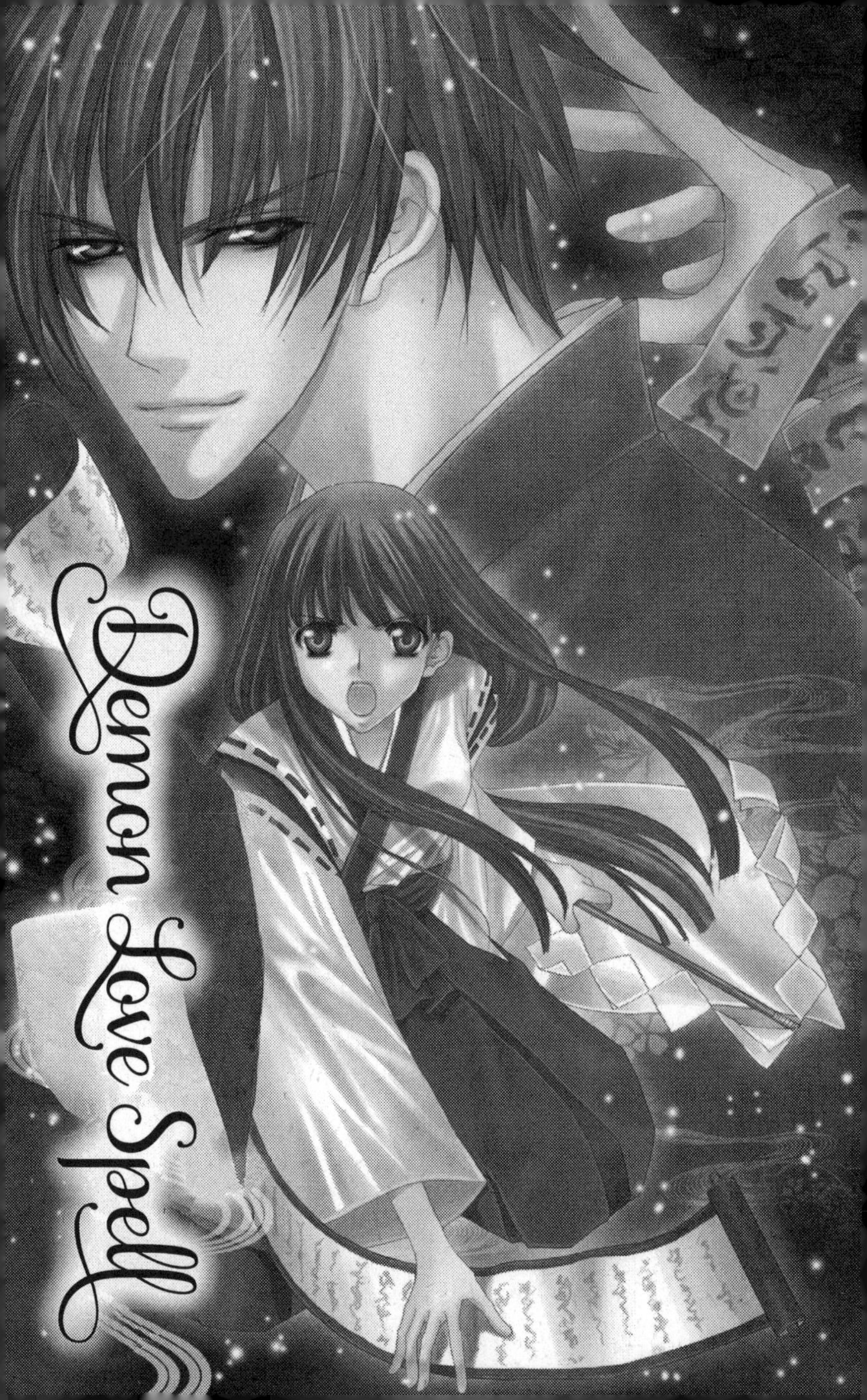
Demon Love Spell

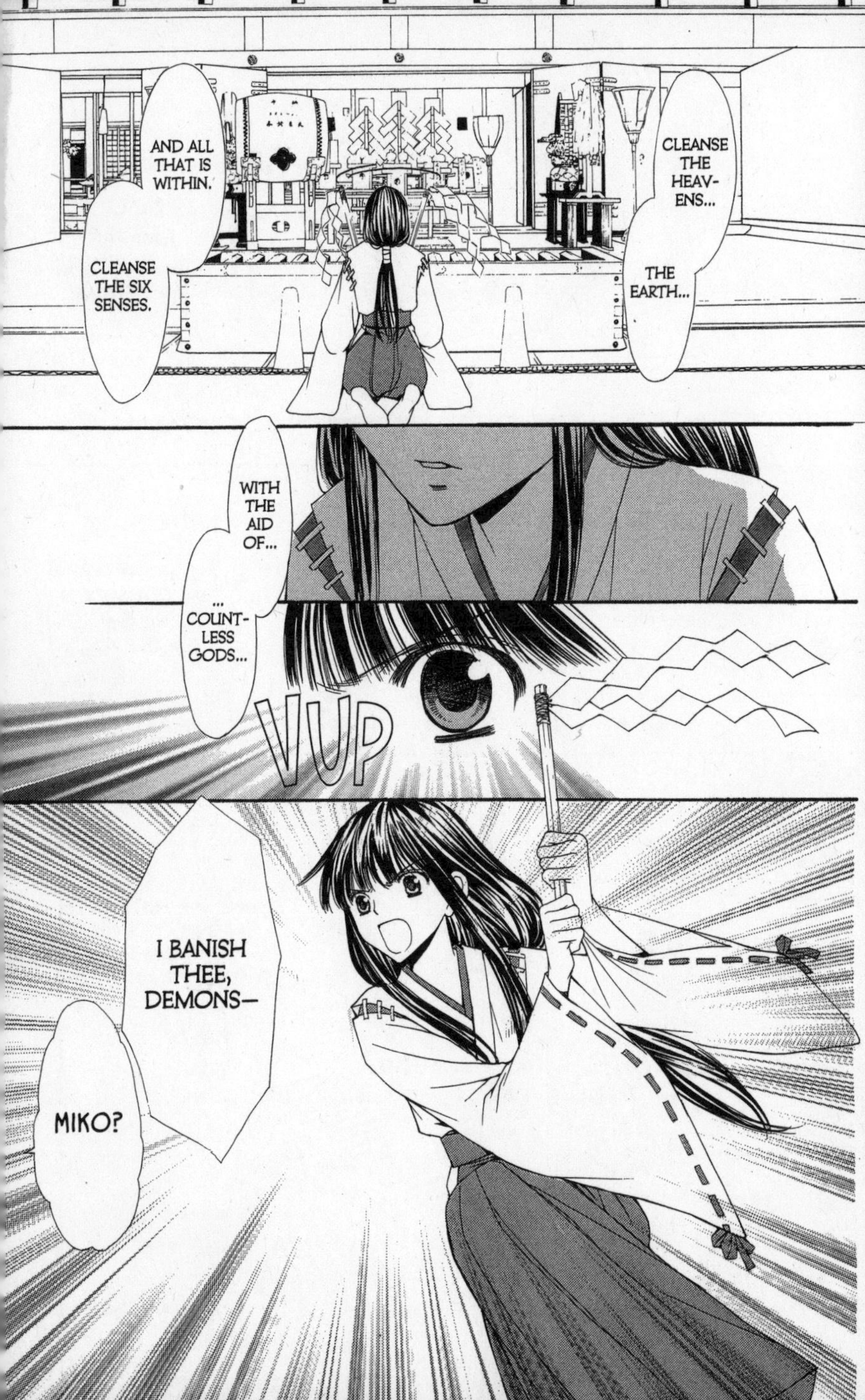

CLEANSE THE HEAVENS...
THE EARTH...
AND ALL THAT IS WITHIN.
CLEANSE THE SIX SENSES.
WITH THE AID OF...
... COUNTLESS GODS...
VUP
I BANISH THEE, DEMONS—
MIKO?

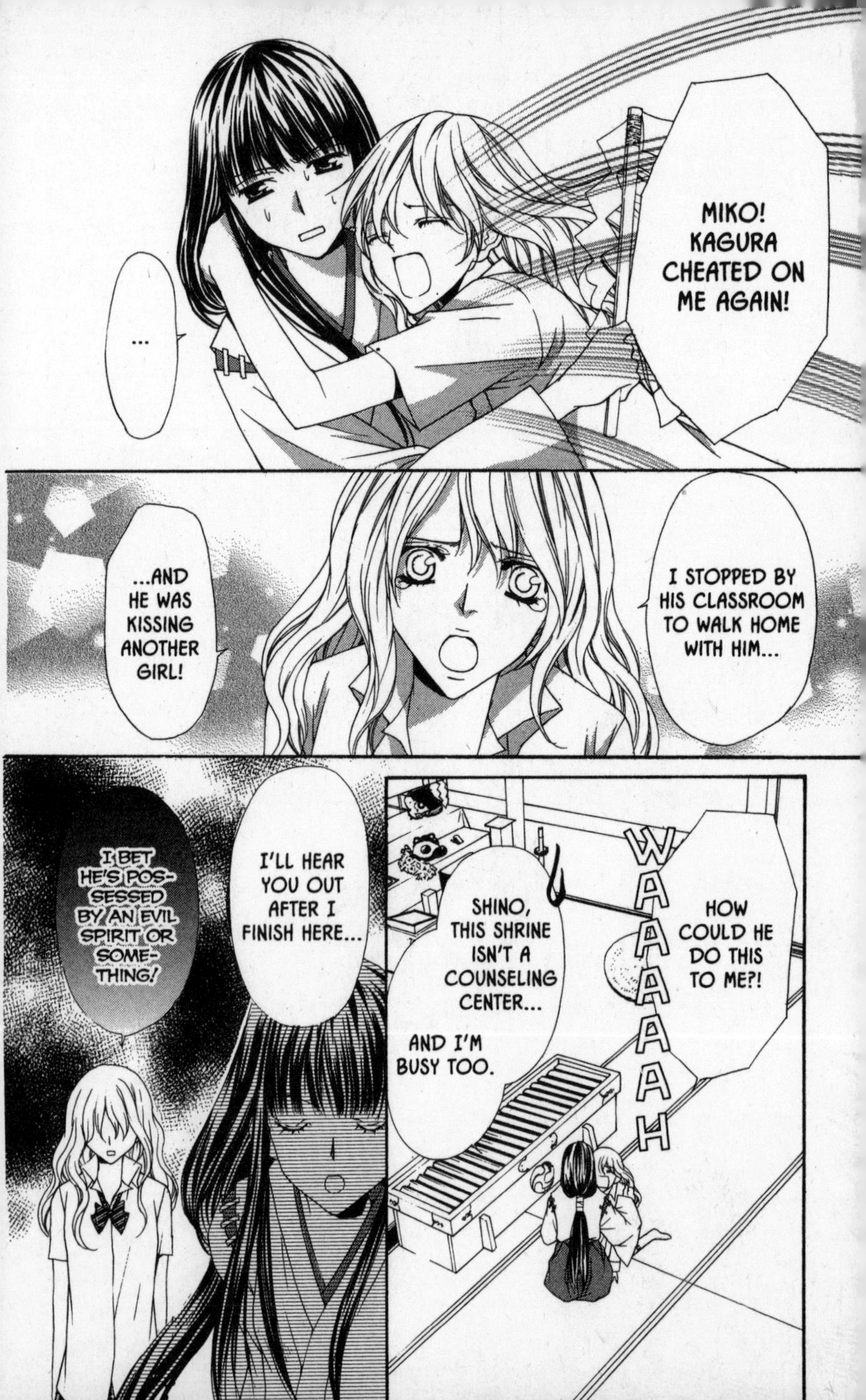
MIKO! KAGURA CHEATED ON ME AGAIN!
...
I STOPPED BY HIS CLASSROOM TO WALK HOME WITH HIM...
...AND HE WAS KISSING ANOTHER GIRL!
HOW COULD HE DO THIS TO ME?!
WAAAAAH
SHINO, THIS SHRINE ISN'T A COUNSELING CENTER...
AND I'M BUSY TOO.
I'LL HEAR YOU OUT AFTER I FINISH HERE...
I BET HE'S POS-SESSED BY AN EVIL SPIRIT OR SOME-THING!

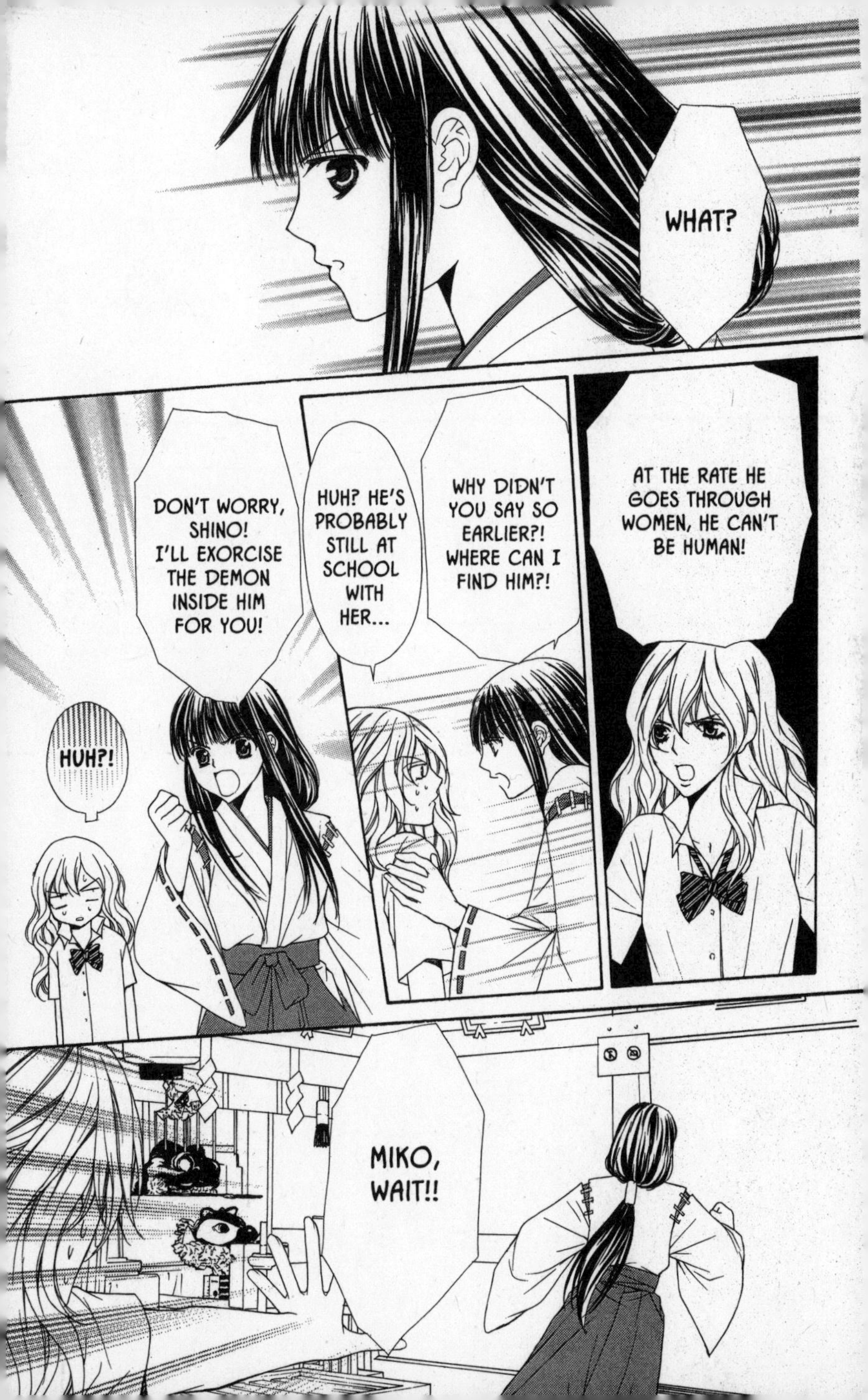
WHAT?
AT THE RATE HE GOES THROUGH WOMEN, HE CAN'T BE HUMAN!
WHY DIDN'T YOU SAY SO EARLIER?! WHERE CAN I FIND HIM?!
HUH? HE'S PROBABLY STILL AT SCHOOL WITH HER...
DON'T WORRY, SHINO! I'LL EXORCISE THE DEMON INSIDE HIM FOR YOU!
HUH?!
MIKO, WAIT!!

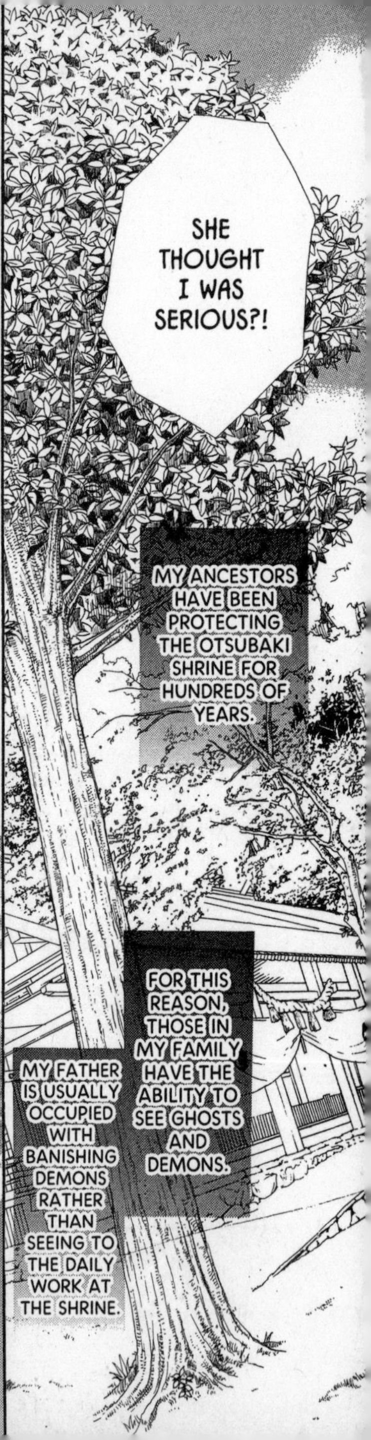
SHE THOUGHT I WAS SERIOUS?!
MY ANCESTORS HAVE BEEN PROTECTING THE OTSUBAKI SHRINE FOR HUNDREDS OF YEARS.
FOR THIS REASON, THOSE IN MY FAMILY HAVE THE ABILITY TO SEE GHOSTS AND DEMONS.
MY FATHER IS USUALLY OCCUPIED WITH BANISHING DEMONS RATHER THAN SEEING TO THE DAILY WORK AT THE SHRINE.

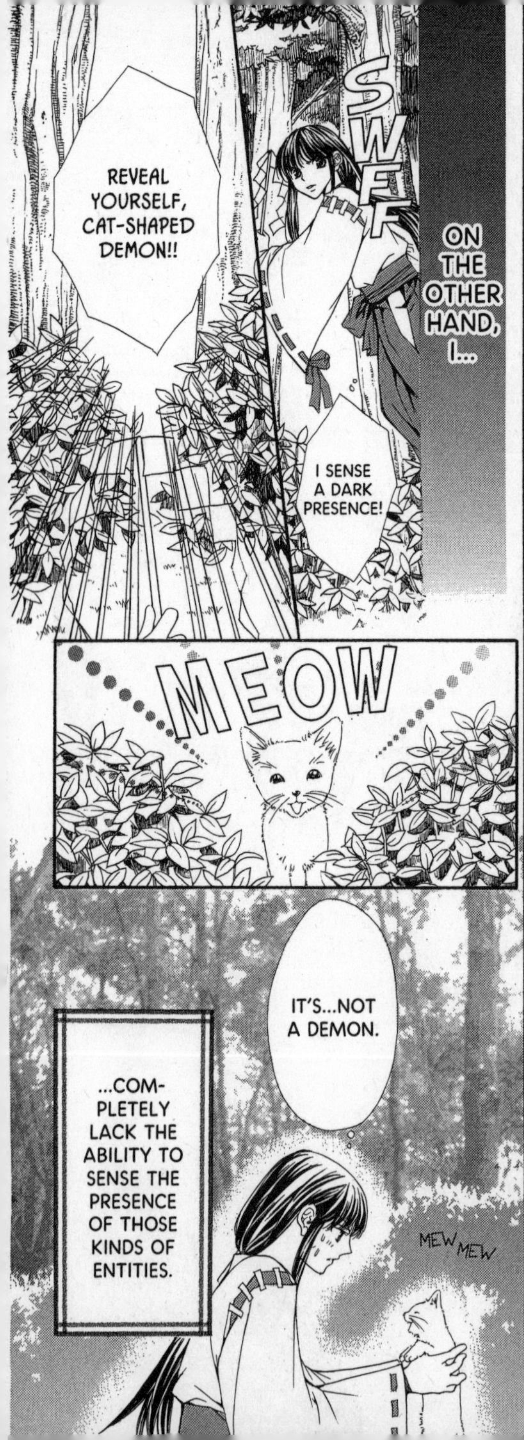
ON THE OTHER HAND, I...
SWFF
I SENSE A DARK PRESENCE!
REVEAL YOURSELF, CAT-SHAPED DEMON!!
MEOW
IT'S...NOT A DEMON.
MEW MEW
...COM-PLETELY LACK THE ABILITY TO SENSE THE PRESENCE OF THOSE KINDS OF ENTITIES.

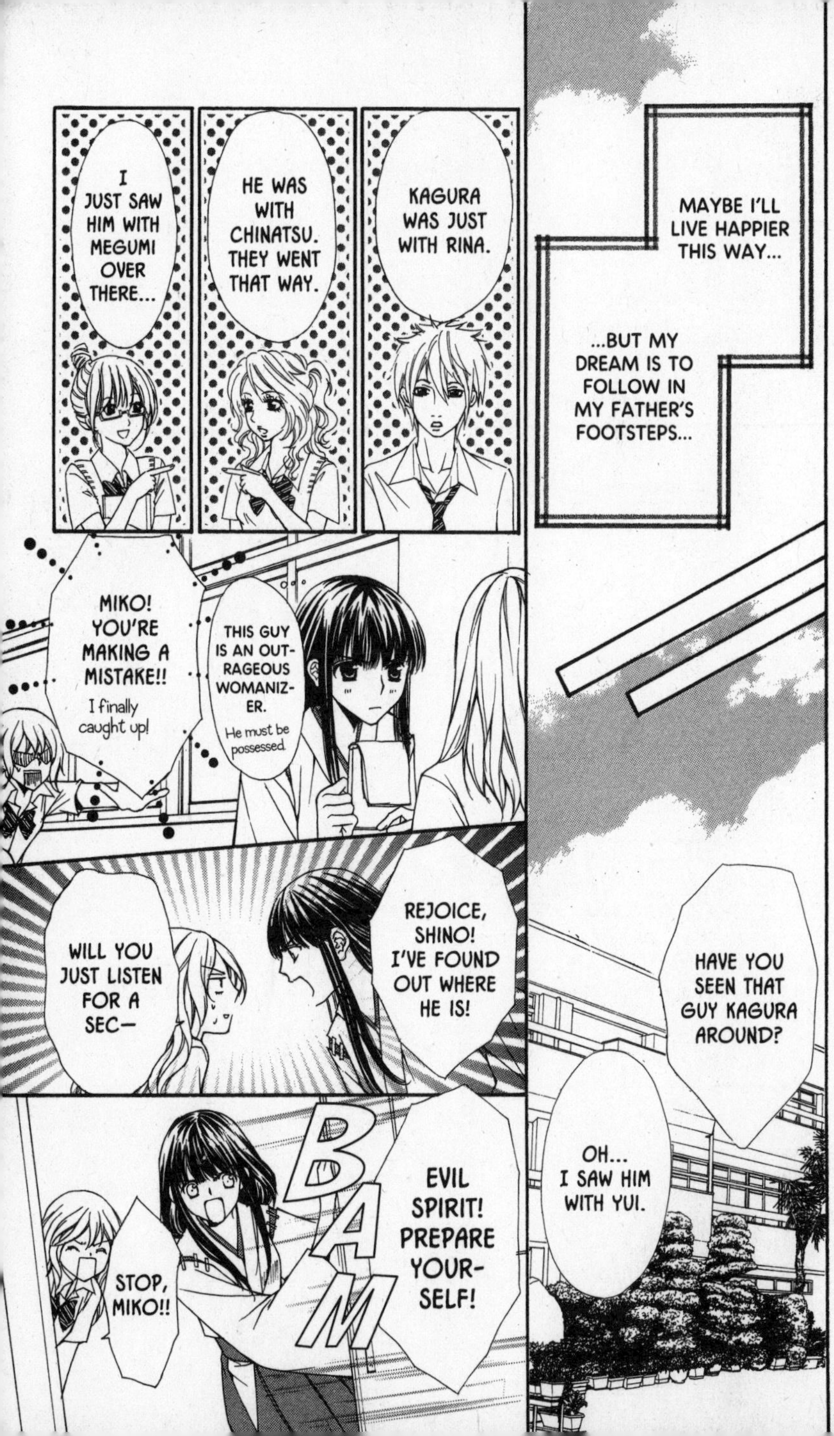
MAYBE I'LL LIVE HAPPIER THIS WAY...
...BUT MY DREAM IS TO FOLLOW IN MY FATHER'S FOOTSTEPS...
HAVE YOU SEEN THAT GUY KAGURA AROUND?
OH... I SAW HIM WITH YUI.
KAGURA WAS JUST WITH RINA.
HE WAS WITH CHINATSU. THEY WENT THAT WAY.
I JUST SAW HIM WITH MEGUMI OVER THERE...
THIS GUY IS AN OUTRAGEOUS WOMANIZER.
He must be possessed.
MIKO! YOU'RE MAKING A MISTAKE!!
I finally caught up!
REJOICE, SHINO! I'VE FOUND OUT WHERE HE IS!
WILL YOU JUST LISTEN FOR A SEC—
EVIL SPIRIT! PREPARE YOURSELF!
BAM
STOP, MIKO!!

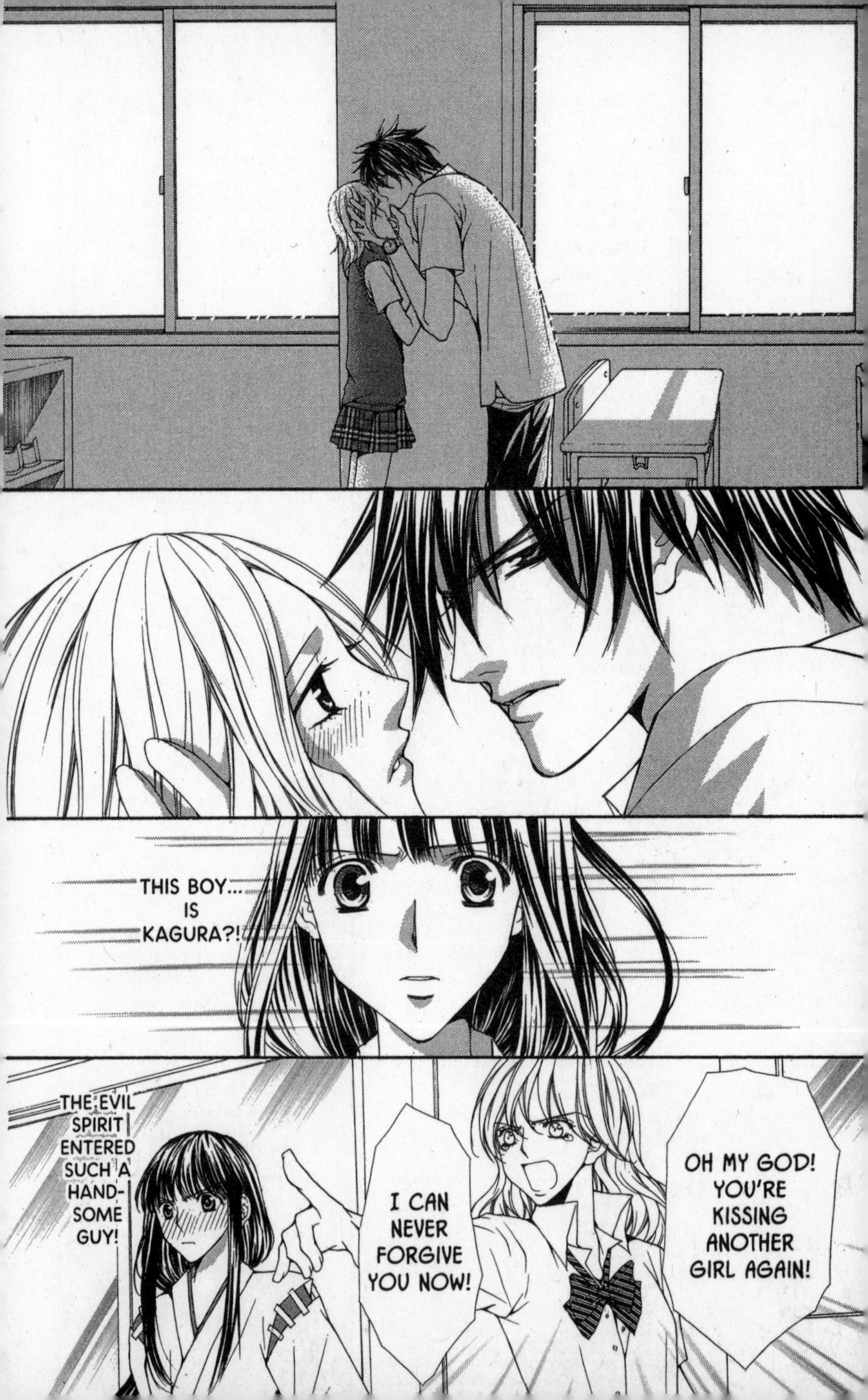
THIS BOY... IS KAGURA?!
OH MY GOD! YOU'RE KISSING ANOTHER GIRL AGAIN!
I CAN NEVER FORGIVE YOU NOW!
THE EVIL SPIRIT ENTERED SUCH A HAND-SOME GUY!

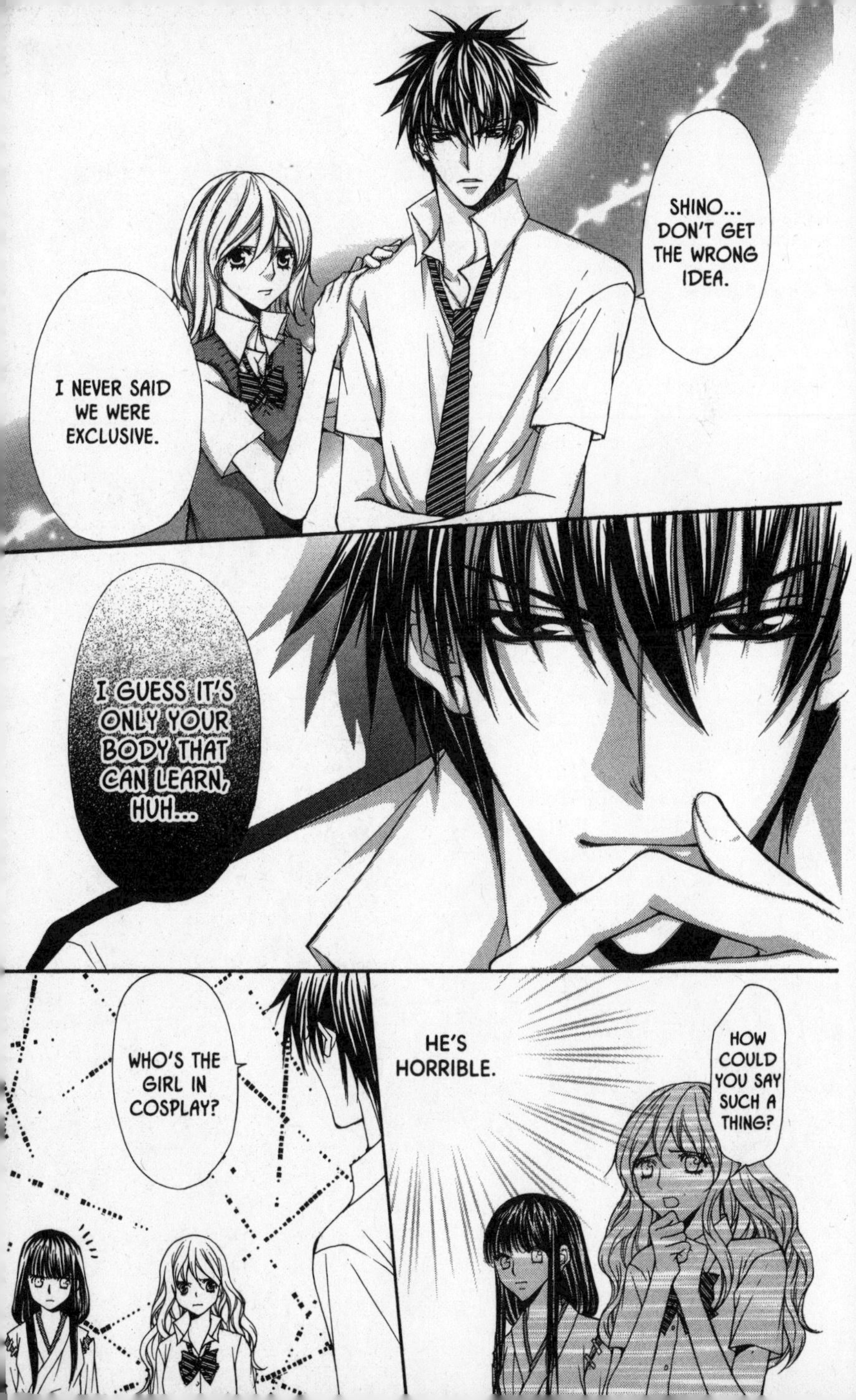
SHINO... DON'T GET THE WRONG IDEA.
I NEVER SAID WE WERE EXCLUSIVE.
I GUESS IT'S ONLY YOUR BODY THAT CAN LEARN, HUH...
HOW COULD YOU SAY SUCH A THING?
HE'S HORRIBLE.
WHO'S THE GIRL IN COSPLAY?

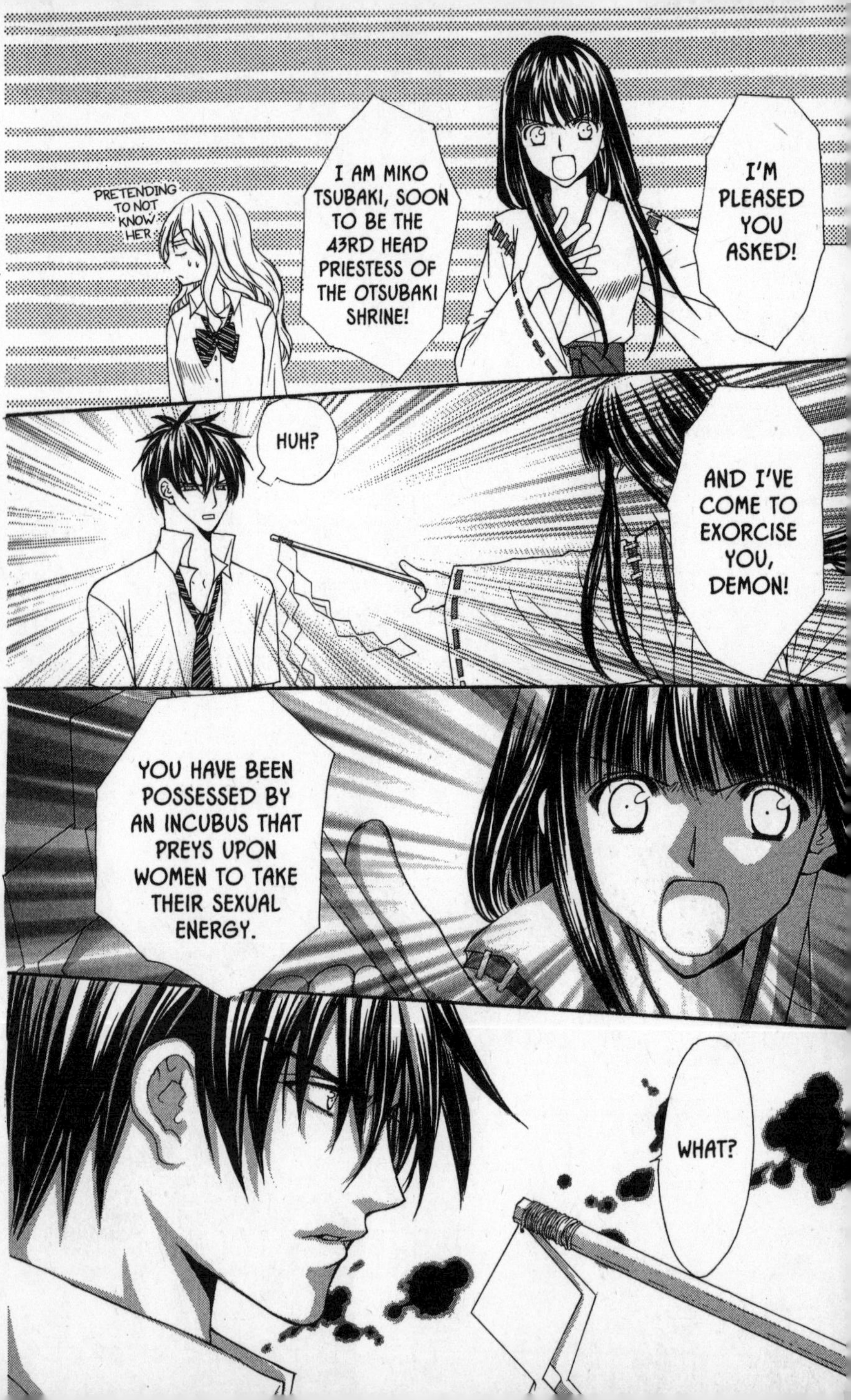
I'M PLEASED YOU ASKED!
I AM MIKO TSUBAKI, SOON TO BE THE 43RD HEAD PRIESTESS OF THE OTSUBAKI SHRINE!
PRETENDING TO NOT KNOW HER
AND I'VE COME TO EXORCISE YOU, DEMON!
HUH?
YOU HAVE BEEN POSSESSED BY AN INCUBUS THAT PREYS UPON WOMEN TO TAKE THEIR SEXUAL ENERGY.
WHAT?

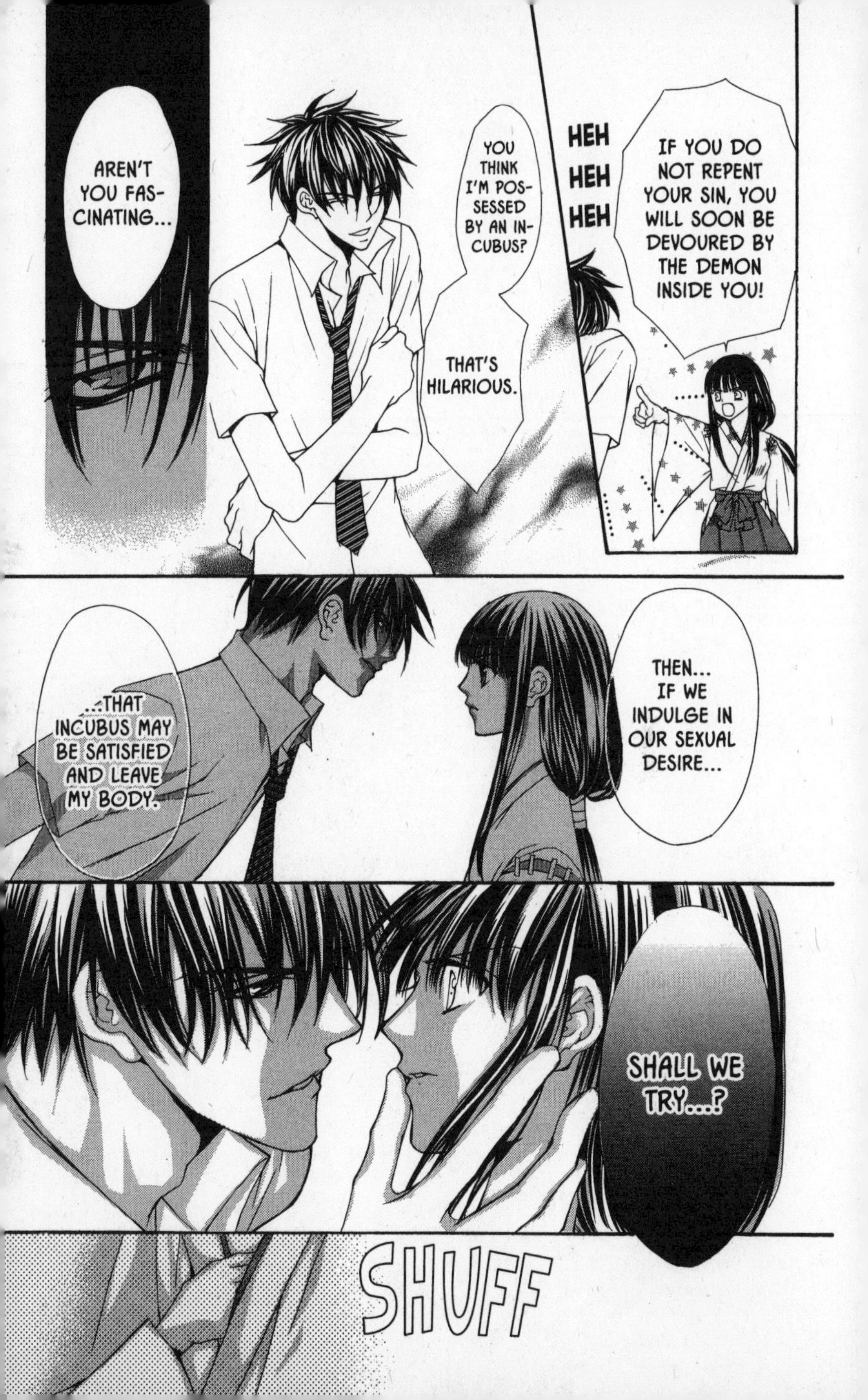
IF YOU DO NOT REPENT YOUR SIN, YOU WILL SOON BE DEVOURED BY THE DEMON INSIDE YOU!
HEH HEH HEH
YOU THINK I'M POS-SESSED BY AN IN-CUBUS?
THAT'S HILARIOUS.
AREN'T YOU FAS-CINATING...
THEN... IF WE INDULGE IN OUR SEXUAL DESIRE...
...THAT INCUBUS MAY BE SATISFIED AND LEAVE MY BODY.
SHALL WE TRY...?
SHUFF

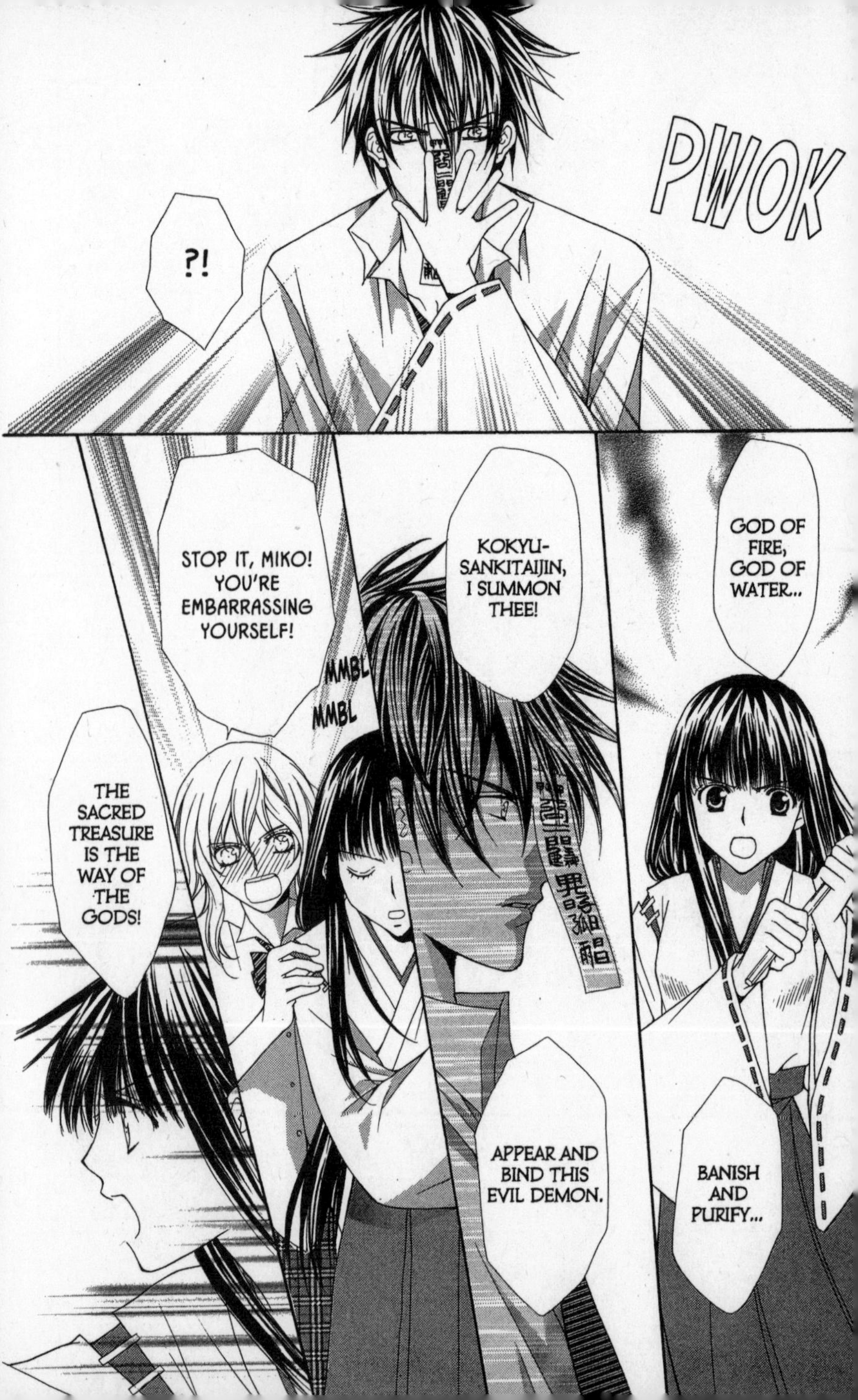
PWOK
?!
GOD OF FIRE, GOD OF WATER...
BANISH AND PURIFY...
KOKYU-SANKITAIJIN, I SUMMON THEE!
APPEAR AND BIND THIS EVIL DEMON.
STOP IT, MIKO! YOU'RE EMBARRASSING YOURSELF!
MMBL
MMBL
THE SACRED TREASURE IS THE WAY OF THE GODS!

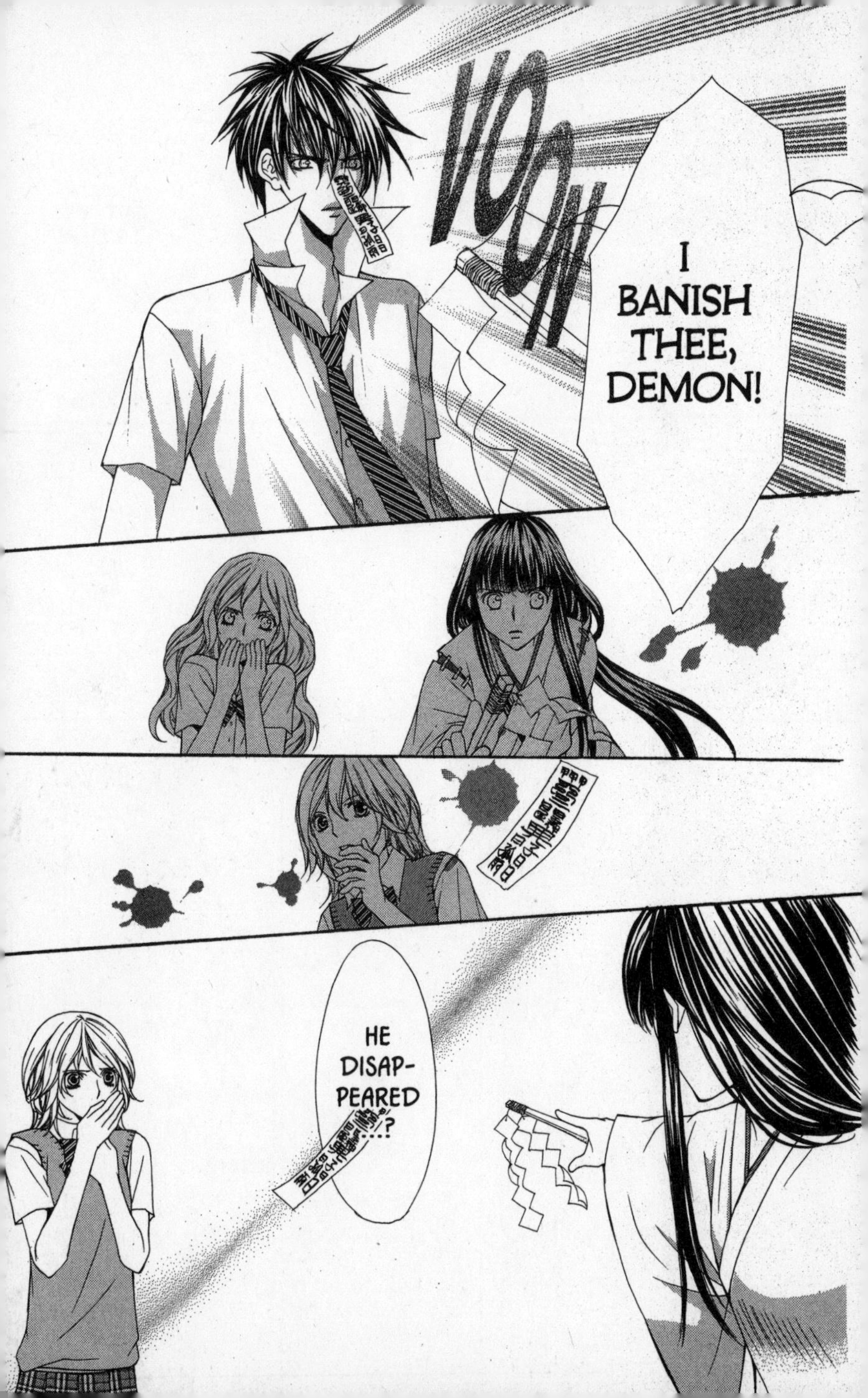
VOOM
I BANISH THEE, DEMON!
HE DISAP-PEARED ......?

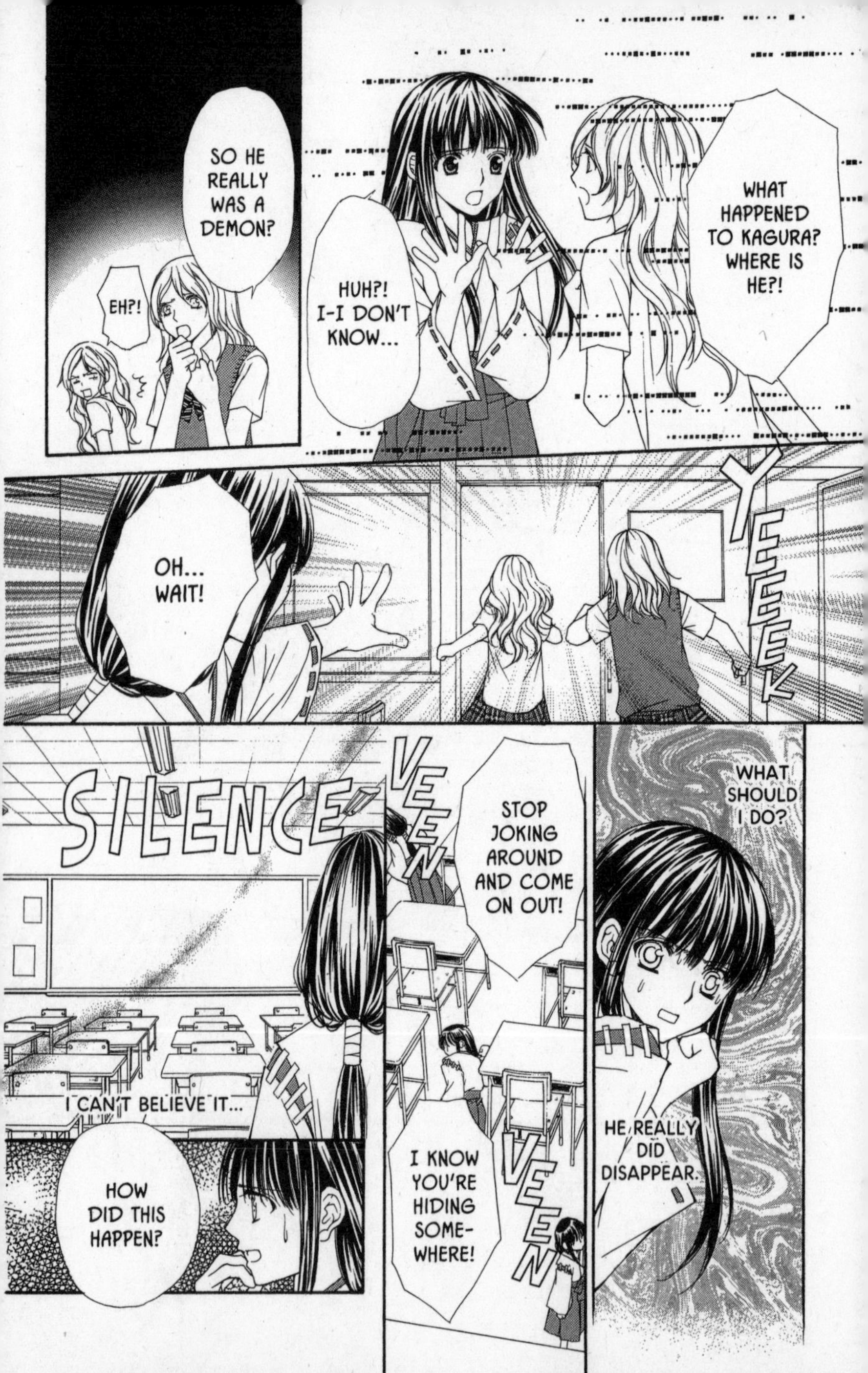
WHAT HAPPENED TO KAGURA? WHERE IS HE?!
HUH?! I-I DON'T KNOW...
SO HE REALLY WAS A DEMON?
EH?!
YEEEEK
OH... WAIT!
WHAT SHOULD I DO?
HE REALLY DID DISAPPEAR.
STOP JOKING AROUND AND COME ON OUT!
VEEN
I KNOW YOU'RE HIDING SOME-WHERE!
VEEN
SILENCE
I CAN'T BELIEVE IT...
HOW DID THIS HAPPEN?

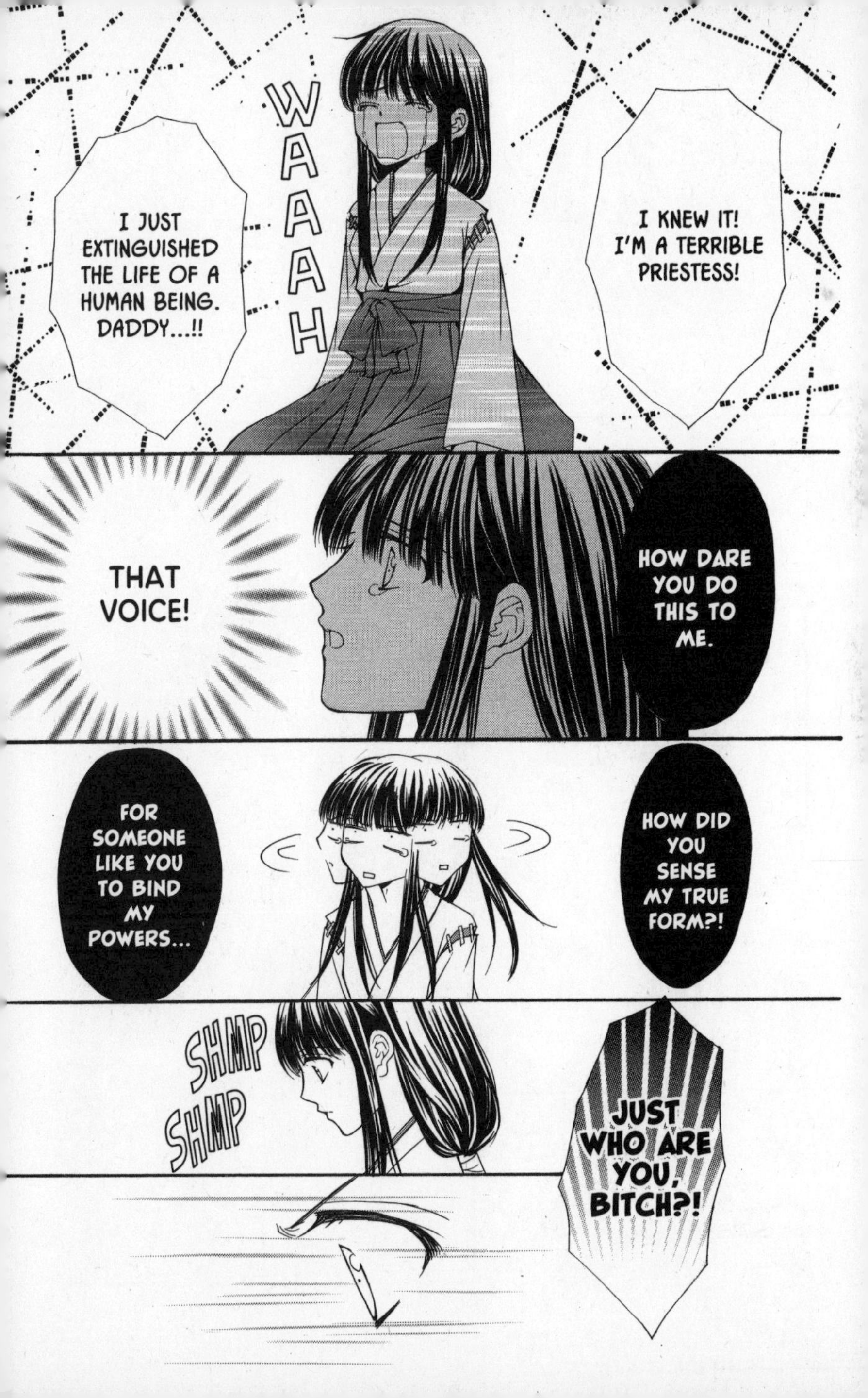
I KNEW IT! I'M A TERRIBLE PRIESTESS!
WAAAH
I JUST EXTINGUISHED THE LIFE OF A HUMAN BEING. DADDY...!!
HOW DARE YOU DO THIS TO ME.
THAT VOICE!
HOW DID YOU SENSE MY TRUE FORM?!
FOR SOMEONE LIKE YOU TO BIND MY POWERS...
JUST WHO ARE YOU, BITCH?!
SHMP SHMP

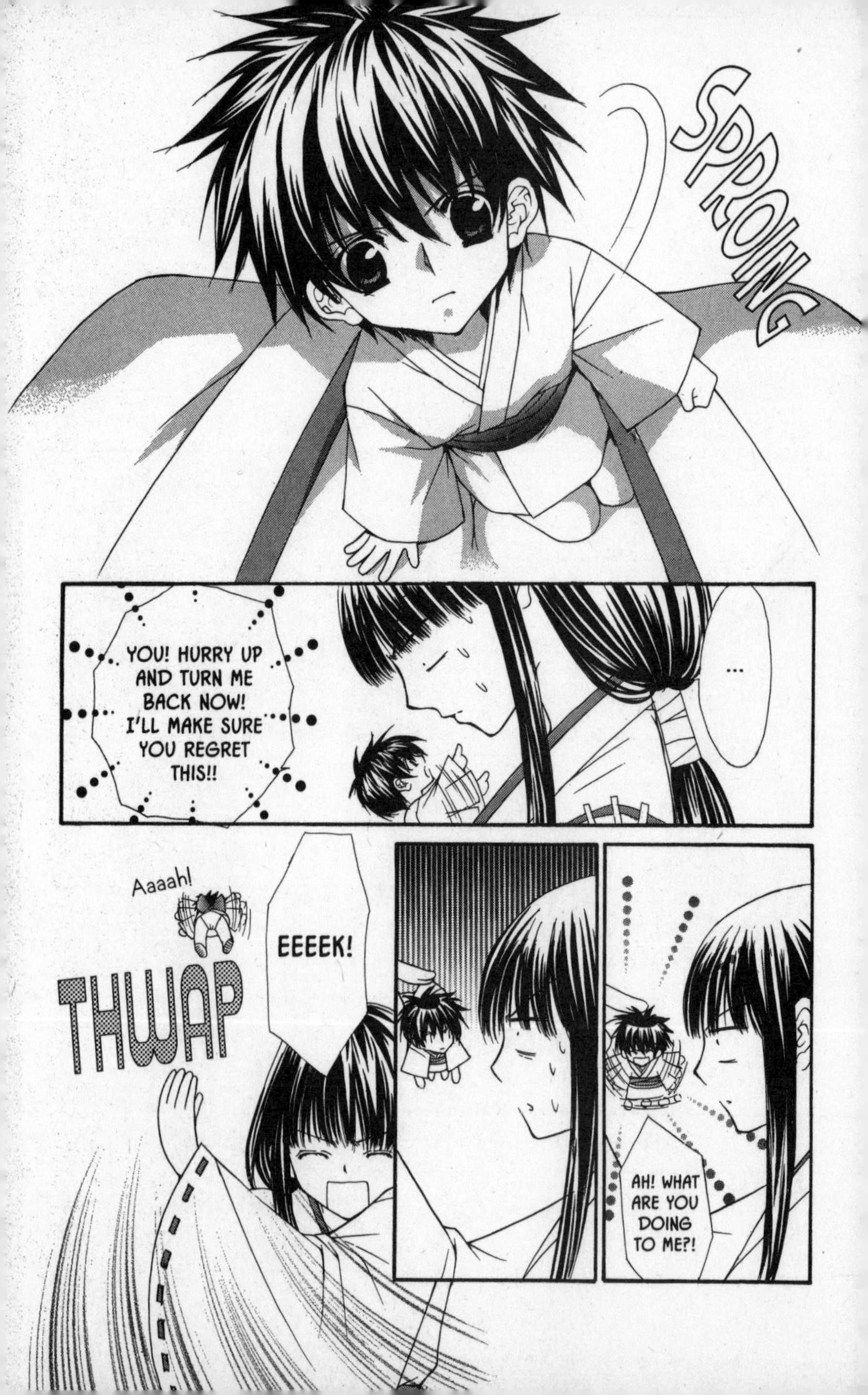
SPROING
...
YOU! HURRY UP AND TURN ME BACK NOW! I'LL MAKE SURE YOU REGRET THIS!!
AH! WHAT ARE YOU DOING TO ME?!
EEEEK!
THWAP
Aaaah!

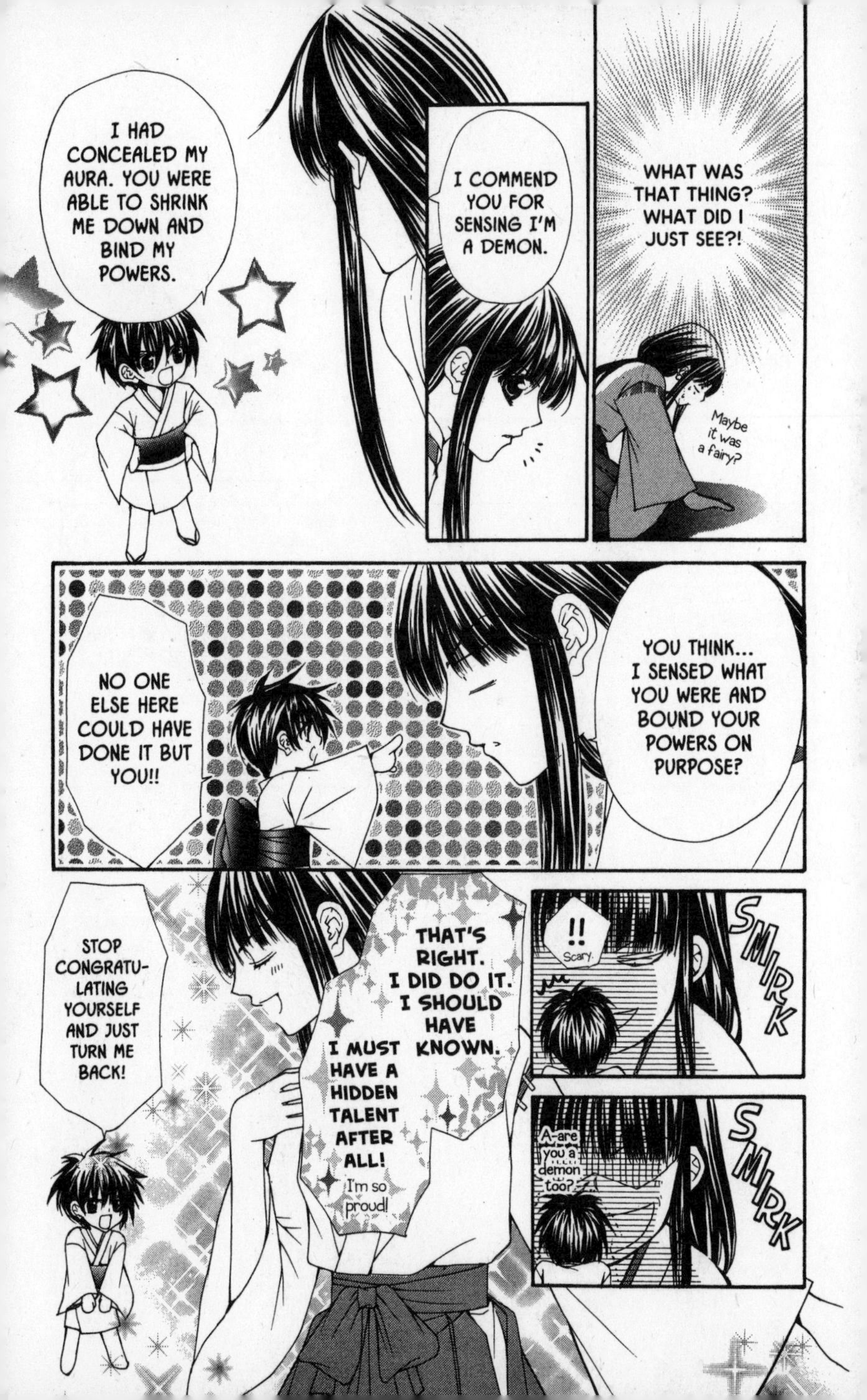
WHAT WAS THAT THING? WHAT DID I JUST SEE?!
Maybe it was a fairy?
I COMMEND YOU FOR SENSING I'M A DEMON.
I HAD CONCEALED MY AURA. YOU WERE ABLE TO SHRINK ME DOWN AND BIND MY POWERS.
YOU THINK... I SENSED WHAT YOU WERE AND BOUND YOUR POWERS ON PURPOSE?
NO ONE ELSE HERE COULD HAVE DONE IT BUT YOU!!
!!
Scary.
SMIRK
A-are you a demon too?
SMIRK
THAT'S RIGHT. I DID DO IT. I SHOULD HAVE KNOWN.
I MUST HAVE A HIDDEN TALENT AFTER ALL!
I'm so proud!
STOP CONGRATULATING YOURSELF AND JUST TURN ME BACK!

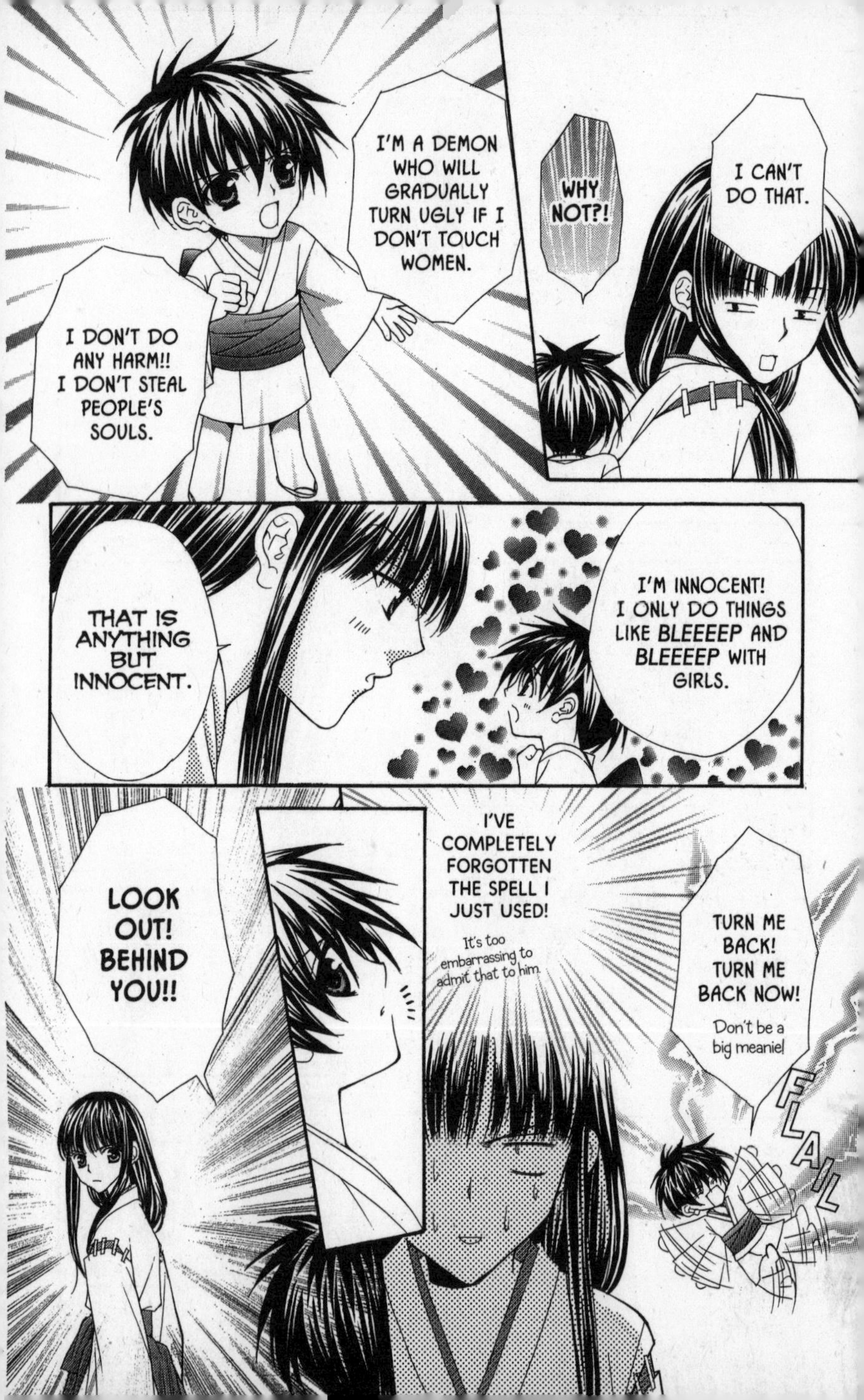
I CAN'T DO THAT.
WHY NOT?!
I'M A DEMON WHO WILL GRADUALLY TURN UGLY IF I DON'T TOUCH WOMEN.
I DON'T DO ANY HARM!! I DON'T STEAL PEOPLE'S SOULS.
I'M INNOCENT! I ONLY DO THINGS LIKE BLEEEEP AND BLEEEEP WITH GIRLS.
THAT IS ANYTHING BUT INNOCENT.
TURN ME BACK! TURN ME BACK NOW!
Don't be a big meanie!
FLAIL
I'VE COMPLETELY FORGOTTEN THE SPELL I JUST USED!
It's too embarrassing to admit that to him.
LOOK OUT! BEHIND YOU!!

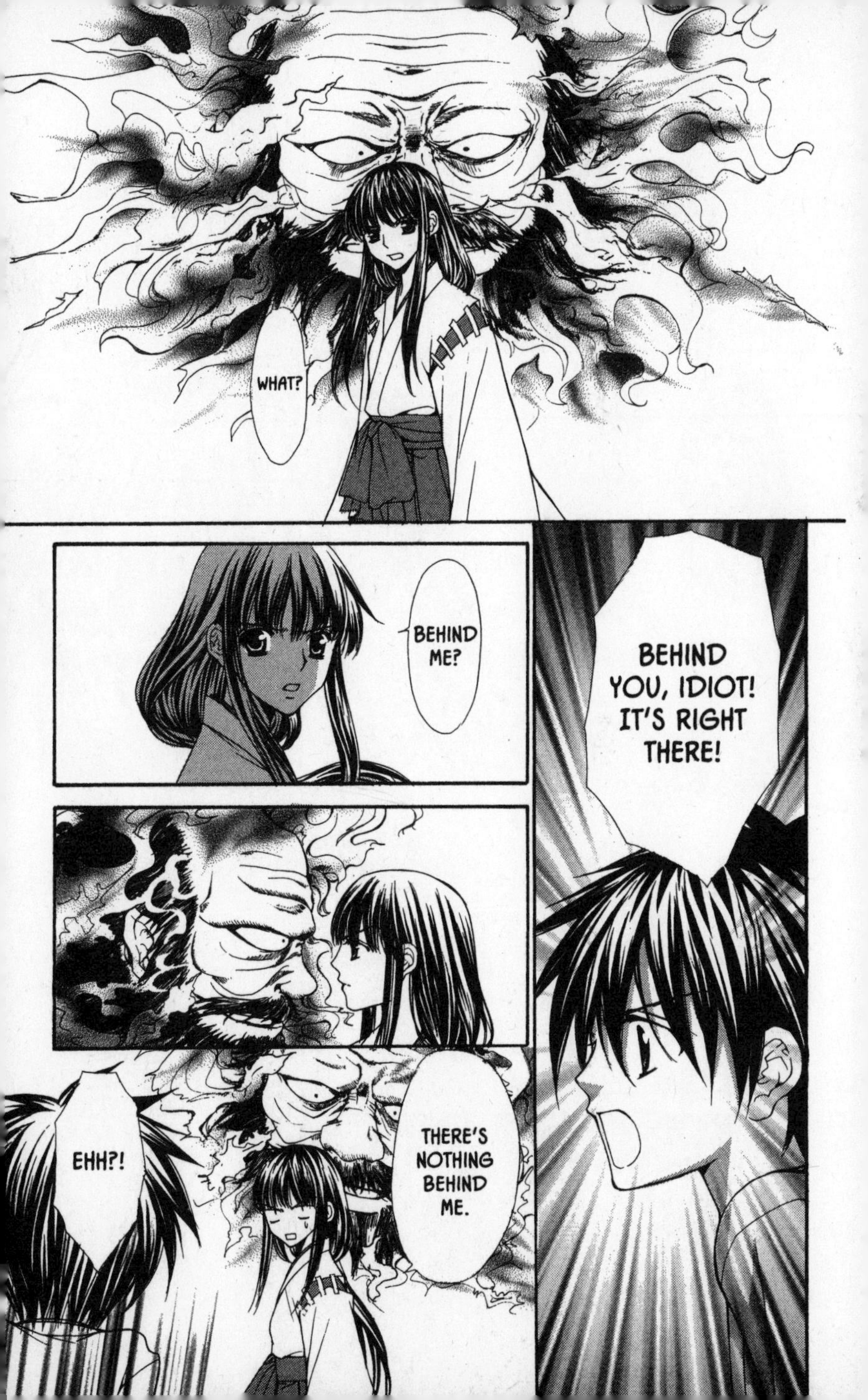
WHAT?
BEHIND YOU, IDIOT! IT'S RIGHT THERE!
BEHIND ME?
THERE'S NOTHING BEHIND ME.
EHH?!

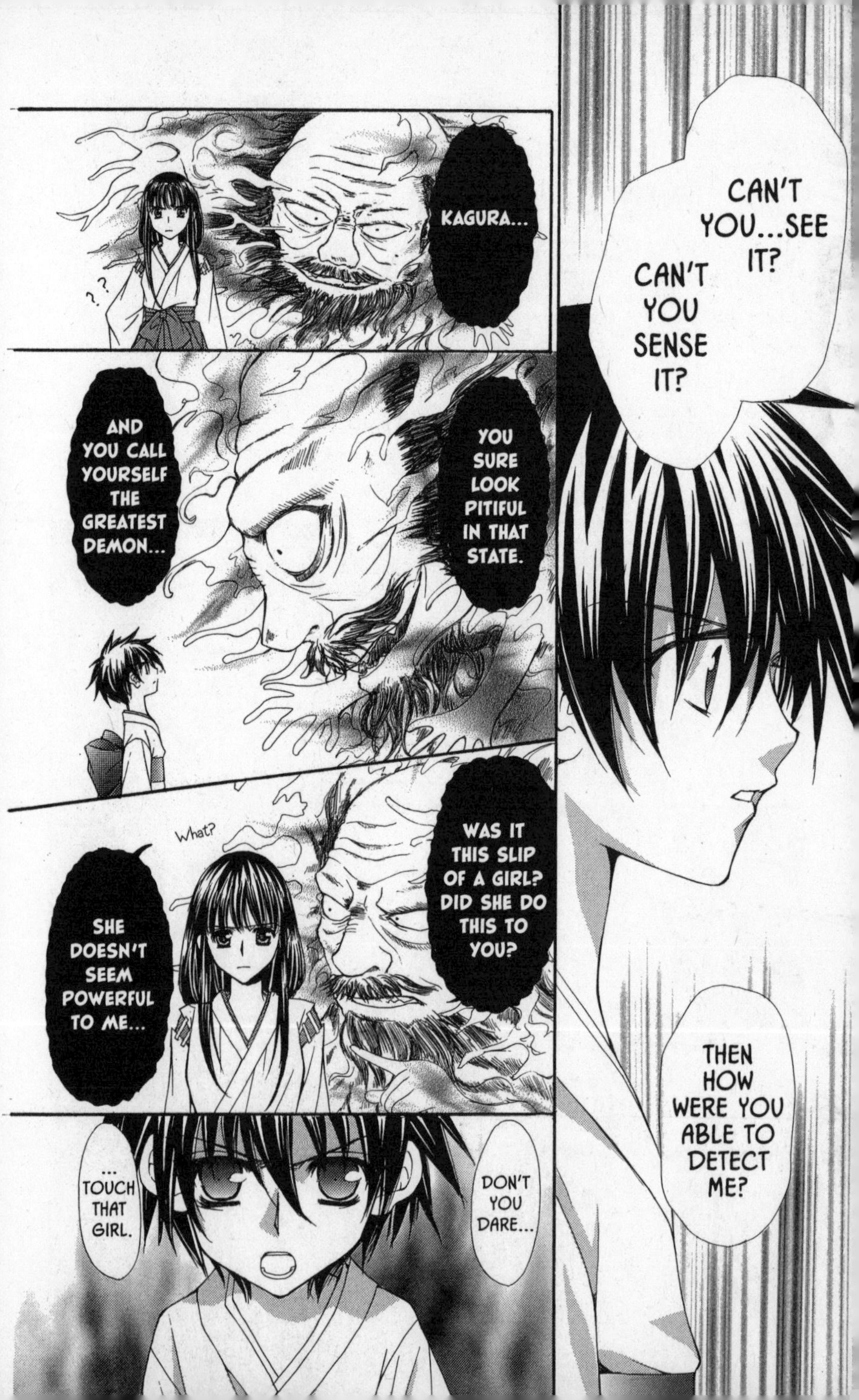
CAN'T YOU...SEE IT?
CAN'T YOU SENSE IT?
THEN HOW WERE YOU ABLE TO DETECT ME?
KAGURA...
YOU SURE LOOK PITIFUL IN THAT STATE.
AND YOU CALL YOURSELF THE GREATEST DEMON...
WAS IT THIS SLIP OF A GIRL? DID SHE DO THIS TO YOU?
What?
SHE DOESN'T SEEM POWERFUL TO ME...
DON'T YOU DARE...
...TOUCH THAT GIRL.

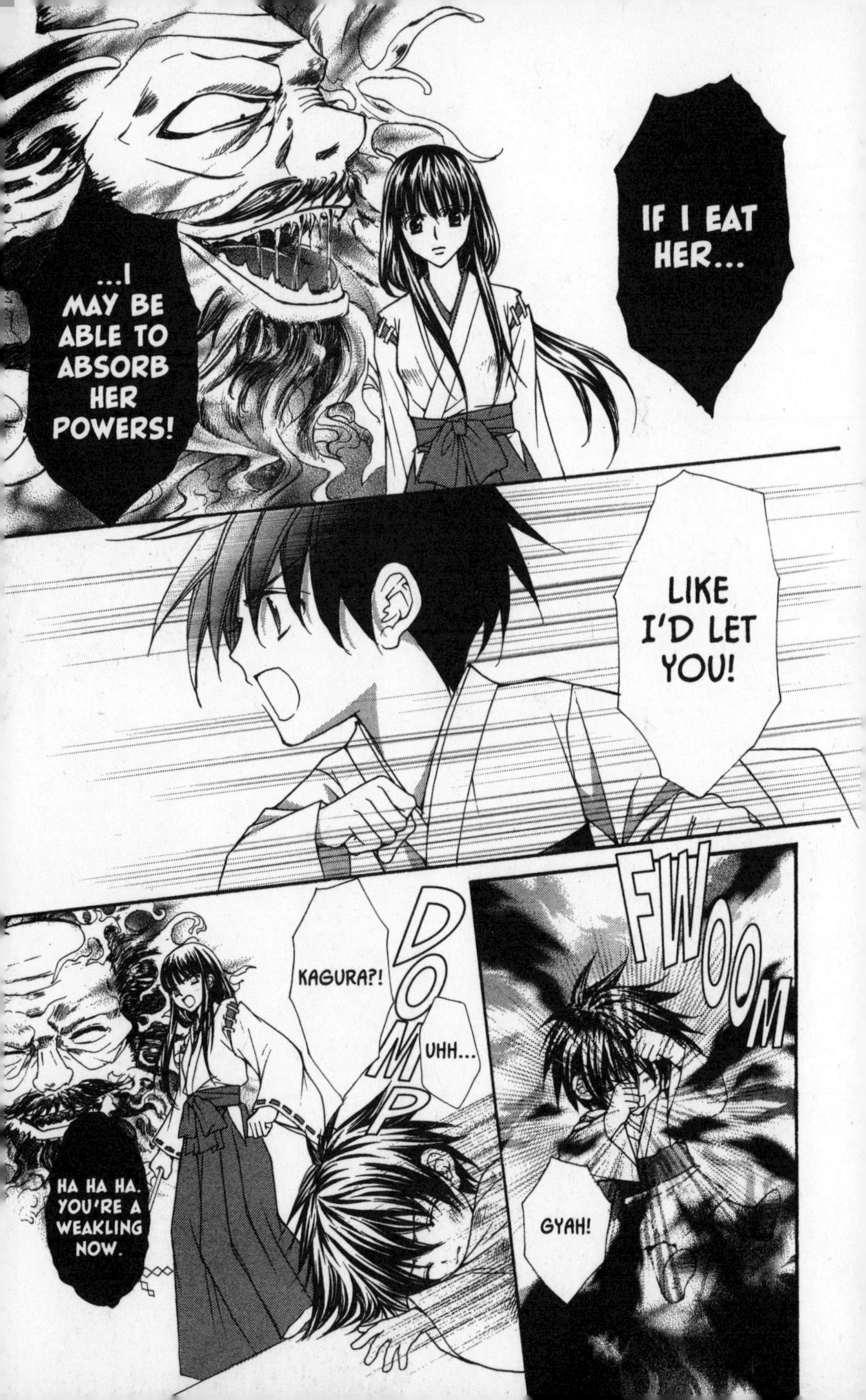
IF I EAT HER...
...I MAY BE ABLE TO ABSORB HER POWERS!
LIKE I'D LET YOU!
FWOOM
GYAH!
DOMP
KAGURA?!
UHH...
HA HA HA. YOU'RE A WEAKLING NOW.

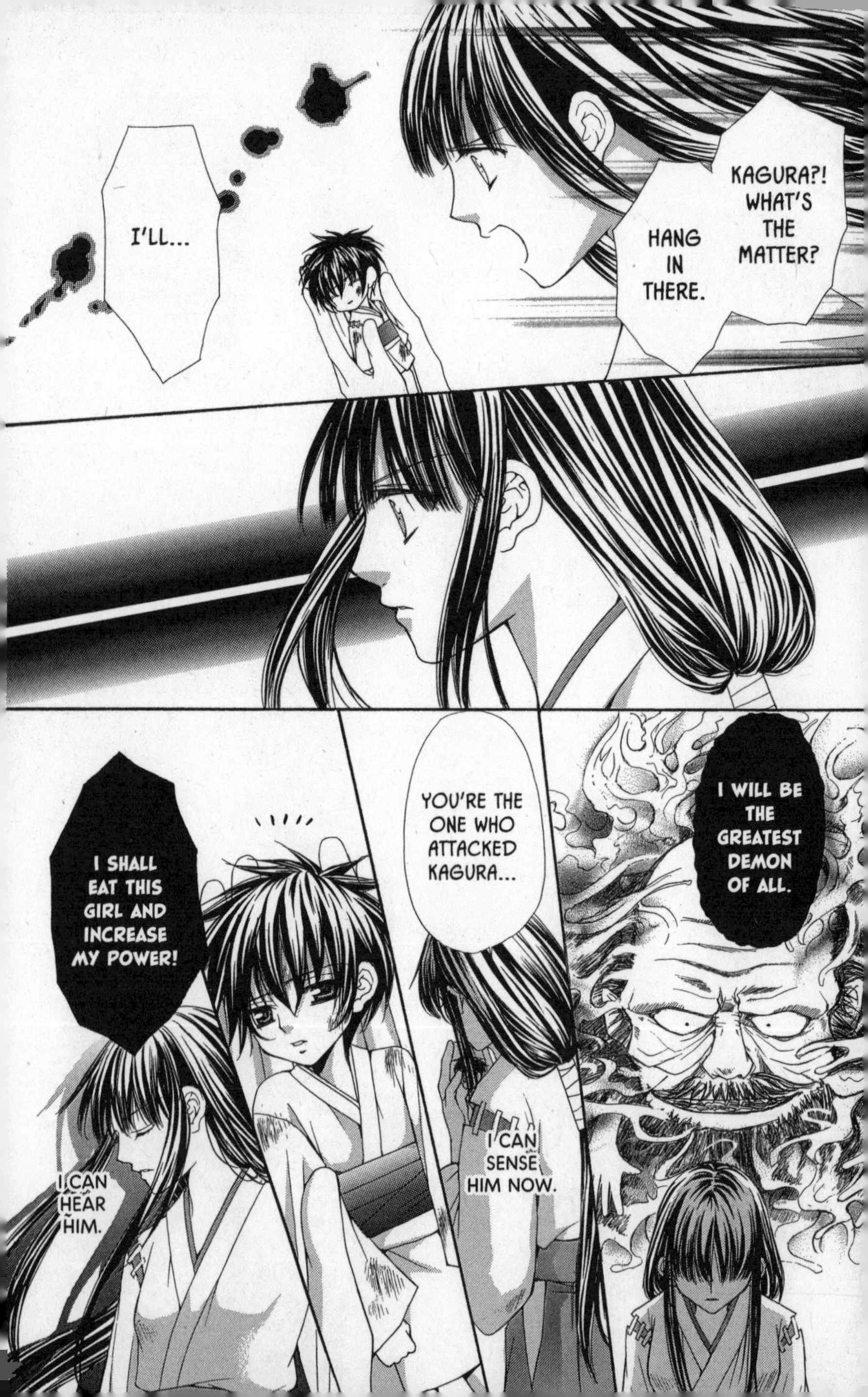
KAGURA?! WHAT'S THE MATTER?
HANG IN THERE.
I'LL...
I WILL BE THE GREATEST DEMON OF ALL.
YOU'RE THE ONE WHO ATTACKED KAGURA...
I CAN SENSE HIM NOW.
I SHALL EAT THIS GIRL AND INCREASE MY POWER!
I CAN HEAR HIM.

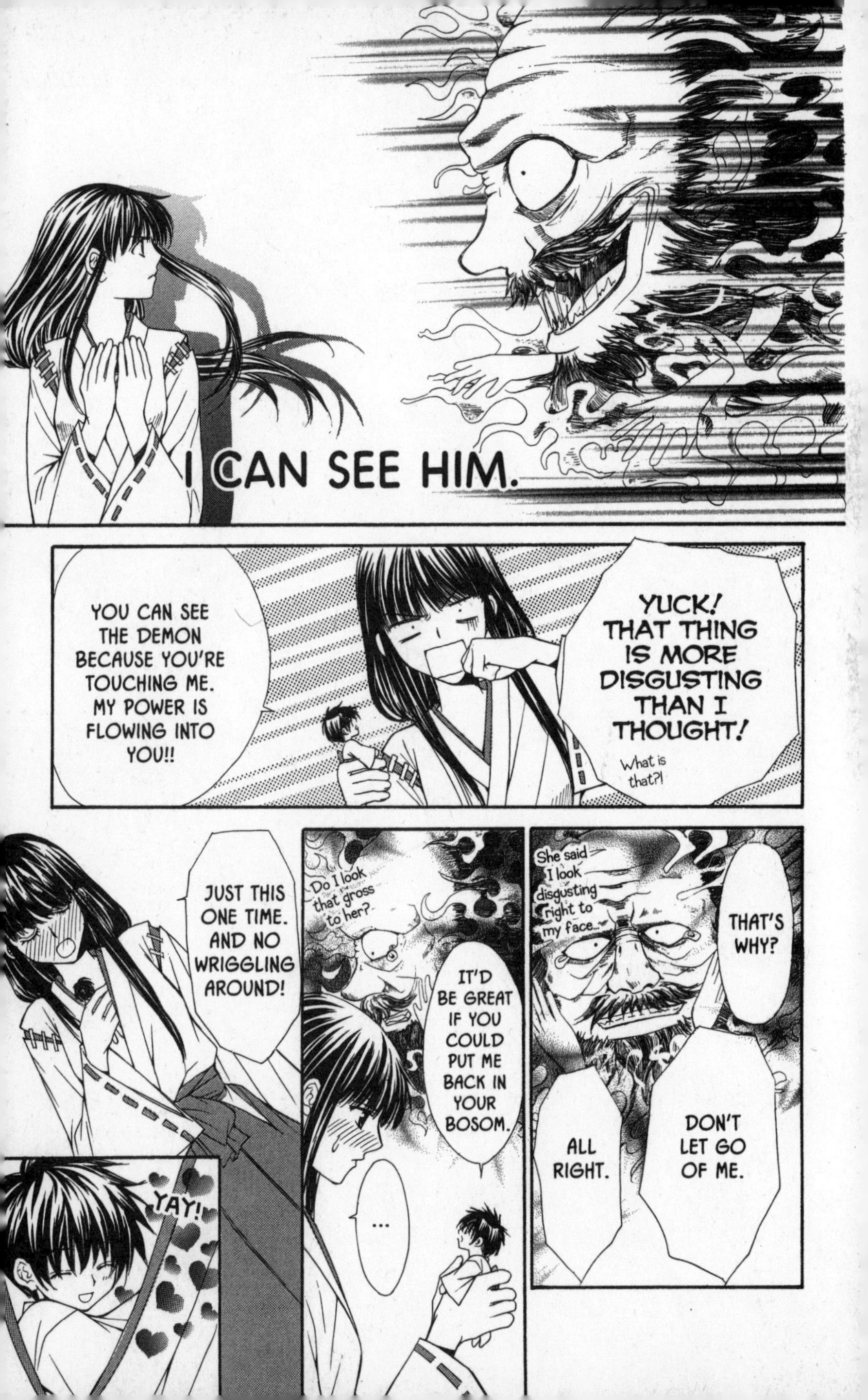
I CAN SEE HIM.
YUCK! THAT THING IS MORE DISGUSTING THAN I THOUGHT!
What is that?!
YOU CAN SEE THE DEMON BECAUSE YOU'RE TOUCHING ME. MY POWER IS FLOWING INTO YOU!!
THAT'S WHY?
She said I look disgusting right to my face...
DON'T LET GO OF ME.
ALL RIGHT.
Do I look that gross to her?
IT'D BE GREAT IF YOU COULD PUT ME BACK IN YOUR BOSOM.
...
JUST THIS ONE TIME. AND NO WRIGGLING AROUND!
YAY!

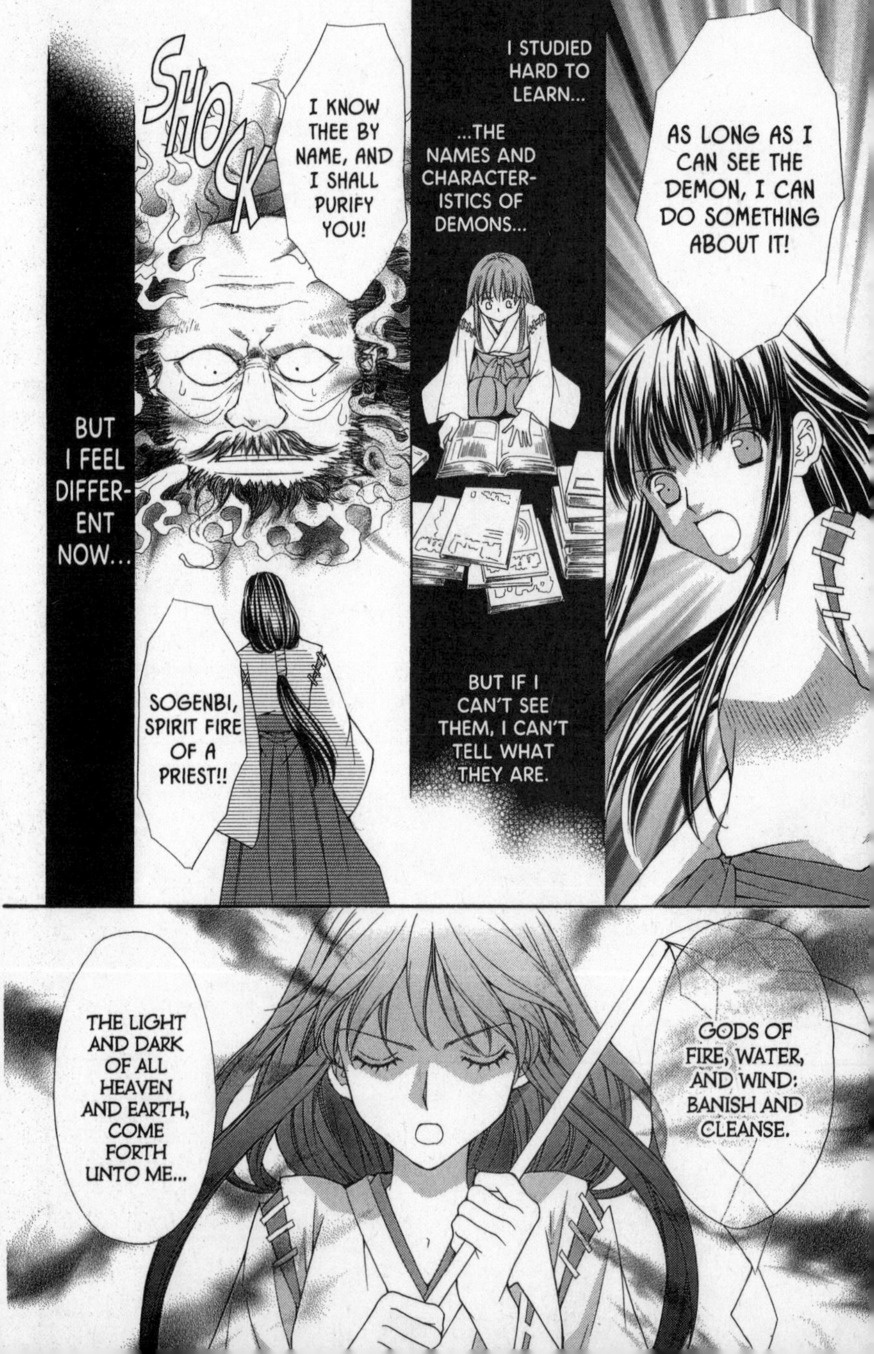
AS LONG AS I CAN SEE THE DEMON, I CAN DO SOMETHING ABOUT IT!
I STUDIED HARD TO LEARN...
...THE NAMES AND CHARACTER-ISTICS OF DEMONS...
BUT IF I CAN'T SEE THEM, I CAN'T TELL WHAT THEY ARE.
I KNOW THEE BY NAME, AND I SHALL PURIFY YOU!
SHOCK
BUT I FEEL DIFFER-ENT NOW...
SOGENBI, SPIRIT FIRE OF A PRIEST!!
GODS OF FIRE, WATER, AND WIND: BANISH AND CLEANSE.
THE LIGHT AND DARK OF ALL HEAVEN AND EARTH, COME FORTH UNTO ME...

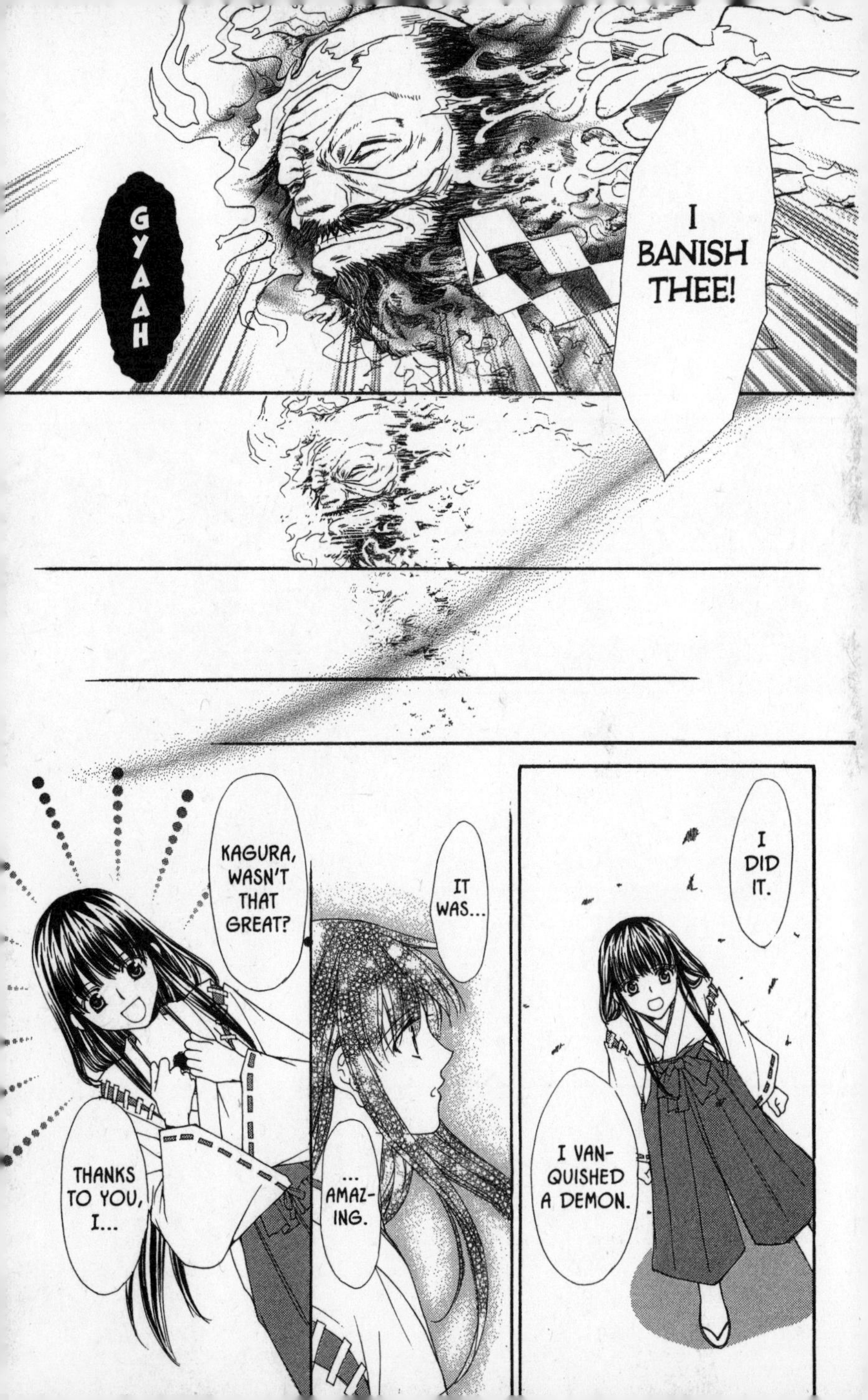
I BANISH THEE!
GYAAH
I DID IT.
I VAN-QUISHED A DEMON.
IT WAS...
...AMAZ-ING.
KAGURA, WASN'T THAT GREAT?
THANKS TO YOU, I...

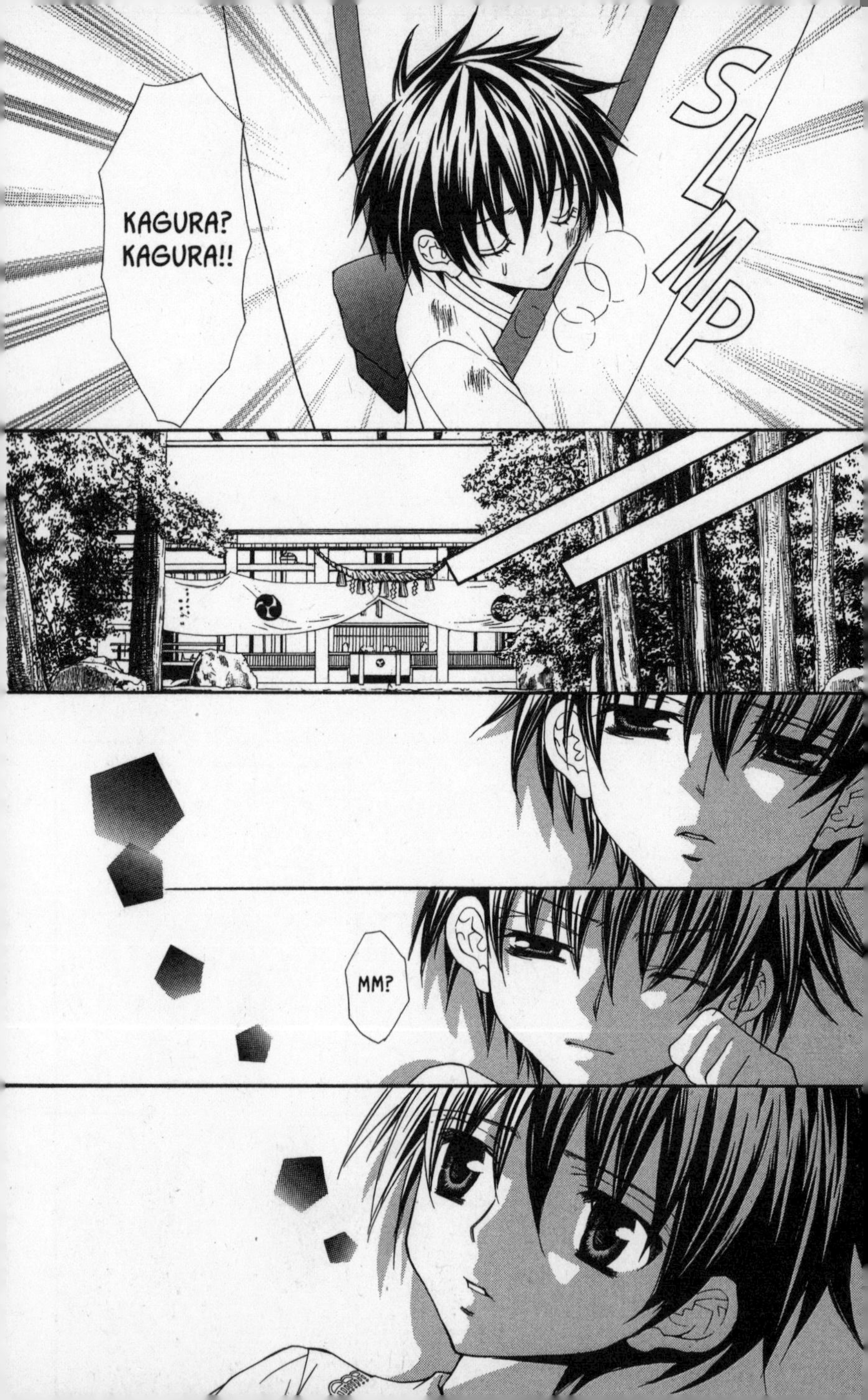
SLMP
KAGURA? KAGURA!!
MM?

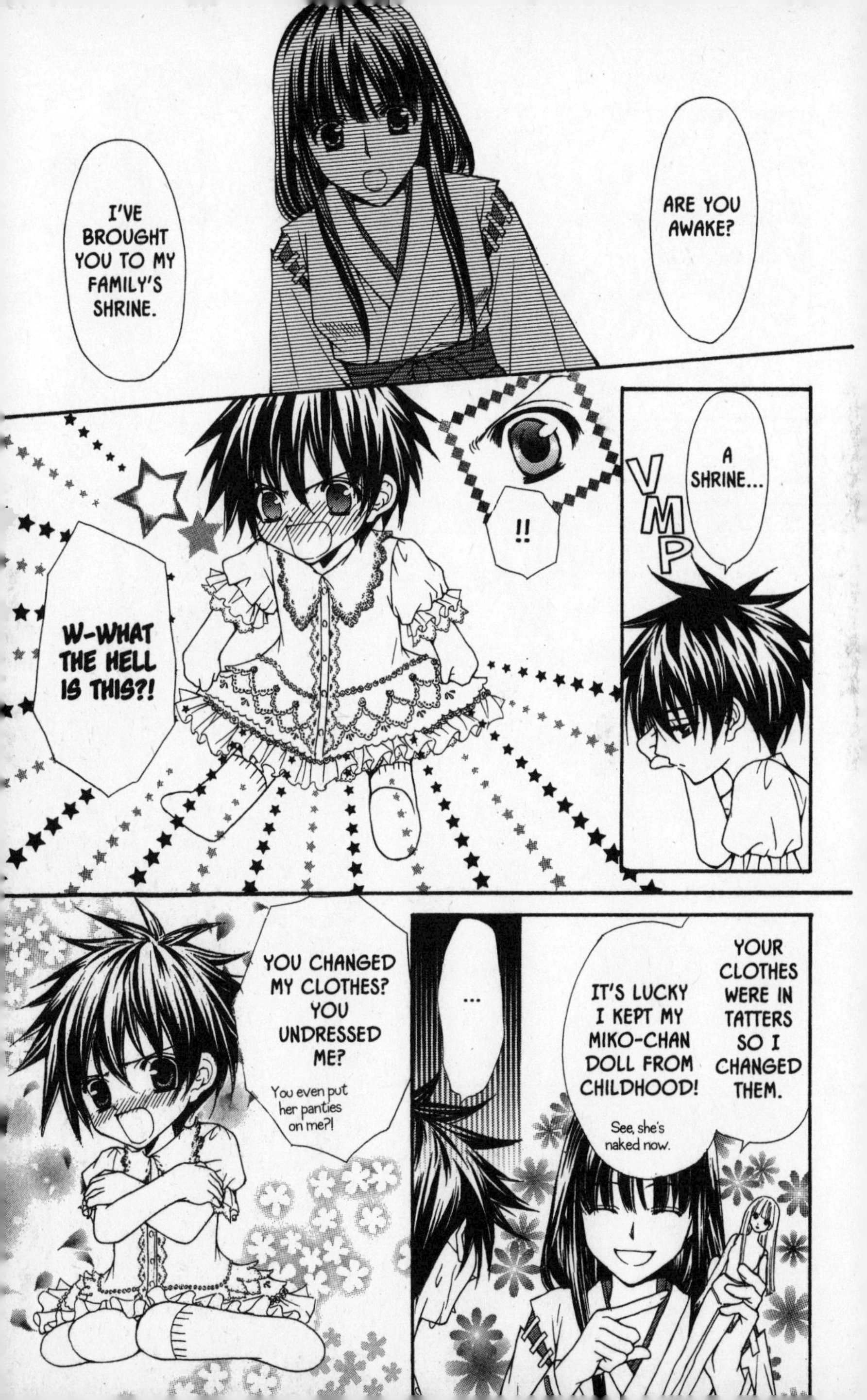
ARE YOU AWAKE?
I'VE BROUGHT YOU TO MY FAMILY'S SHRINE.
A SHRINE...
VMP
!!
W-WHAT THE HELL IS THIS?!
YOUR CLOTHES WERE IN TATTERS SO I CHANGED THEM.
IT'S LUCKY I KEPT MY MIKO-CHAN DOLL FROM CHILDHOOD!
See, she's naked now.
...
YOU CHANGED MY CLOTHES? YOU UNDRESSED ME?
You even put her panties on me?!

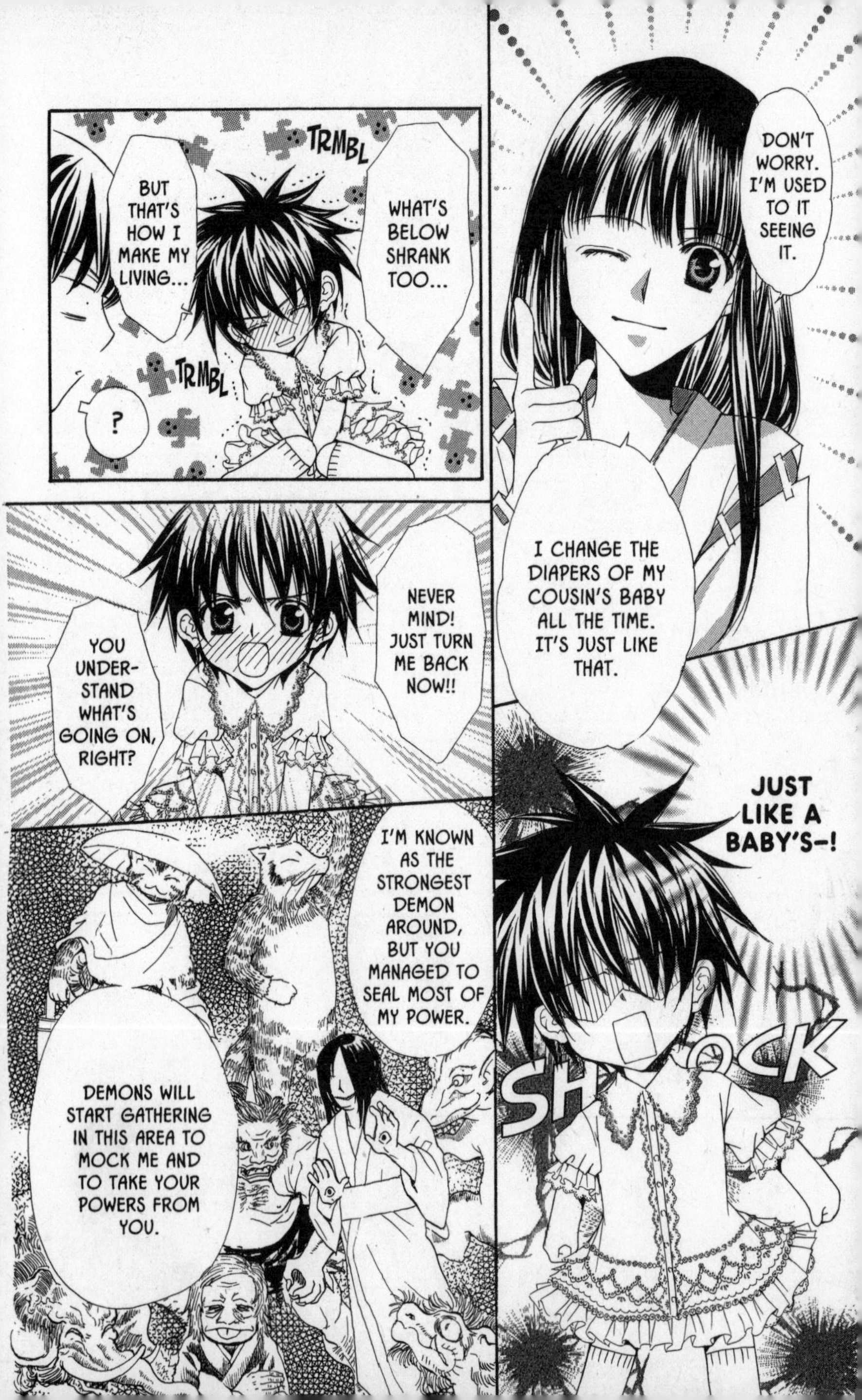
DON'T WORRY. I'M USED TO IT SEEING IT.
I CHANGE THE DIAPERS OF MY COUSIN'S BABY ALL THE TIME. IT'S JUST LIKE THAT.
JUST LIKE A BABY'S-!
SHOCK
TRMBL
WHAT'S BELOW SHRANK TOO...
BUT THAT'S HOW I MAKE MY LIVING...
TRMBL
?
NEVER MIND! JUST TURN ME BACK NOW!!
YOU UNDER-STAND WHAT'S GOING ON, RIGHT?
I'M KNOWN AS THE STRONGEST DEMON AROUND, BUT YOU MANAGED TO SEAL MOST OF MY POWER.
DEMONS WILL START GATHERING IN THIS AREA TO MOCK ME AND TO TAKE YOUR POWERS FROM YOU.

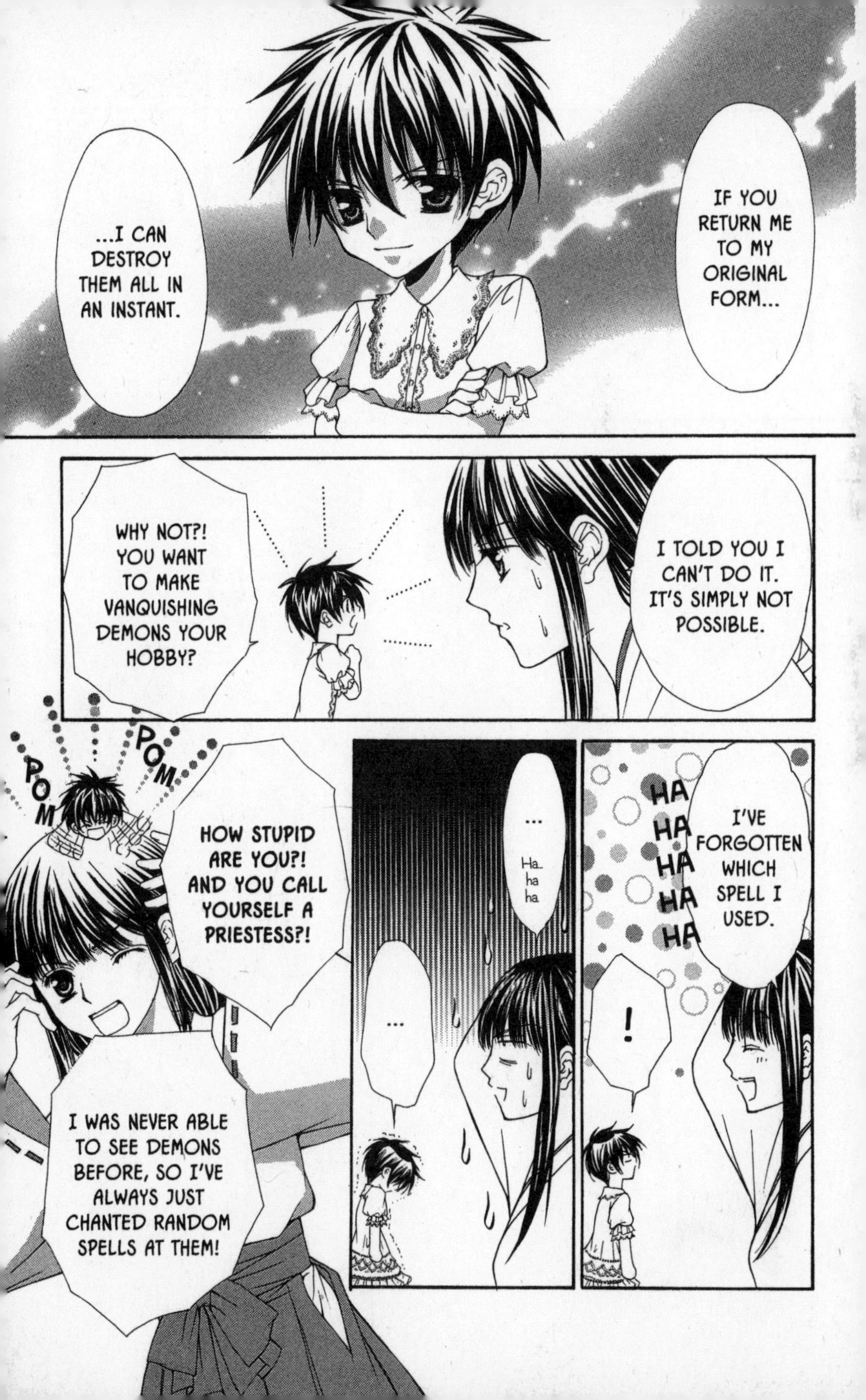
IF YOU RETURN ME TO MY ORIGINAL FORM...
...I CAN DESTROY THEM ALL IN AN INSTANT.
I TOLD YOU I CAN'T DO IT. IT'S SIMPLY NOT POSSIBLE.
WHY NOT?! YOU WANT TO MAKE VANQUISHING DEMONS YOUR HOBBY?
HA HA HA HA HA
I'VE FORGOTTEN WHICH SPELL I USED.
!
...
Ha.. ha ha
...
POM POM POM
HOW STUPID ARE YOU?! AND YOU CALL YOURSELF A PRIESTESS?!
I WAS NEVER ABLE TO SEE DEMONS BEFORE, SO I'VE ALWAYS JUST CHANTED RANDOM SPELLS AT THEM!

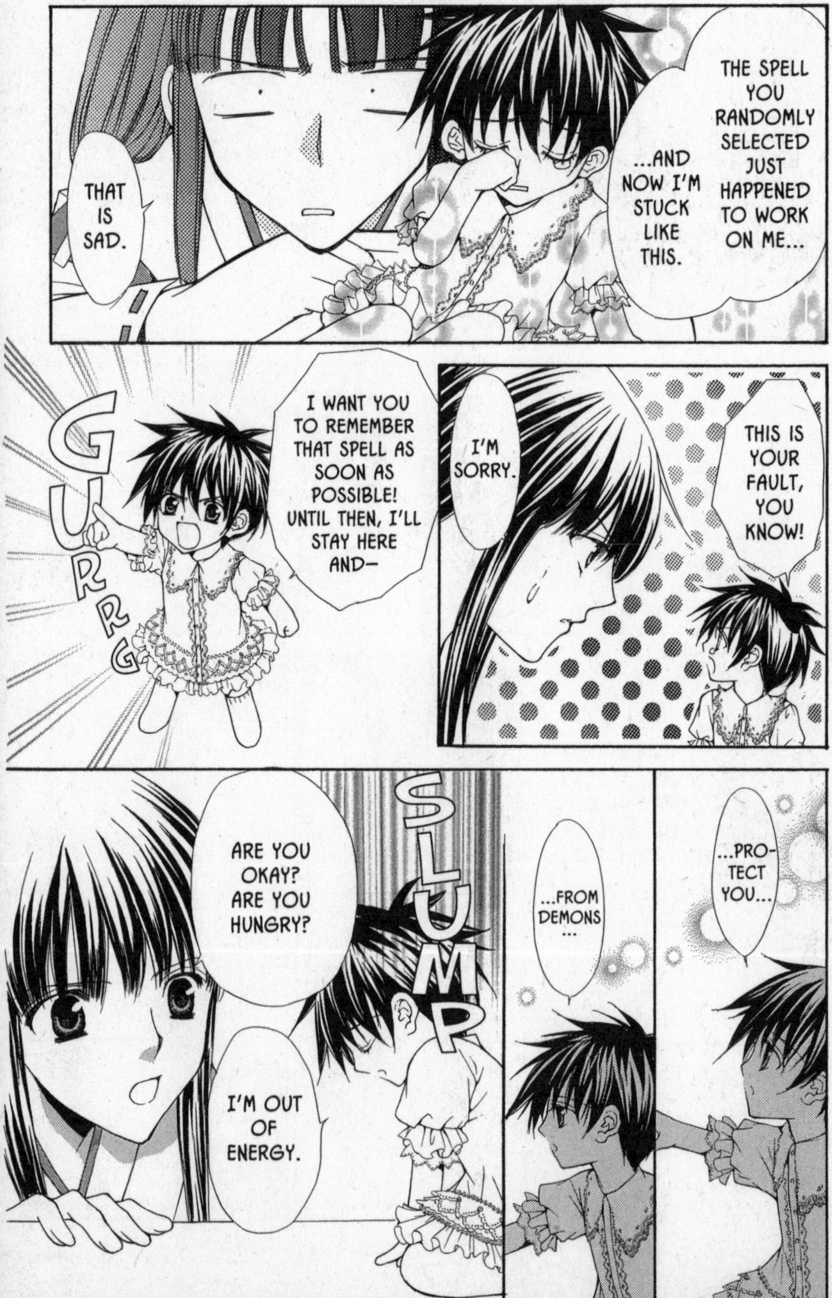
THE SPELL YOU RANDOMLY SELECTED JUST HAPPENED TO WORK ON ME...
...AND NOW I'M STUCK LIKE THIS.
THAT IS SAD.
THIS IS YOUR FAULT, YOU KNOW!
I'M SORRY.
I WANT YOU TO REMEMBER THAT SPELL AS SOON AS POSSIBLE! UNTIL THEN, I'LL STAY HERE AND—
GURRG
...PRO-TECT YOU...
...FROM DEMONS...
SLUMP
ARE YOU OKAY? ARE YOU HUNGRY?
I'M OUT OF ENERGY.

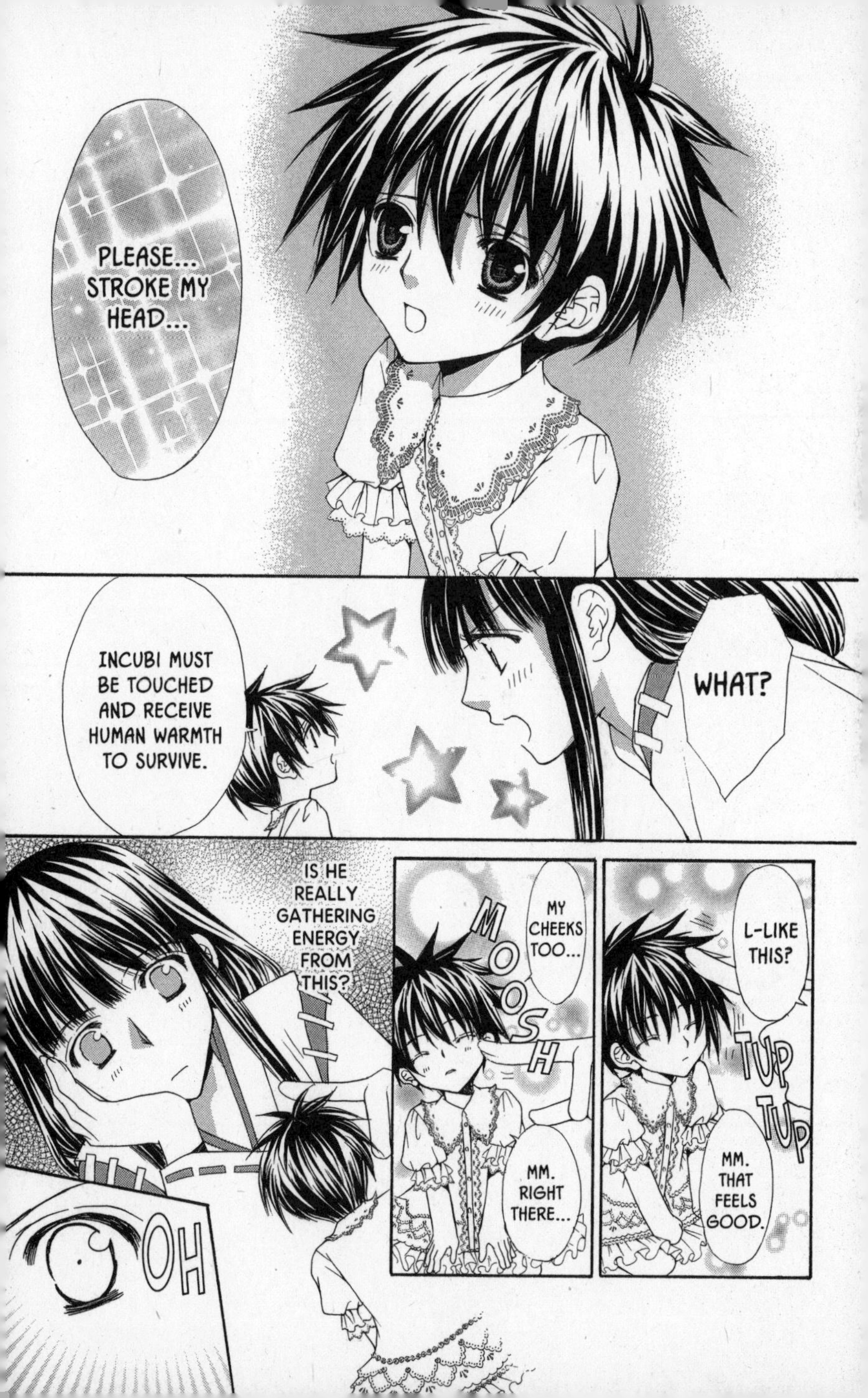
PLEASE... STROKE MY HEAD...
WHAT?
INCUBI MUST BE TOUCHED AND RECEIVE HUMAN WARMTH TO SURVIVE.
L-LIKE THIS?
TUP TUP
MM. THAT FEELS GOOD.
MY CHEEKS TOO...
MOOSH
MM. RIGHT THERE...
IS HE REALLY GATHERING ENERGY FROM THIS?
OH

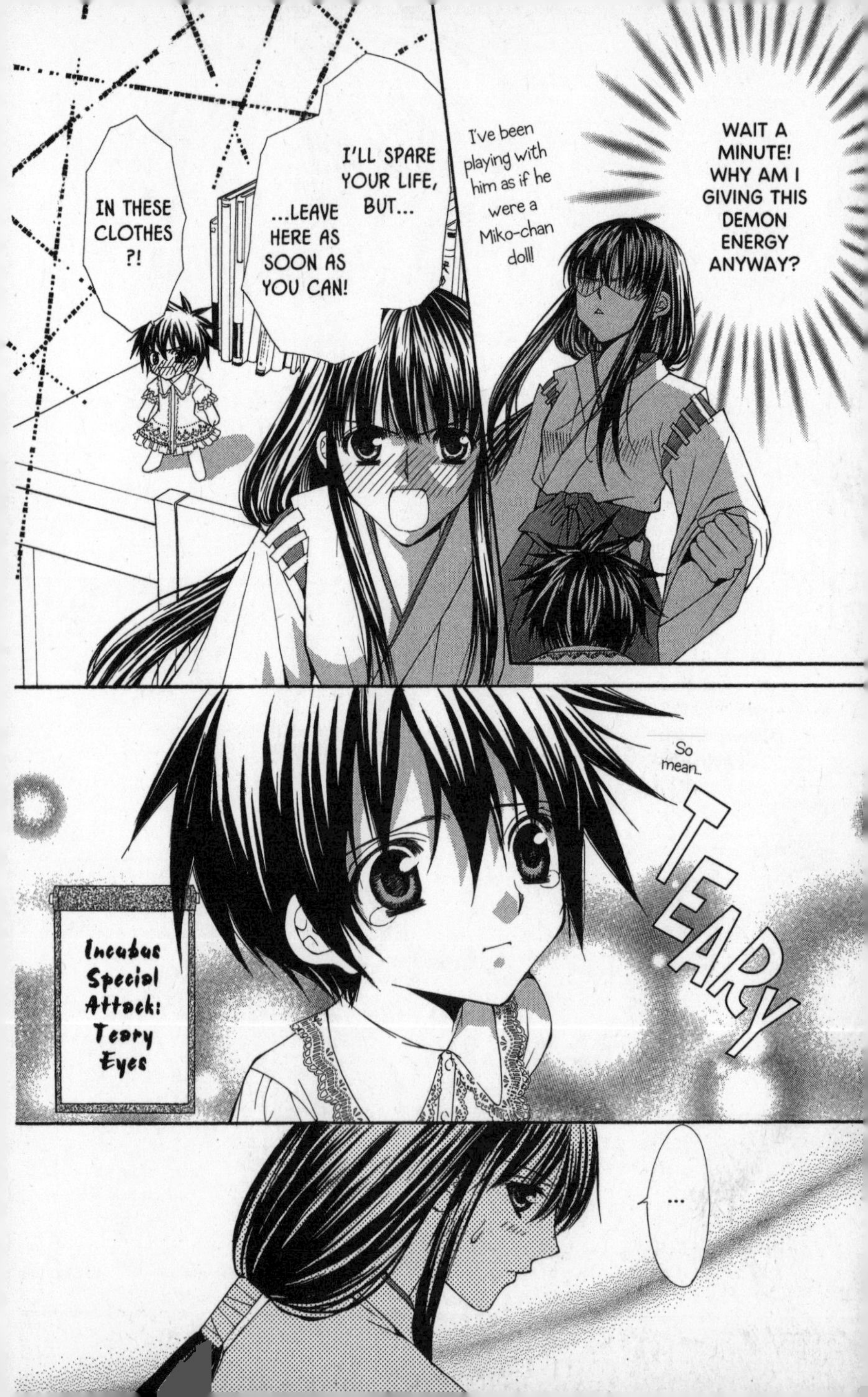
WAIT A MINUTE! WHY AM I GIVING THIS DEMON ENERGY ANYWAY?
I've been playing with him as if he were a Miko-chan doll!
I'LL SPARE YOUR LIFE, BUT...
...LEAVE HERE AS SOON AS YOU CAN!
IN THESE CLOTHES ?!
So mean..
TEARY
Incubus Special Attack: Teary Eyes
...

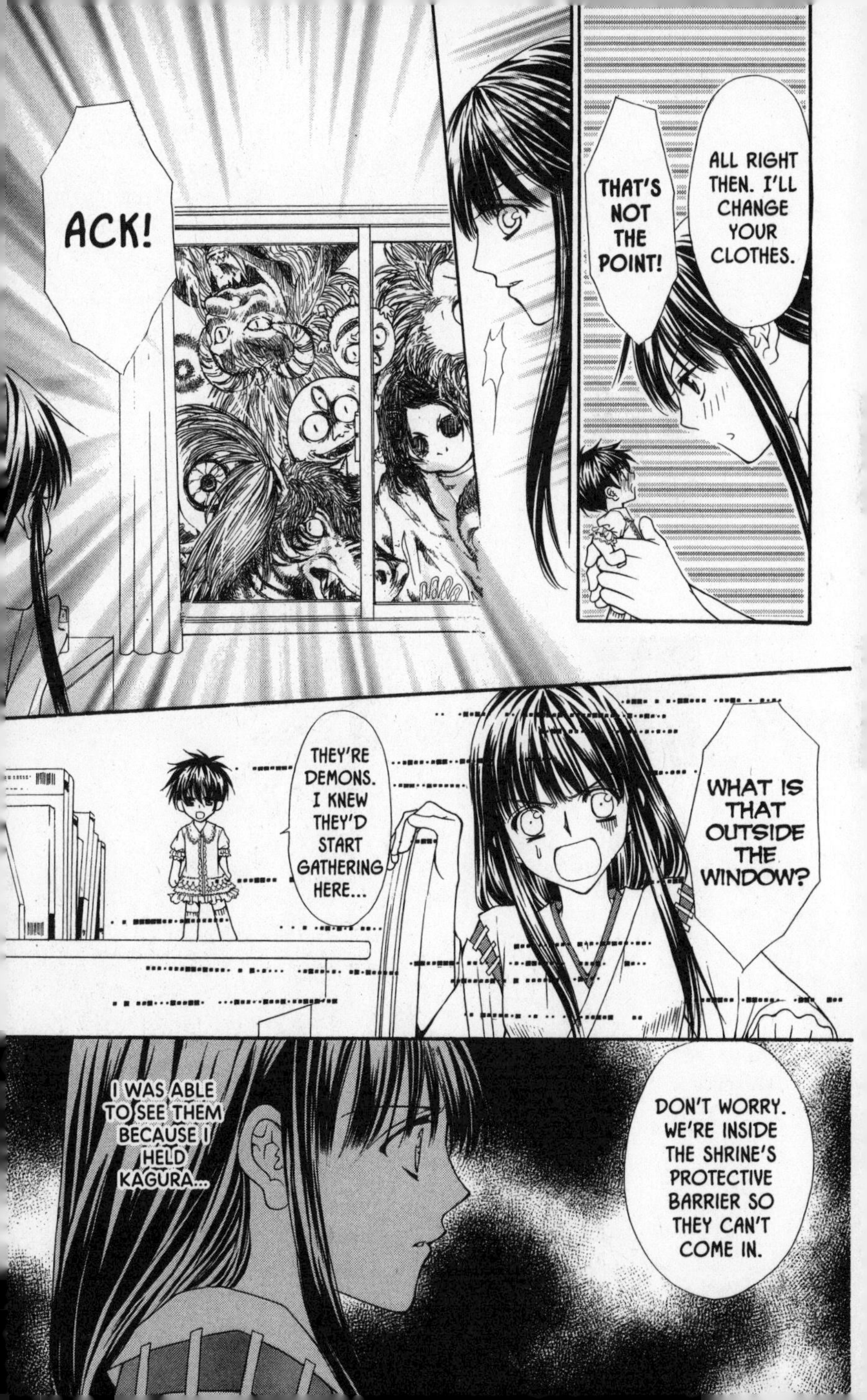
ALL RIGHT THEN. I'LL CHANGE YOUR CLOTHES.
THAT'S NOT THE POINT!
ACK!
WHAT IS THAT OUTSIDE THE WINDOW?
THEY'RE DEMONS. I KNEW THEY'D START GATHERING HERE...
DON'T WORRY. WE'RE INSIDE THE SHRINE'S PROTECTIVE BARRIER SO THEY CAN'T COME IN.
I WAS ABLE TO SEE THEM BECAUSE I HELD KAGURA...

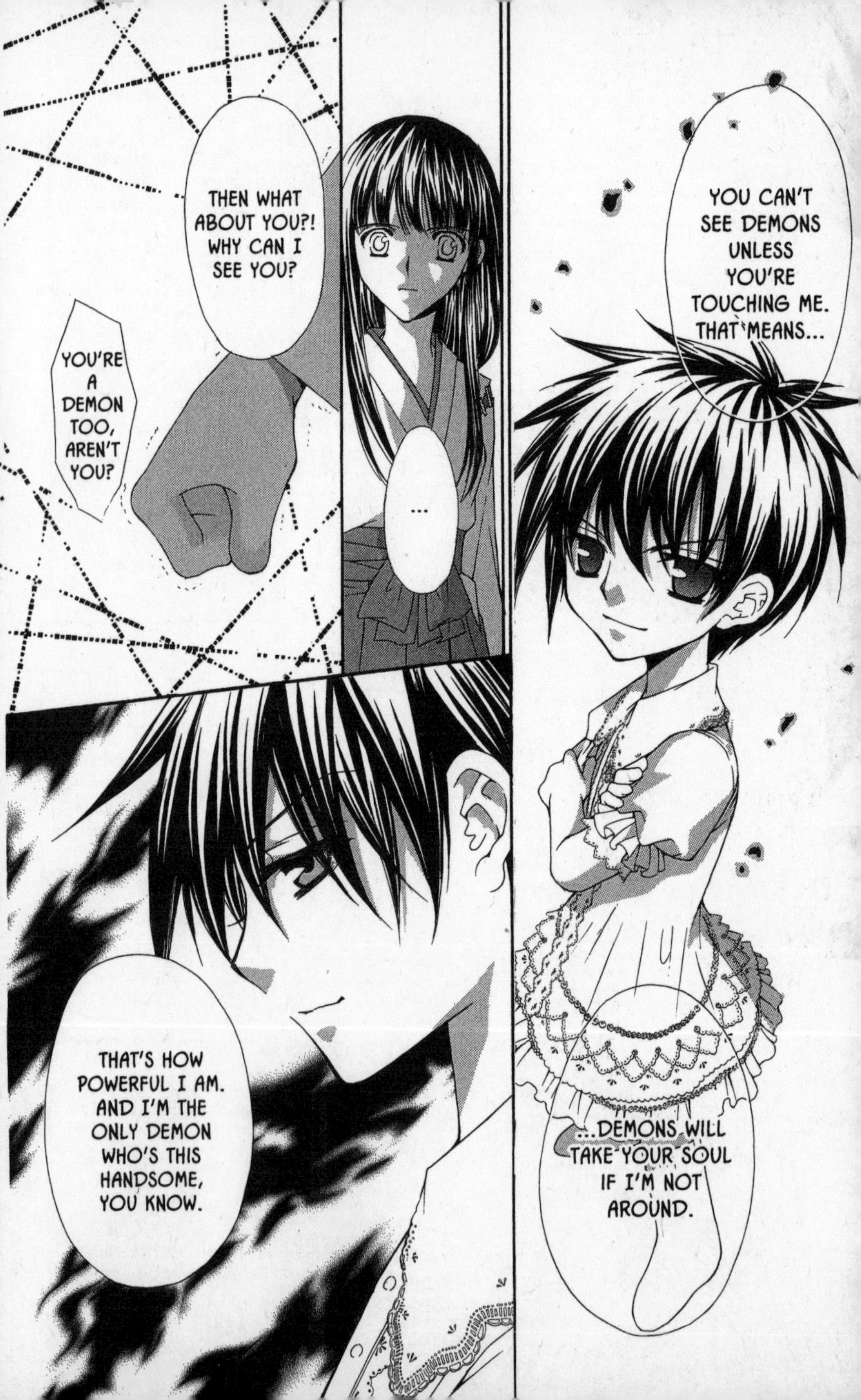
YOU CAN'T SEE DEMONS UNLESS YOU'RE TOUCHING ME. THAT MEANS...
...DEMONS WILL TAKE YOUR SOUL IF I'M NOT AROUND.
...
THEN WHAT ABOUT YOU?! WHY CAN I SEE YOU?
YOU'RE A DEMON TOO, AREN'T YOU?
THAT'S HOW POWERFUL I AM. AND I'M THE ONLY DEMON WHO'S THIS HANDSOME, YOU KNOW.

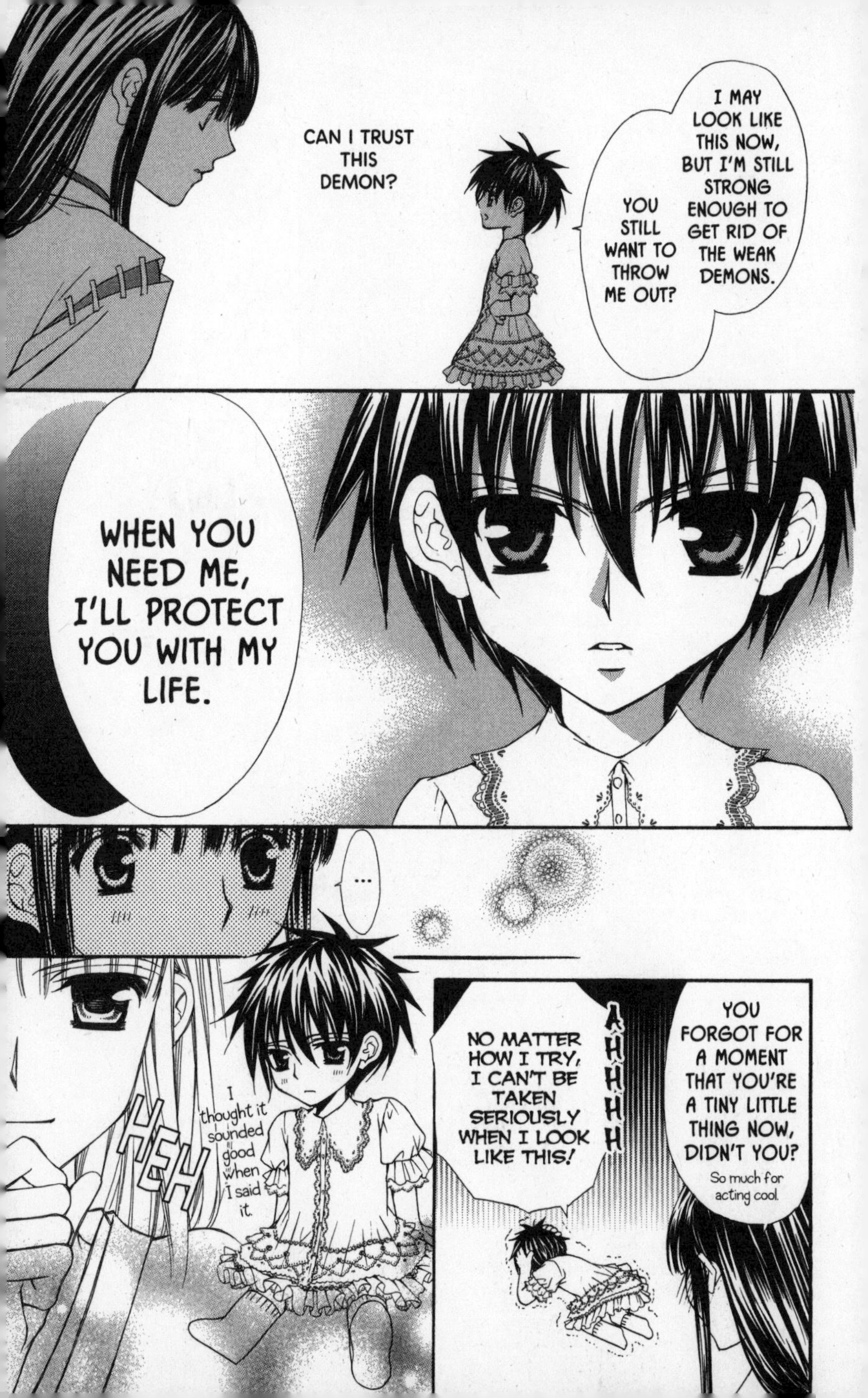

I MAY LOOK LIKE THIS NOW, BUT I'M STILL STRONG ENOUGH TO GET RID OF THE WEAK DEMONS.
YOU STILL WANT TO THROW ME OUT?
CAN I TRUST THIS DEMON?
WHEN YOU NEED ME, I'LL PROTECT YOU WITH MY LIFE.
...
YOU FORGOT FOR A MOMENT THAT YOU'RE A TINY LITTLE THING NOW, DIDN'T YOU?
So much for acting cool.
AHHHH
NO MATTER HOW I TRY, I CAN'T BE TAKEN SERIOUSLY WHEN I LOOK LIKE THIS!
I thought it sounded good when I said it.
HEH

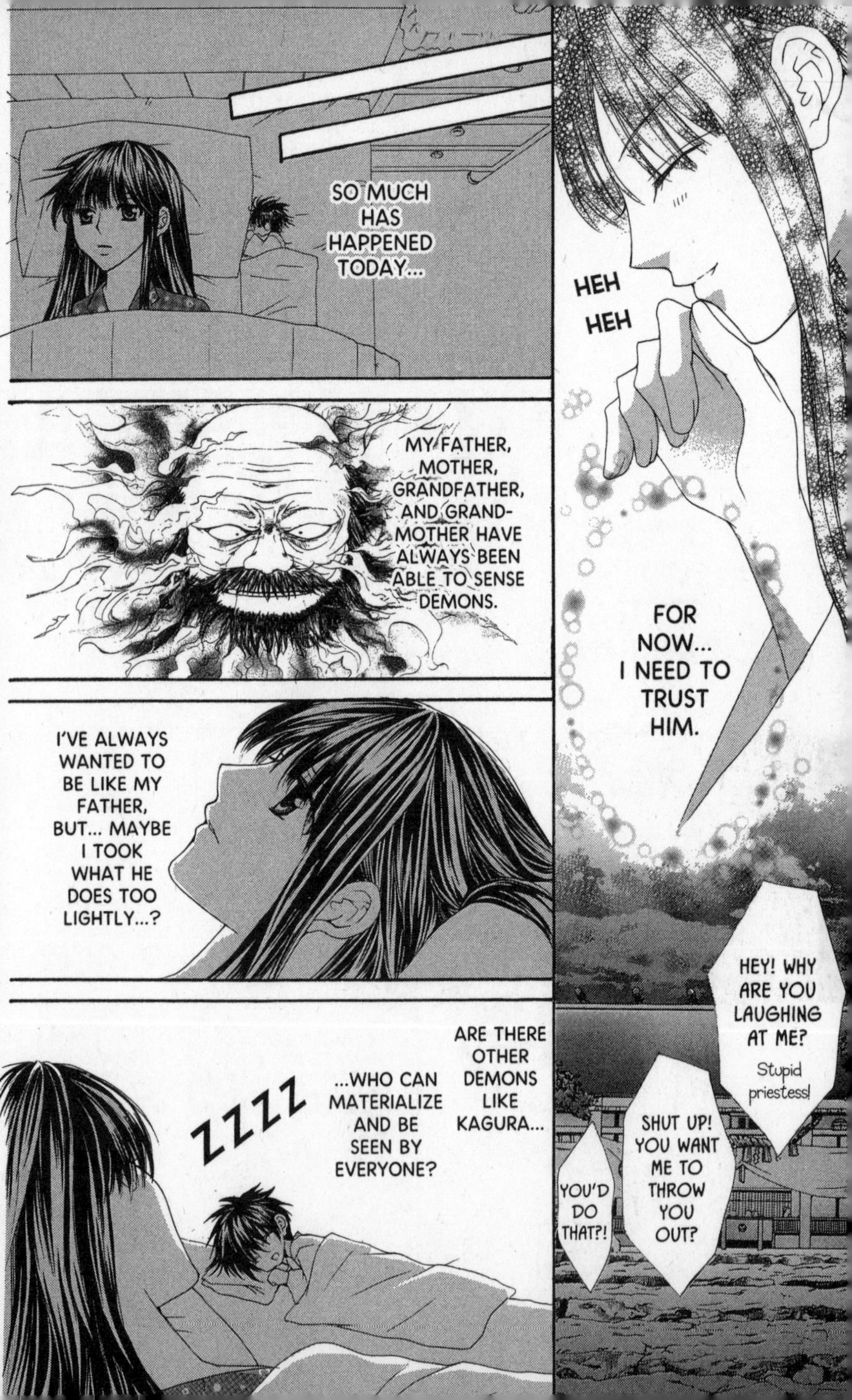
HEH HEH
FOR NOW... I NEED TO TRUST HIM.
HEY! WHY ARE YOU LAUGHING AT ME?
Stupid priestess!
SHUT UP! YOU WANT ME TO THROW YOU OUT?
YOU'D DO THAT?!
SO MUCH HAS HAPPENED TODAY...
MY FATHER, MOTHER, GRANDFATHER, AND GRAND-MOTHER HAVE ALWAYS BEEN ABLE TO SENSE DEMONS.
I'VE ALWAYS WANTED TO BE LIKE MY FATHER, BUT... MAYBE I TOOK WHAT HE DOES TOO LIGHTLY...?
ARE THERE OTHER DEMONS LIKE KAGURA...
...WHO CAN MATERIALIZE AND BE SEEN BY EVERYONE?
ZZZZ

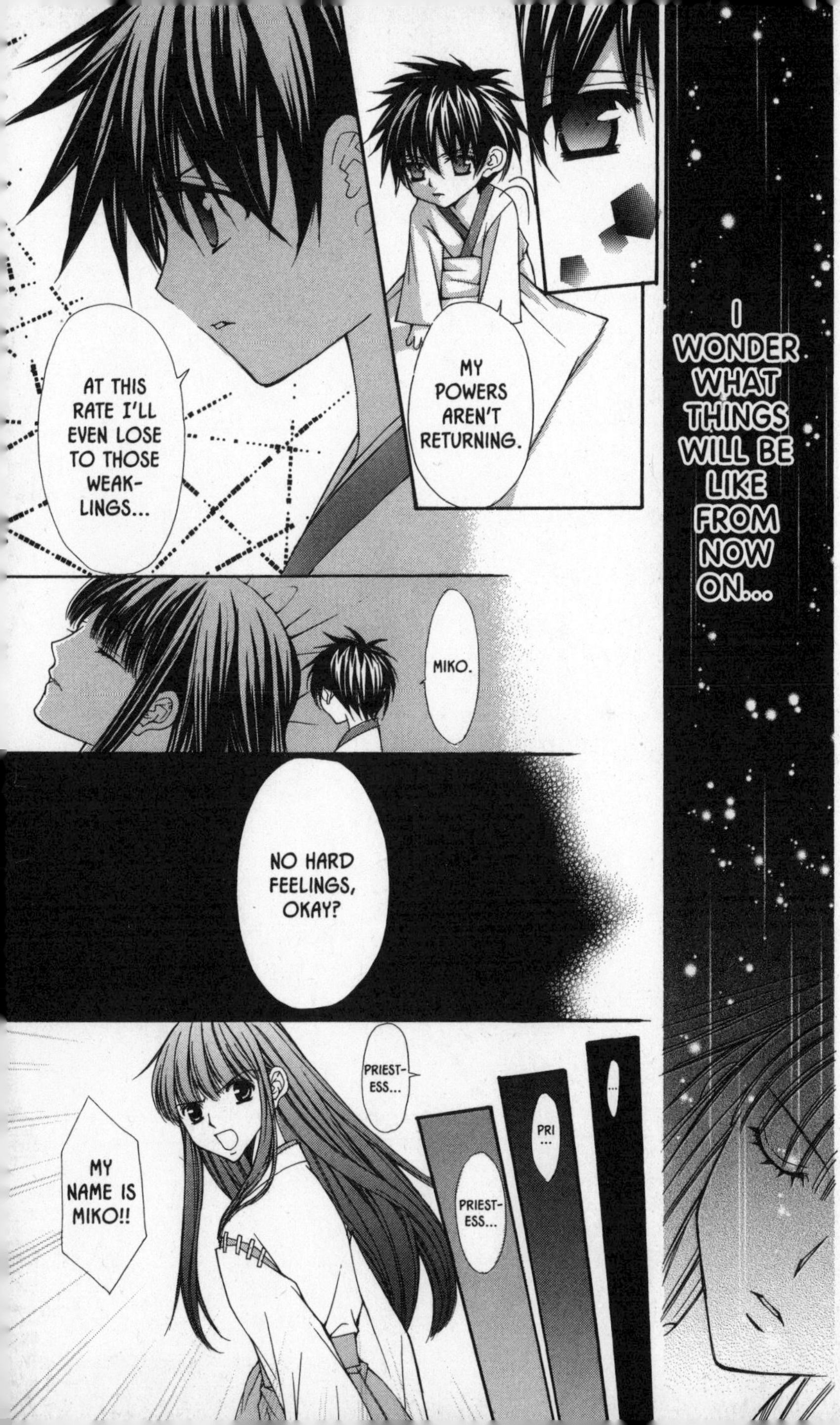

I WONDER WHAT THINGS WILL BE LIKE FROM NOW ON...
MY POWERS AREN'T RETURNING.
AT THIS RATE I'LL EVEN LOSE TO THOSE WEAK-LINGS...
MIKO.
NO HARD FEELINGS, OKAY?
...
PRI...
PRIEST-ESS...
PRIEST-ESS...
MY NAME IS MIKO!!

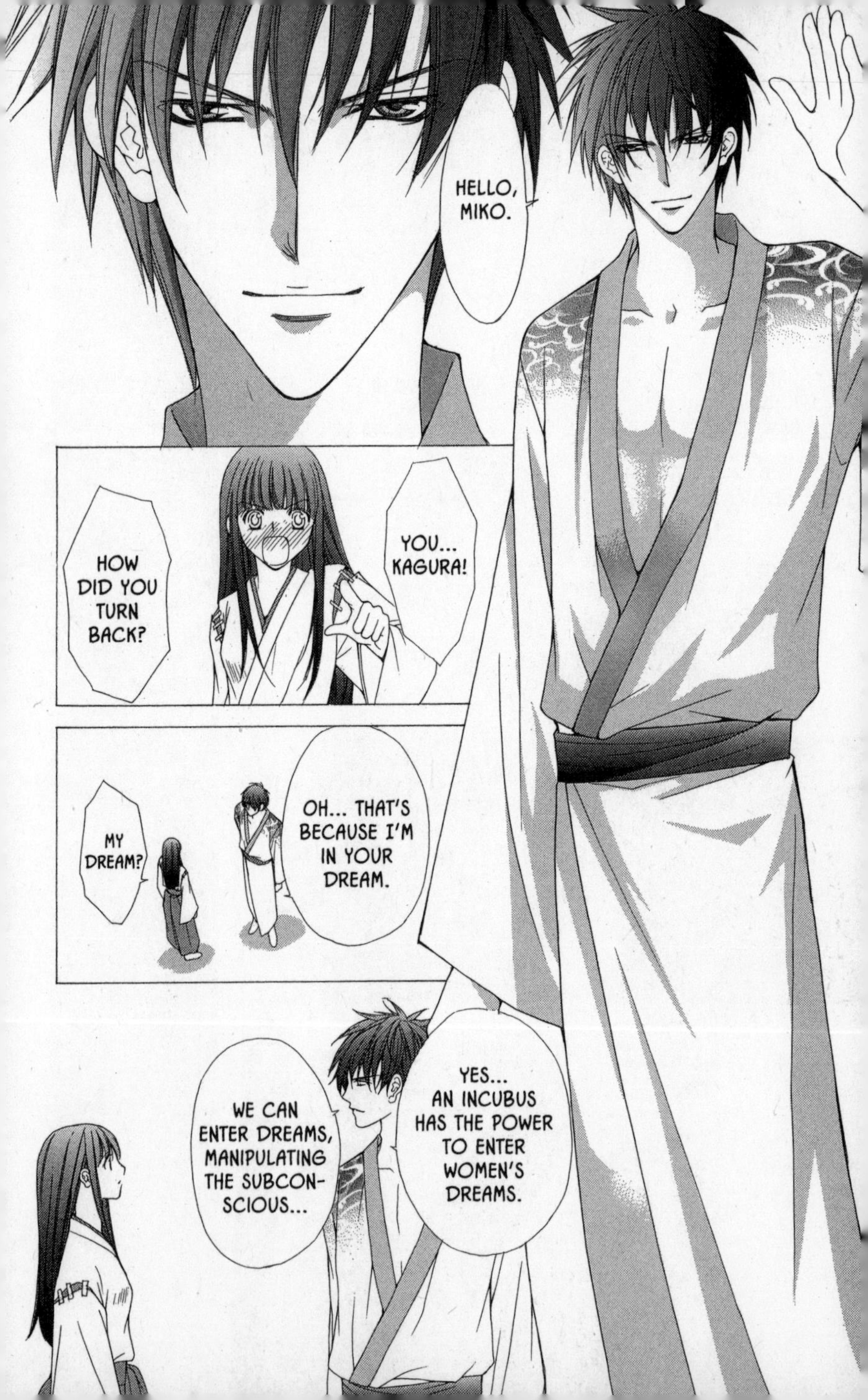
HELLO, MIKO.
YOU... KAGURA!
HOW DID YOU TURN BACK?
OH... THAT'S BECAUSE I'M IN YOUR DREAM.
MY DREAM?
YES... AN INCUBUS HAS THE POWER TO ENTER WOMEN'S DREAMS.
WE CAN ENTER DREAMS, MANIPULATING THE SUBCONSCIOUS...

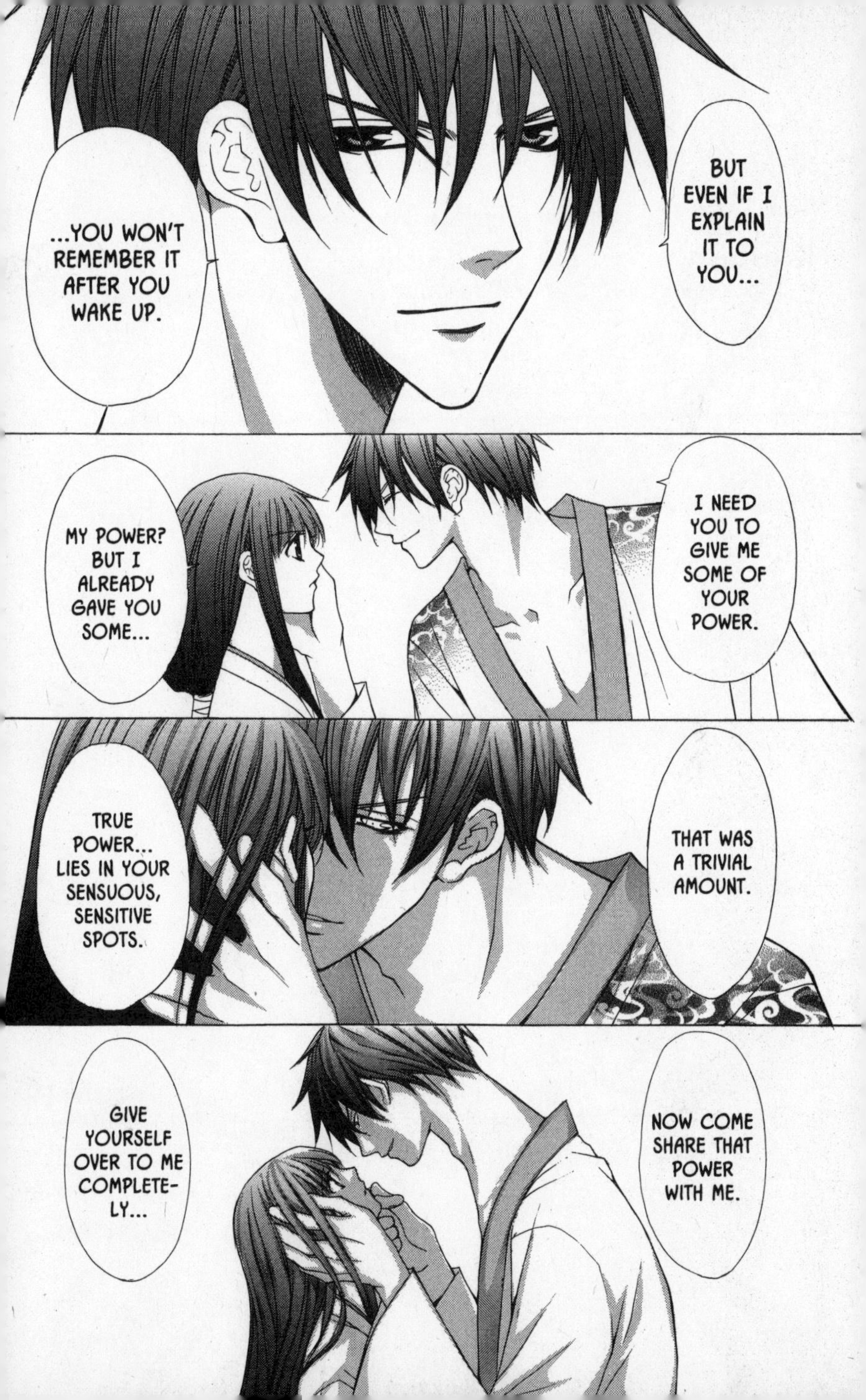
BUT EVEN IF I EXPLAIN IT TO YOU...
...YOU WON'T REMEMBER IT AFTER YOU WAKE UP.
I NEED YOU TO GIVE ME SOME OF YOUR POWER.
MY POWER? BUT I ALREADY GAVE YOU SOME...
THAT WAS A TRIVIAL AMOUNT.
TRUE POWER... LIES IN YOUR SENSUOUS, SENSITIVE SPOTS.
NOW COME SHARE THAT POWER WITH ME.
GIVE YOURSELF OVER TO ME COMPLETE-LY...

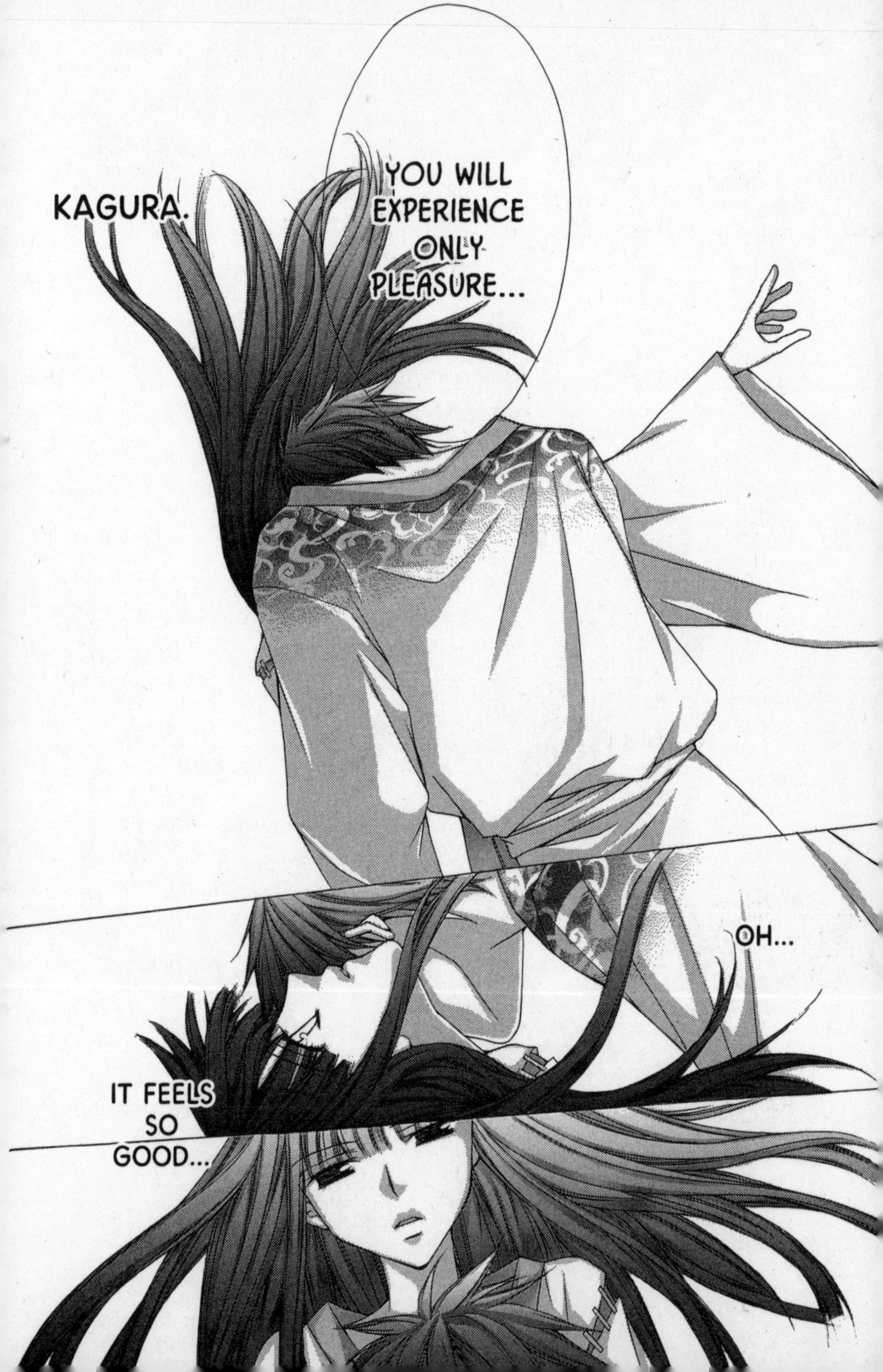
YOU WILL EXPERIENCE ONLY PLEASURE...
KAGURA.
OH...
IT FEELS SO GOOD...

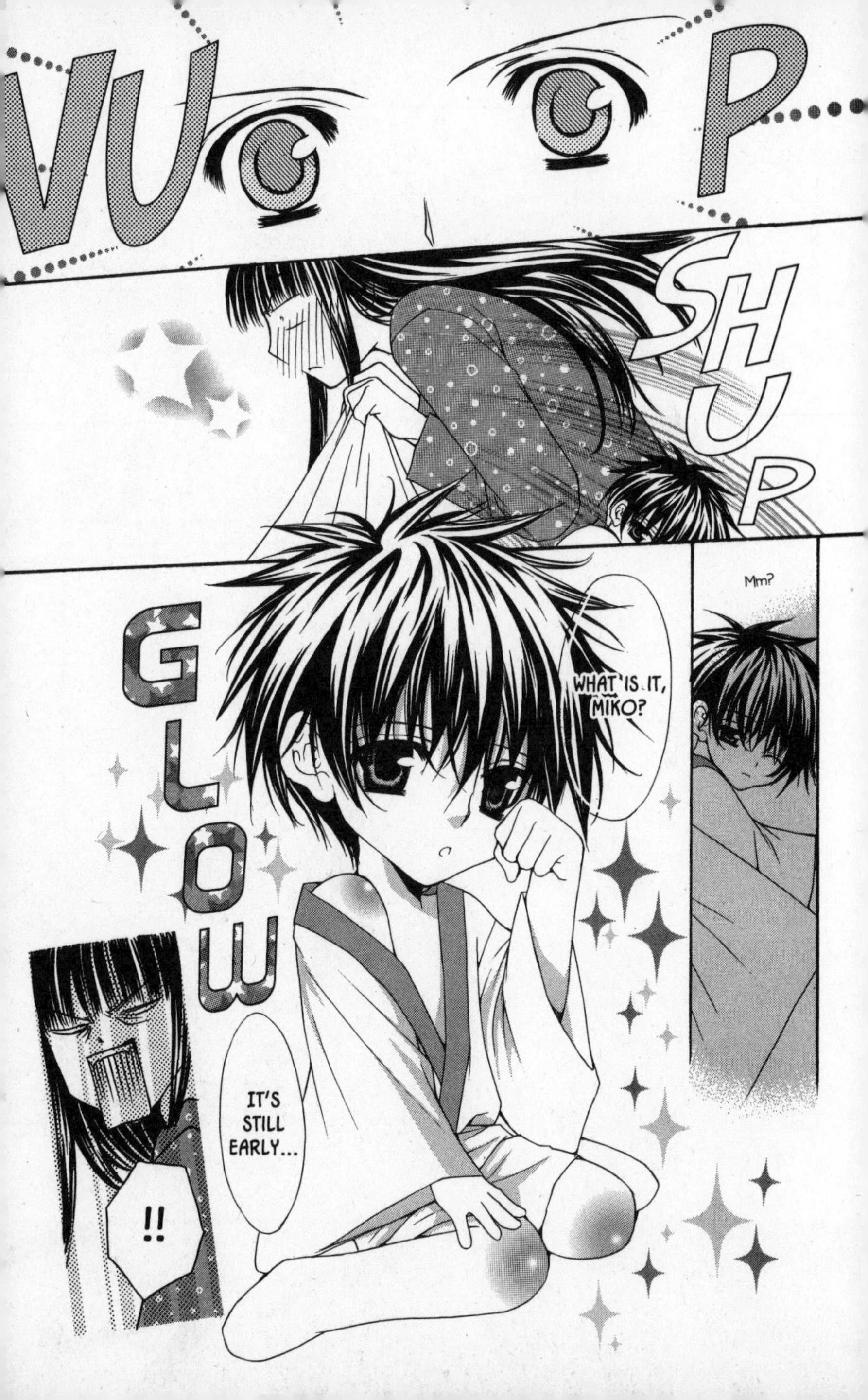
VUOOP
SHUP
Mm?
WHAT IS IT, MIKO?
GLOW
IT'S STILL EARLY...
!!

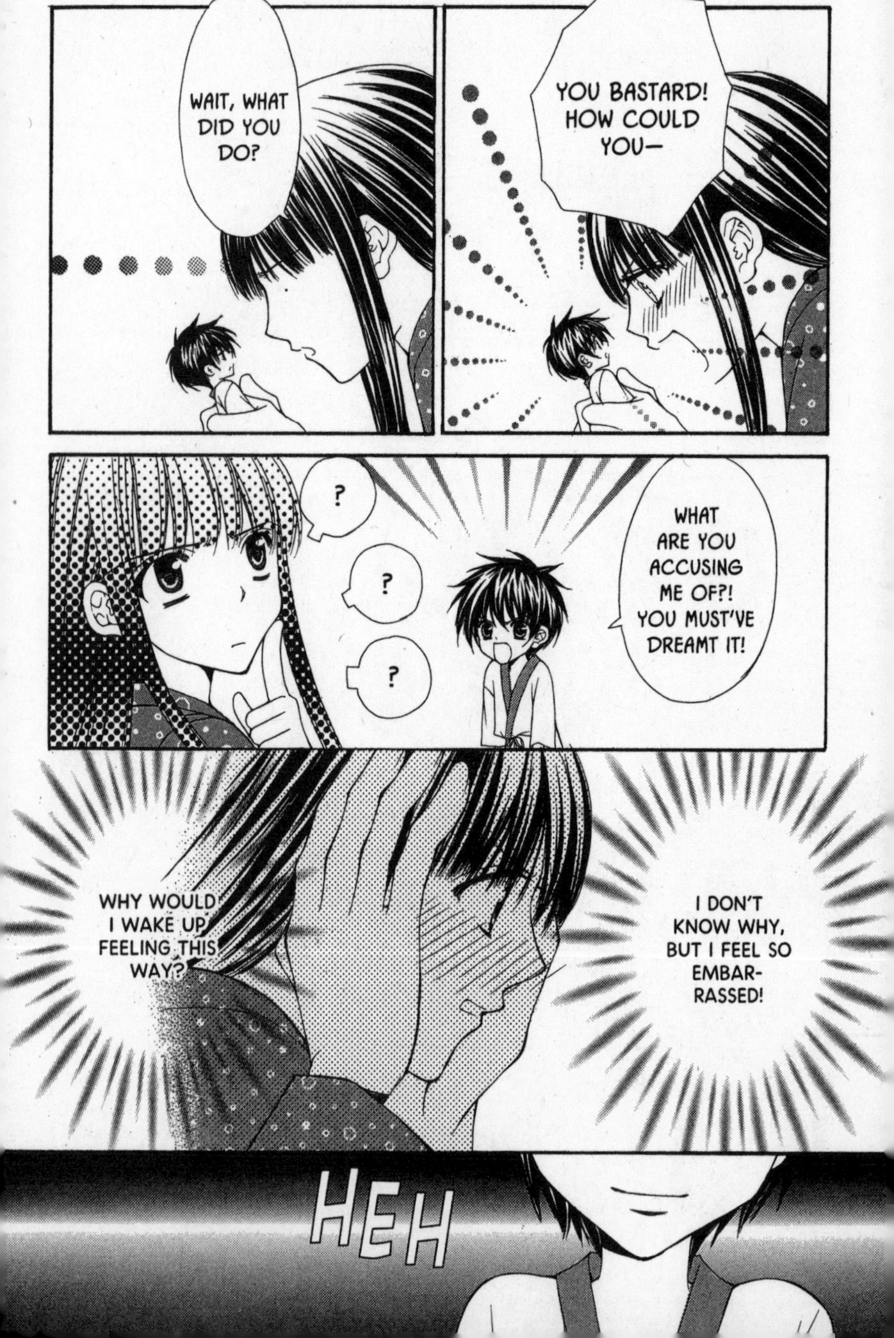
YOU BASTARD! HOW COULD YOU—
WAIT, WHAT DID YOU DO?
WHAT ARE YOU ACCUSING ME OF?! YOU MUST'VE DREAMT IT!
?
?
?
I DON'T KNOW WHY, BUT I FEEL SO EMBARRASSED!
WHY WOULD I WAKE UP FEELING THIS WAY?
HEH

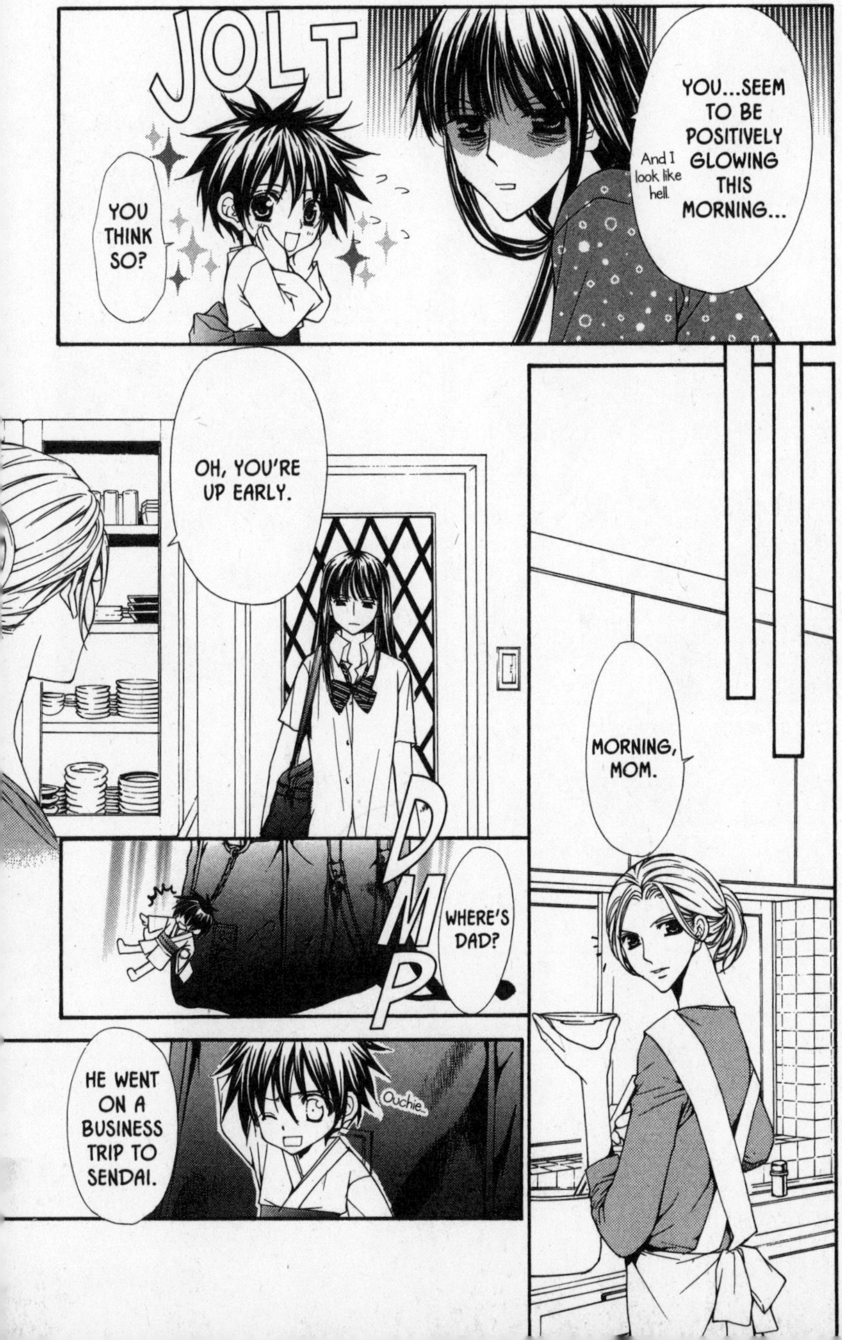

YOU...SEEM TO BE POSITIVELY GLOWING THIS MORNING...
And I look like hell.
JOLT
YOU THINK SO?
MORNING, MOM.
OH, YOU'RE UP EARLY.
WHERE'S DAD?
DMP
HE WENT ON A BUSINESS TRIP TO SENDAI.
Ouchie...

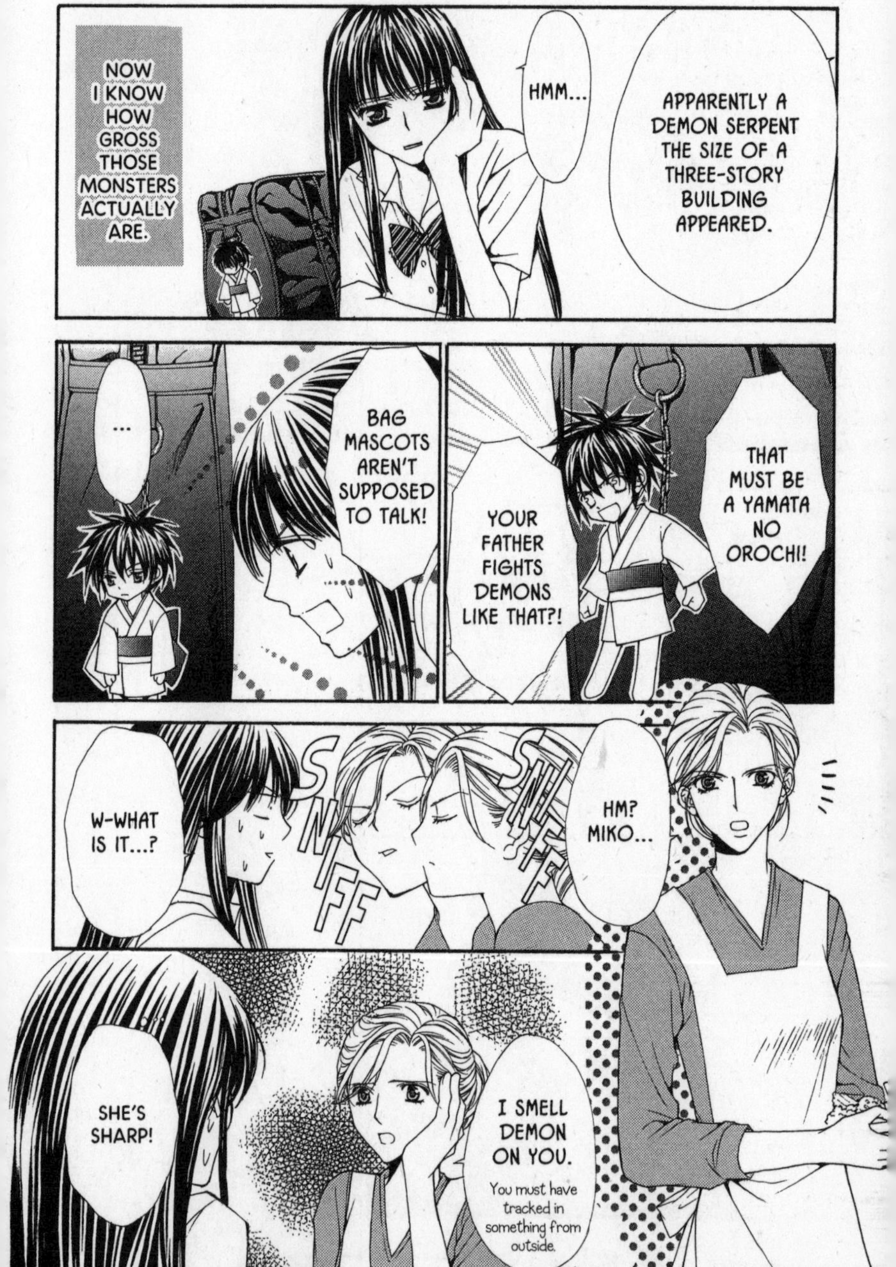
APPARENTLY A DEMON SERPENT THE SIZE OF A THREE-STORY BUILDING APPEARED.
HMM...
NOW I KNOW HOW GROSS THOSE MONSTERS ACTUALLY ARE.
THAT MUST BE A YAMATA NO OROCHI!
YOUR FATHER FIGHTS DEMONS LIKE THAT?!
BAG MASCOTS AREN'T SUPPOSED TO TALK!
...
HM? MIKO...
SNIFF
SNIFF
W-WHAT IS IT...?
I SMELL DEMON ON YOU.
You must have tracked in something from outside.
SHE'S SHARP!

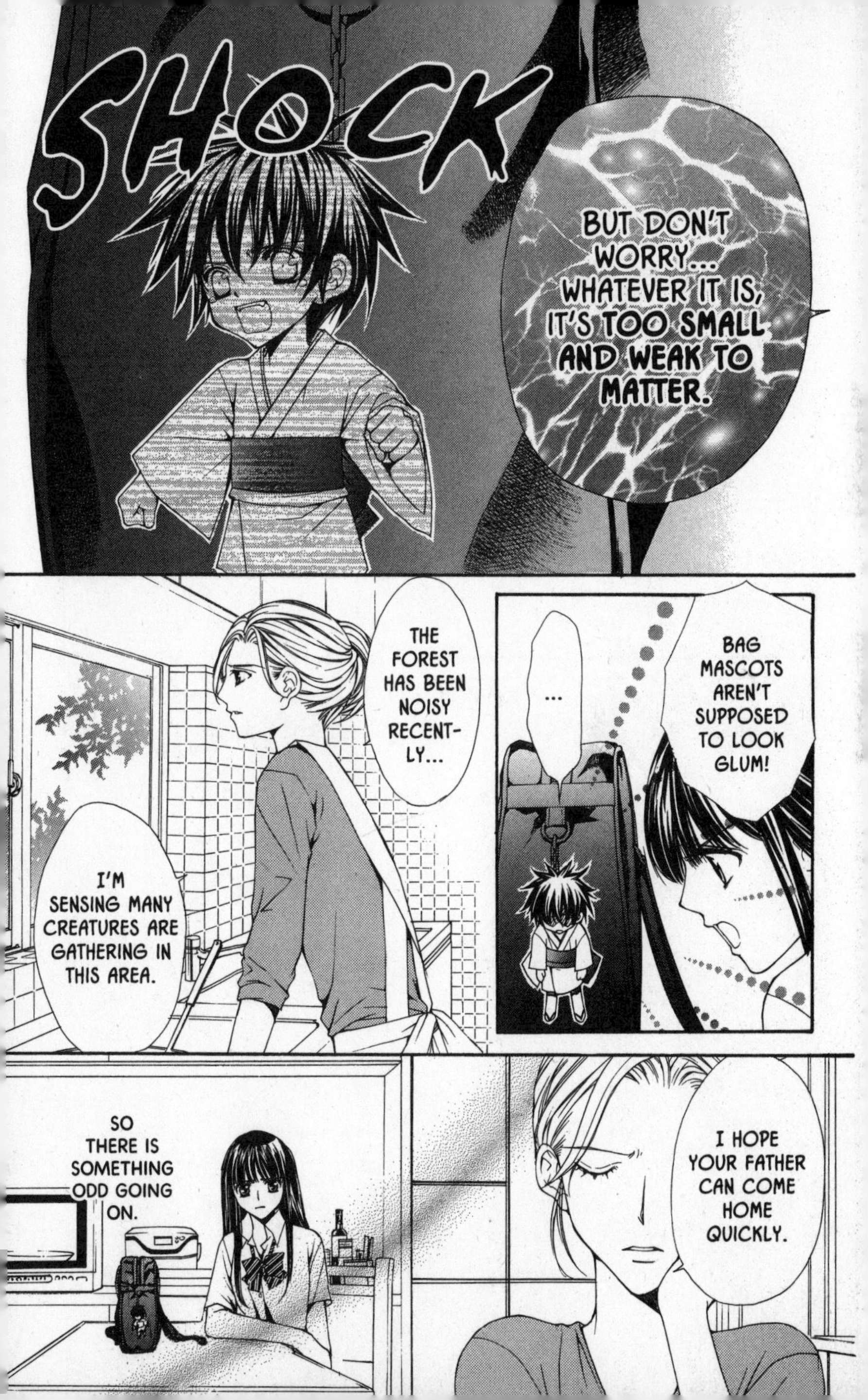
SHOCK
BUT DON'T WORRY... WHATEVER IT IS, IT'S TOO SMALL AND WEAK TO MATTER.
BAG MASCOTS AREN'T SUPPOSED TO LOOK GLUM!
...
THE FOREST HAS BEEN NOISY RECENT-LY...
I'M SENSING MANY CREATURES ARE GATHERING IN THIS AREA.
I HOPE YOUR FATHER CAN COME HOME QUICKLY.
SO THERE IS SOMETHING ODD GOING ON.

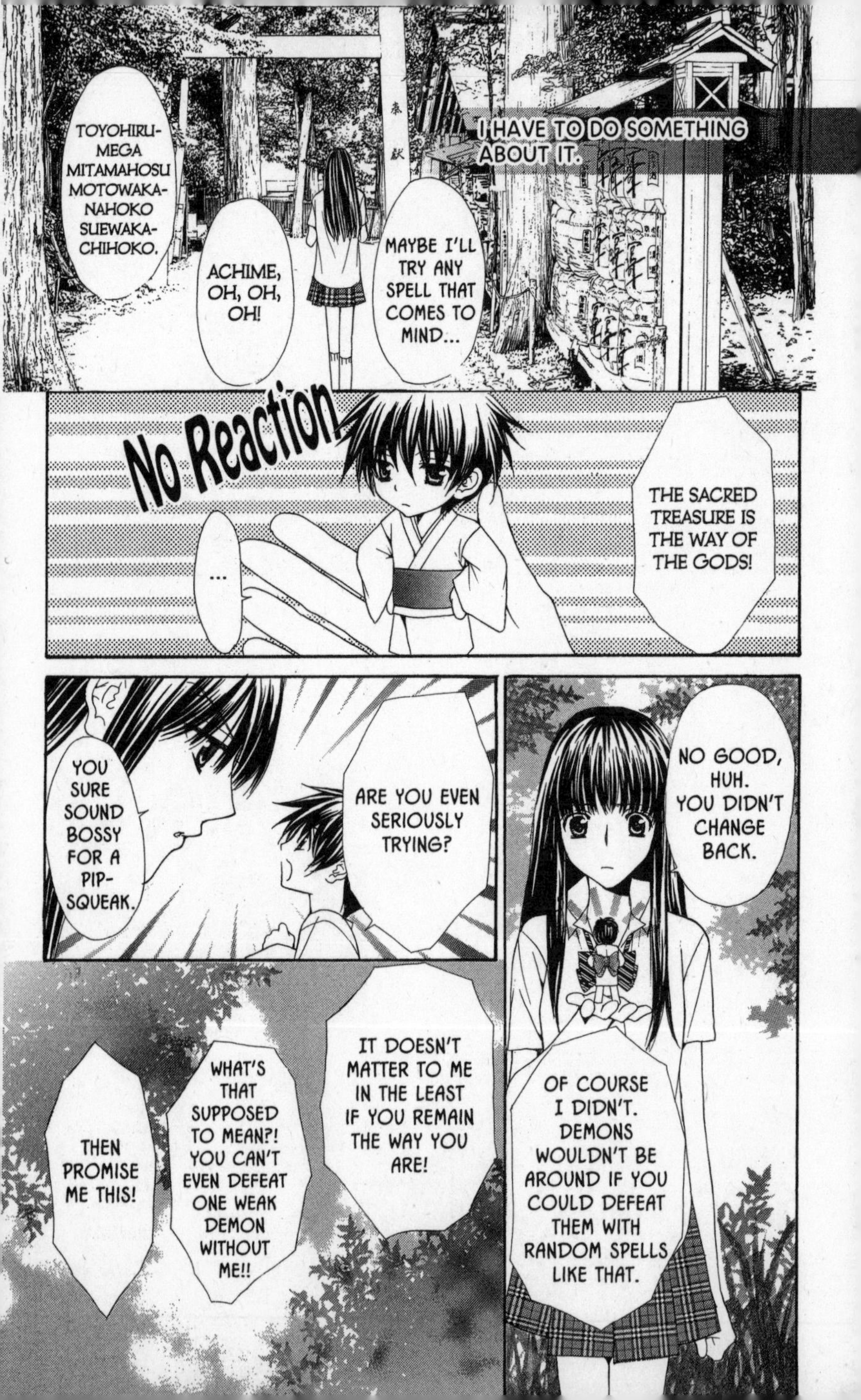
I HAVE TO DO SOMETHING ABOUT IT.
MAYBE I'LL TRY ANY SPELL THAT COMES TO MIND...
ACHIME, OH, OH, OH!
TOYOHIRU-MEGA MITAMAHOSU MOTOWAKA-NAHOKO SUEWAKA-CHIHOKO.
THE SACRED TREASURE IS THE WAY OF THE GODS!
No Reaction
...
NO GOOD, HUH. YOU DIDN'T CHANGE BACK.
ARE YOU EVEN SERIOUSLY TRYING?
YOU SURE SOUND BOSSY FOR A PIP-SQUEAK.
OF COURSE I DIDN'T. DEMONS WOULDN'T BE AROUND IF YOU COULD DEFEAT THEM WITH RANDOM SPELLS LIKE THAT.
IT DOESN'T MATTER TO ME IN THE LEAST IF YOU REMAIN THE WAY YOU ARE!
WHAT'S THAT SUPPOSED TO MEAN?! YOU CAN'T EVEN DEFEAT ONE WEAK DEMON WITHOUT ME!!
THEN PROMISE ME THIS!

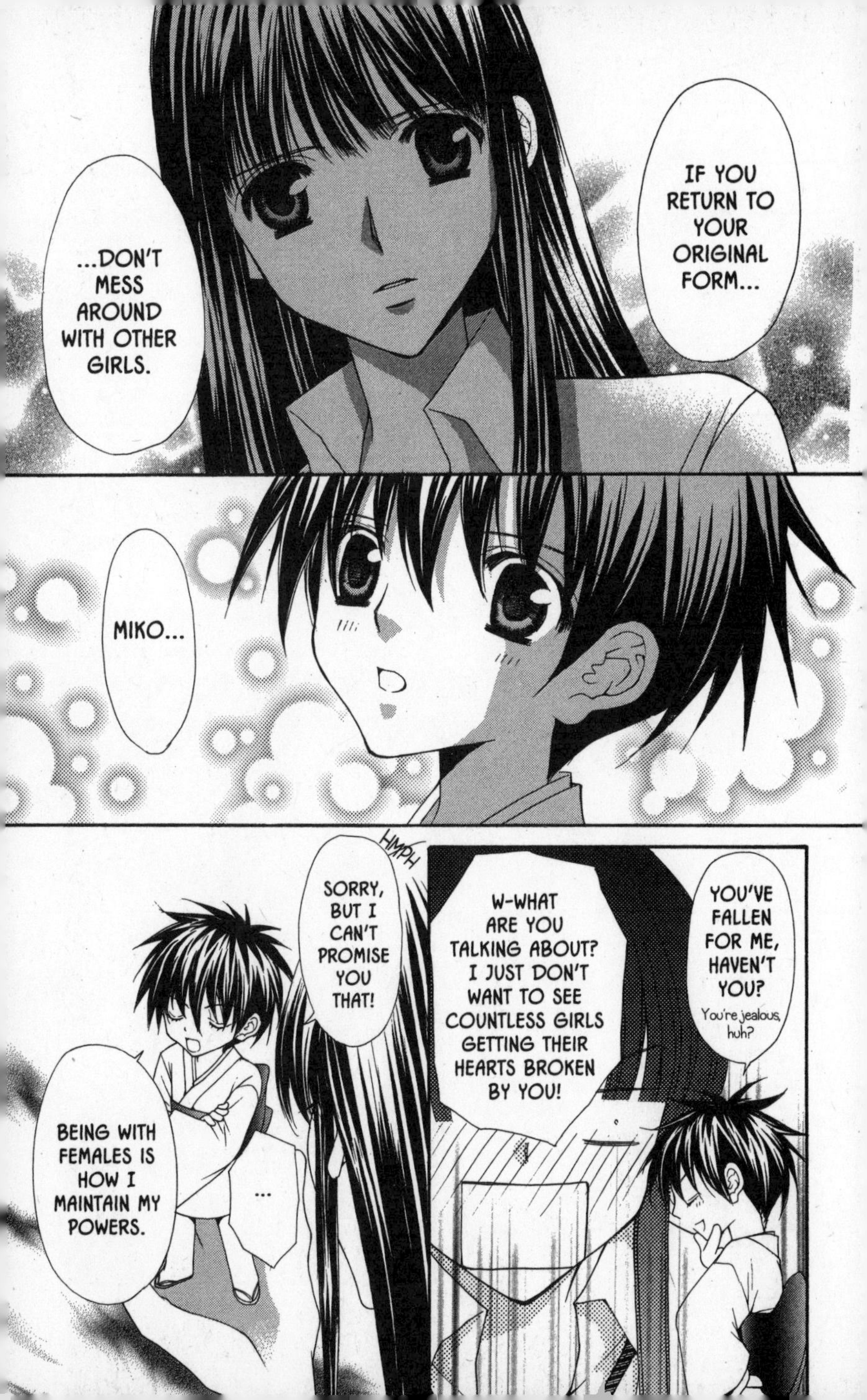
IF YOU RETURN TO YOUR ORIGINAL FORM...
...DON'T MESS AROUND WITH OTHER GIRLS.
MIKO...
YOU'VE FALLEN FOR ME, HAVEN'T YOU?
You're jealous, huh?
W-WHAT ARE YOU TALKING ABOUT? I JUST DON'T WANT TO SEE COUNTLESS GIRLS GETTING THEIR HEARTS BROKEN BY YOU!
HMPH
SORRY, BUT I CAN'T PROMISE YOU THAT!
...
BEING WITH FEMALES IS HOW I MAINTAIN MY POWERS.

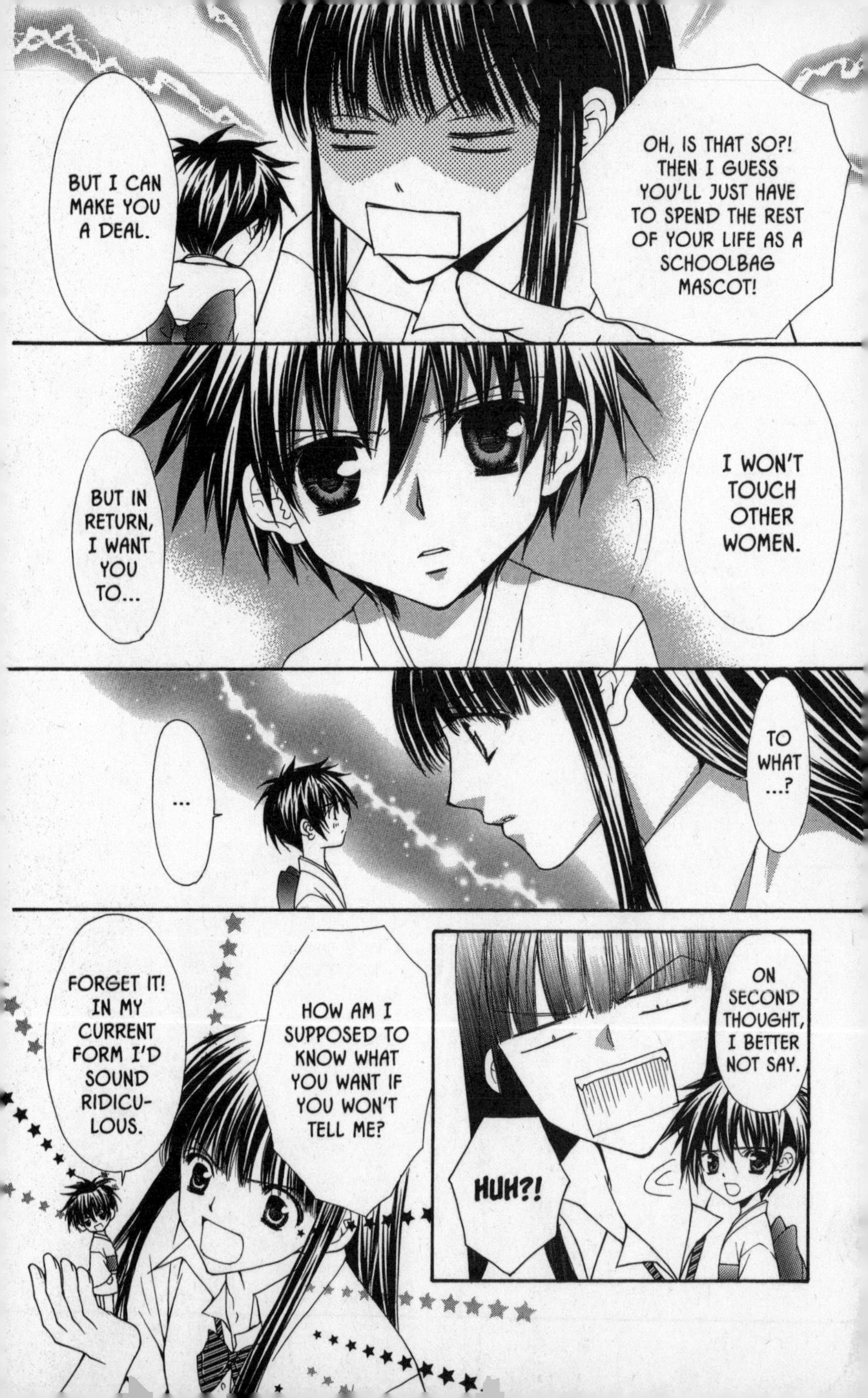
OH, IS THAT SO?! THEN I GUESS YOU'LL JUST HAVE TO SPEND THE REST OF YOUR LIFE AS A SCHOOLBAG MASCOT!
BUT I CAN MAKE YOU A DEAL.
I WON'T TOUCH OTHER WOMEN.
BUT IN RETURN, I WANT YOU TO...
TO WHAT ...?
...
ON SECOND THOUGHT, I BETTER NOT SAY.
HUH?!
HOW AM I SUPPOSED TO KNOW WHAT YOU WANT IF YOU WON'T TELL ME?
FORGET IT! IN MY CURRENT FORM I'D SOUND RIDICU-LOUS.

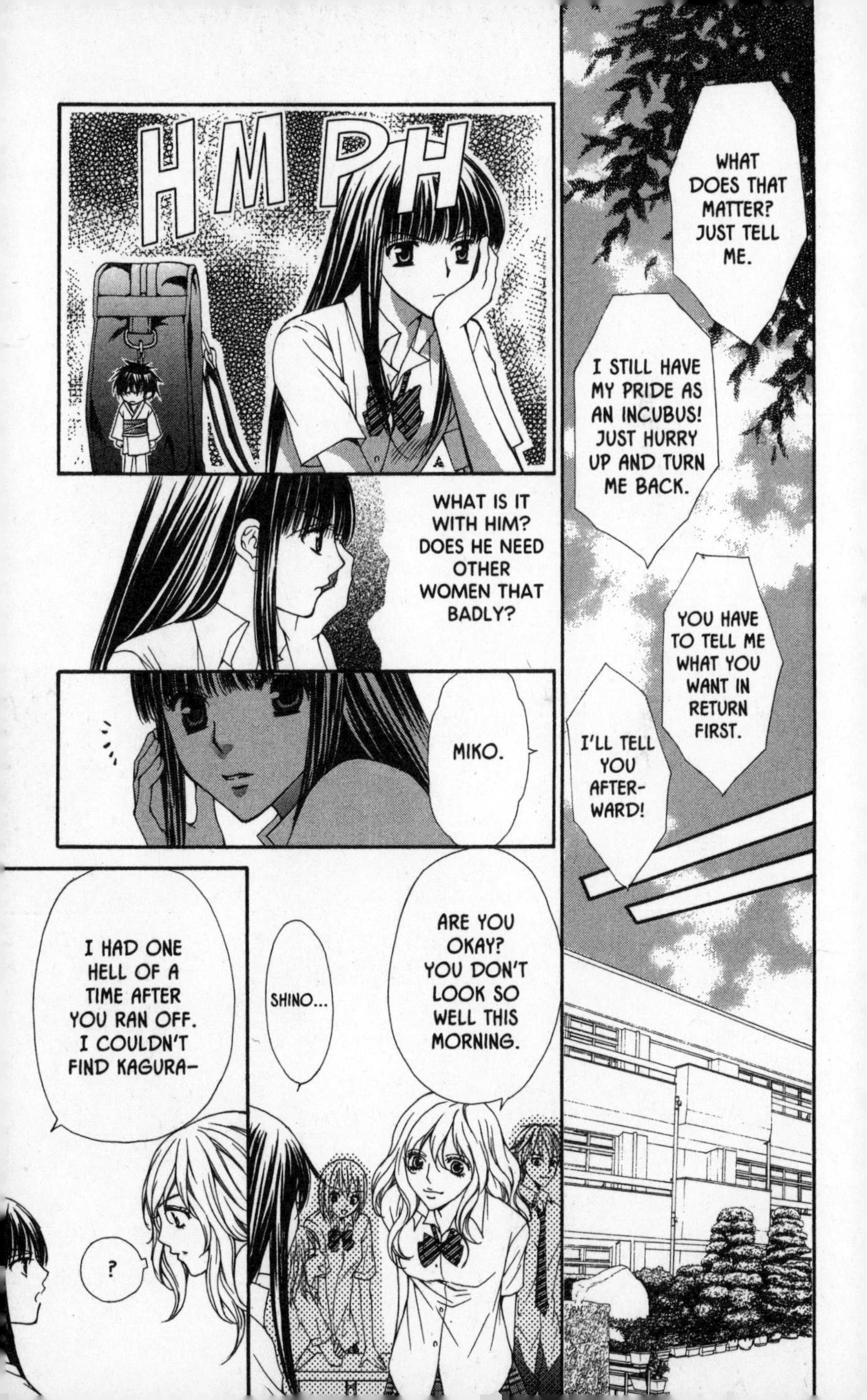
WHAT DOES THAT MATTER? JUST TELL ME.
I STILL HAVE MY PRIDE AS AN INCUBUS! JUST HURRY UP AND TURN ME BACK.
YOU HAVE TO TELL ME WHAT YOU WANT IN RETURN FIRST.
I'LL TELL YOU AFTER-WARD!
HMPH
WHAT IS IT WITH HIM? DOES HE NEED OTHER WOMEN THAT BADLY?
MIKO.
ARE YOU OKAY? YOU DON'T LOOK SO WELL THIS MORNING.
SHINO...
I HAD ONE HELL OF A TIME AFTER YOU RAN OFF. I COULDN'T FIND KAGURA-
?

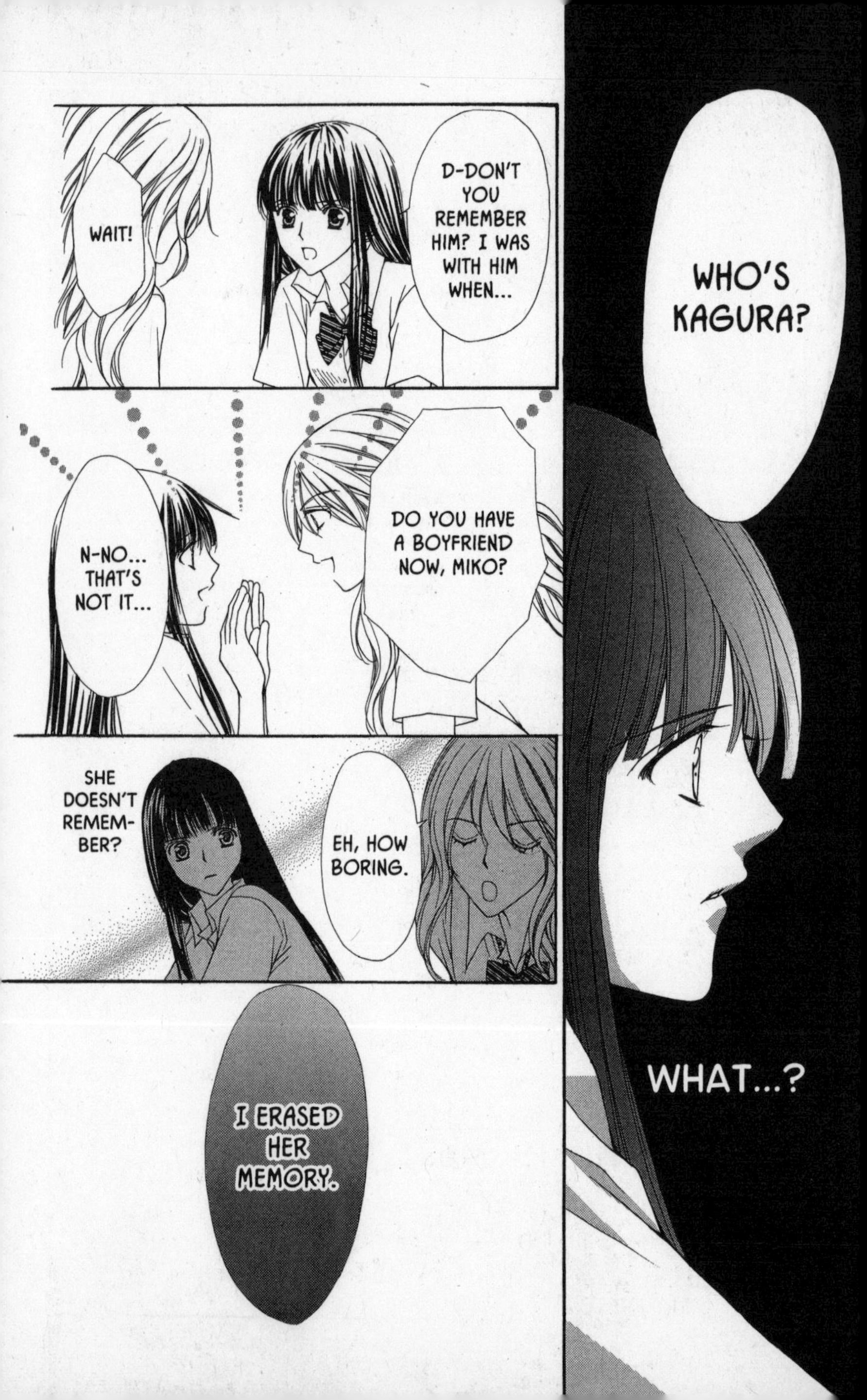
WHO'S KAGURA?
WHAT...?
D-DON'T YOU REMEMBER HIM? I WAS WITH HIM WHEN...
WAIT!
DO YOU HAVE A BOYFRIEND NOW, MIKO?
N-NO... THAT'S NOT IT...
EH, HOW BORING.
SHE DOESN'T REMEMBER?
I ERASED HER MEMORY.

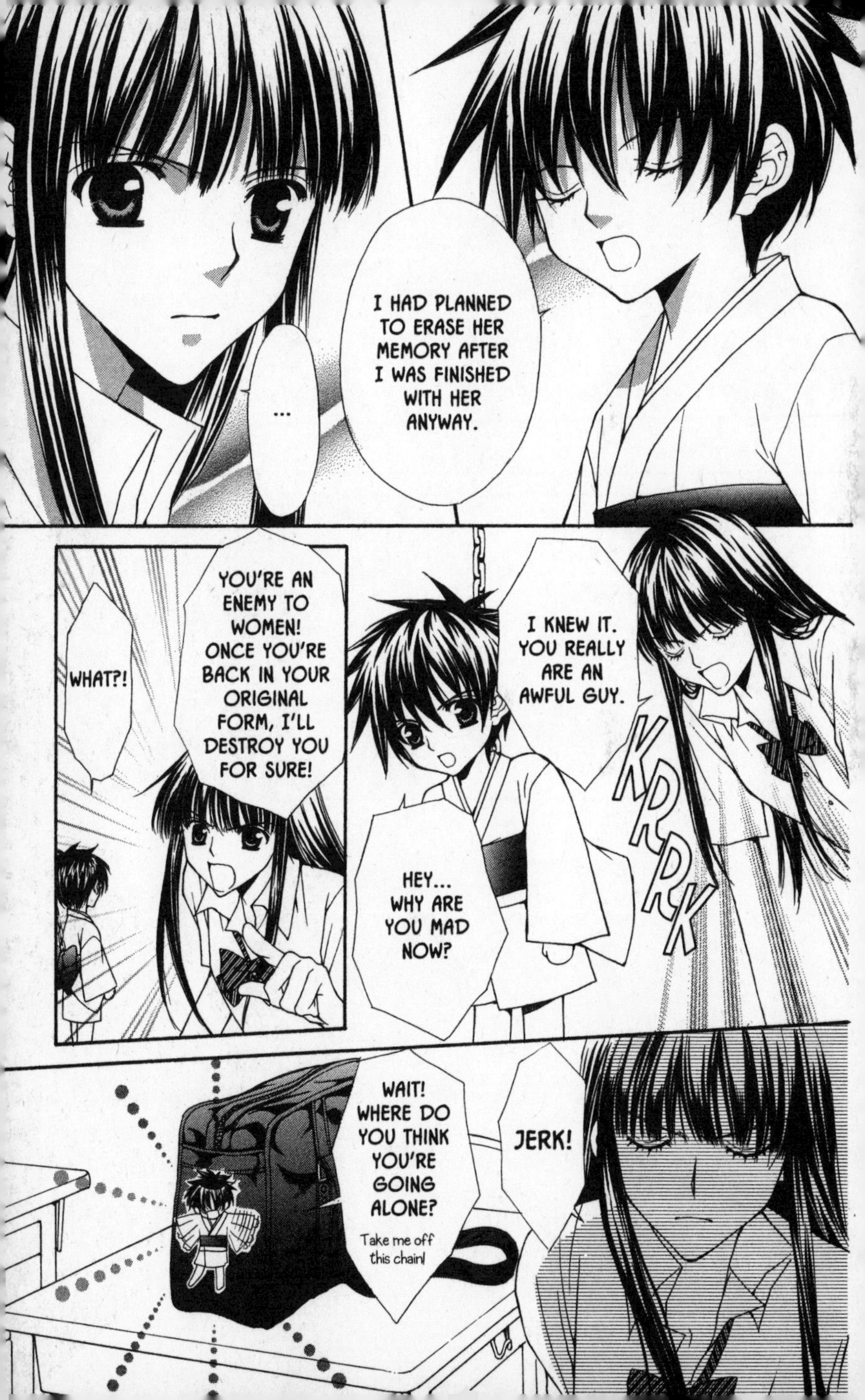
I HAD PLANNED TO ERASE HER MEMORY AFTER I WAS FINISHED WITH HER ANYWAY.
...
I KNEW IT. YOU REALLY ARE AN AWFUL GUY.
KRRK
HEY... WHY ARE YOU MAD NOW?
YOU'RE AN ENEMY TO WOMEN! ONCE YOU'RE BACK IN YOUR ORIGINAL FORM, I'LL DESTROY YOU FOR SURE!
WHAT?!
JERK!
WAIT! WHERE DO YOU THINK YOU'RE GOING ALONE?
Take me off this chain!

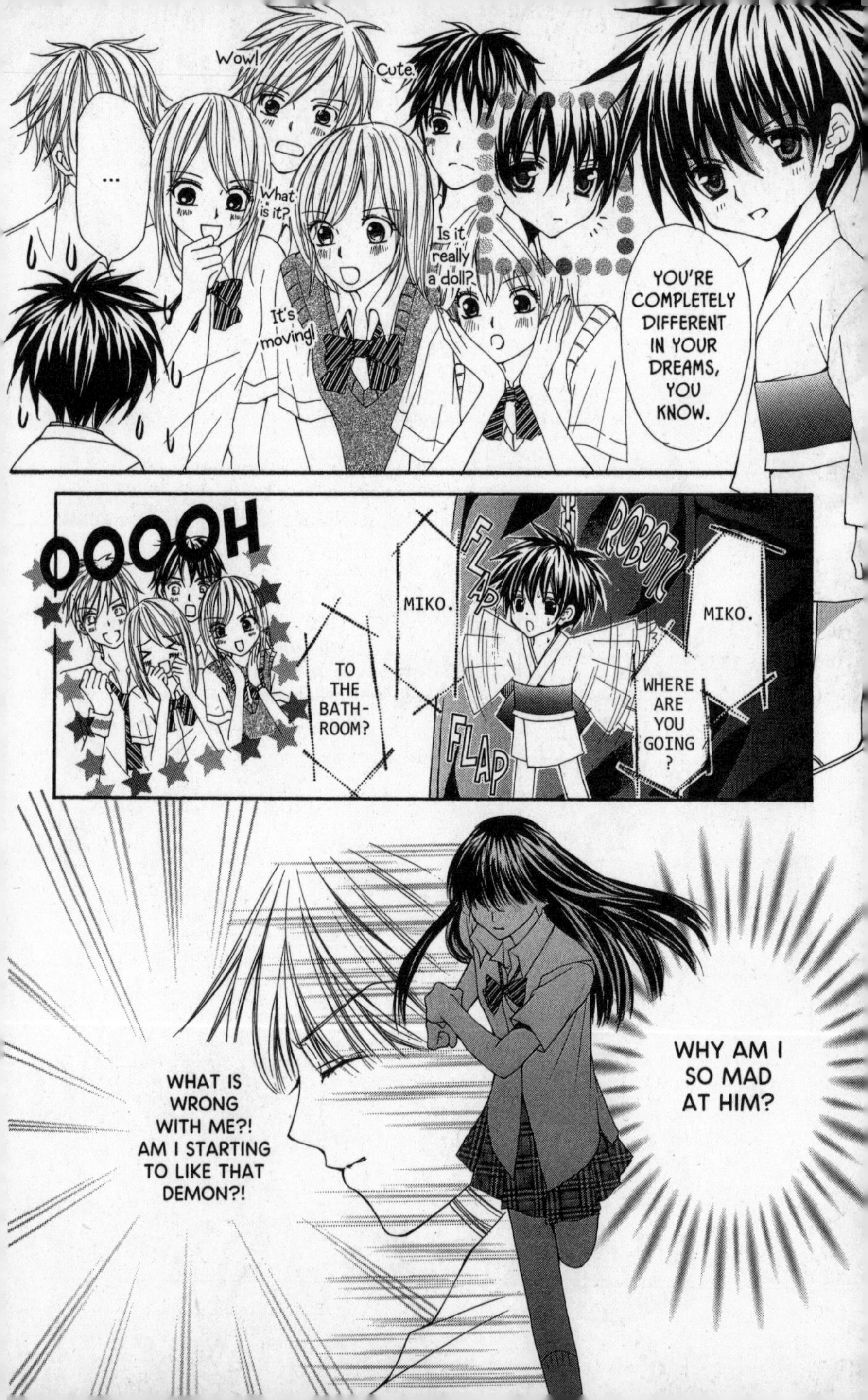
YOU'RE COMPLETELY DIFFERENT IN YOUR DREAMS, YOU KNOW.
Is it really a doll?
Cute.
What is it?
It's moving!
Wow!
...
MIKO.
WHERE ARE YOU GOING?
ROBOTIC
FLAP
FLAP
MIKO.
TO THE BATH-ROOM?
OOOOH
WHY AM I SO MAD AT HIM?
WHAT IS WRONG WITH ME?! AM I STARTING TO LIKE THAT DEMON?!

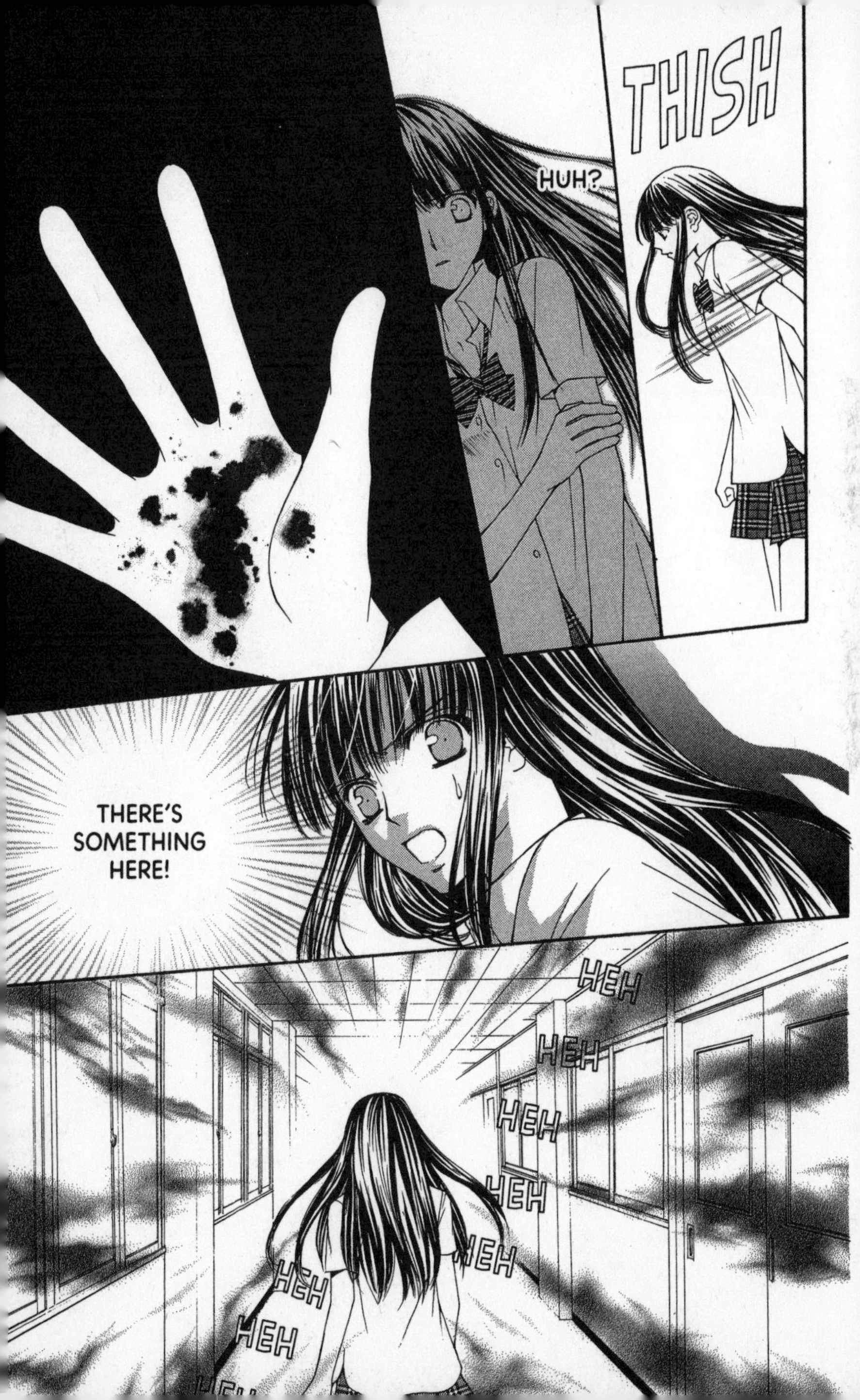
THISH
HUH?
THERE'S SOMETHING HERE!
HEH
HEH
HEH
HEH
HEH
HEH
HEH

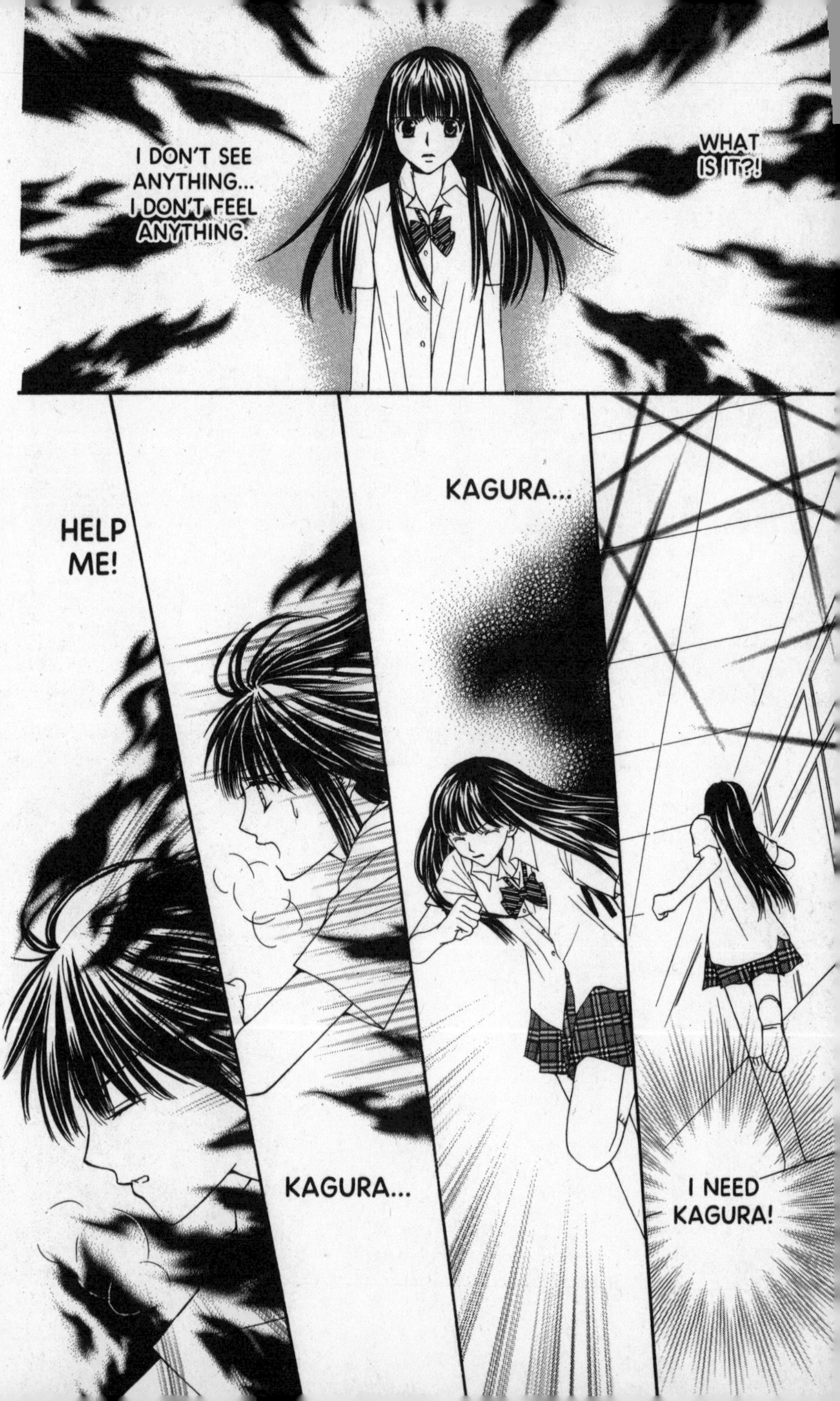
WHAT IS IT?!
I DON'T SEE ANYTHING... I DON'T FEEL ANYTHING.
I NEED KAGURA!
KAGURA...
KAGURA...
HELP ME!

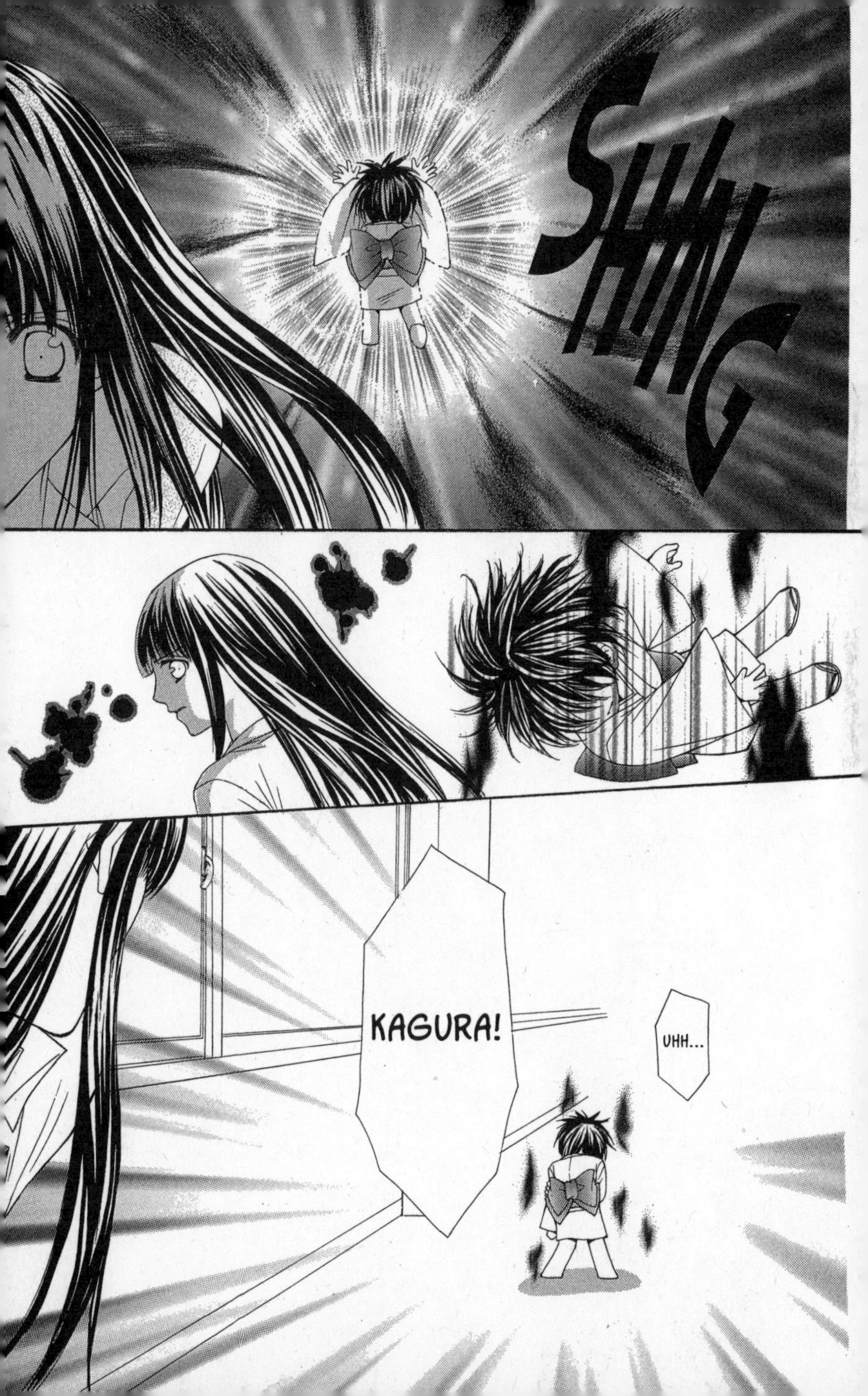
SHING
KAGURA!
UHH...

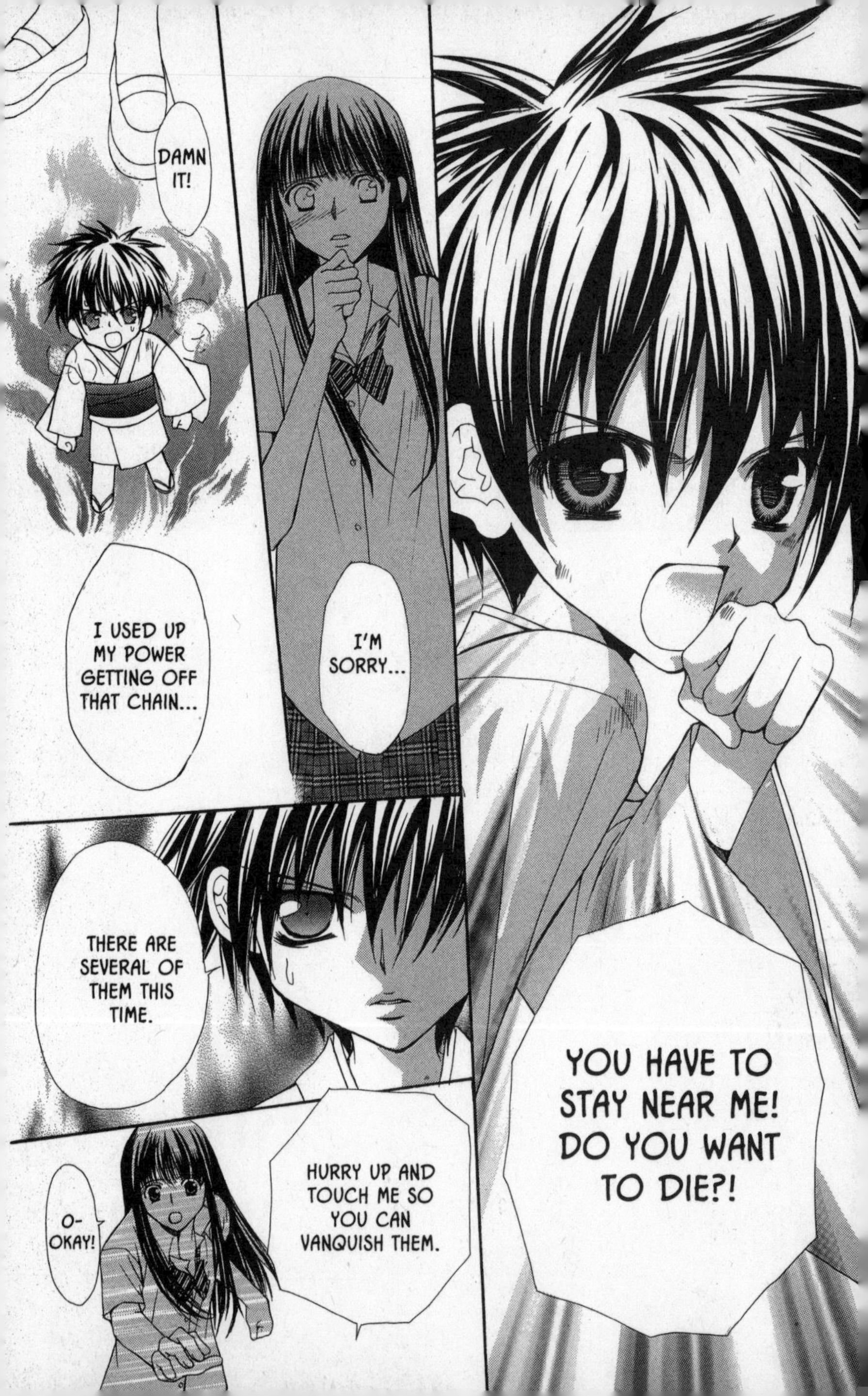
YOU HAVE TO STAY NEAR ME! DO YOU WANT TO DIE?!
I'M SORRY...
DAMN IT!
I USED UP MY POWER GETTING OFF THAT CHAIN...
THERE ARE SEVERAL OF THEM THIS TIME.
HURRY UP AND TOUCH ME SO YOU CAN VANQUISH THEM.
O-OKAY!

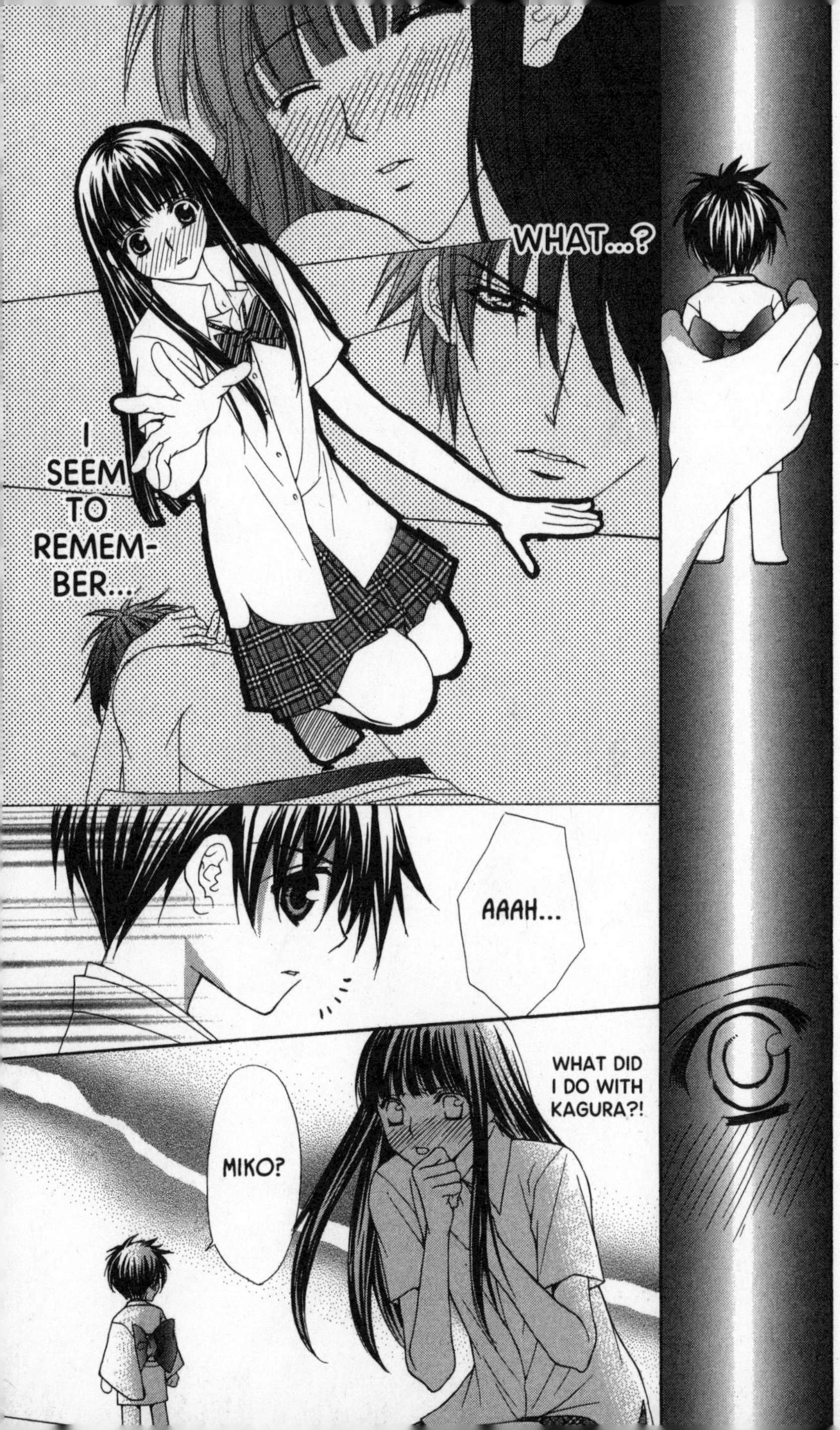
WHAT...?
I SEEM TO REMEMBER...
AAAH...
WHAT DID I DO WITH KAGURA?!
MIKO?

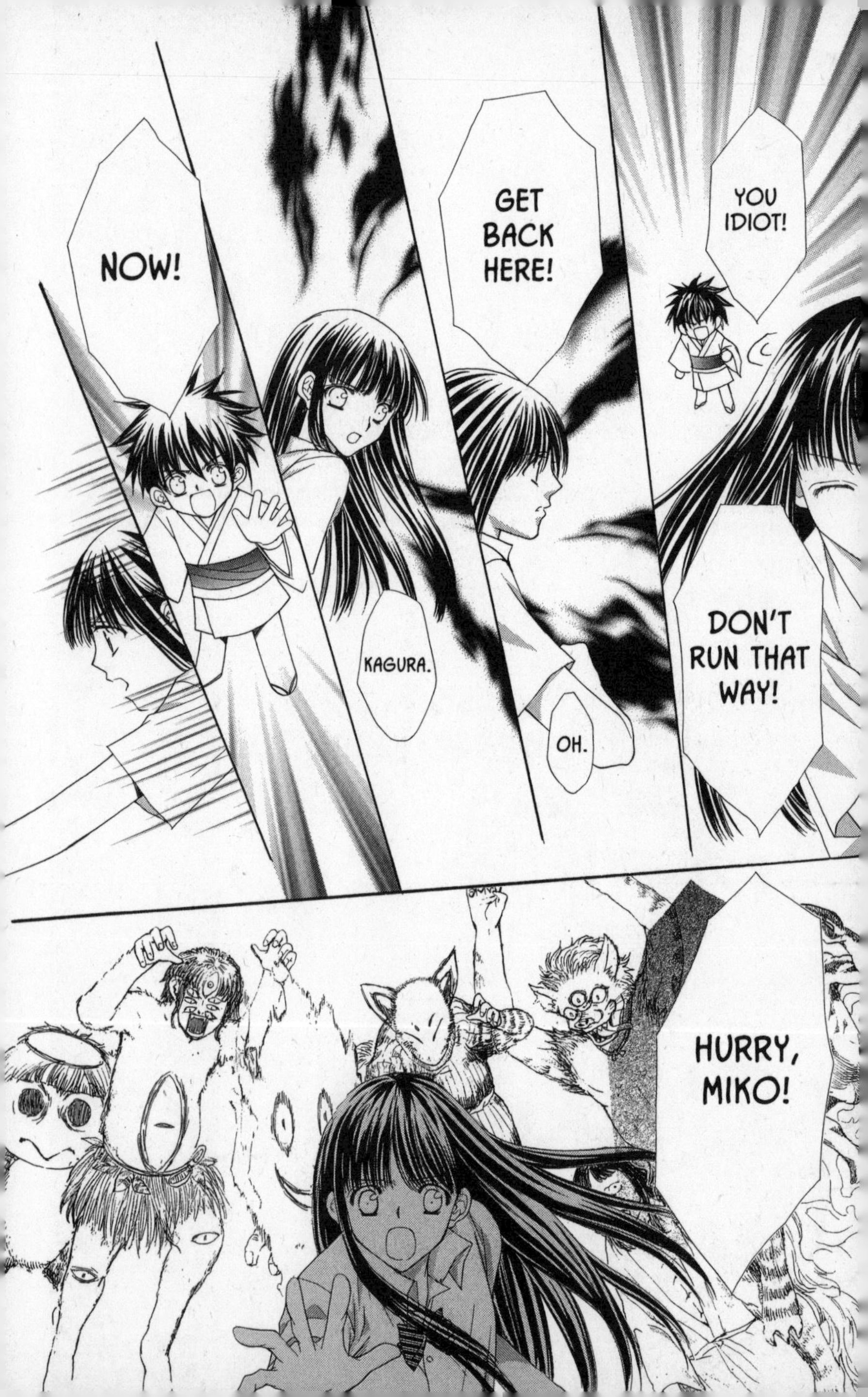
YOU IDIOT!
DON'T RUN THAT WAY!
GET BACK HERE!
OH.
KAGURA.
NOW!
HURRY, MIKO!

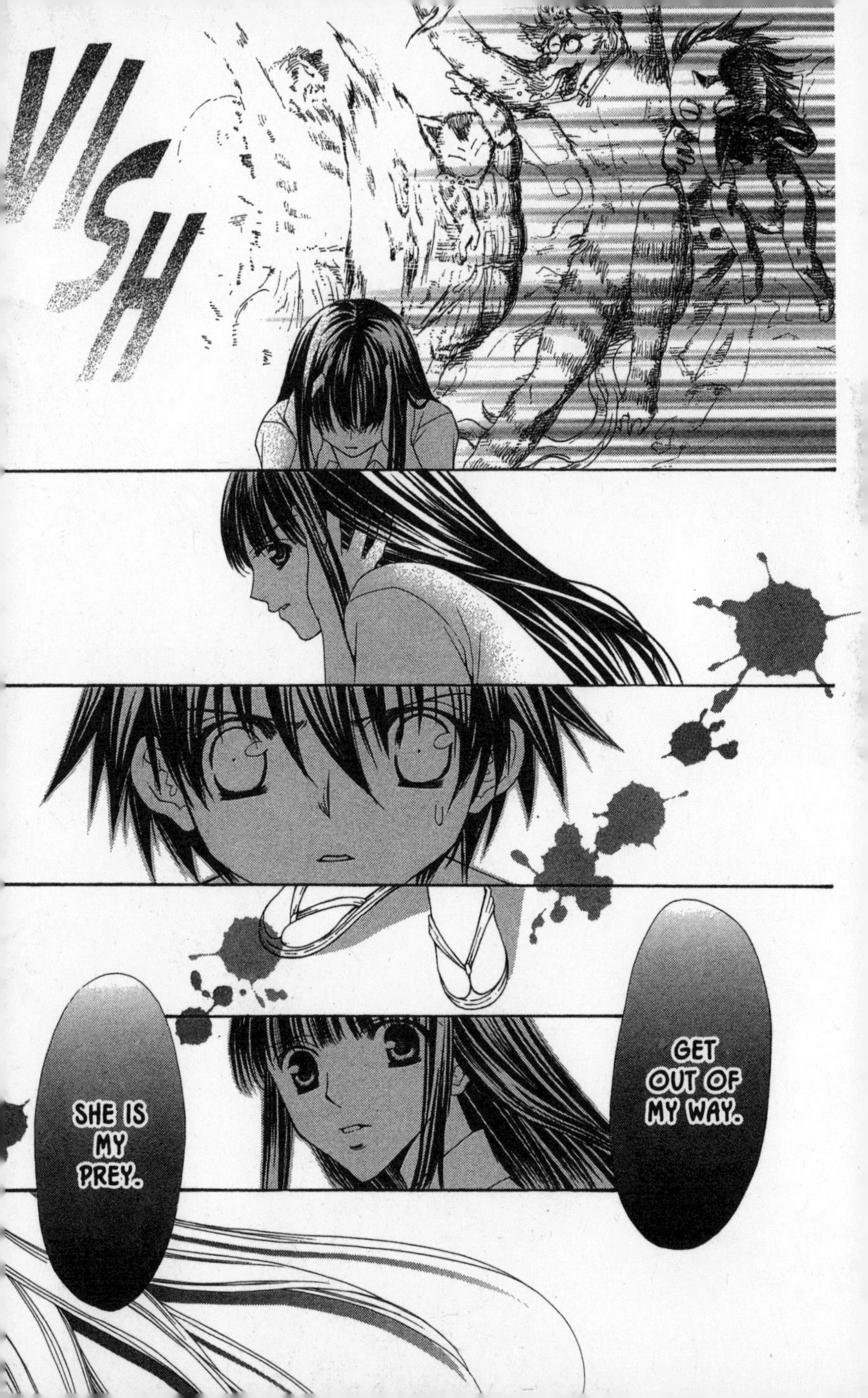
VISH
GET OUT OF MY WAY.
SHE IS MY PREY.

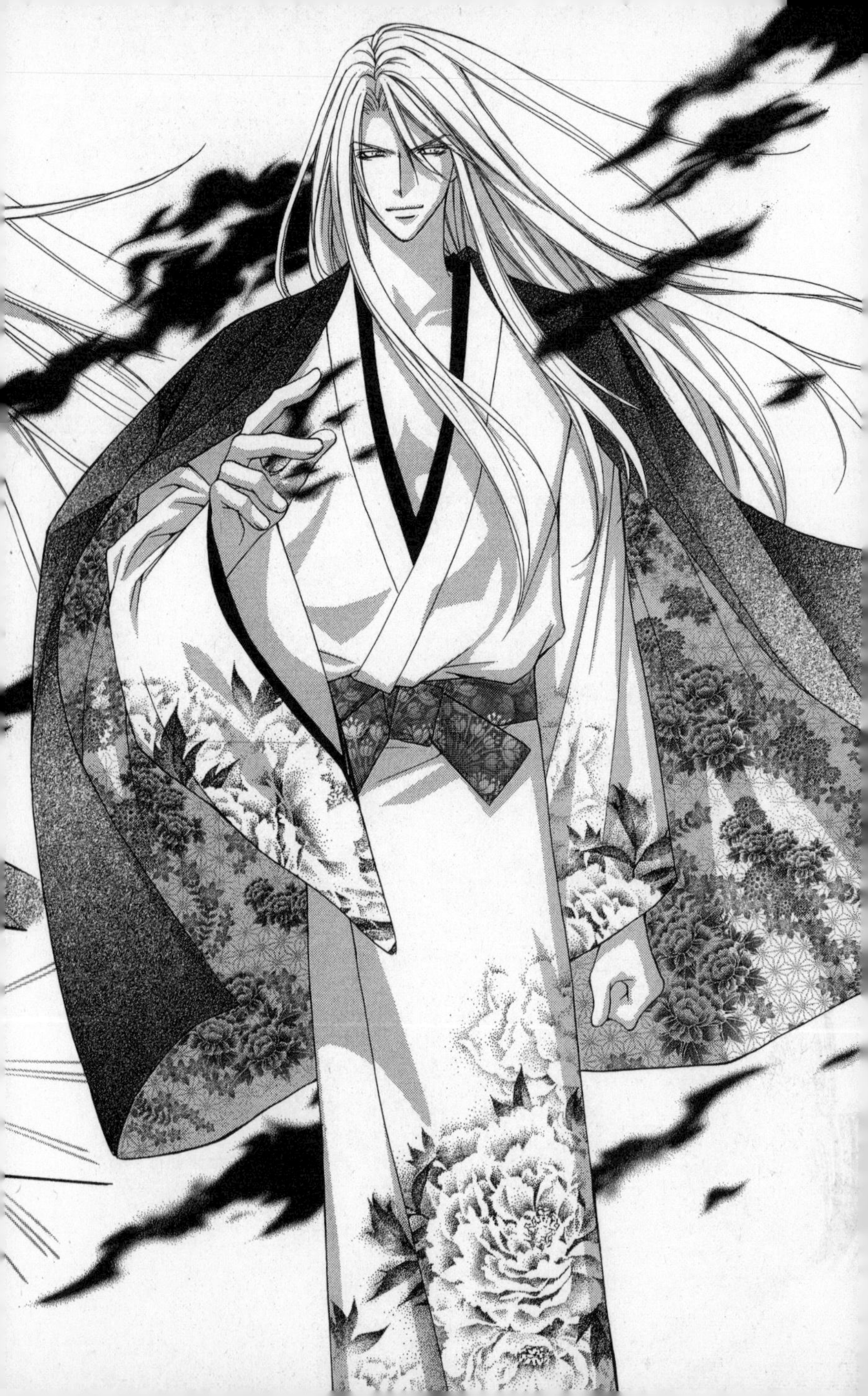

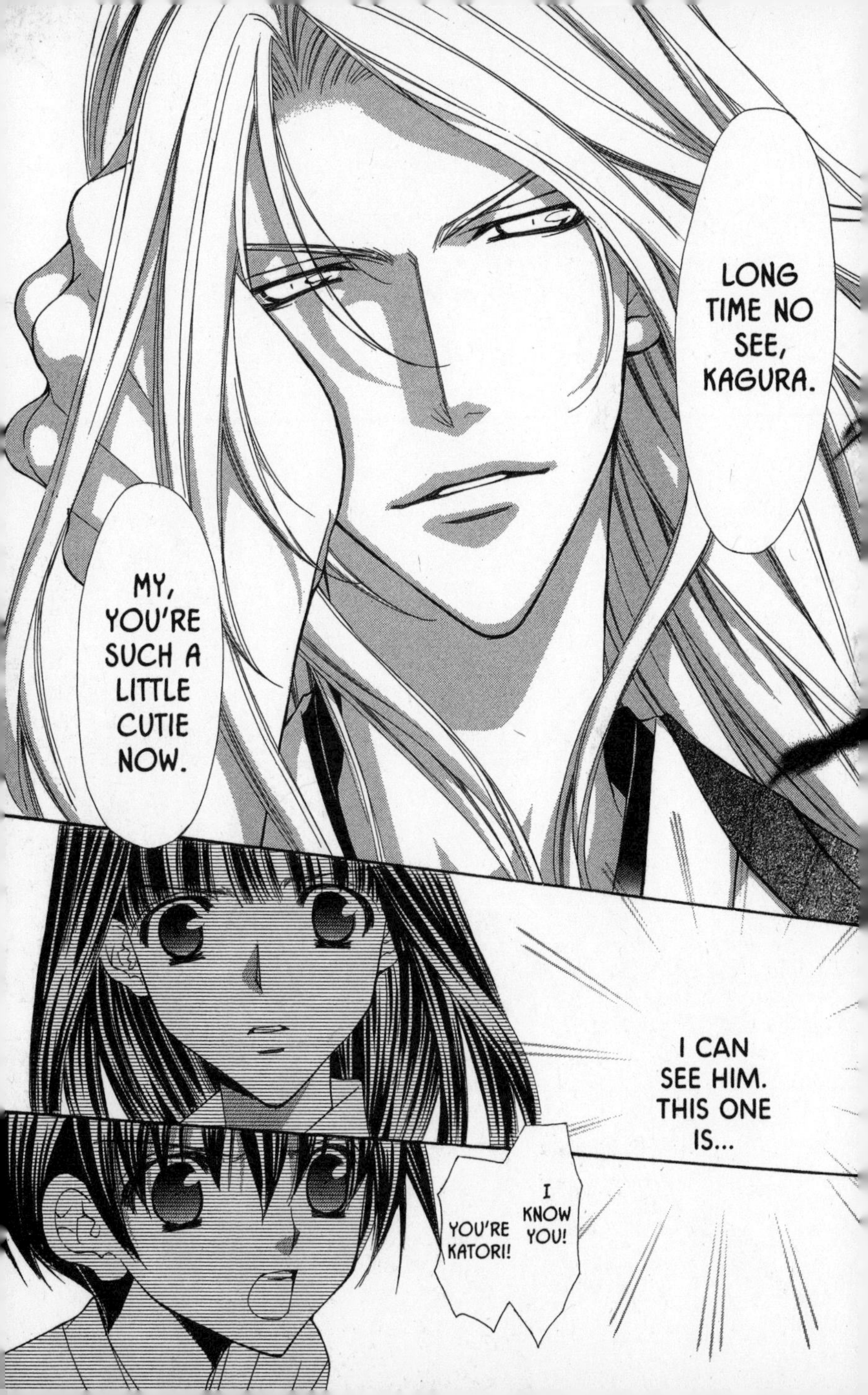
LONG TIME NO SEE, KAGURA.
MY, YOU'RE SUCH A LITTLE CUTIE NOW.
I CAN SEE HIM. THIS ONE IS...
I KNOW YOU!
YOU'RE KATORI!

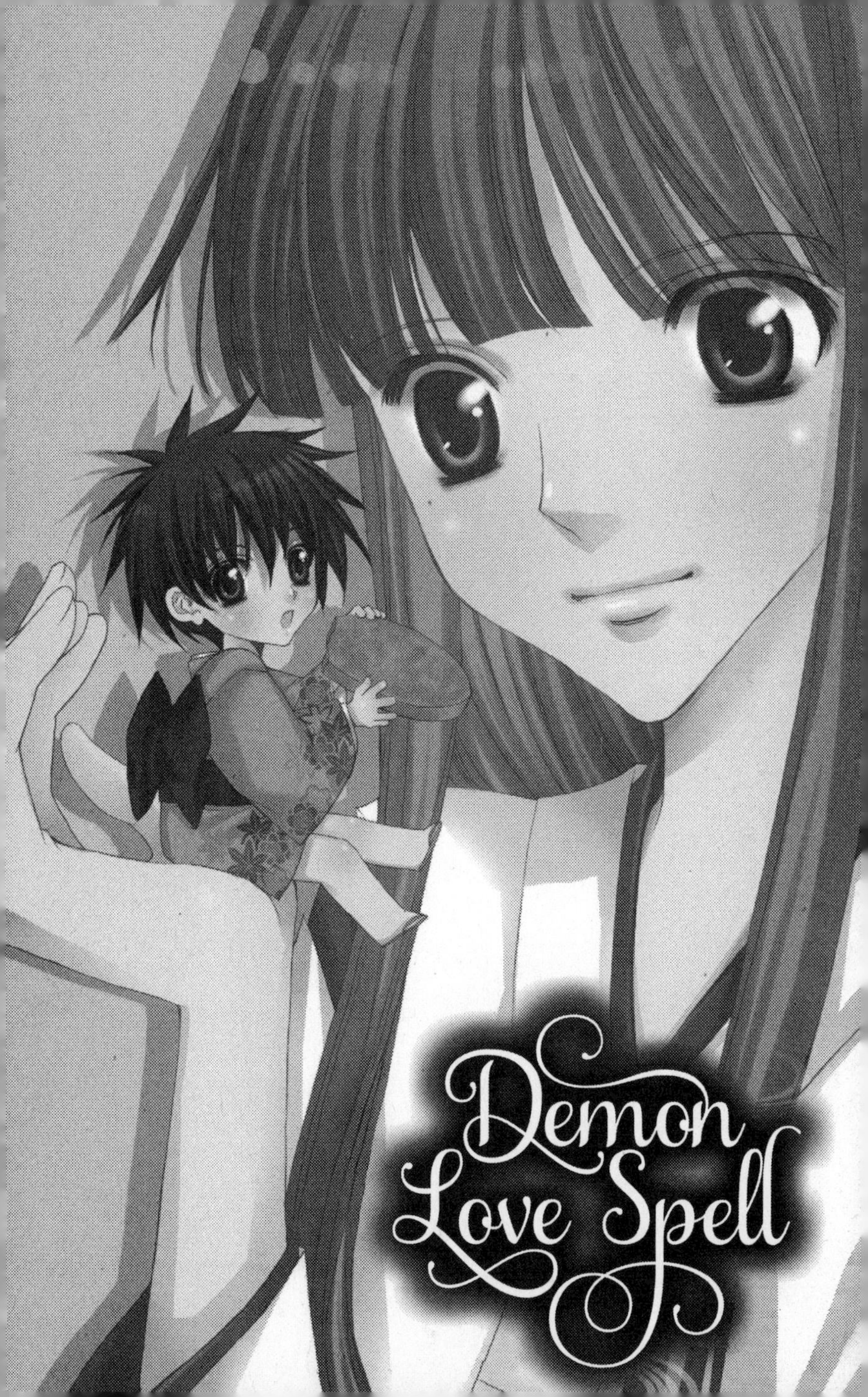
Demon
Love Spell

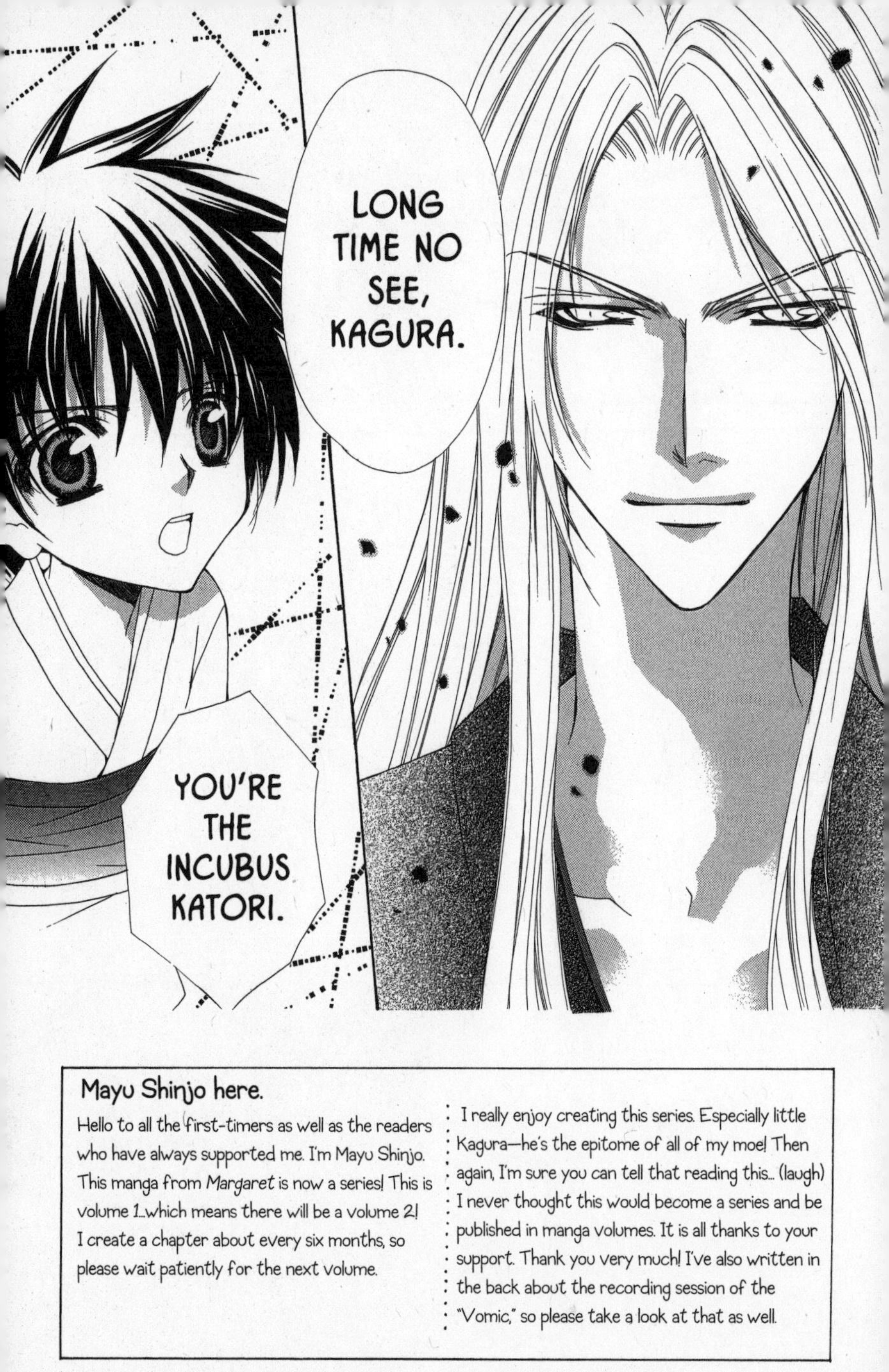
LONG TIME NO SEE, KAGURA.
YOU'RE THE INCUBUS KATORI.

Mayu Shinjo here.

Hello to all the first-timers as well as the readers who have always supported me. I'm Mayu Shinjo. This manga from *Margaret* is now a series! This is volume 1...which means there will be a volume 2! I create a chapter about every six months, so please wait patiently for the next volume.

I really enjoy creating this series. Especially little Kagura—he's the epitome of all of my moe! Then again, I'm sure you can tell that reading this... (laugh) I never thought this would become a series and be published in manga volumes. It is all thanks to your support. Thank you very much! I've also written in the back about the recording session of the "Vomic," so please take a look at that as well.

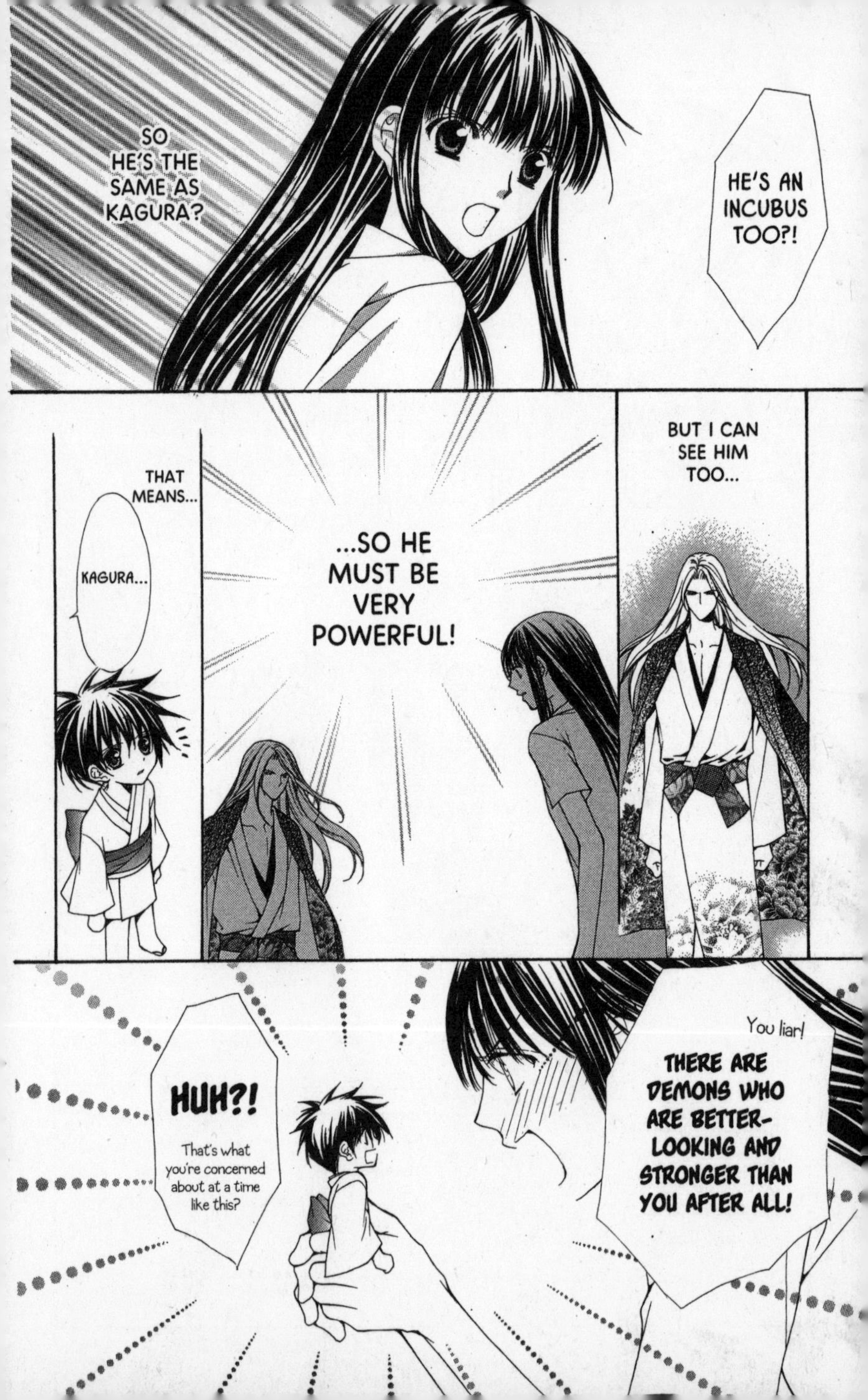
HE'S AN INCUBUS TOO?!
SO HE'S THE SAME AS KAGURA?
BUT I CAN SEE HIM TOO...
...SO HE MUST BE VERY POWERFUL!
THAT MEANS...
KAGURA...
You liar!
THERE ARE DEMONS WHO ARE BETTER-LOOKING AND STRONGER THAN YOU AFTER ALL!
HUH?!
That's what you're concerned about at a time like this?

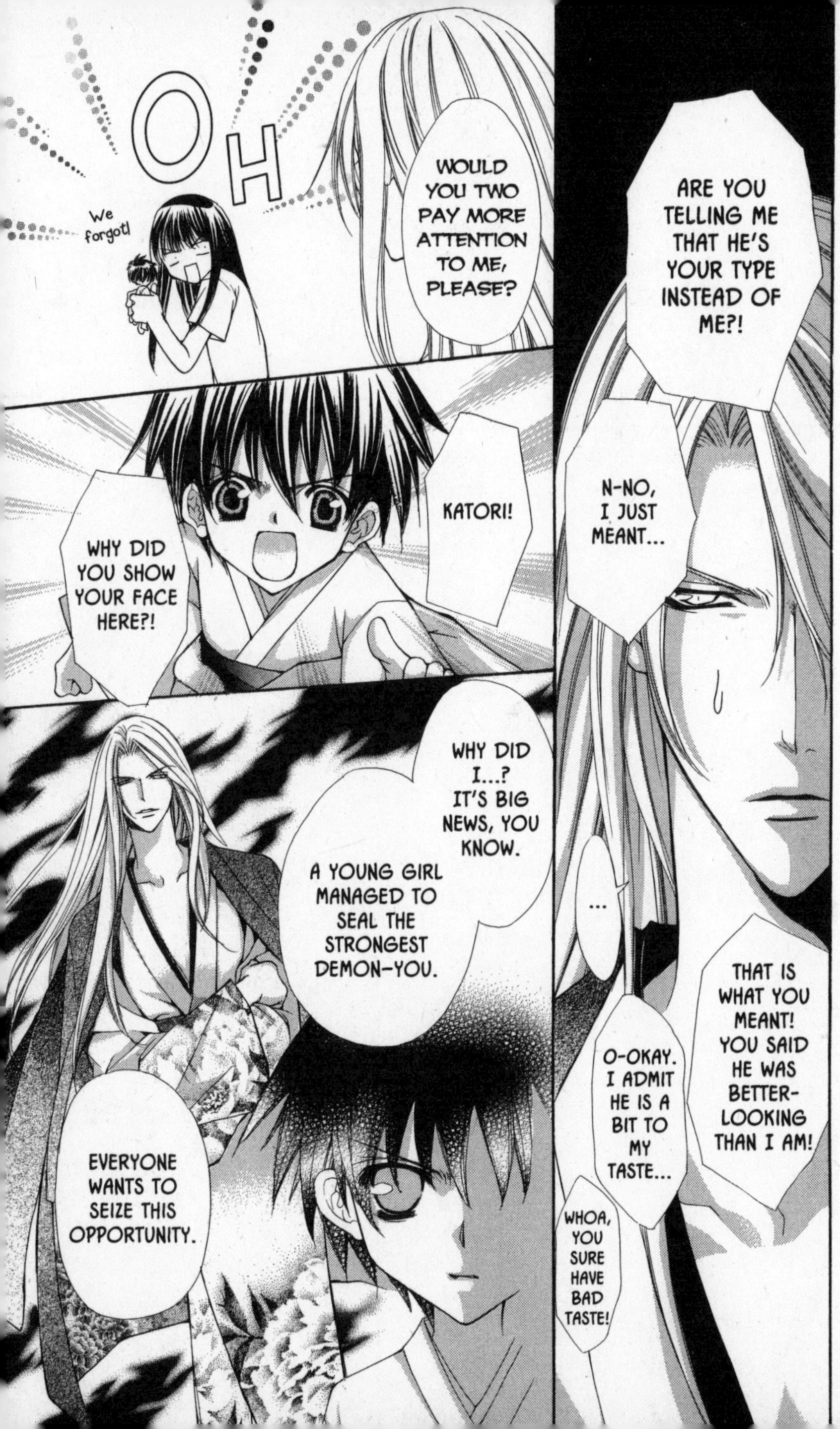
ARE YOU TELLING ME THAT HE'S YOUR TYPE INSTEAD OF ME?!
N-NO, I JUST MEANT...
...
THAT IS WHAT YOU MEANT! YOU SAID HE WAS BETTER-LOOKING THAN I AM!
O-OKAY. I ADMIT HE IS A BIT TO MY TASTE...
WHOA, YOU SURE HAVE BAD TASTE!
WOULD YOU TWO PAY MORE ATTENTION TO ME, PLEASE?
OH
We forgot!
KATORI!
WHY DID YOU SHOW YOUR FACE HERE?!
WHY DID I...? IT'S BIG NEWS, YOU KNOW.
A YOUNG GIRL MANAGED TO SEAL THE STRONGEST DEMON—YOU.
EVERYONE WANTS TO SEIZE THIS OPPORTUNITY.

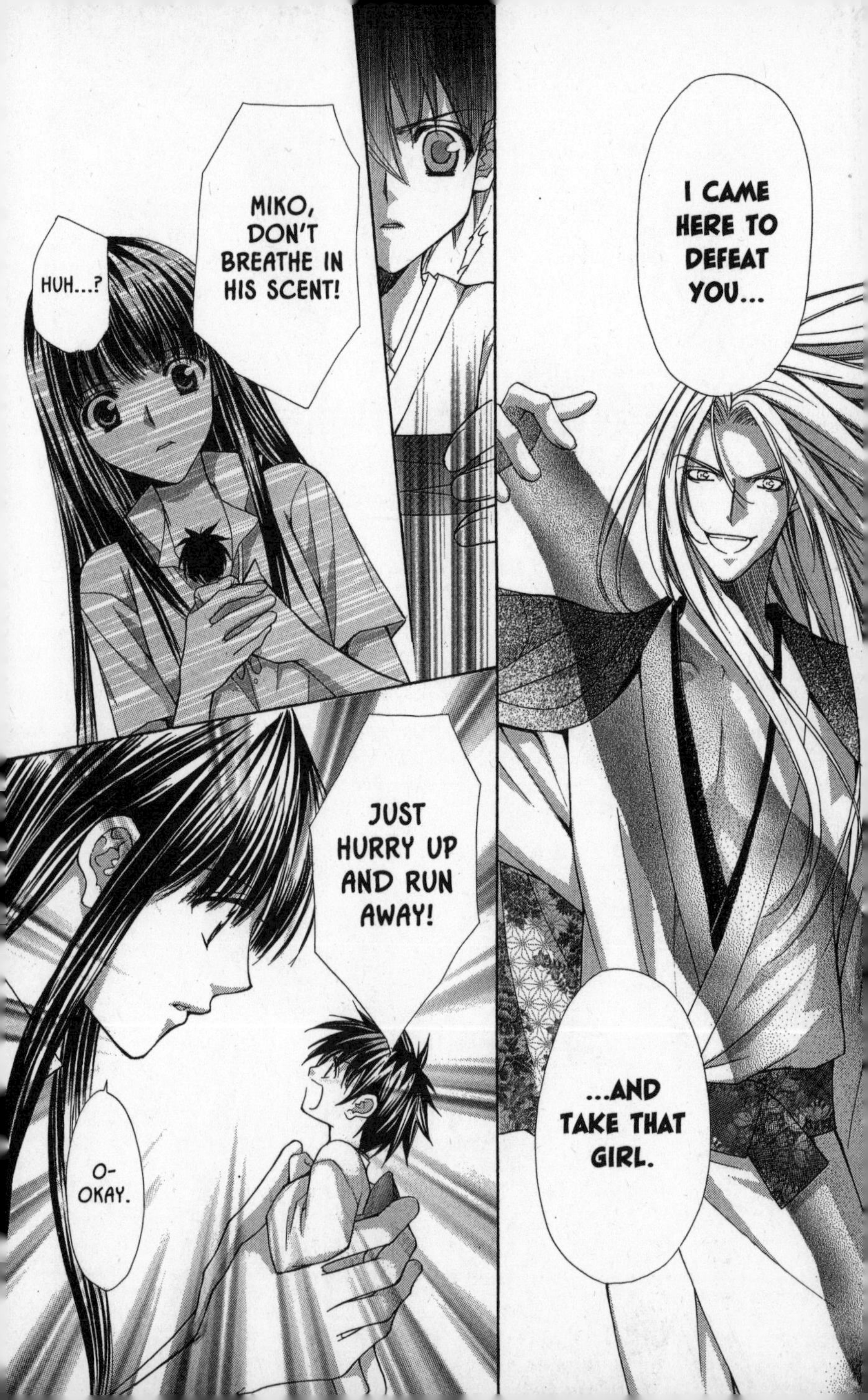
I CAME HERE TO DEFEAT YOU...
...AND TAKE THAT GIRL.
MIKO, DON'T BREATHE IN HIS SCENT!
HUH...?
JUST HURRY UP AND RUN AWAY!
O-OKAY.

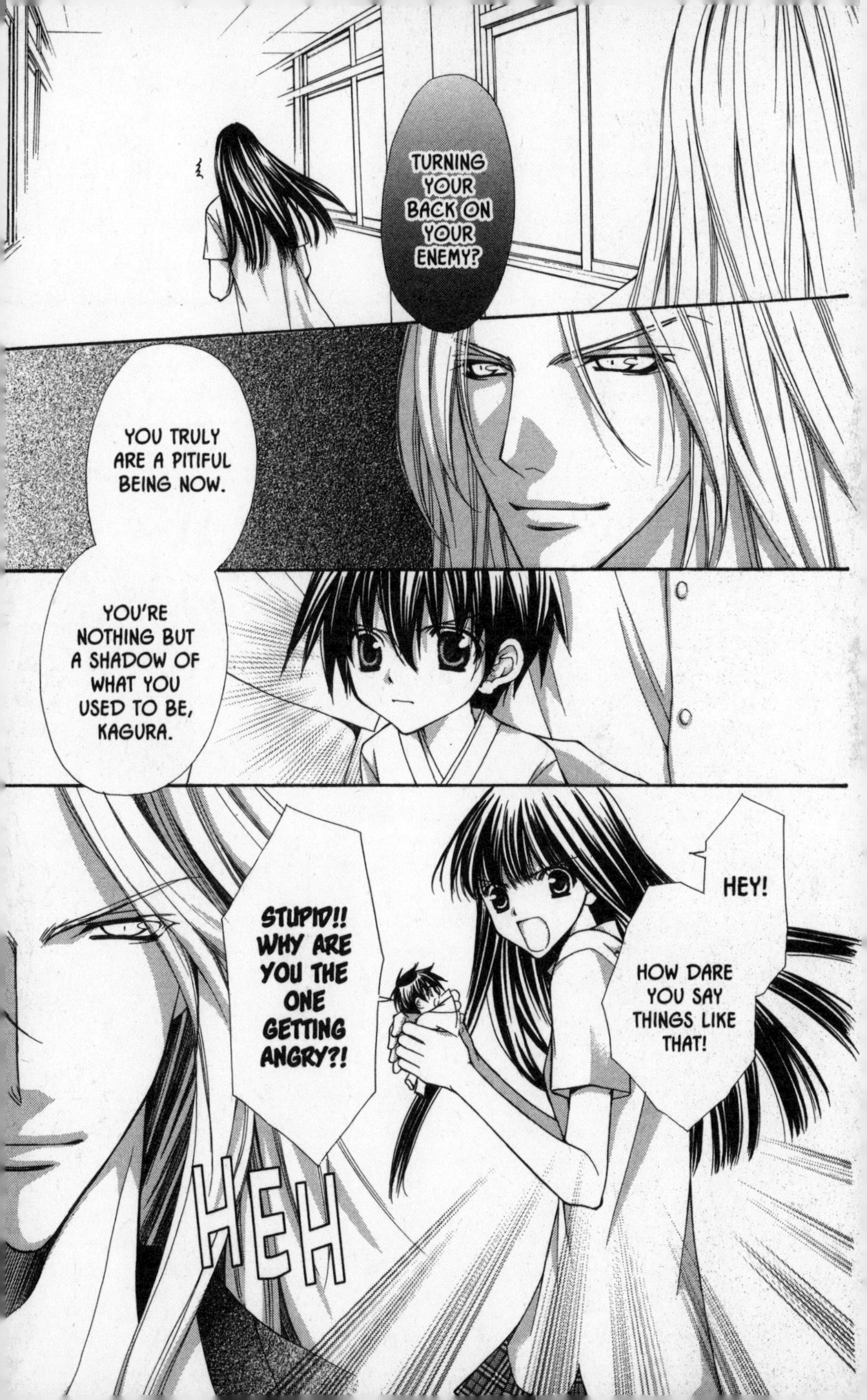
TURNING YOUR BACK ON YOUR ENEMY?
YOU TRULY ARE A PITIFUL BEING NOW.
YOU'RE NOTHING BUT A SHADOW OF WHAT YOU USED TO BE, KAGURA.
HEY!
HOW DARE YOU SAY THINGS LIKE THAT!
STUPID!! WHY ARE YOU THE ONE GETTING ANGRY?!
HEH

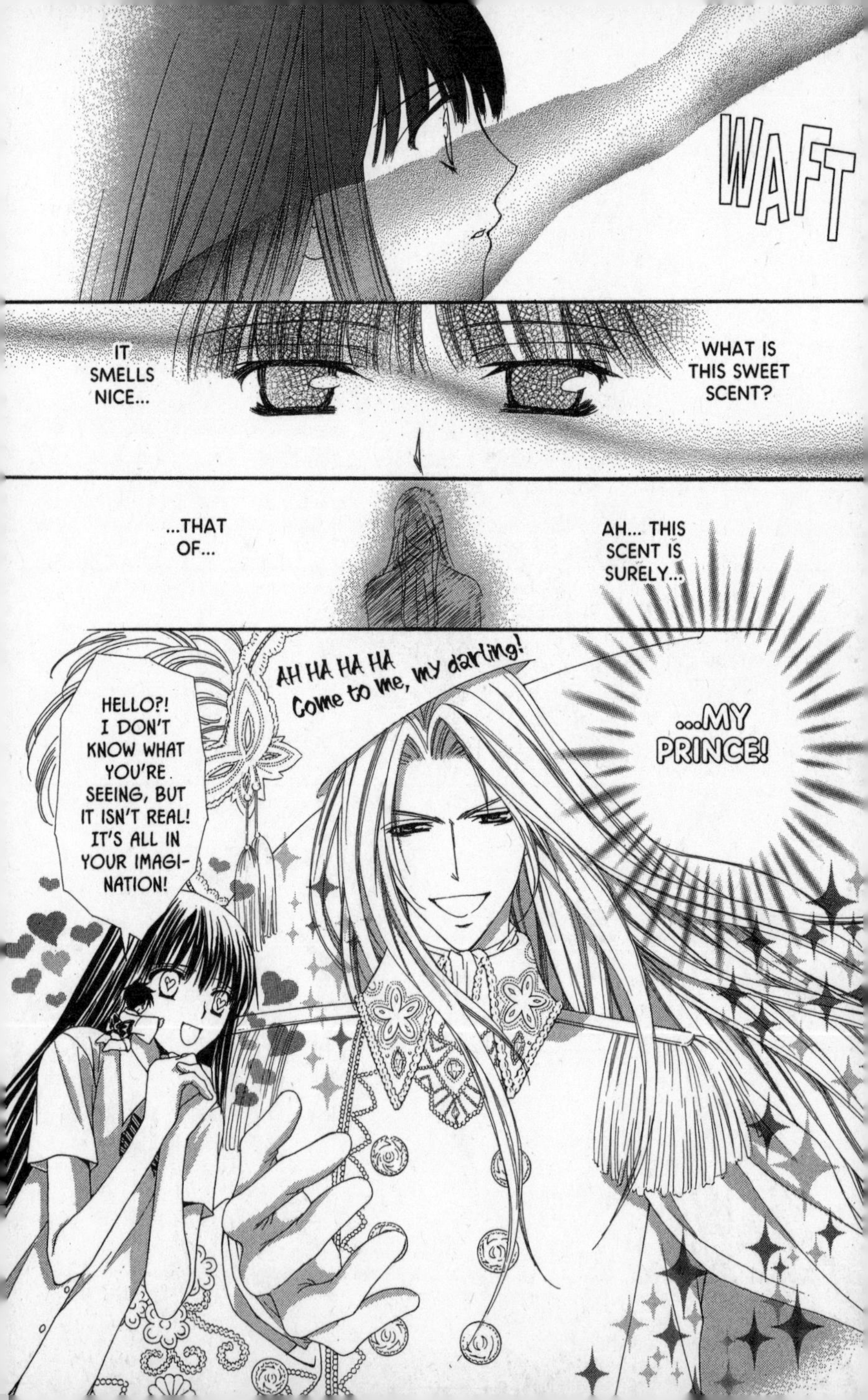
WAFT
WHAT IS THIS SWEET SCENT?
IT SMELLS NICE...
AH... THIS SCENT IS SURELY...
...THAT OF...
...MY PRINCE!
AH HA HA HA Come to me, my darling!
HELLO?! I DON'T KNOW WHAT YOU'RE SEEING, BUT IT ISN'T REAL! IT'S ALL IN YOUR IMAGINATION!

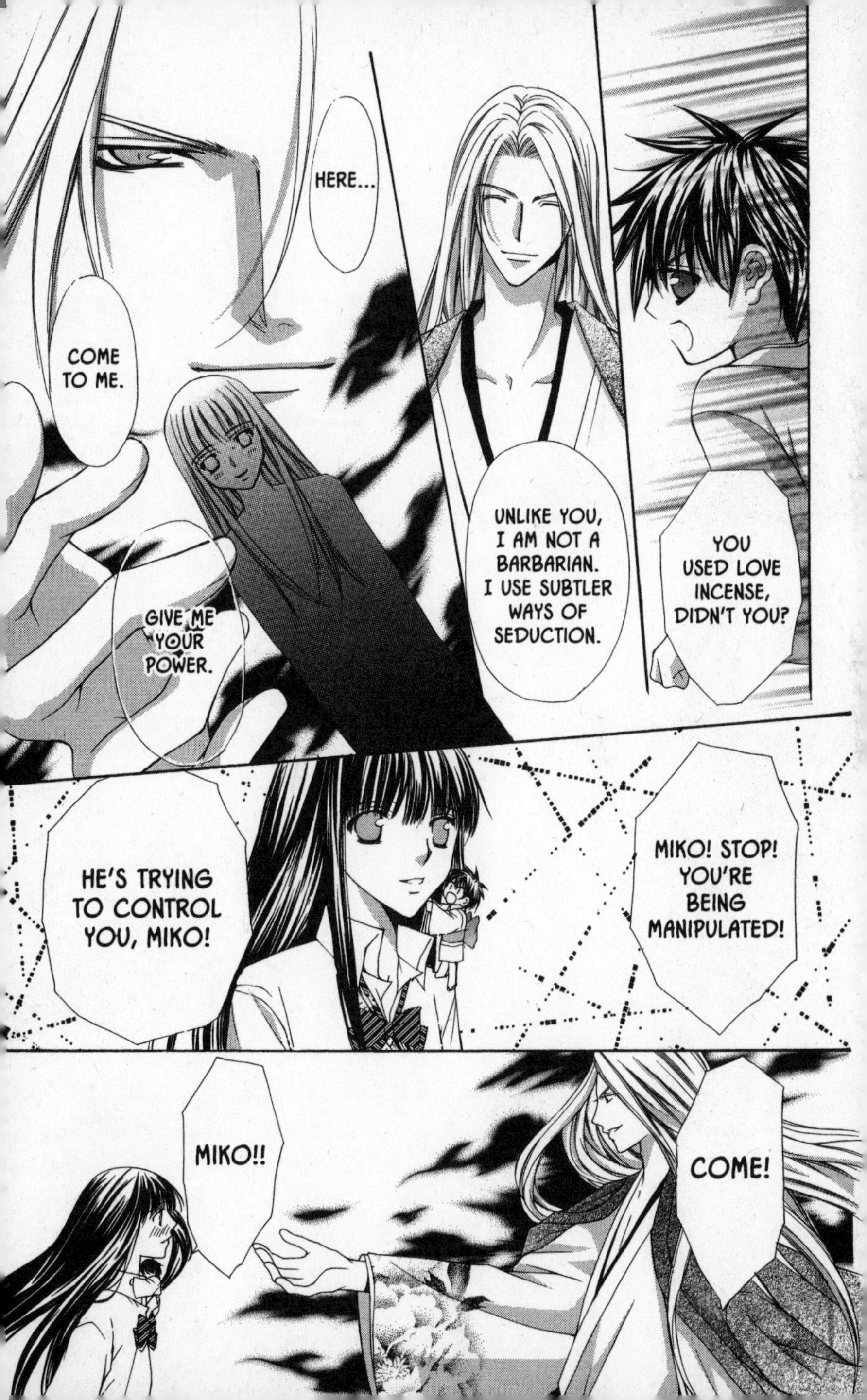
YOU USED LOVE INCENSE, DIDN'T YOU?
UNLIKE YOU, I AM NOT A BARBARIAN. I USE SUBTLER WAYS OF SEDUCTION.
HERE...
COME TO ME.
GIVE ME YOUR POWER.
MIKO! STOP! YOU'RE BEING MANIPULATED!
HE'S TRYING TO CONTROL YOU, MIKO!
COME!
MIKO!!

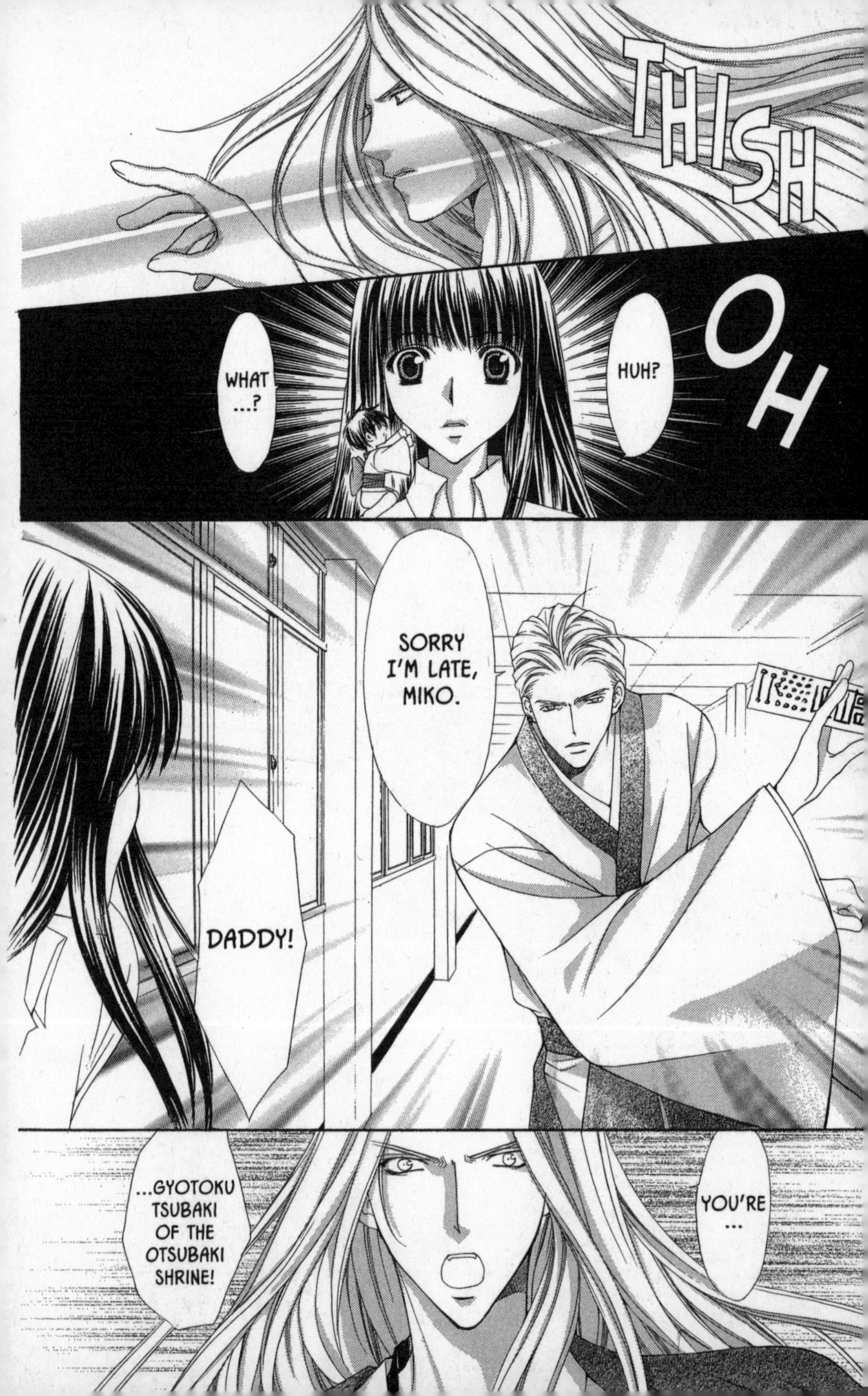
THISH
OH
HUH?
WHAT ...?
SORRY I'M LATE, MIKO.
DADDY!
YOU'RE ...
...GYOTOKU TSUBAKI OF THE OTSUBAKI SHRINE!

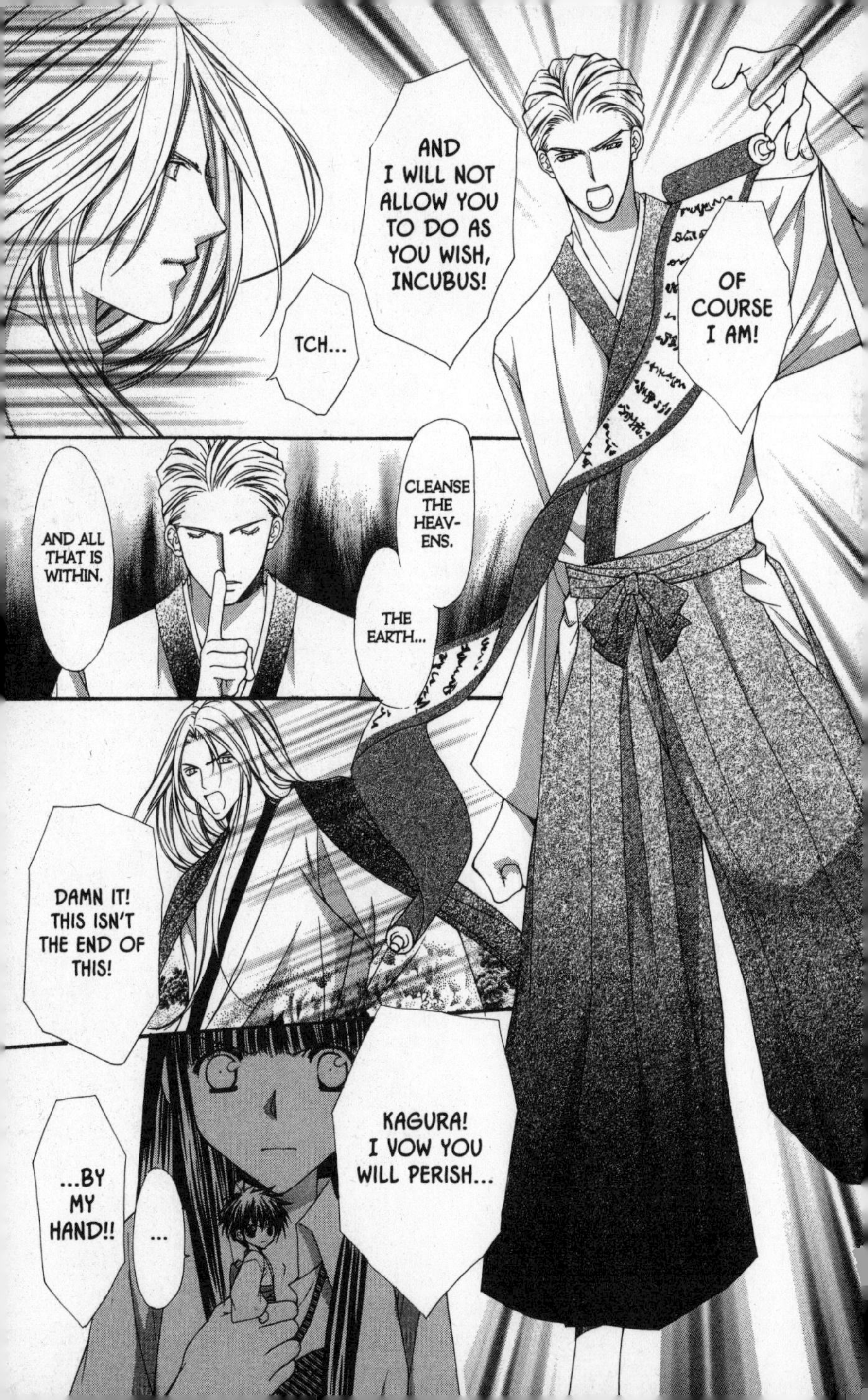
OF COURSE I AM!
AND I WILL NOT ALLOW YOU TO DO AS YOU WISH, INCUBUS!
TCH...
CLEANSE THE HEAVENS.
THE EARTH...
AND ALL THAT IS WITHIN.
DAMN IT! THIS ISN'T THE END OF THIS!
KAGURA! I VOW YOU WILL PERISH...
...BY MY HAND!!
...

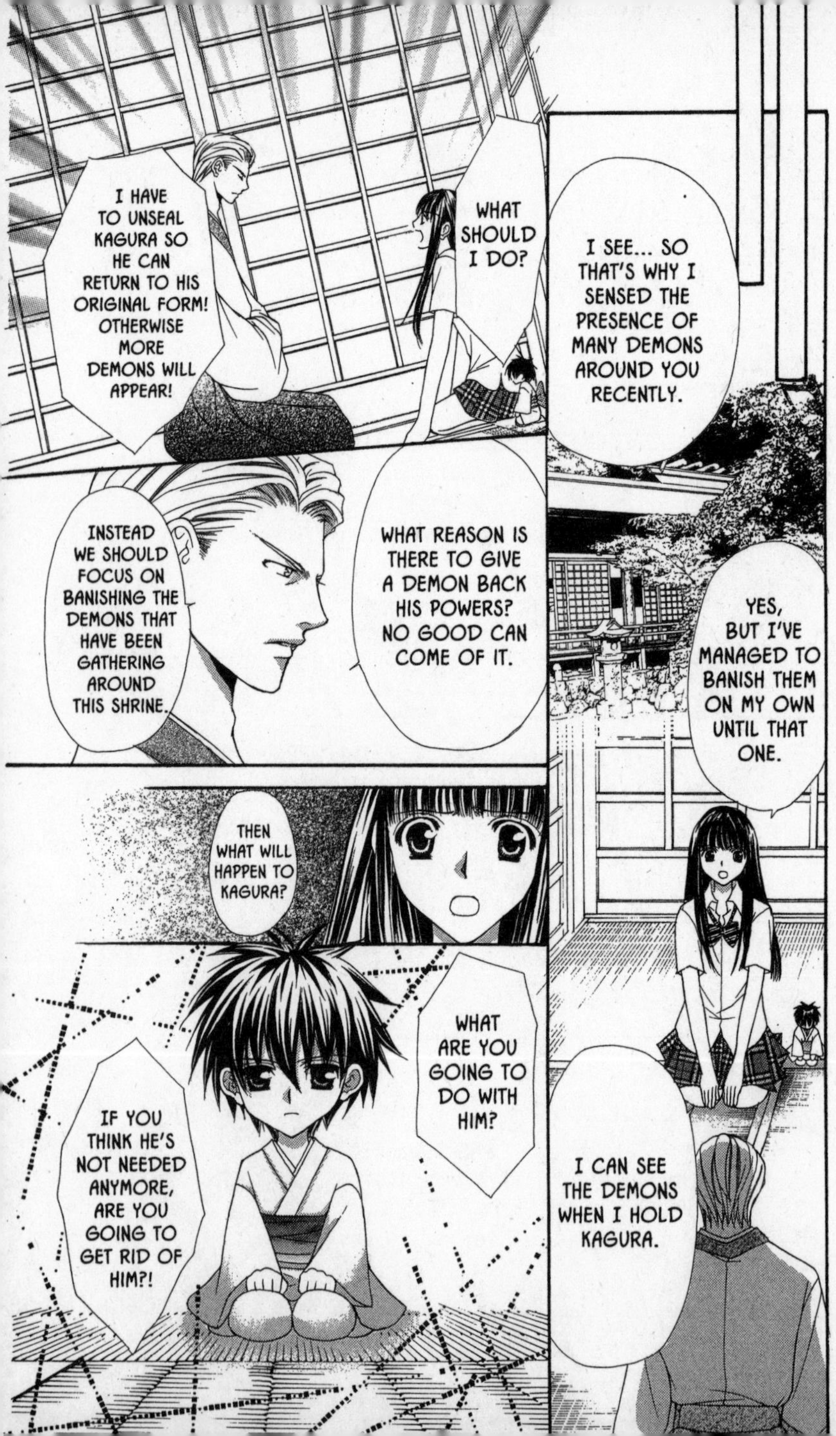
I SEE... SO THAT'S WHY I SENSED THE PRESENCE OF MANY DEMONS AROUND YOU RECENTLY.
YES, BUT I'VE MANAGED TO BANISH THEM ON MY OWN UNTIL THAT ONE.
I CAN SEE THE DEMONS WHEN I HOLD KAGURA.
WHAT SHOULD I DO?
I HAVE TO UNSEAL KAGURA SO HE CAN RETURN TO HIS ORIGINAL FORM! OTHERWISE MORE DEMONS WILL APPEAR!
WHAT REASON IS THERE TO GIVE A DEMON BACK HIS POWERS? NO GOOD CAN COME OF IT.
INSTEAD WE SHOULD FOCUS ON BANISHING THE DEMONS THAT HAVE BEEN GATHERING AROUND THIS SHRINE.
THEN WHAT WILL HAPPEN TO KAGURA?
WHAT ARE YOU GOING TO DO WITH HIM?
IF YOU THINK HE'S NOT NEEDED ANYMORE, ARE YOU GOING TO GET RID OF HIM?!

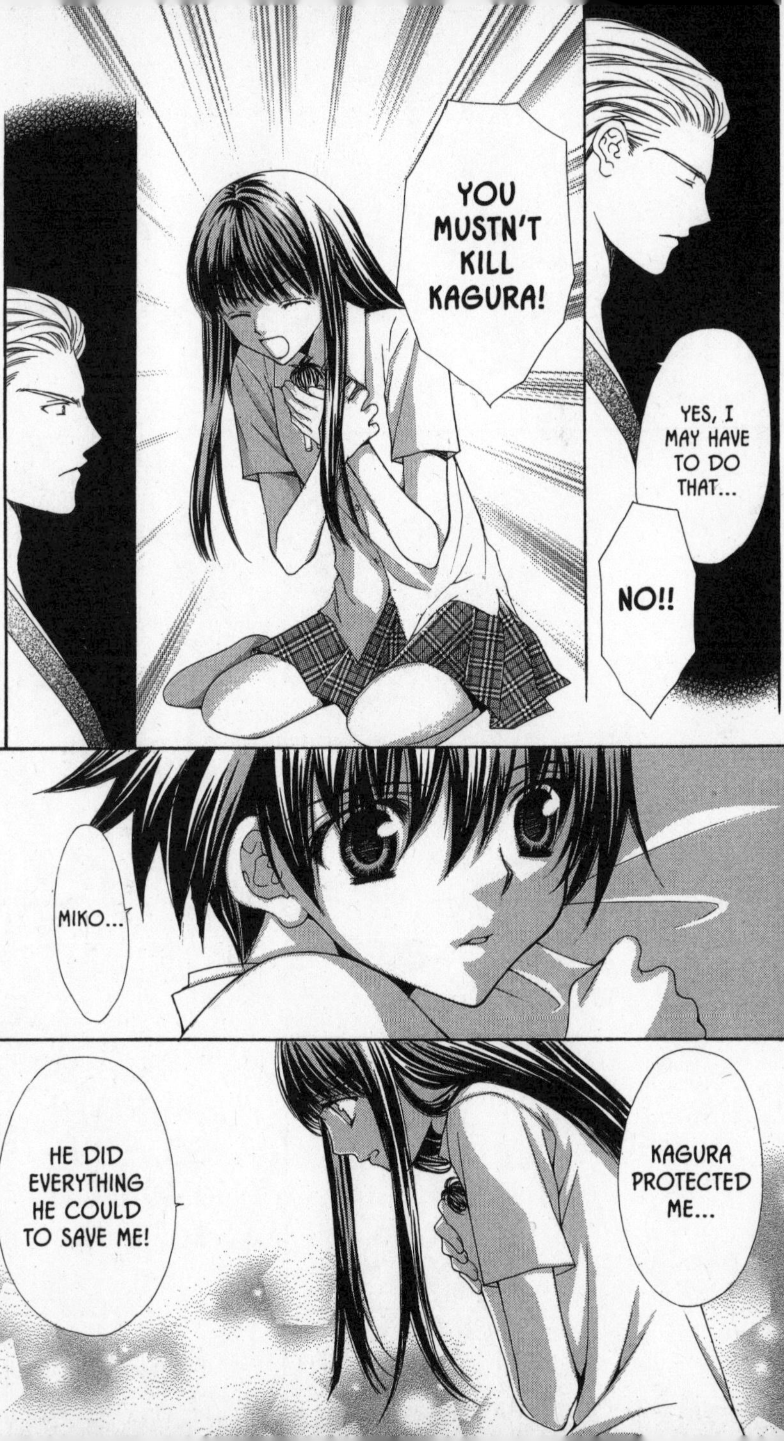
YES, I MAY HAVE TO DO THAT...
NO!!
YOU MUSTN'T KILL KAGURA!
MIKO...
KAGURA PROTECTED ME...
HE DID EVERYTHING HE COULD TO SAVE ME!

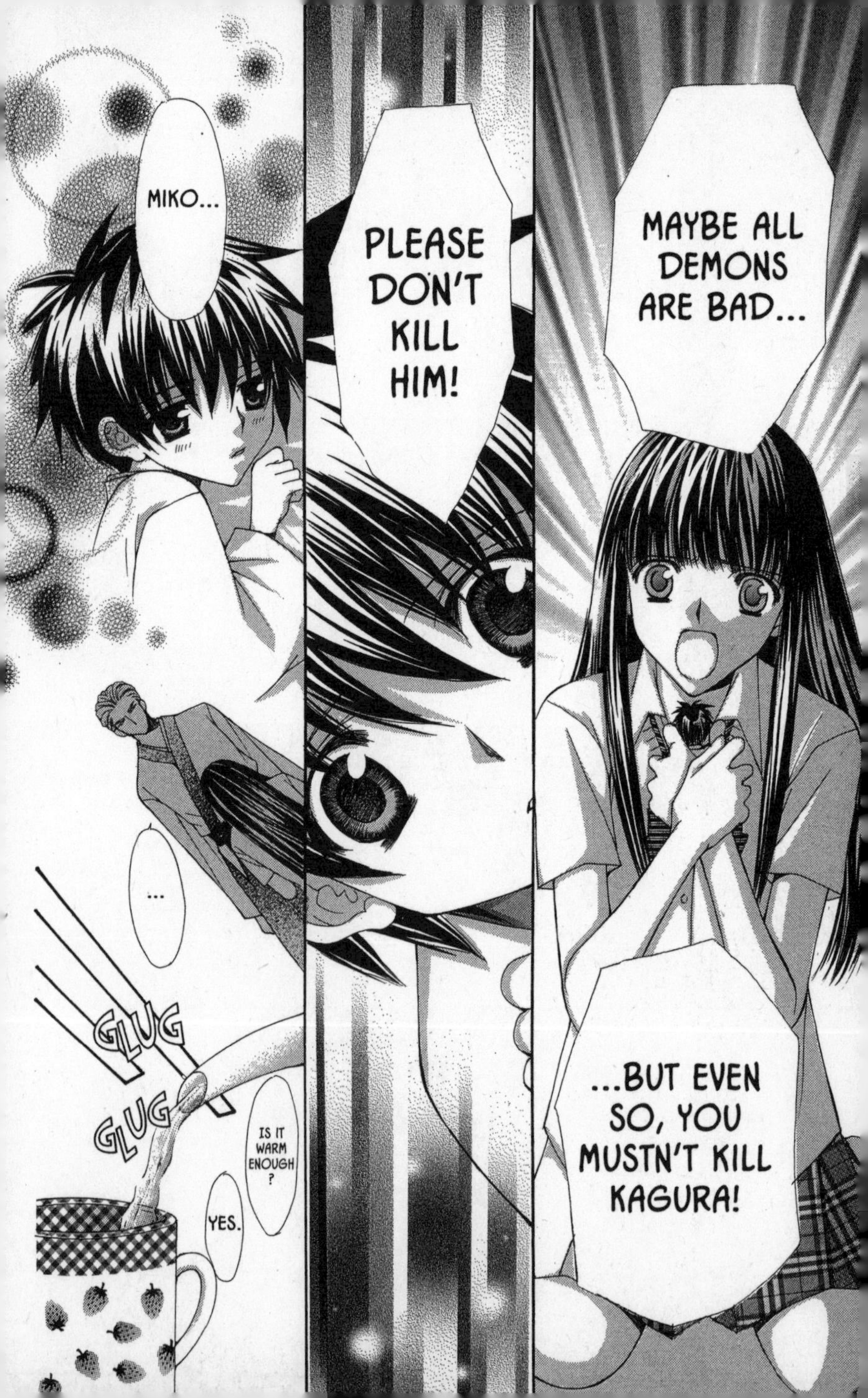
MAYBE ALL DEMONS ARE BAD...
...BUT EVEN SO, YOU MUSTN'T KILL KAGURA!
PLEASE DON'T KILL HIM!
MIKO...
...
GLUG
GLUG
IS IT WARM ENOUGH?
YES.

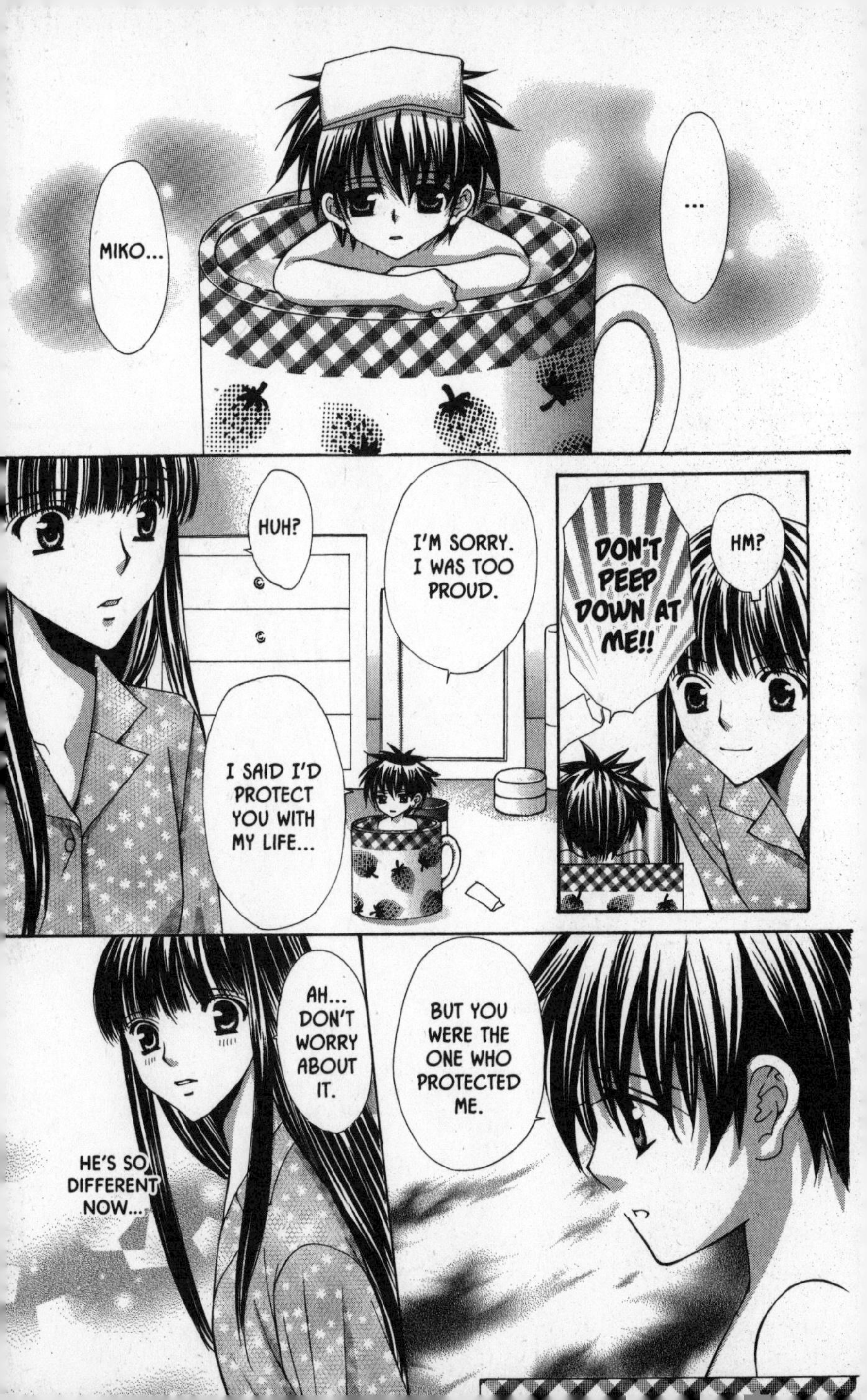
...
MIKO...
HM?
DON'T PEEP DOWN AT ME!!
I'M SORRY. I WAS TOO PROUD.
HUH?
I SAID I'D PROTECT YOU WITH MY LIFE...
BUT YOU WERE THE ONE WHO PROTECTED ME.
AH... DON'T WORRY ABOUT IT.
HE'S SO DIFFERENT NOW...

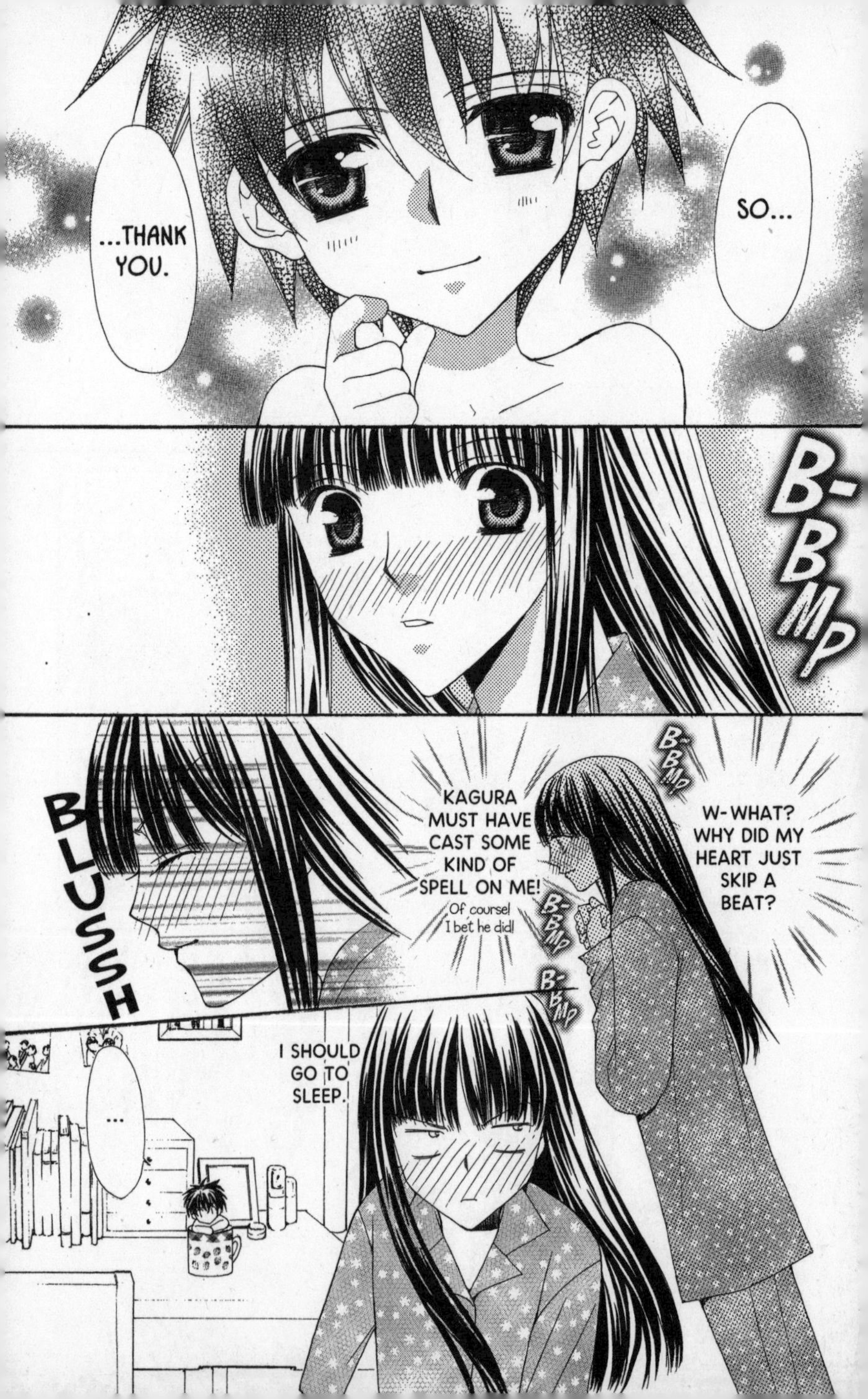
SO...
...THANK YOU.
B-BMP
W-WHAT? WHY DID MY HEART JUST SKIP A BEAT?
B-BMP
KAGURA MUST HAVE CAST SOME KIND OF SPELL ON ME!
Of course! I bet he did!
B-BMP
B-BMP
BLUSSH
I SHOULD GO TO SLEEP.
...

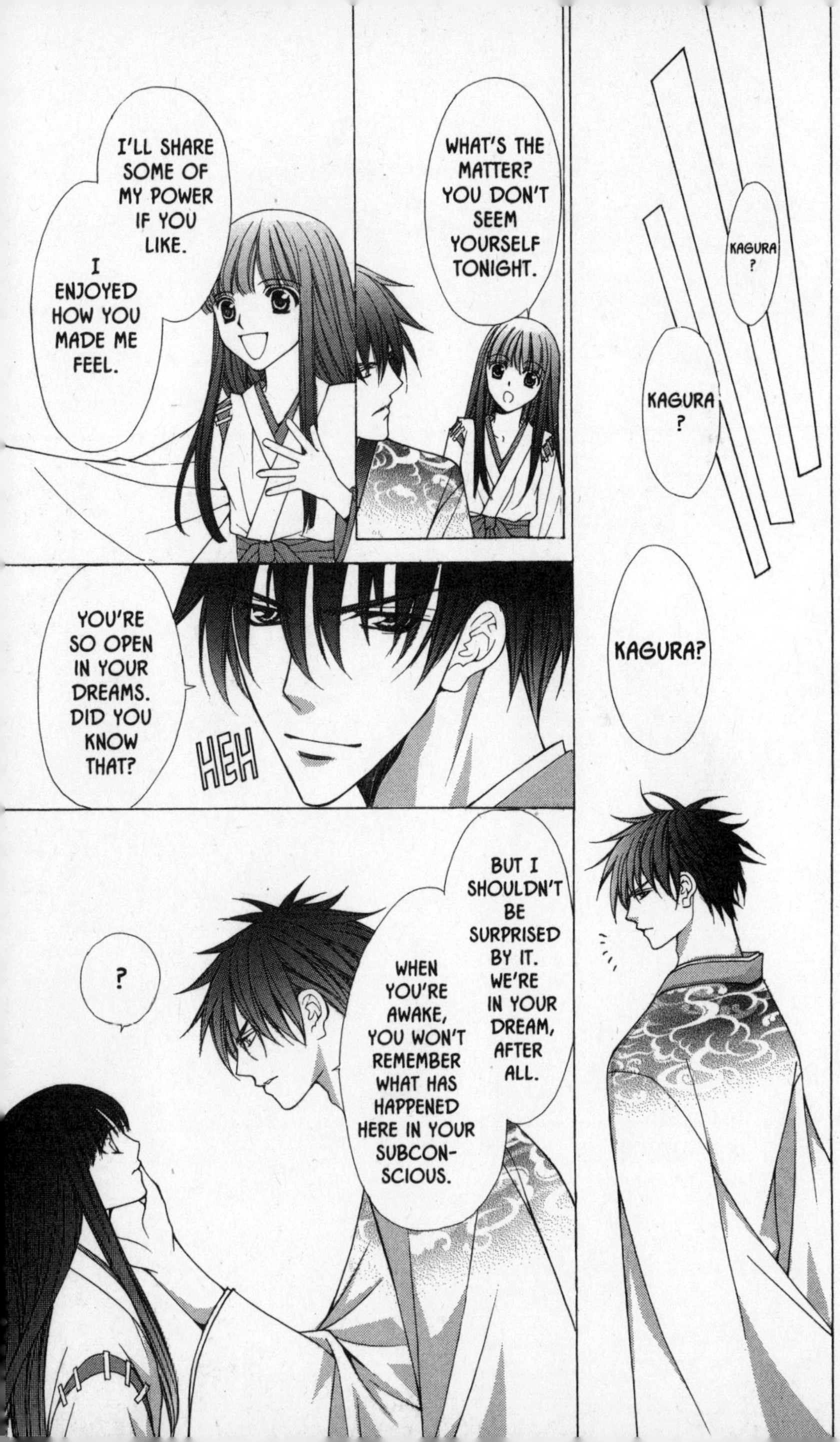
KAGURA ?
KAGURA ?
KAGURA?
WHAT'S THE MATTER? YOU DON'T SEEM YOURSELF TONIGHT.
I'LL SHARE SOME OF MY POWER IF YOU LIKE.
I ENJOYED HOW YOU MADE ME FEEL.
YOU'RE SO OPEN IN YOUR DREAMS. DID YOU KNOW THAT?
HEH
BUT I SHOULDN'T BE SURPRISED BY IT. WE'RE IN YOUR DREAM, AFTER ALL.
WHEN YOU'RE AWAKE, YOU WON'T REMEMBER WHAT HAS HAPPENED HERE IN YOUR SUBCON-SCIOUS.
?

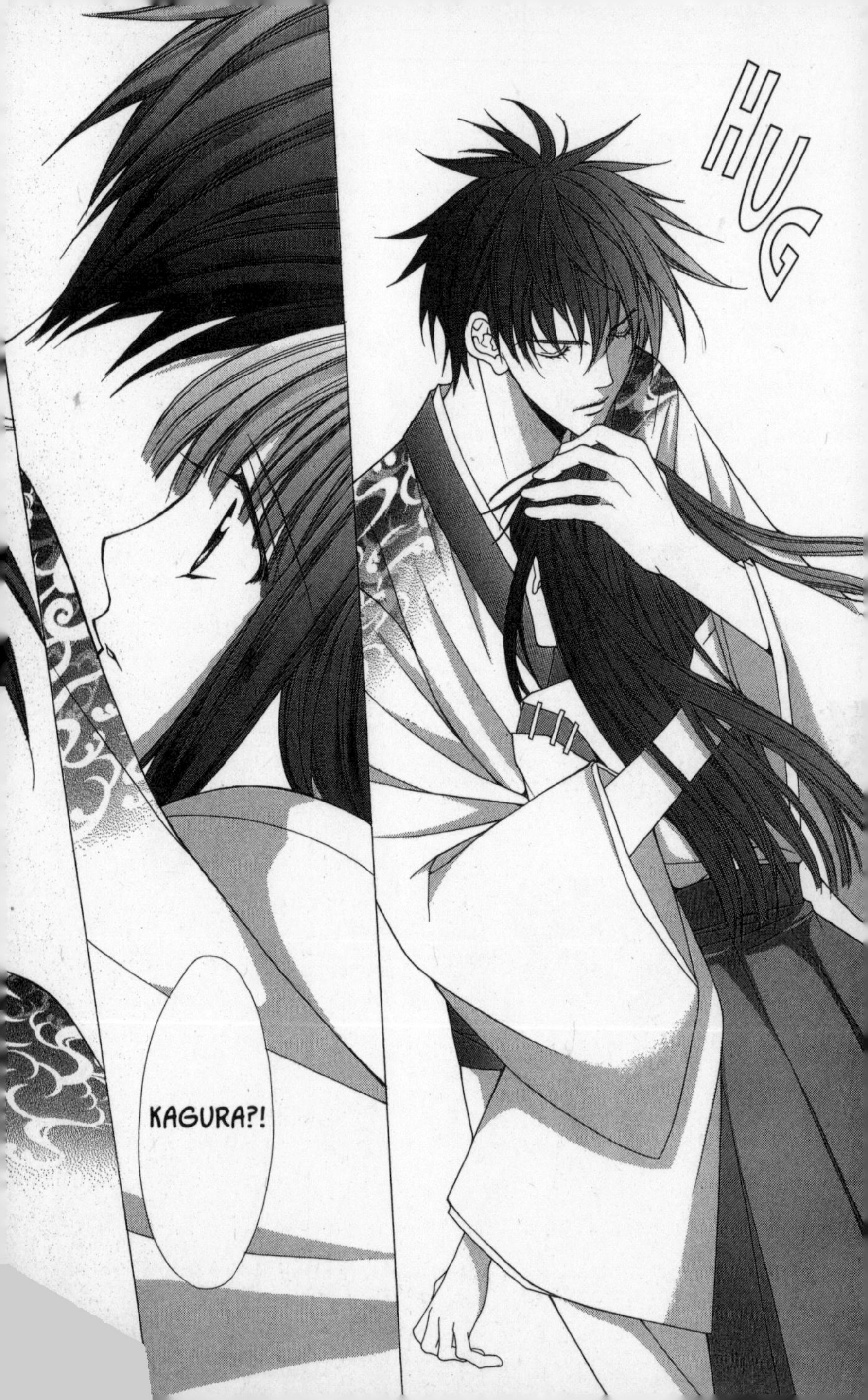
HUG
KAGURA?!

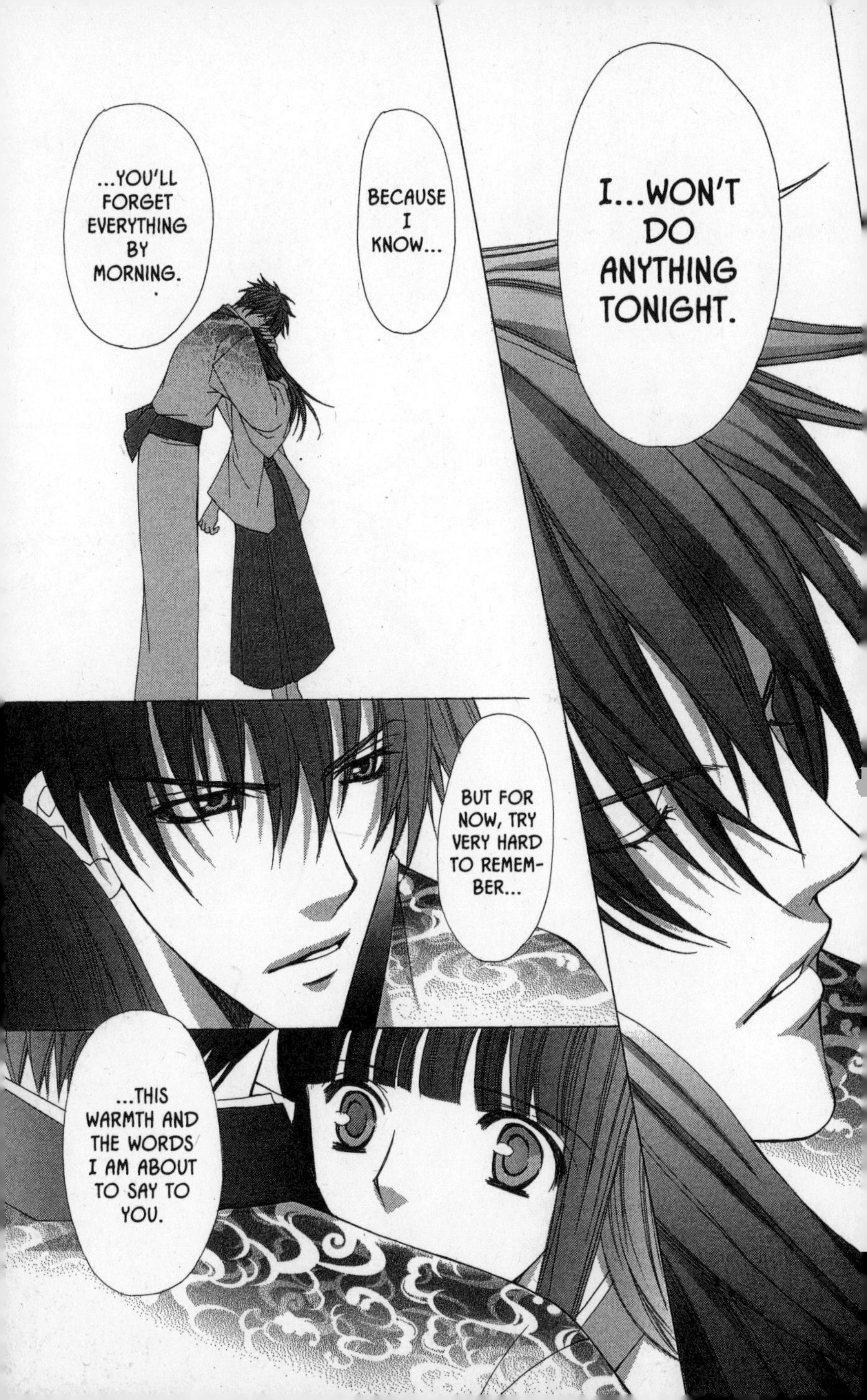
I...WON'T DO ANYTHING TONIGHT.
BECAUSE I KNOW...
...YOU'LL FORGET EVERYTHING BY MORNING.
BUT FOR NOW, TRY VERY HARD TO REMEM-BER...
...THIS WARMTH AND THE WORDS I AM ABOUT TO SAY TO YOU.

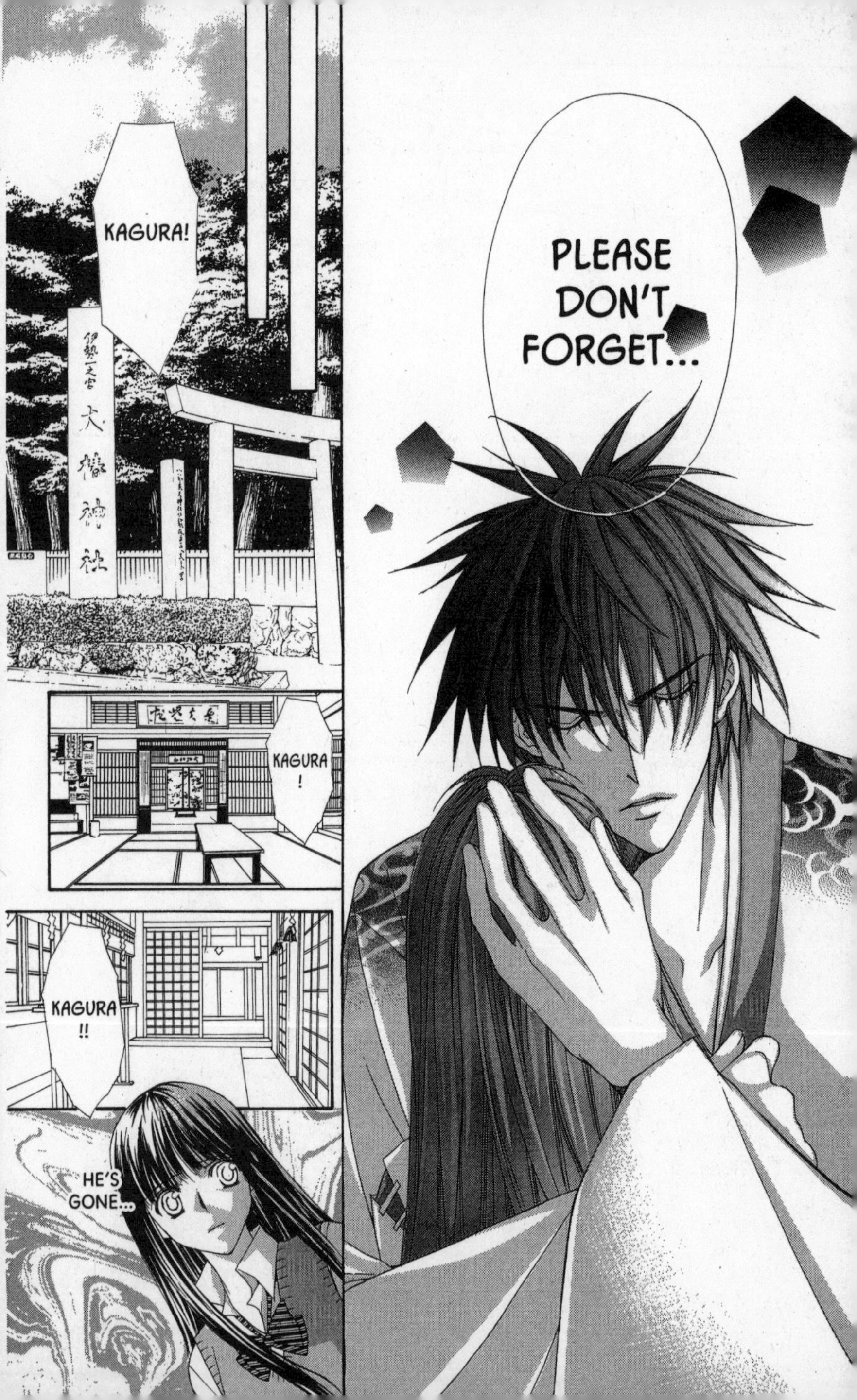
PLEASE DON'T FORGET...
KAGURA!
KAGURA !
KAGURA !!
HE'S GONE...

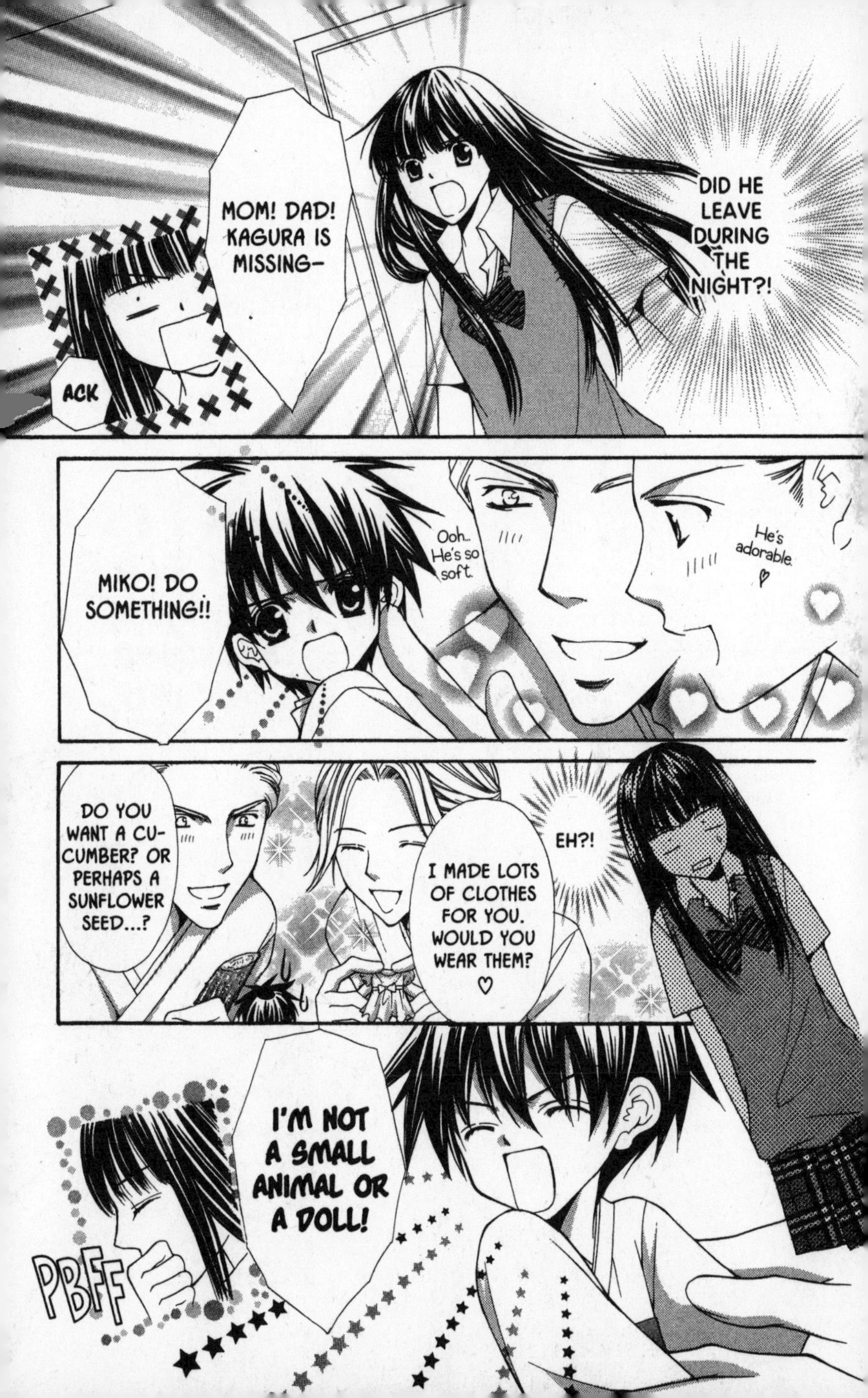
DID HE LEAVE DURING THE NIGHT?!
MOM! DAD! KAGURA IS MISSING–
ACK
He's adorable. ♡
Ooh... He's so soft.
MIKO! DO SOMETHING!!
EH?!
I MADE LOTS OF CLOTHES FOR YOU. WOULD YOU WEAR THEM? ♡
DO YOU WANT A CU-CUMBER? OR PERHAPS A SUNFLOWER SEED...?
I'M NOT A SMALL ANIMAL OR A DOLL!
PBFF

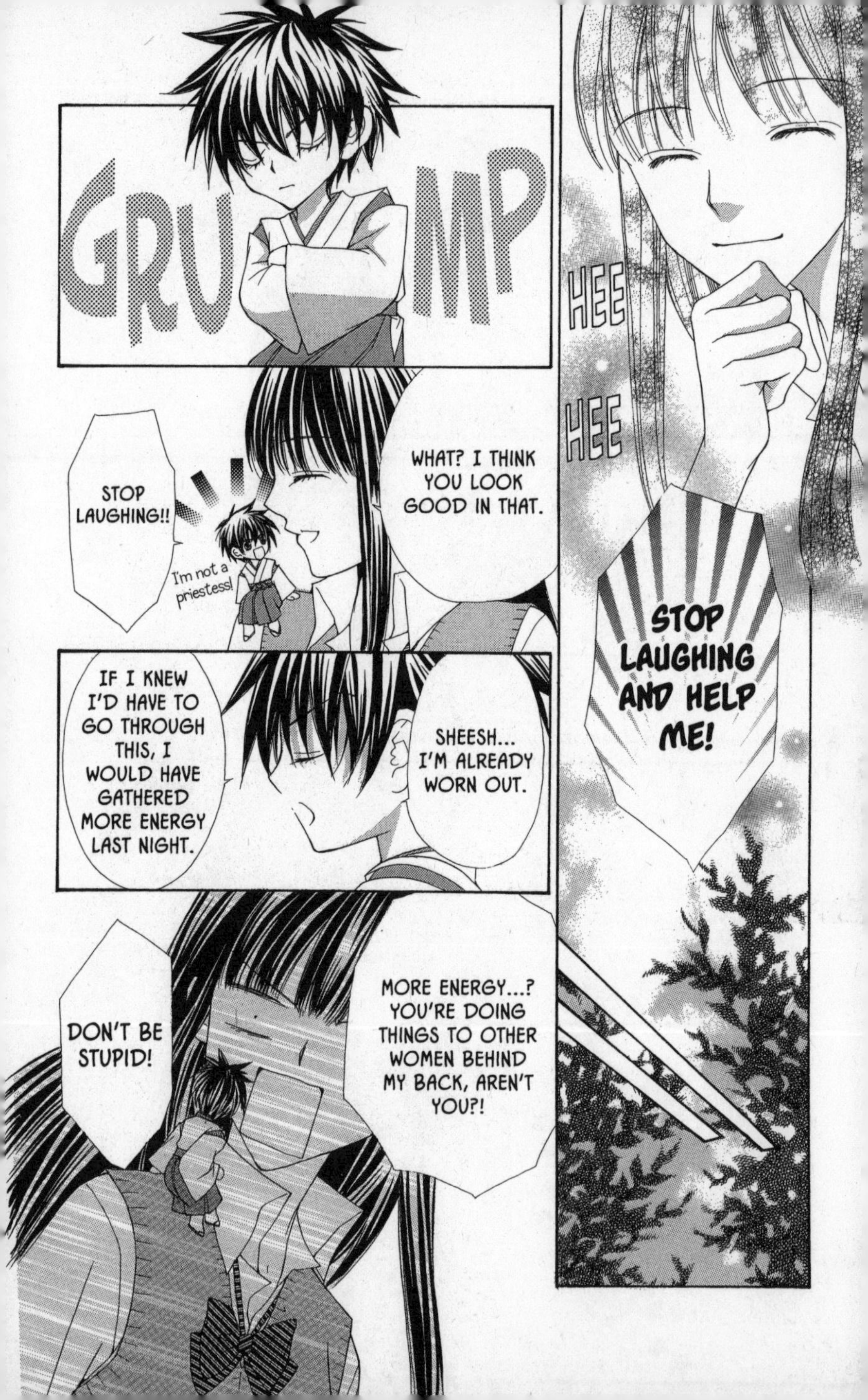
HEE
HEE
STOP LAUGHING AND HELP ME!
GRUMP
WHAT? I THINK YOU LOOK GOOD IN THAT.
STOP LAUGHING!!
I'm not a priestess!
SHEESH... I'M ALREADY WORN OUT.
IF I KNEW I'D HAVE TO GO THROUGH THIS, I WOULD HAVE GATHERED MORE ENERGY LAST NIGHT.
MORE ENERGY...? YOU'RE DOING THINGS TO OTHER WOMEN BEHIND MY BACK, AREN'T YOU?!
DON'T BE STUPID!

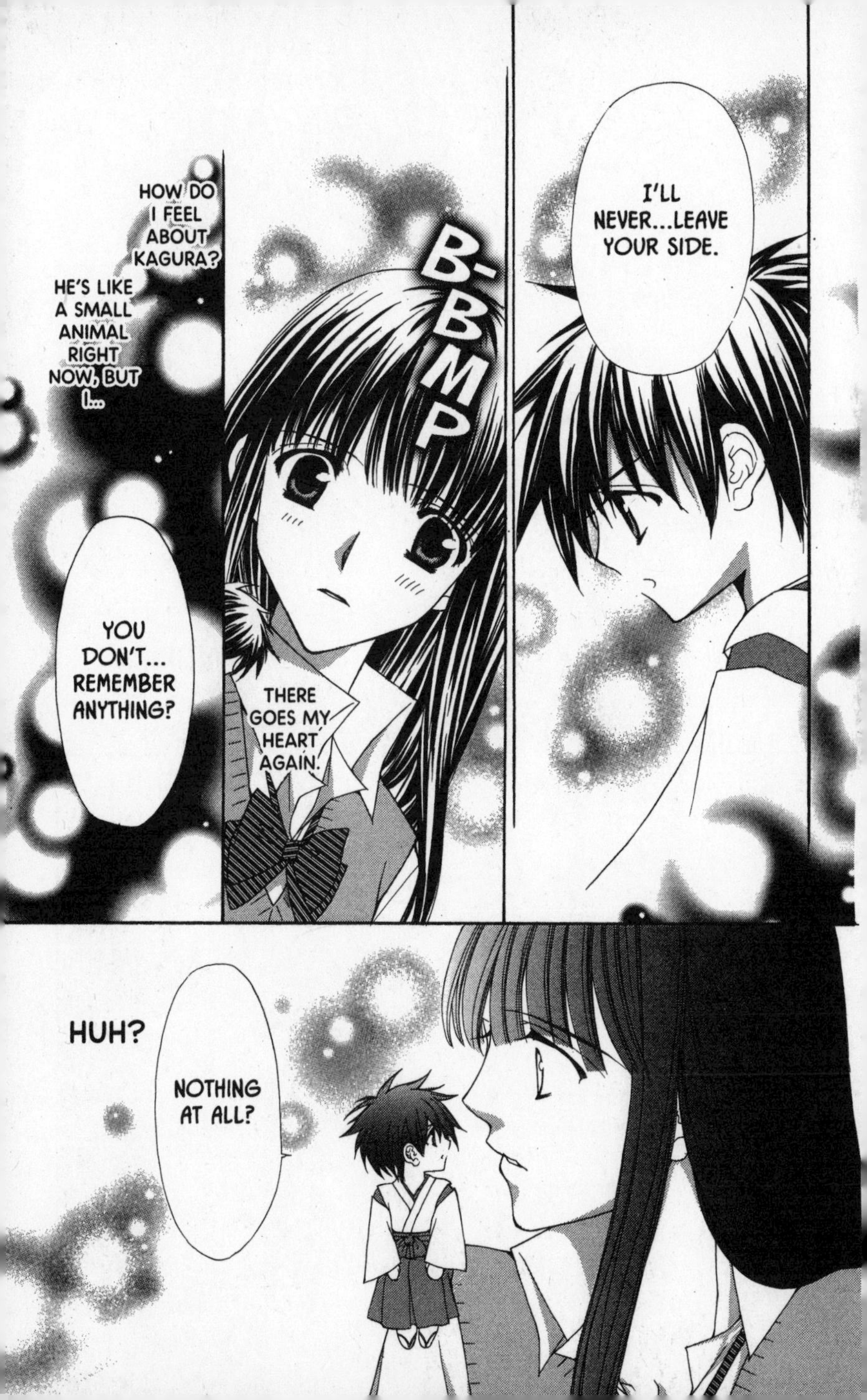
I'LL NEVER...LEAVE YOUR SIDE.
B-BMP
THERE GOES MY HEART AGAIN.
HOW DO I FEEL ABOUT KAGURA?
HE'S LIKE A SMALL ANIMAL RIGHT NOW, BUT I...
YOU DON'T... REMEMBER ANYTHING?
NOTHING AT ALL?
HUH?

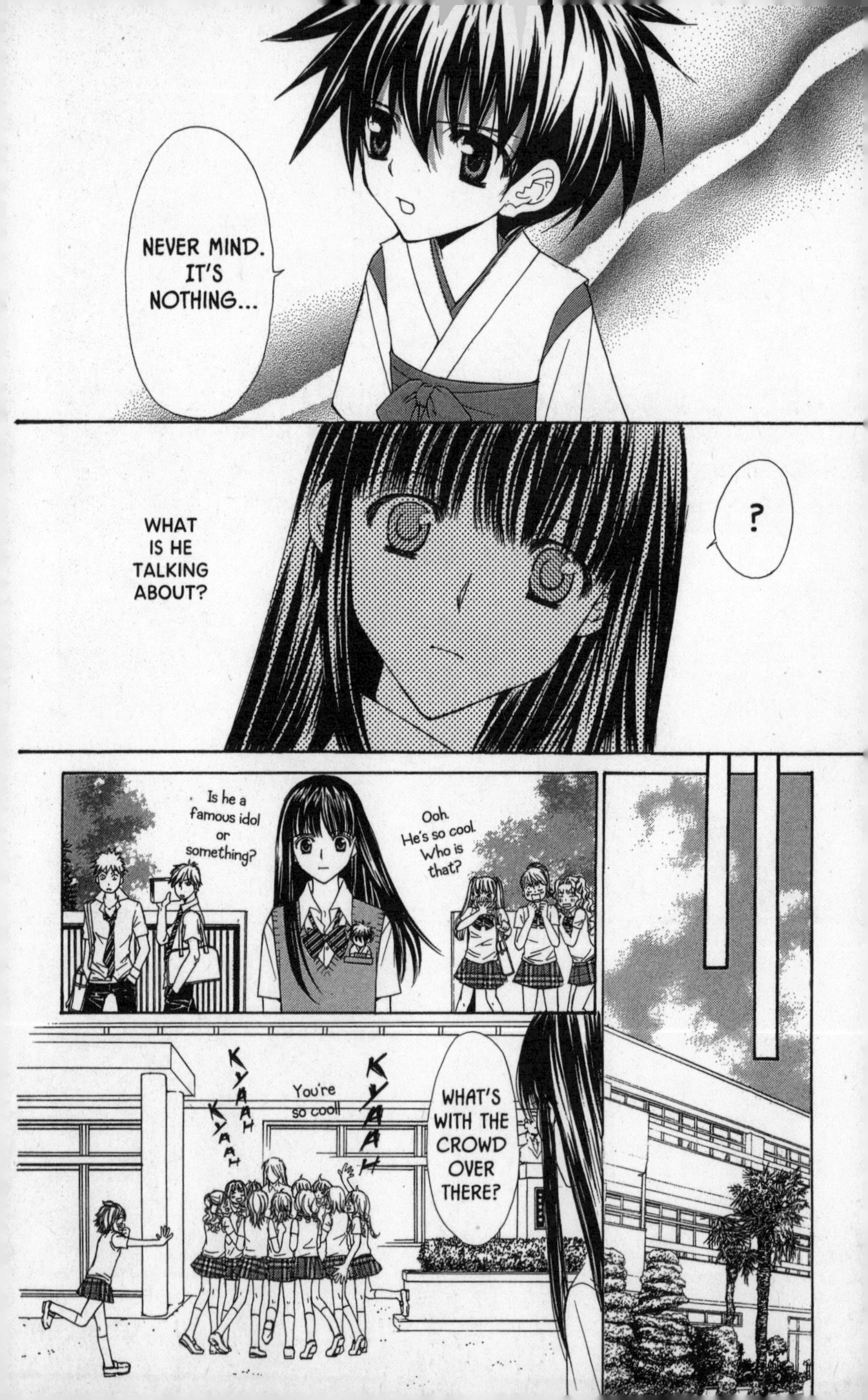
NEVER MIND. IT'S NOTHING...
?
WHAT IS HE TALKING ABOUT?
Ooh. He's so cool. Who is that?
Is he a famous idol or something?
WHAT'S WITH THE CROWD OVER THERE?
KYAAH
You're so cool!
KYAAH
KYAAH

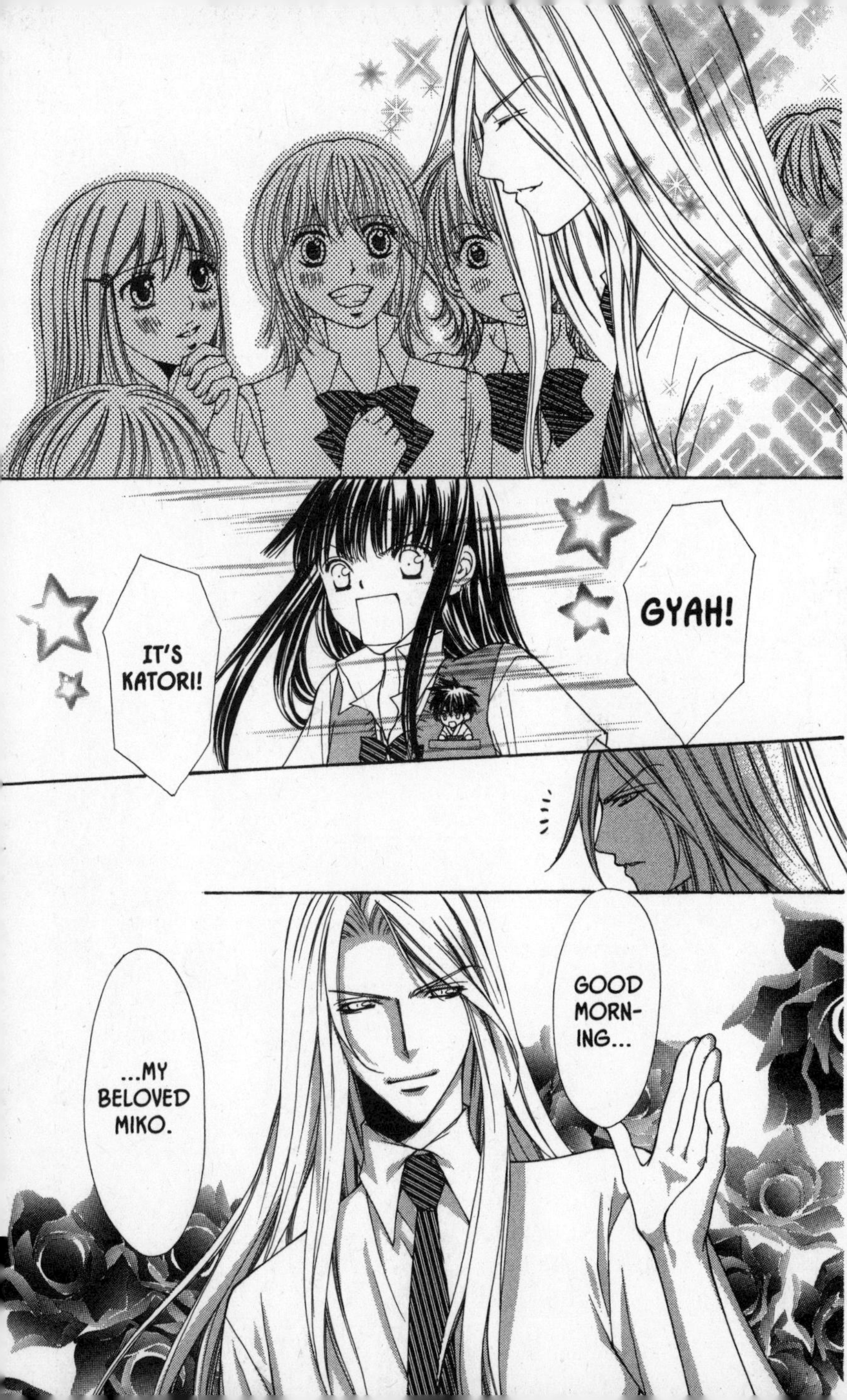
GYAH!
IT'S MY KATORI!
GOOD MORN-ING...
...MY BELOVED MIKO.

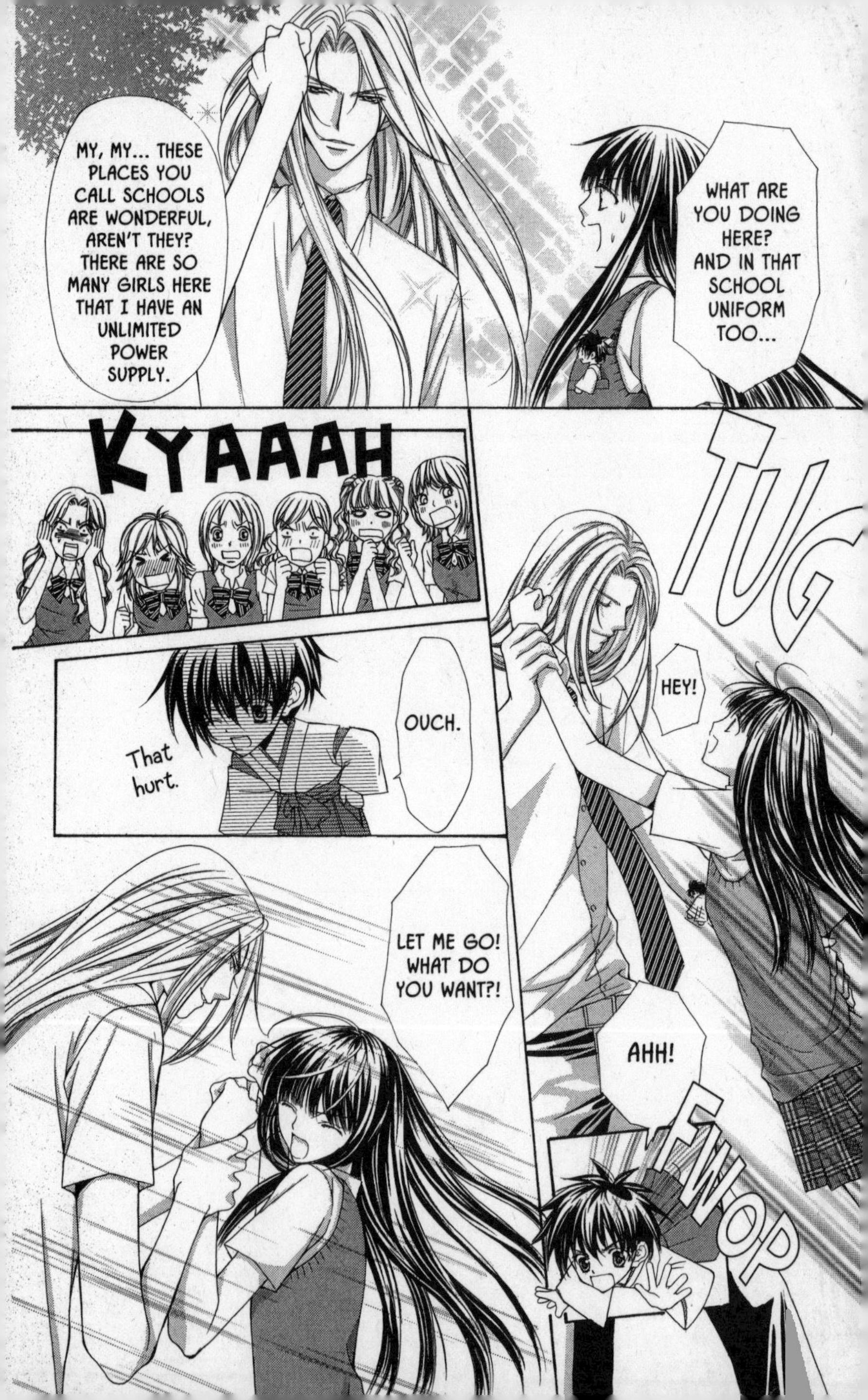
WHAT ARE YOU DOING HERE? AND IN THAT SCHOOL UNIFORM TOO...
MY, MY... THESE PLACES YOU CALL SCHOOLS ARE WONDERFUL, AREN'T THEY? THERE ARE SO MANY GIRLS HERE THAT I HAVE AN UNLIMITED POWER SUPPLY.
TUG
HEY!
AHH!
FWOP
KYAAAH
OUCH.
That hurt.
LET ME GO! WHAT DO YOU WANT?!

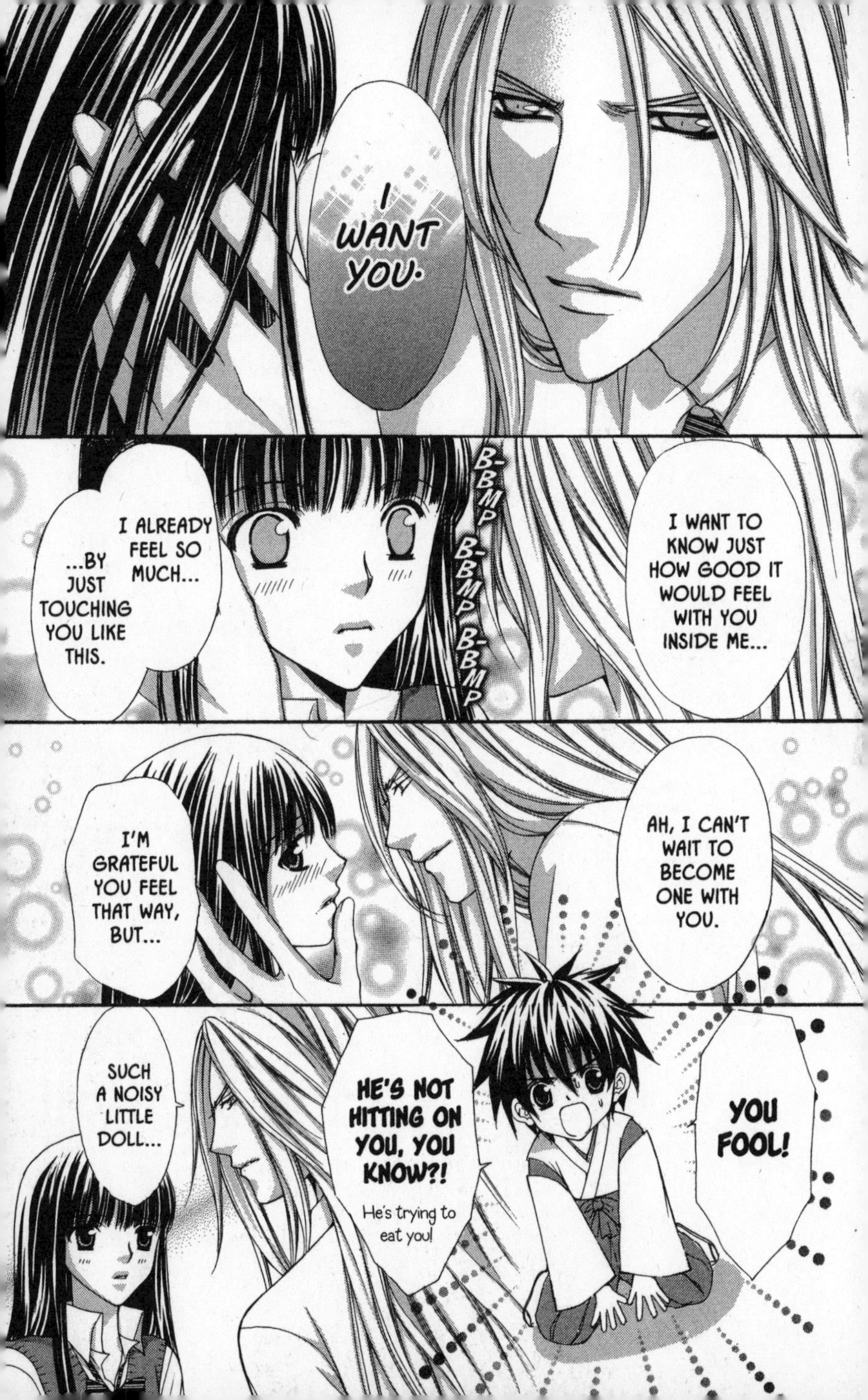
I WANT YOU.
I WANT TO KNOW JUST HOW GOOD IT WOULD FEEL WITH YOU INSIDE ME...
B-BMP B-BMP B-BMP
I ALREADY FEEL SO MUCH...
...BY JUST TOUCHING YOU LIKE THIS.
AH, I CAN'T WAIT TO BECOME ONE WITH YOU.
I'M GRATEFUL YOU FEEL THAT WAY, BUT...
YOU FOOL!
HE'S NOT HITTING ON YOU, YOU KNOW?!
He's trying to eat you!
SUCH A NOISY LITTLE DOLL...

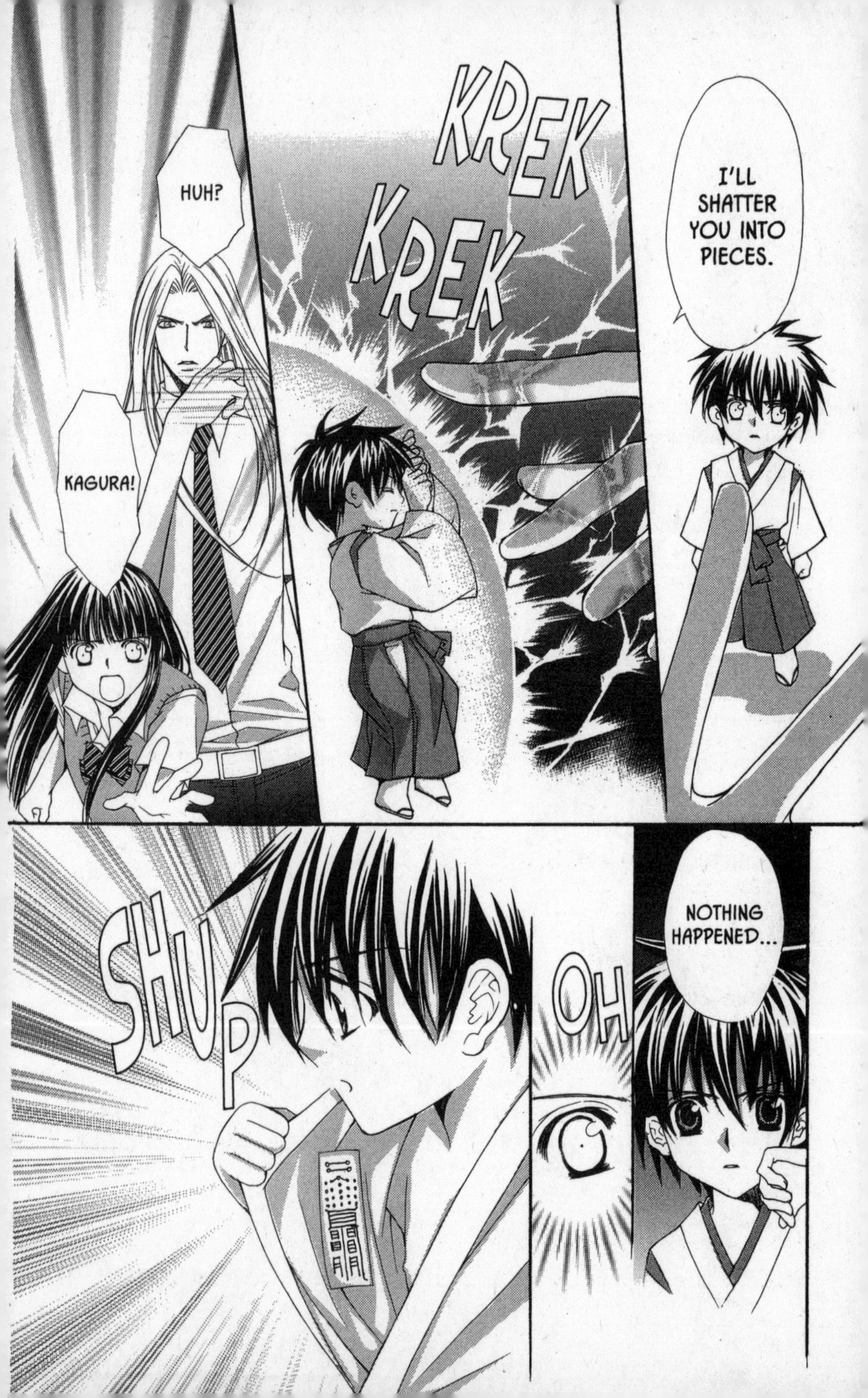
I'LL SHATTER YOU INTO PIECES.
KREK
KREK
HUH?
KAGURA!
NOTHING HAPPENED...
OH
SHUP

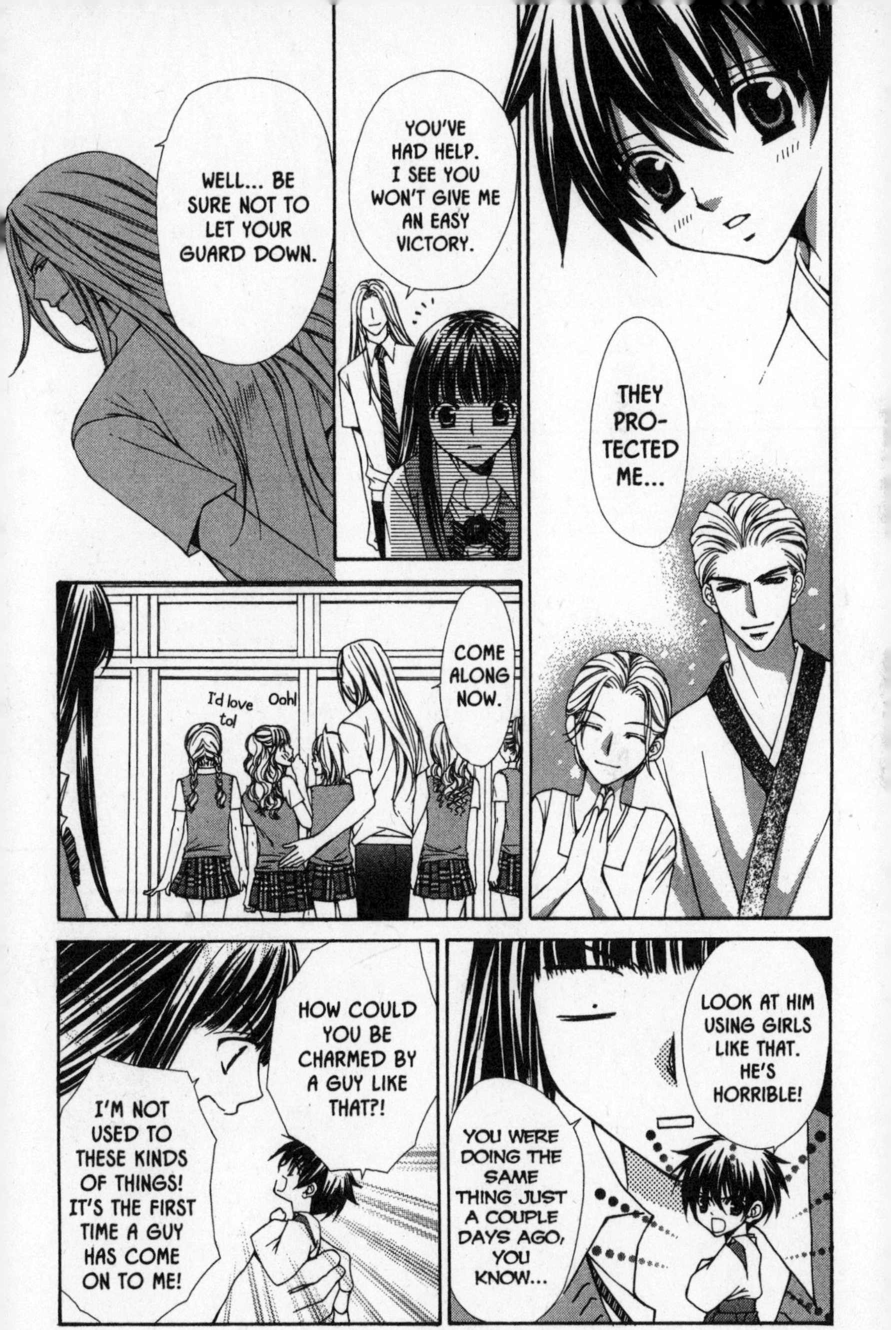
THEY PROTECTED ME...
YOU'VE HAD HELP. I SEE YOU WON'T GIVE ME AN EASY VICTORY.
WELL... BE SURE NOT TO LET YOUR GUARD DOWN.
COME ALONG NOW.
Ooh!
I'd love to!
LOOK AT HIM USING GIRLS LIKE THAT. HE'S HORRIBLE!
YOU WERE DOING THE SAME THING JUST A COUPLE DAYS AGO, YOU KNOW...
HOW COULD YOU BE CHARMED BY A GUY LIKE THAT?!
I'M NOT USED TO THESE KINDS OF THINGS! IT'S THE FIRST TIME A GUY HAS COME ON TO ME!

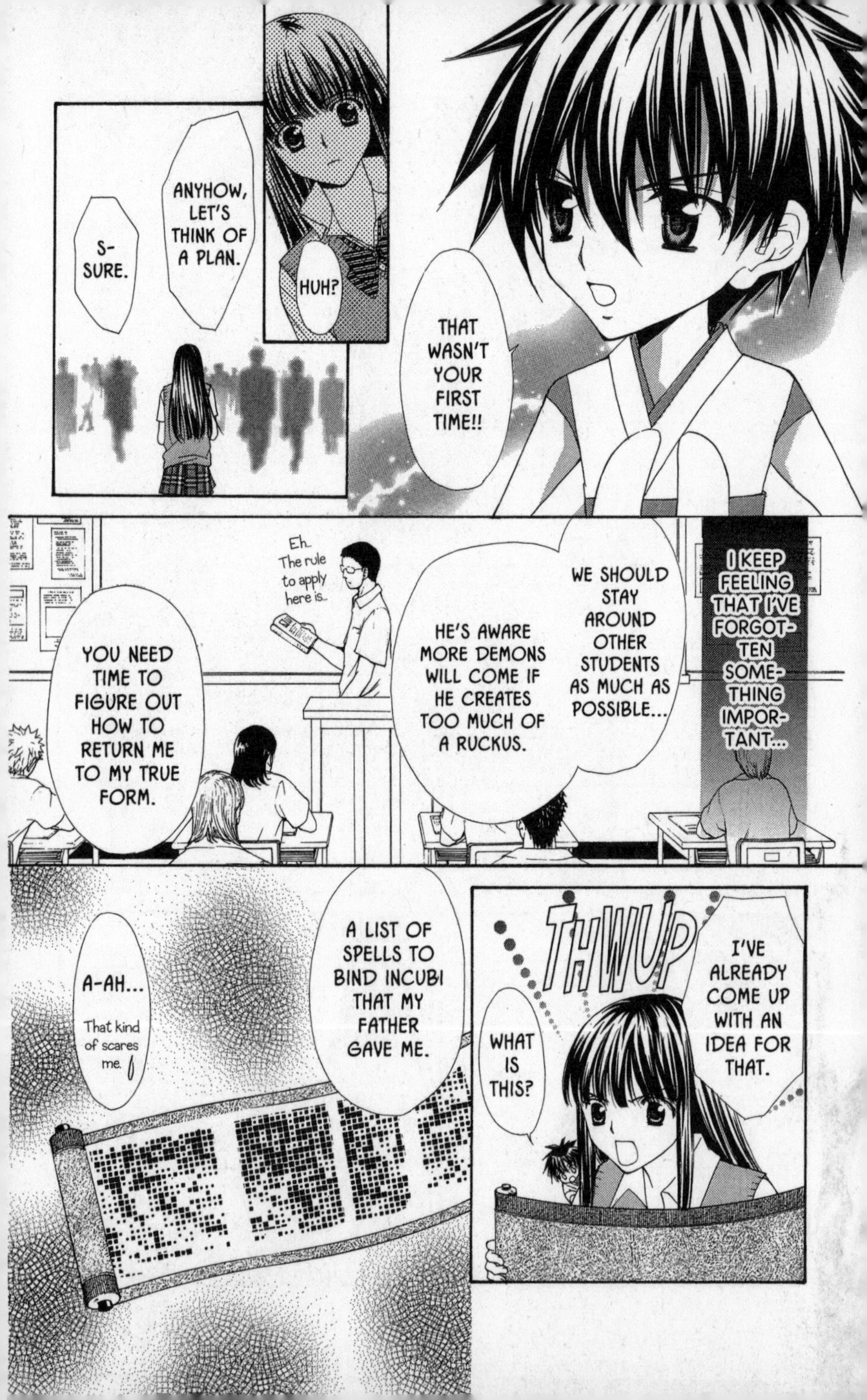
THAT WASN'T YOUR FIRST TIME!!
HUH?
ANYHOW, LET'S THINK OF A PLAN.
S- SURE.
I KEEP FEELING THAT I'VE FORGOT- TEN SOME- THING IMPOR- TANT...
WE SHOULD STAY AROUND OTHER STUDENTS AS MUCH AS POSSIBLE...
HE'S AWARE MORE DEMONS WILL COME IF HE CREATES TOO MUCH OF A RUCKUS.
Eh.. The rule to apply here is..
YOU NEED TIME TO FIGURE OUT HOW TO RETURN ME TO MY TRUE FORM.
THWUP
I'VE ALREADY COME UP WITH AN IDEA FOR THAT.
WHAT IS THIS?
A LIST OF SPELLS TO BIND INCUBI THAT MY FATHER GAVE ME.
A-AH...
That kind of scares me.

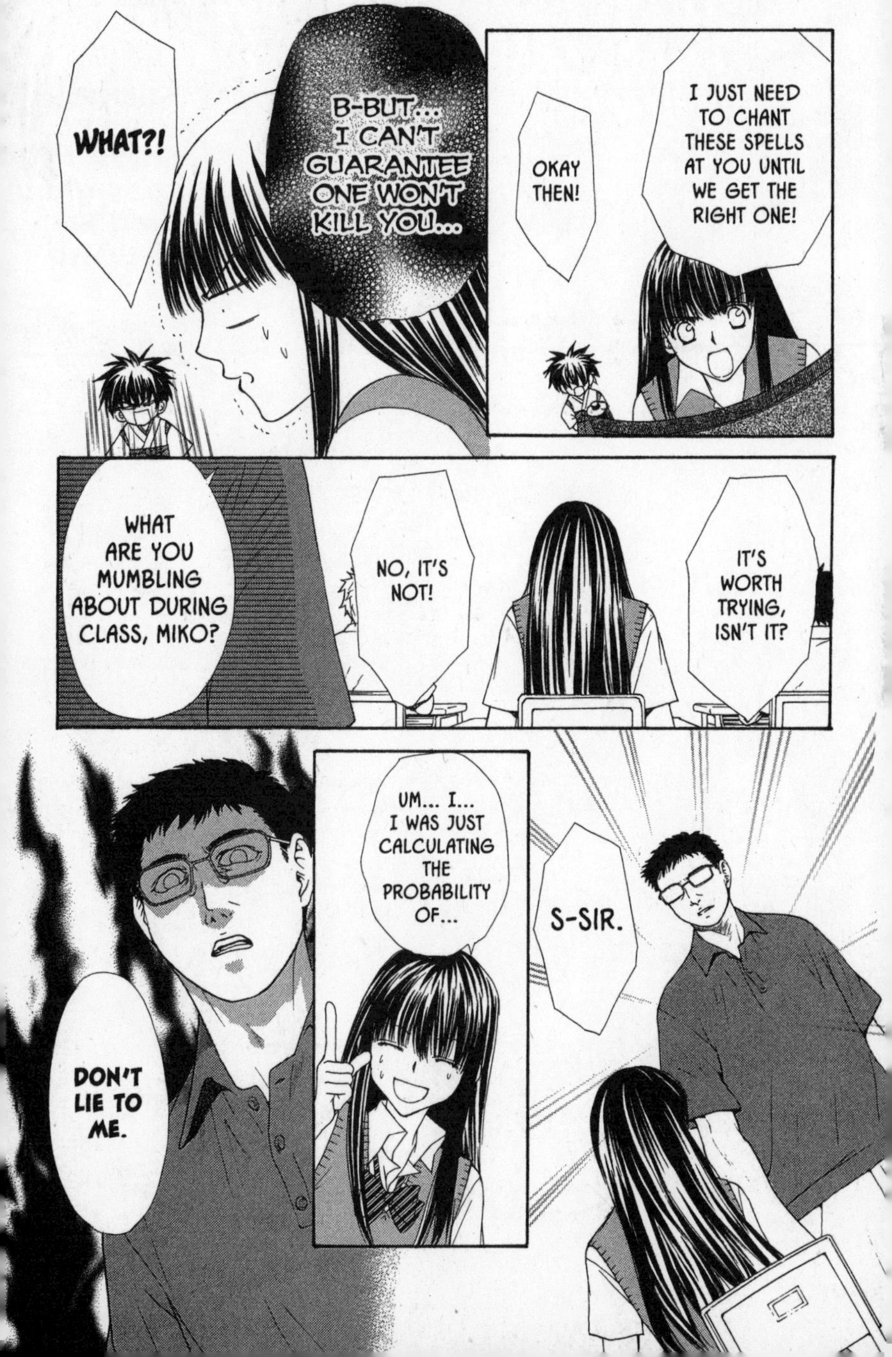
I JUST NEED TO CHANT THESE SPELLS AT YOU UNTIL WE GET THE RIGHT ONE!
OKAY THEN!
B-BUT... I CAN'T GUARANTEE ONE WON'T KILL YOU...
WHAT?!
IT'S WORTH TRYING, ISN'T IT?
NO, IT'S NOT!
WHAT ARE YOU MUMBLING ABOUT DURING CLASS, MIKO?
S-SIR.
UM... I... I WAS JUST CALCULATING THE PROBABILITY OF...
DON'T LIE TO ME.

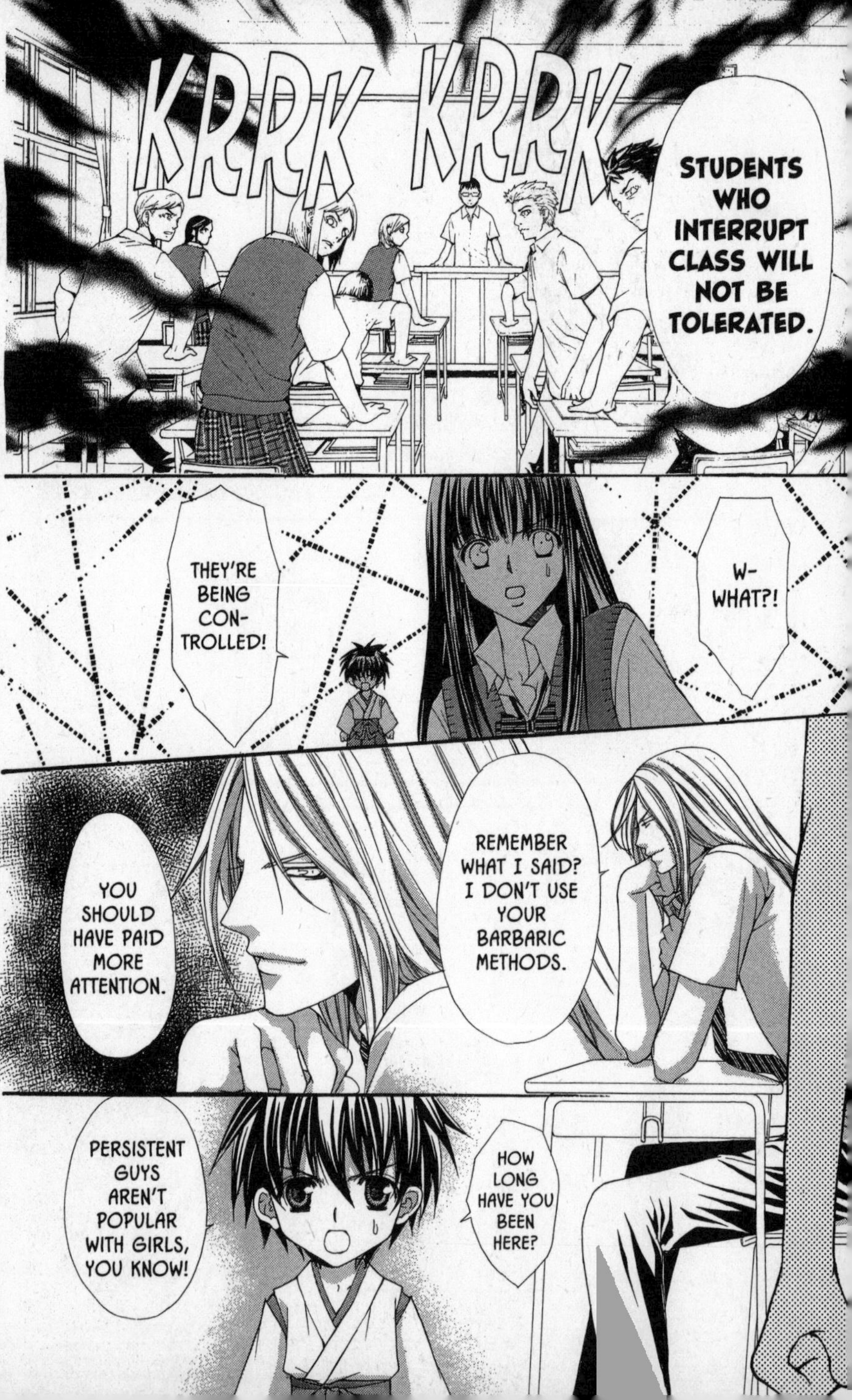
STUDENTS WHO INTERRUPT CLASS WILL NOT BE TOLERATED.
KRRK KRRK
W-WHAT?!
THEY'RE BEING CON-TROLLED!
REMEMBER WHAT I SAID? I DON'T USE YOUR BARBARIC METHODS.
YOU SHOULD HAVE PAID MORE ATTENTION.
HOW LONG HAVE YOU BEEN HERE?
PERSISTENT GUYS AREN'T POPULAR WITH GIRLS, YOU KNOW!

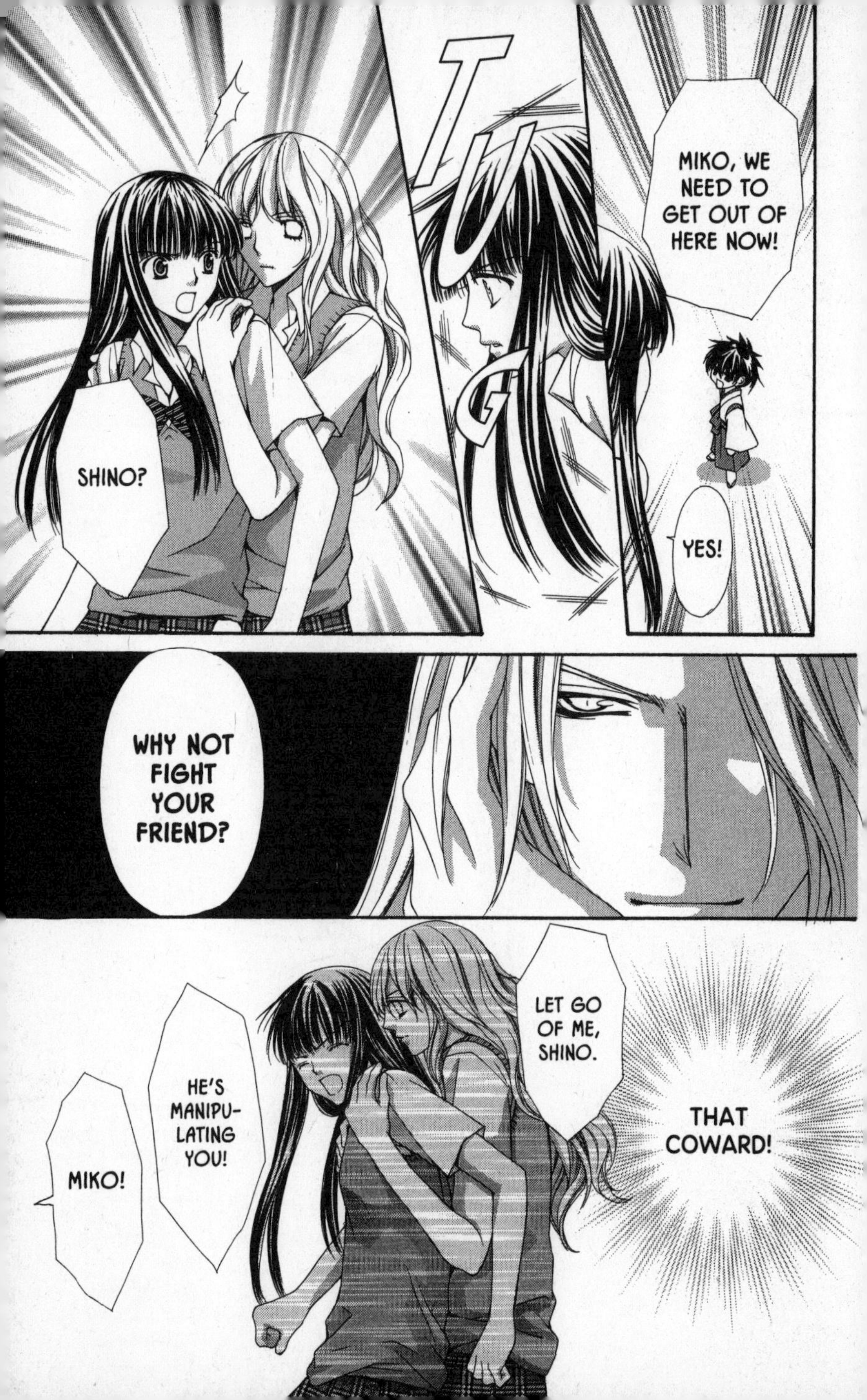
MIKO, WE NEED TO GET OUT OF HERE NOW!
YES!
TUG
SHINO?
WHY NOT FIGHT YOUR FRIEND?
THAT COWARD!
LET GO OF ME, SHINO.
HE'S MANIPU-LATING YOU!
MIKO!

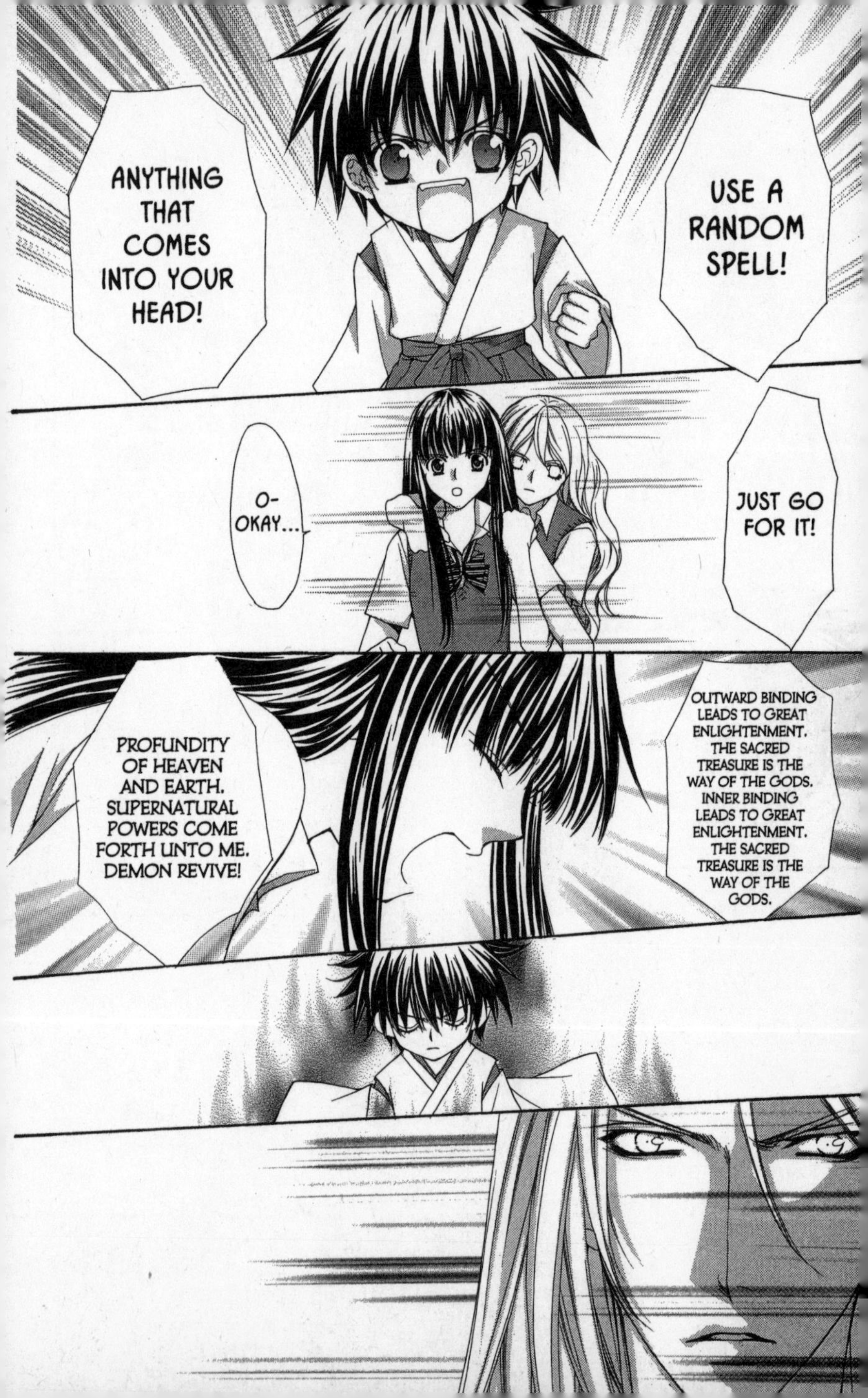
USE A RANDOM SPELL!
ANYTHING THAT COMES INTO YOUR HEAD!
JUST GO FOR IT!
O-OKAY...
OUTWARD BINDING LEADS TO GREAT ENLIGHTENMENT. THE SACRED TREASURE IS THE WAY OF THE GODS. INNER BINDING LEADS TO GREAT ENLIGHTENMENT. THE SACRED TREASURE IS THE WAY OF THE GODS.
PROFUNDITY OF HEAVEN AND EARTH. SUPERNATURAL POWERS COME FORTH UNTO ME. DEMON REVIVE!

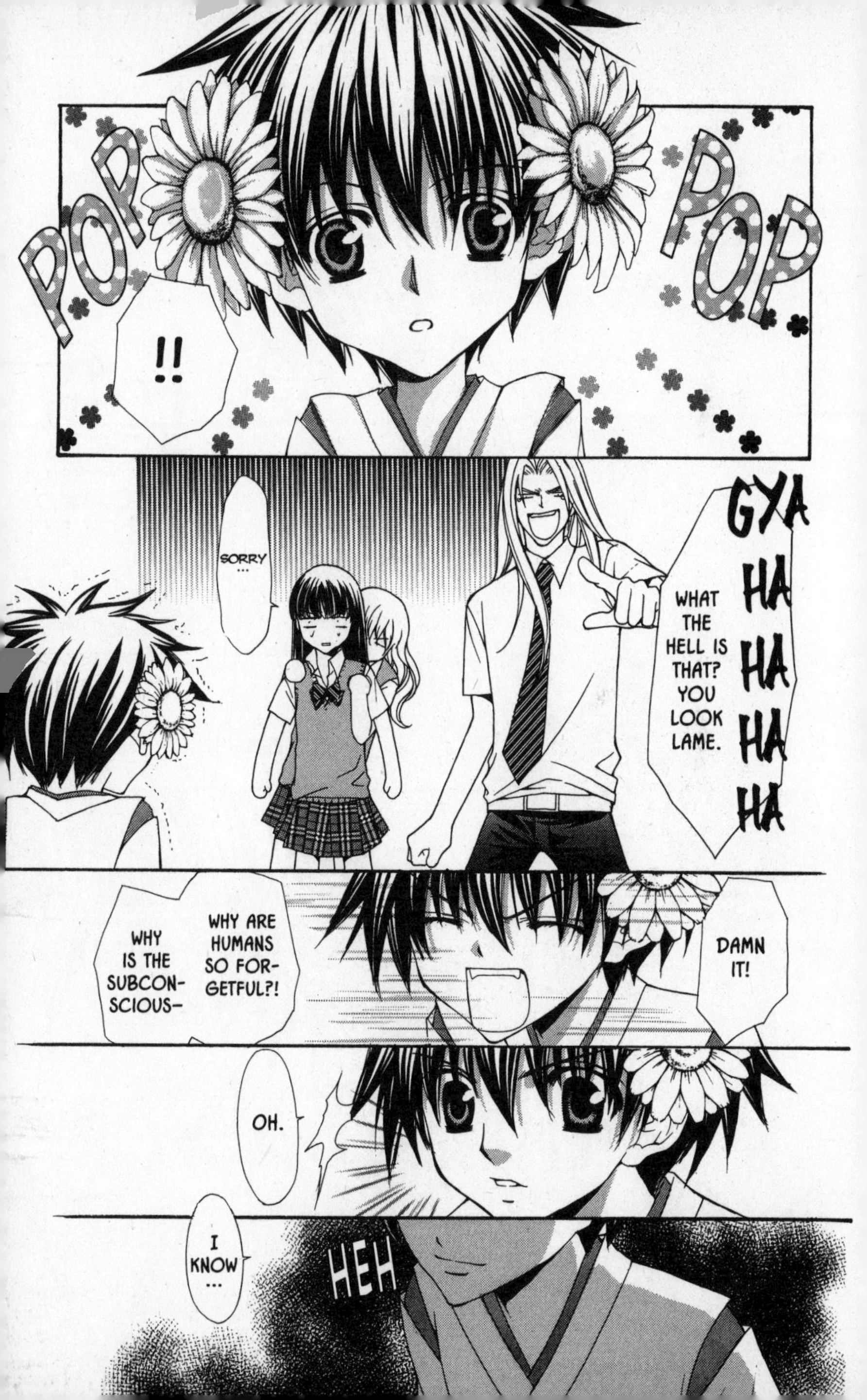
POP POP
POP POP
!!
GYA HA HA HA HA HA
WHAT THE HELL IS THAT? YOU LOOK LAME.
SORRY...
DAMN IT!
WHY ARE HUMANS SO FOR-GETFUL?!
WHY IS THE SUBCON-SCIOUS–
OH.
HEH
I KNOW...

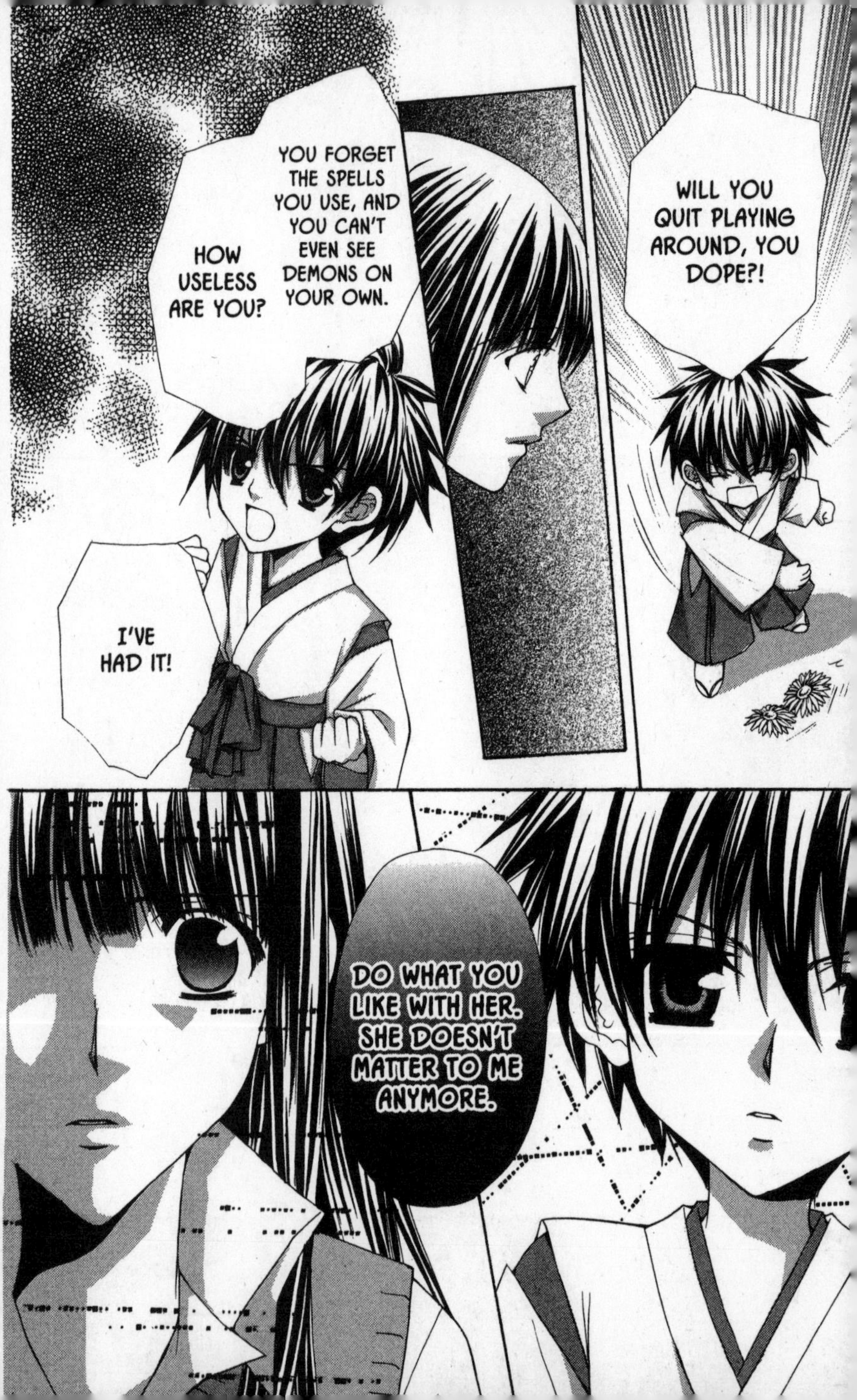
WILL YOU QUIT PLAYING AROUND, YOU DOPE?!
YOU FORGET THE SPELLS YOU USE, AND YOU CAN'T EVEN SEE DEMONS ON YOUR OWN.
HOW USELESS ARE YOU?
I'VE HAD IT!
DO WHAT YOU LIKE WITH HER. SHE DOESN'T MATTER TO ME ANYMORE.

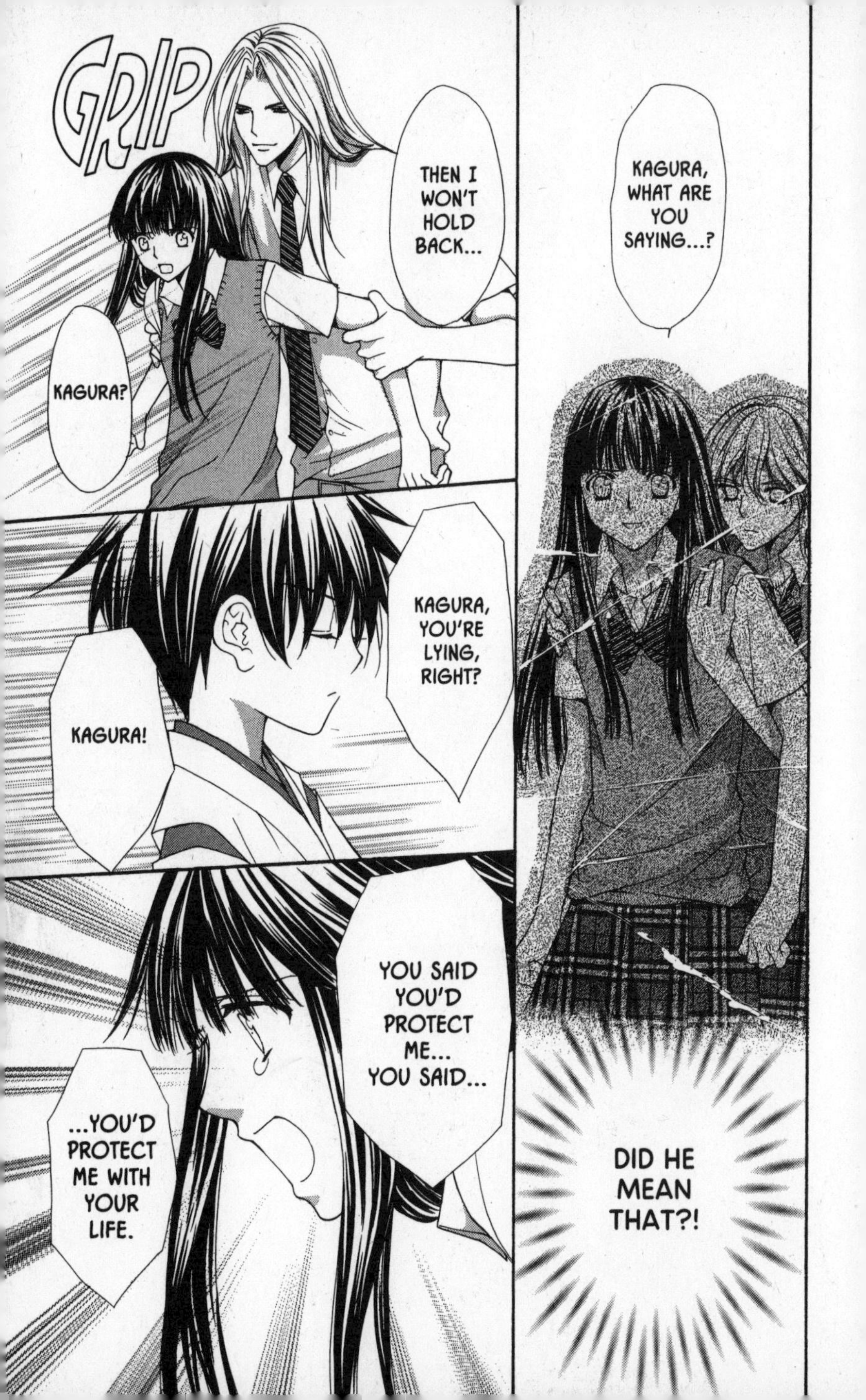
KAGURA, WHAT ARE YOU SAYING...?
DID HE MEAN THAT?!
GRIP
THEN I WON'T HOLD BACK...
KAGURA?
KAGURA, YOU'RE LYING, RIGHT?
KAGURA!
YOU SAID YOU'D PROTECT ME... YOU SAID...
...YOU'D PROTECT ME WITH YOUR LIFE.

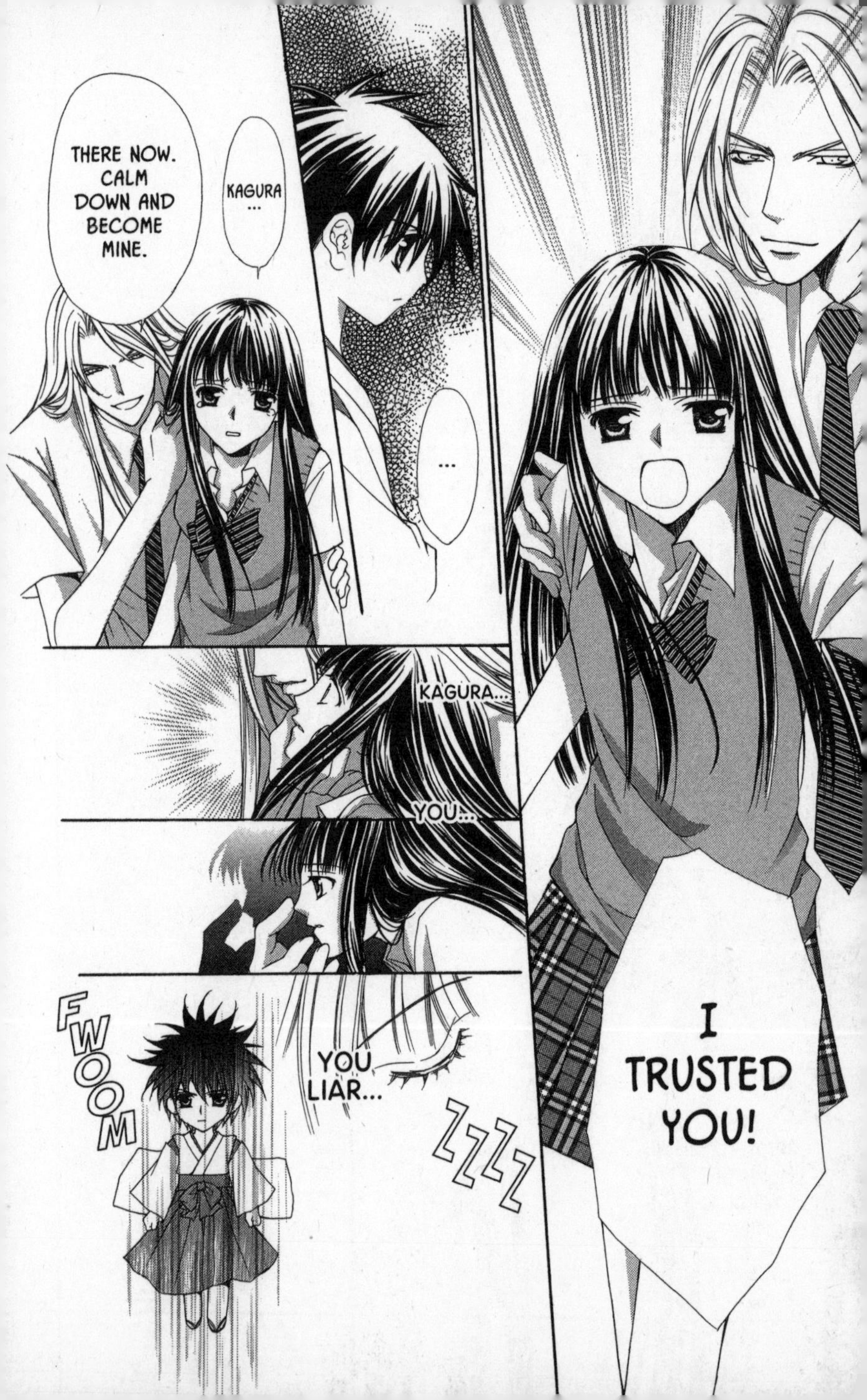
I TRUSTED YOU!
...
KAGURA ...
THERE NOW. CALM DOWN AND BECOME MINE.
KAGURA...
YOU...
YOU LIAR...
ZZZZ
FWOOM

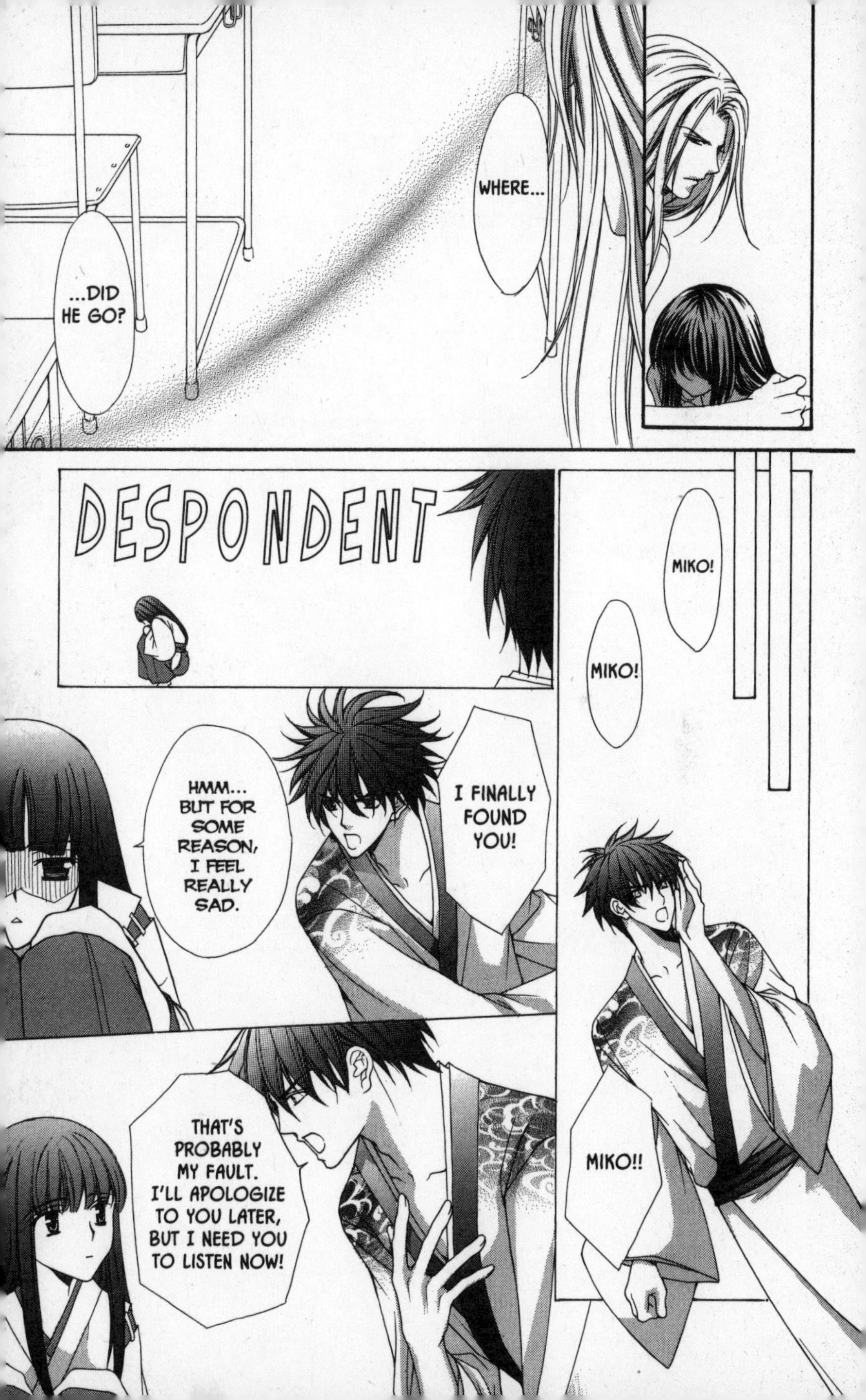
WHERE...
...DID HE GO?
MIKO!
MIKO!
MIKO!!
DESPONDENT
I FINALLY FOUND YOU!
HMM... BUT FOR SOME REASON, I FEEL REALLY SAD.
THAT'S PROBABLY MY FAULT. I'LL APOLOGIZE TO YOU LATER, BUT I NEED YOU TO LISTEN NOW!

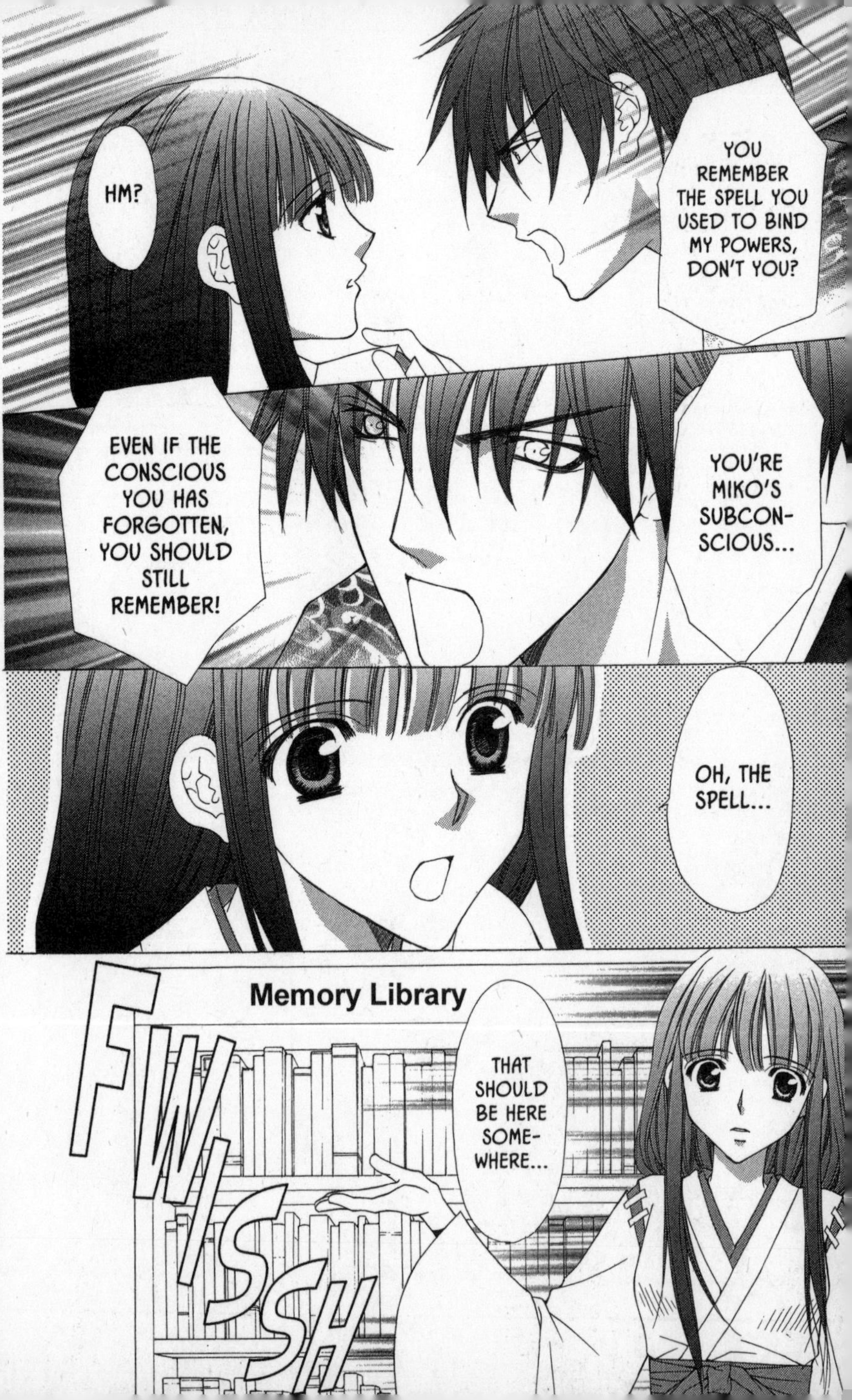
YOU REMEMBER THE SPELL YOU USED TO BIND MY POWERS, DON'T YOU?
HM?
YOU'RE MIKO'S SUBCON-SCIOUS...
EVEN IF THE CONSCIOUS YOU HAS FORGOTTEN, YOU SHOULD STILL REMEMBER!
OH, THE SPELL...
Memory Library
THAT SHOULD BE HERE SOME-WHERE...
FWISSH

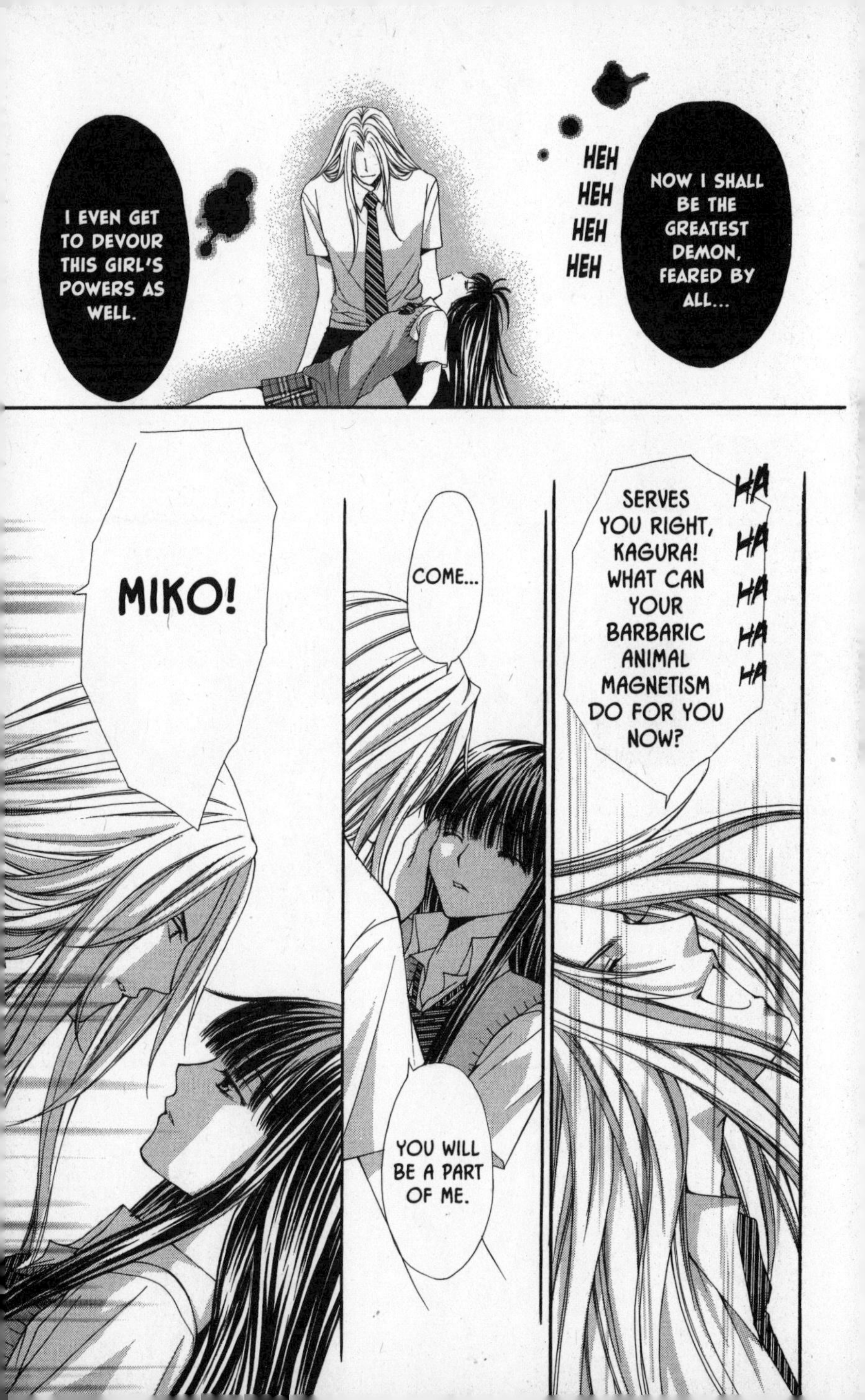
NOW I SHALL BE THE GREATEST DEMON, FEARED BY ALL...
HEH HEH HEH HEH
I EVEN GET TO DEVOUR THIS GIRL'S POWERS AS WELL.
SERVES YOU RIGHT, KAGURA! WHAT CAN YOUR BARBARIC ANIMAL MAGNETISM DO FOR YOU NOW?
HA HA HA HA HA
COME...
YOU WILL BE A PART OF ME.
MIKO!

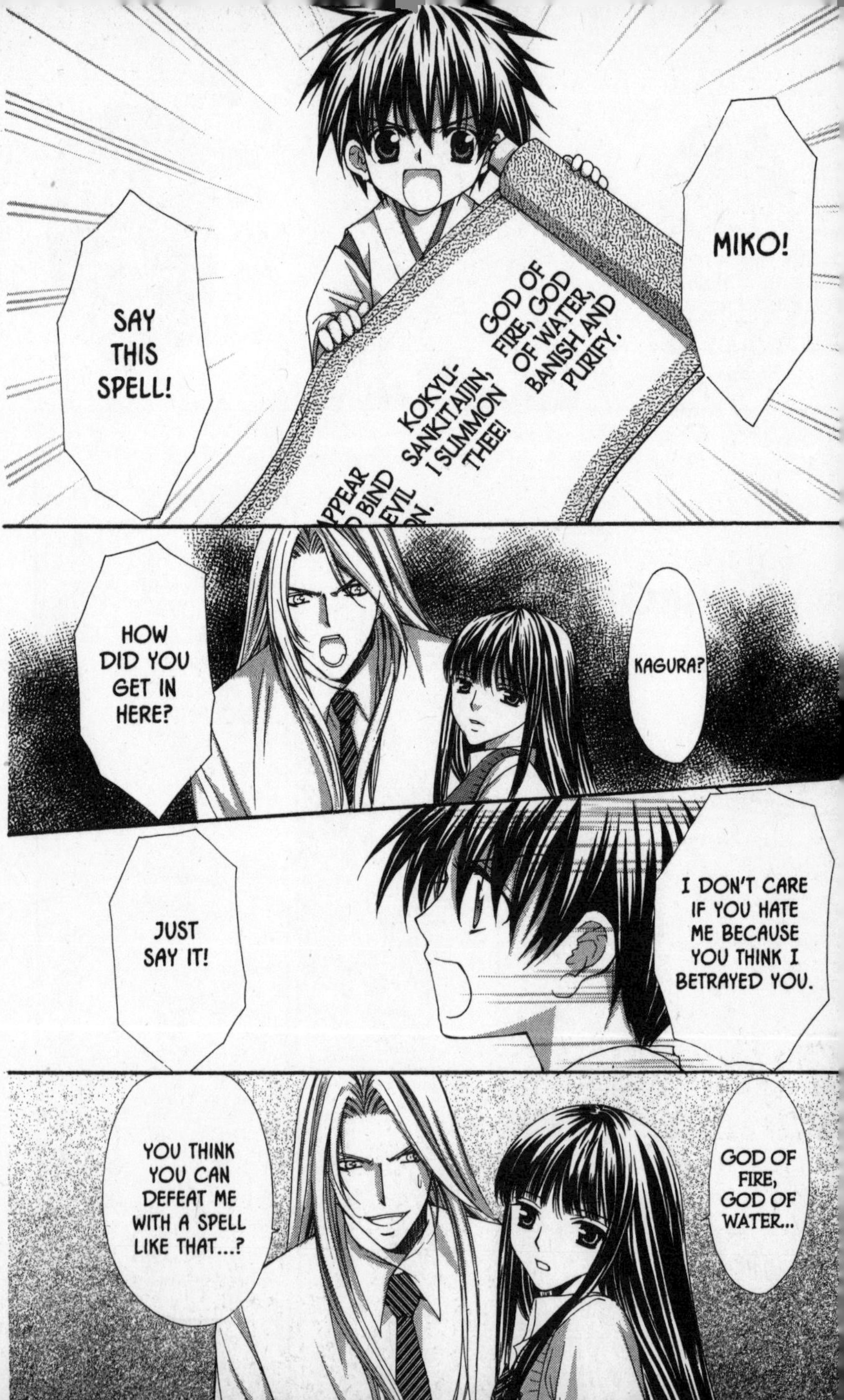
MIKO!
GOD OF FIRE, GOD OF WATER, BANISH AND PURIFY.
KOKYU-SANKITAIJIN, I SUMMON THEE!
SAY THIS SPELL!
KAGURA?
HOW DID YOU GET IN HERE?
I DON'T CARE IF YOU HATE ME BECAUSE YOU THINK I BETRAYED YOU.
JUST SAY IT!
GOD OF FIRE, GOD OF WATER...
YOU THINK YOU CAN DEFEAT ME WITH A SPELL LIKE THAT...?

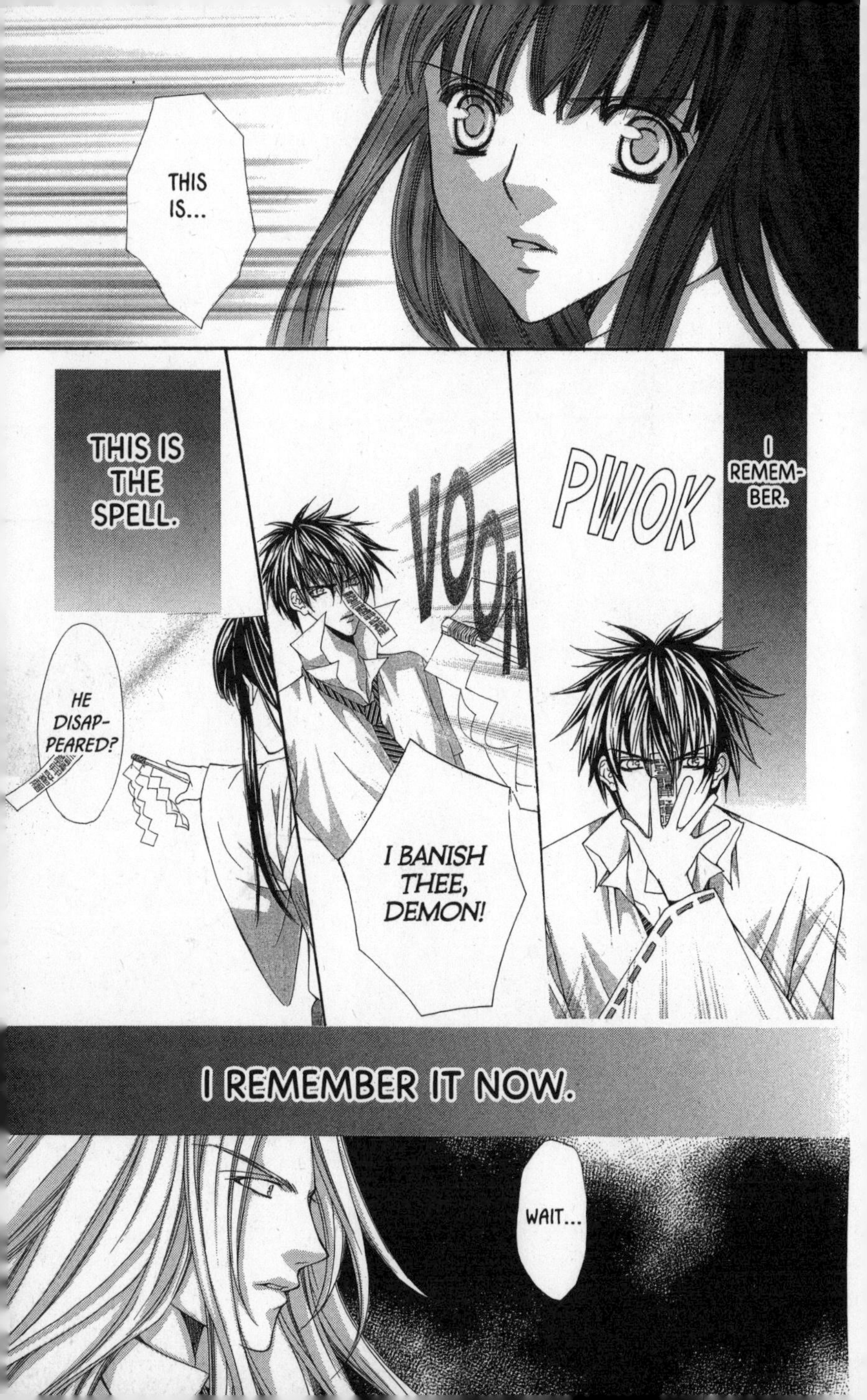
THIS IS...
I REMEMBER.
PWOK
VOON
I BANISH THEE, DEMON!
THIS IS THE SPELL.
HE DISAPPEARED?
I REMEMBER IT NOW.
WAIT...

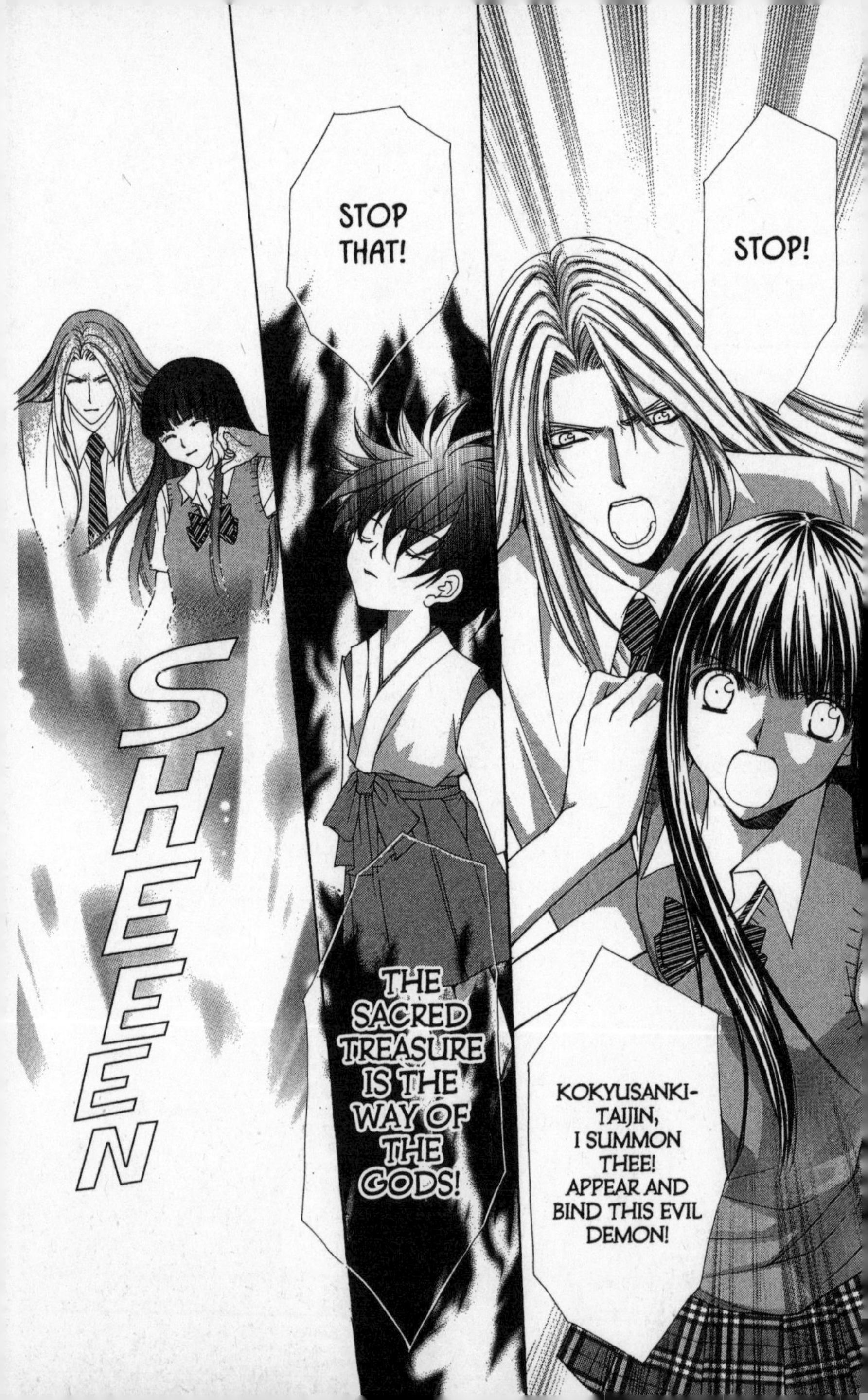
STOP!
KOKYUSANKI-TAIJIN, I SUMMON THEE! APPEAR AND BIND THIS EVIL DEMON!
STOP THAT!
THE SACRED TREASURE IS THE WAY OF THE GODS!
SHEEEN

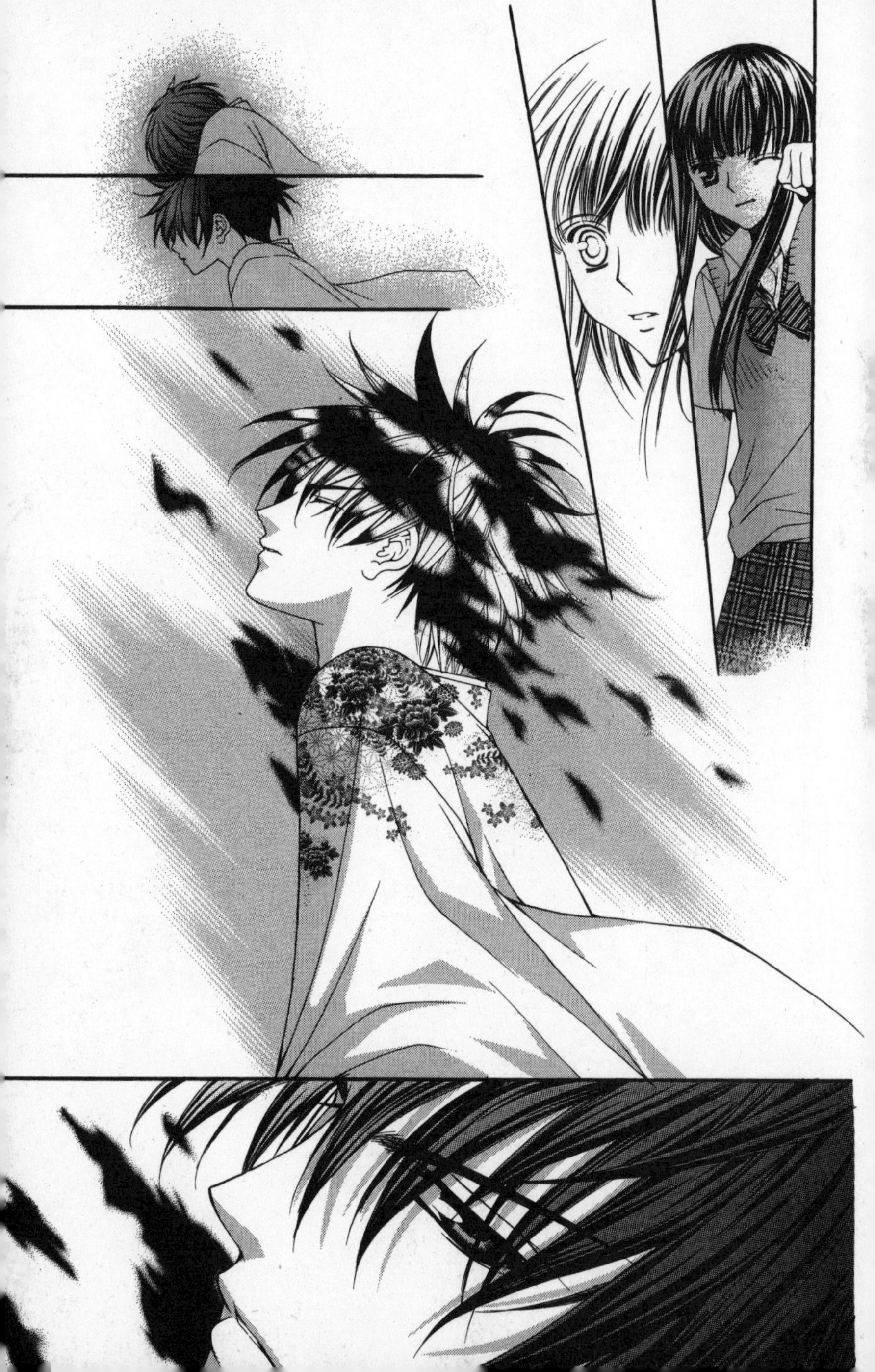

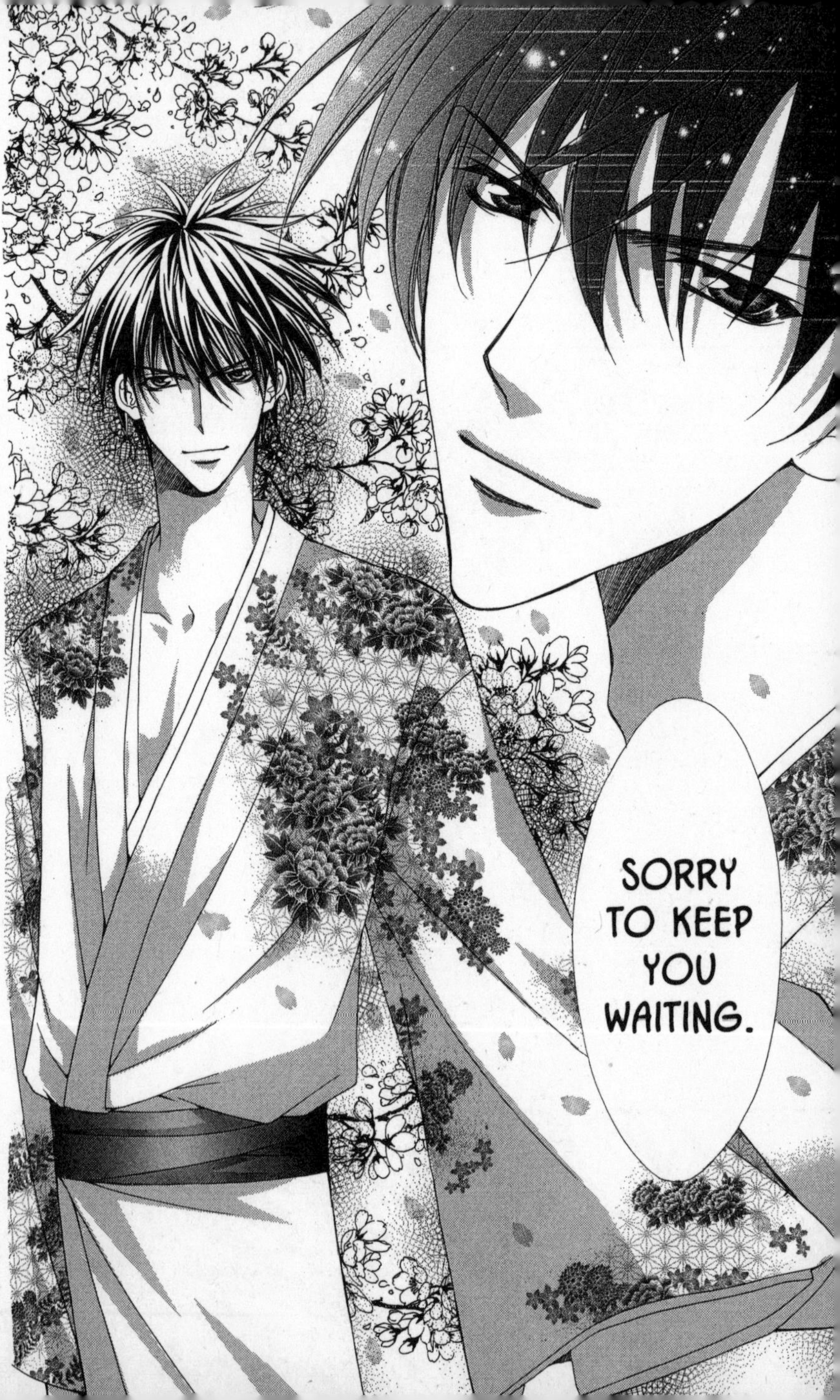
SORRY TO KEEP YOU WAITING.

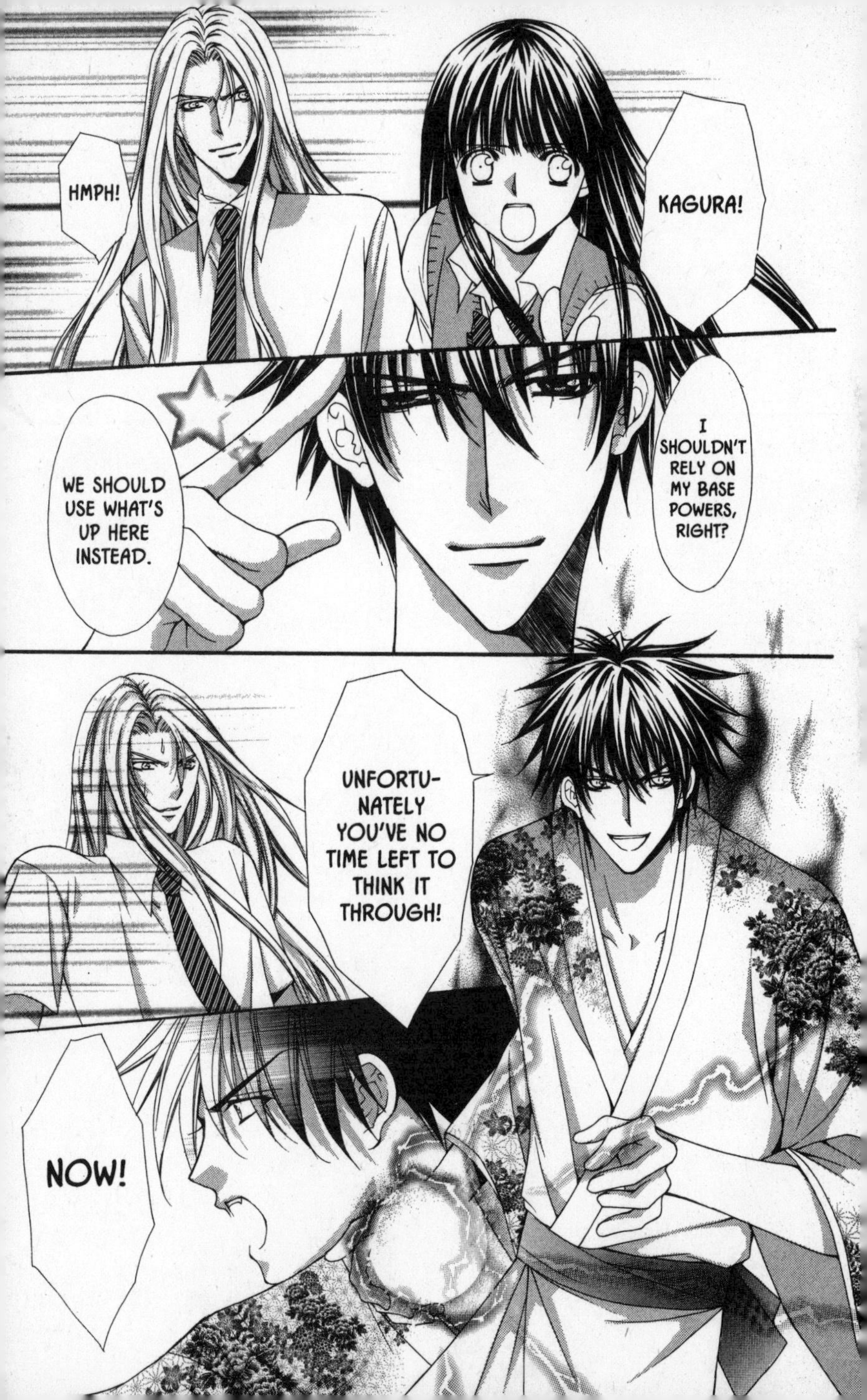
KAGURA!
HMPH!
I SHOULDN'T RELY ON MY BASE POWERS, RIGHT?
WE SHOULD USE WHAT'S UP HERE INSTEAD.
UNFORTU-NATELY YOU'VE NO TIME LEFT TO THINK IT THROUGH!
NOW!

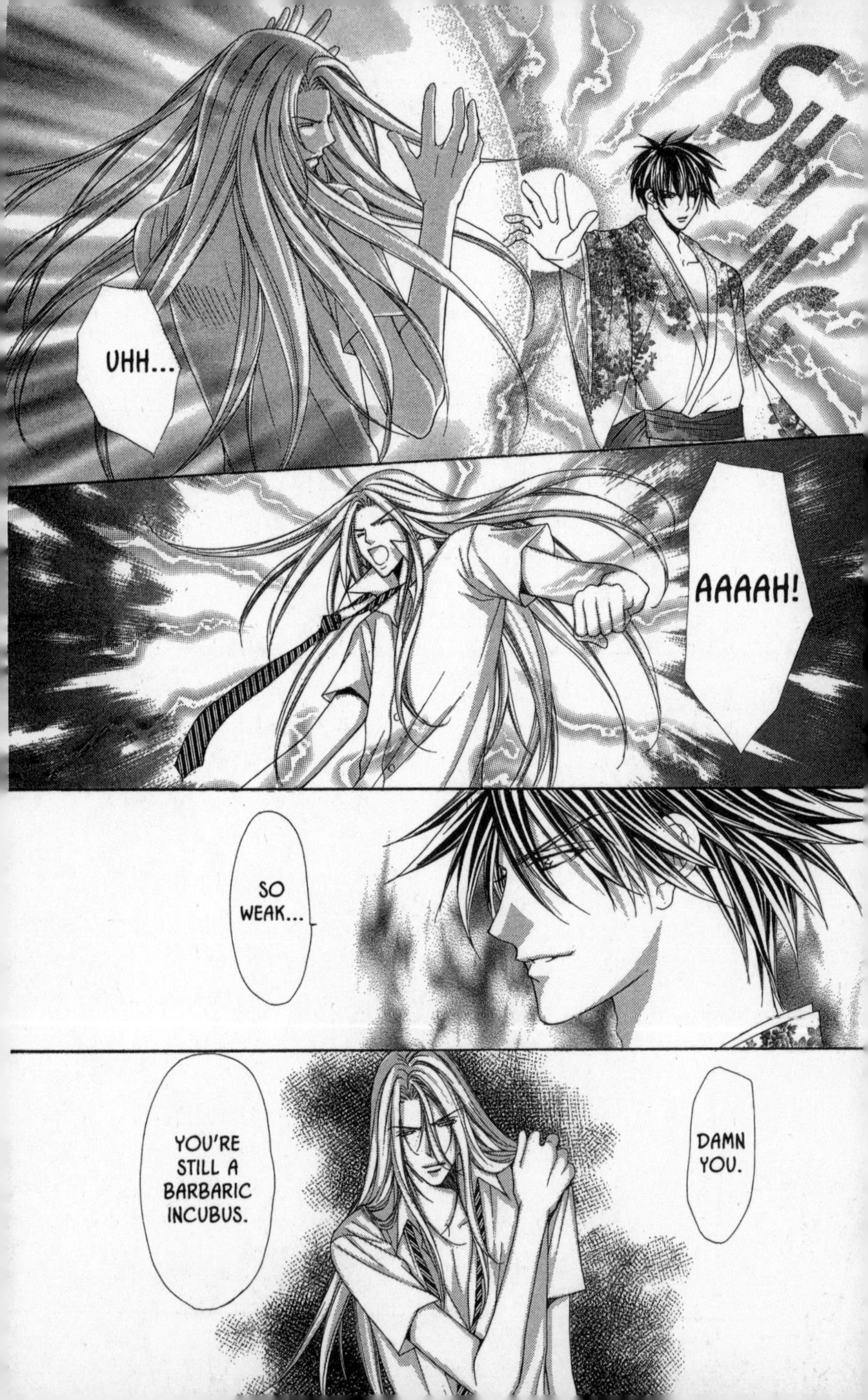
UHH...
AAAAH!
SO WEAK...
DAMN YOU.
YOU'RE STILL A BARBARIC INCUBUS.

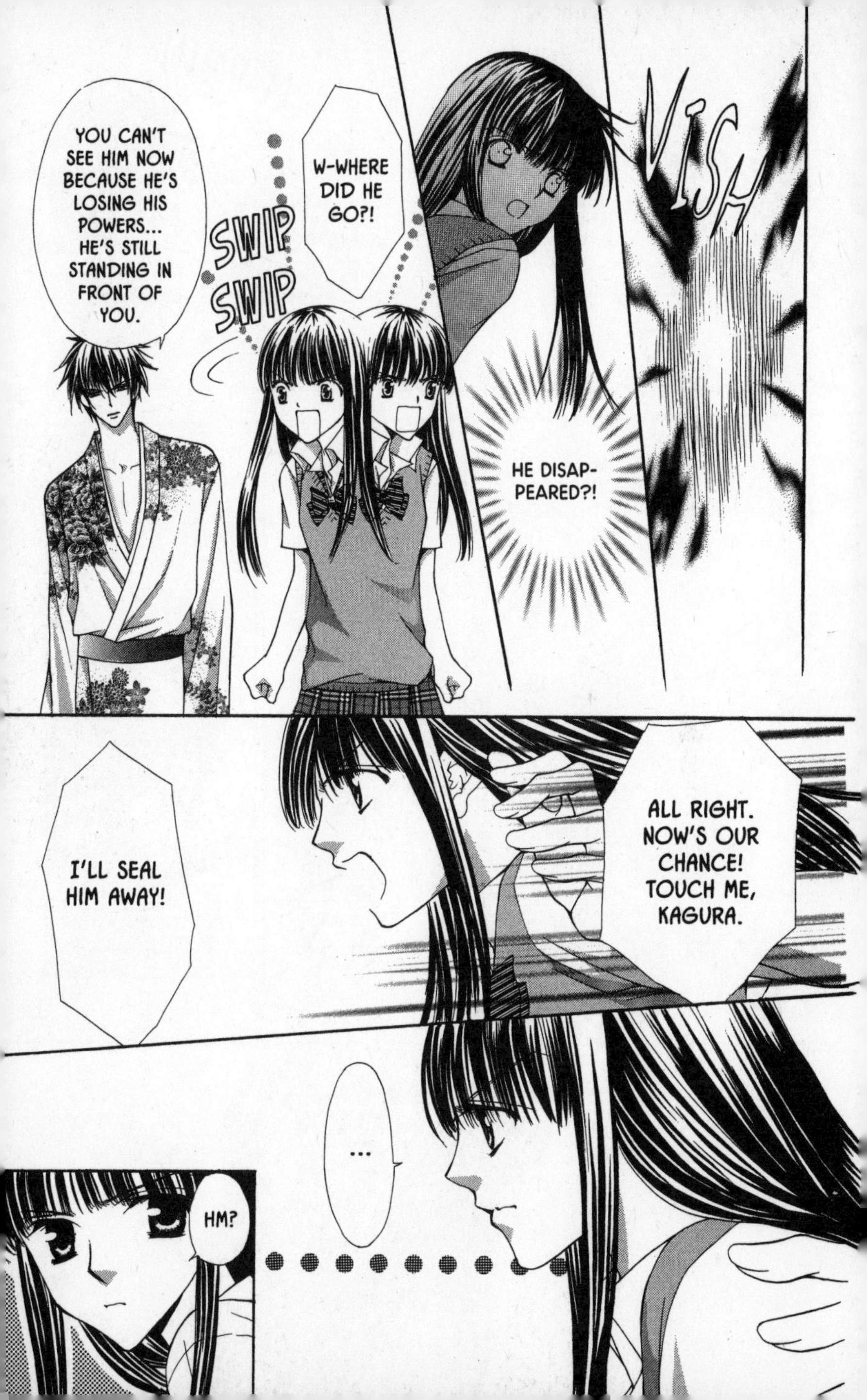
VISH
HE DISAPPEARED?!
W-WHERE DID HE GO?!
SWIP SWIP
YOU CAN'T SEE HIM NOW BECAUSE HE'S LOSING HIS POWERS... HE'S STILL STANDING IN FRONT OF YOU.
ALL RIGHT. NOW'S OUR CHANCE! TOUCH ME, KAGURA.
I'LL SEAL HIM AWAY!
...
HM?

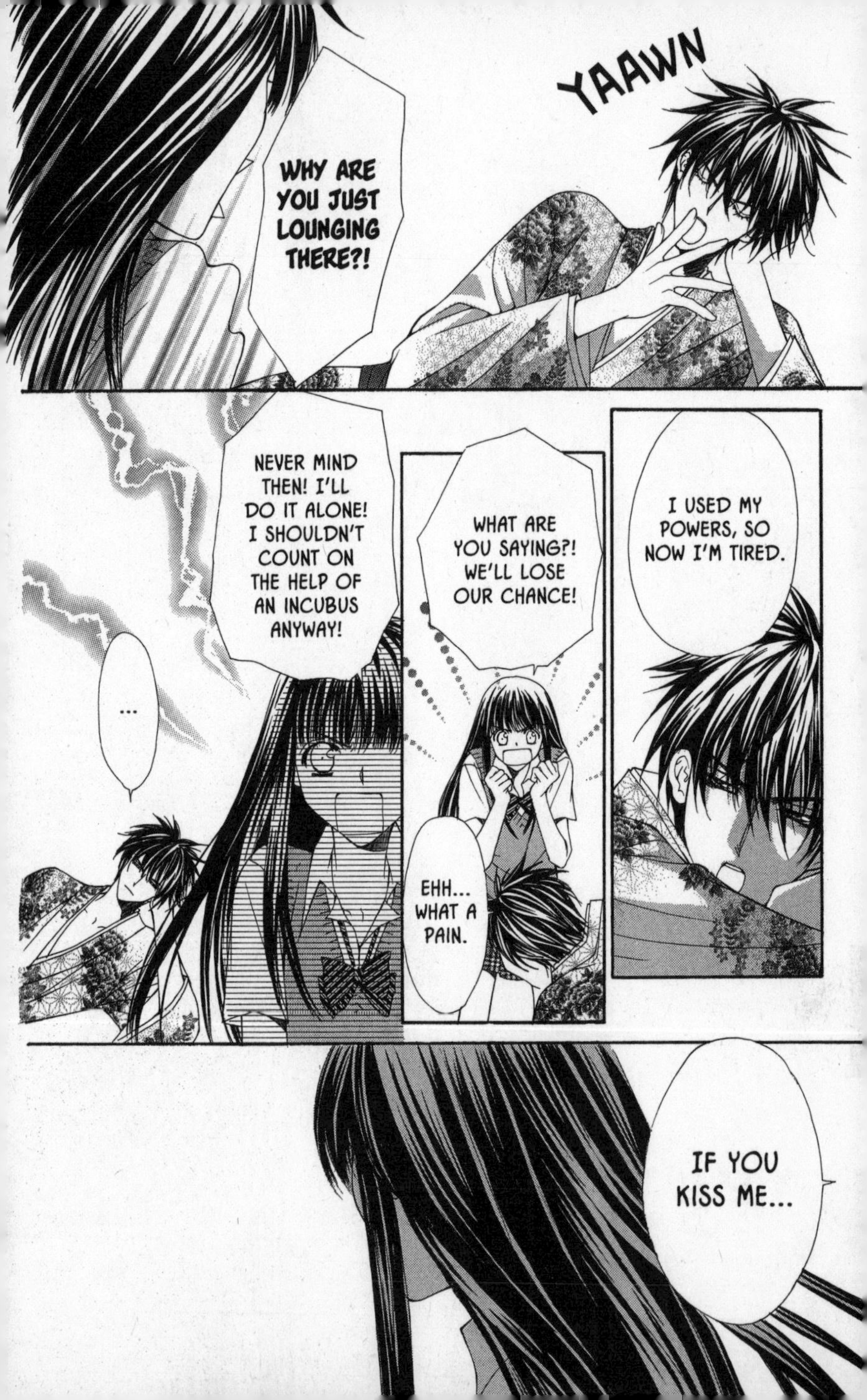
YAAWN
WHY ARE YOU JUST LOUNGING THERE?!
I USED MY POWERS, SO NOW I'M TIRED.
WHAT ARE YOU SAYING?! WE'LL LOSE OUR CHANCE!
EHH... WHAT A PAIN.
NEVER MIND THEN! I'LL DO IT ALONE! I SHOULDN'T COUNT ON THE HELP OF AN INCUBUS ANYWAY!
...
IF YOU KISS ME...

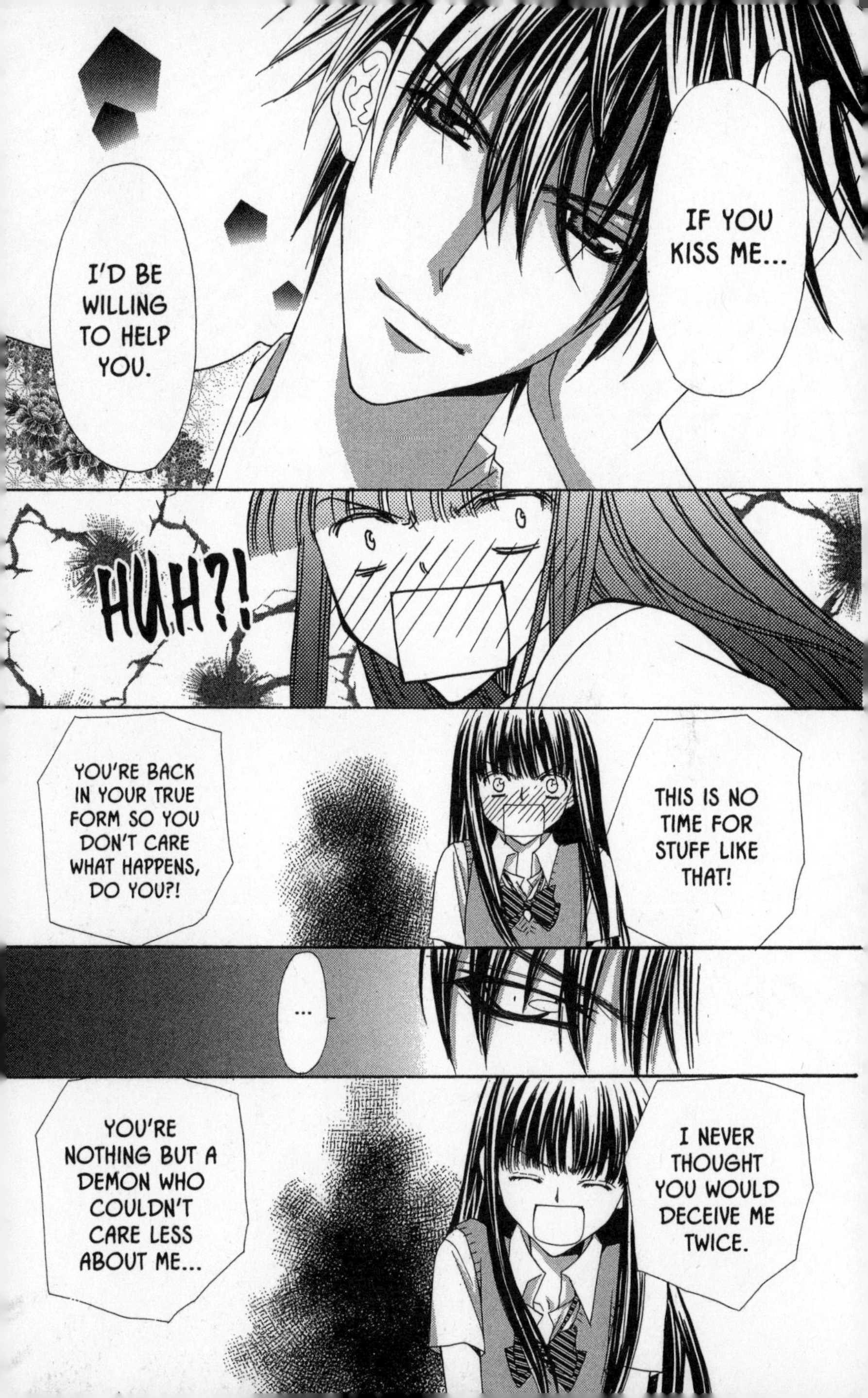
IF YOU KISS ME...
I'D BE WILLING TO HELP YOU.
HUH?!
THIS IS NO TIME FOR STUFF LIKE THAT!
YOU'RE BACK IN YOUR TRUE FORM SO YOU DON'T CARE WHAT HAPPENS, DO YOU?!
...
I NEVER THOUGHT YOU WOULD DECEIVE ME TWICE.
YOU'RE NOTHING BUT A DEMON WHO COULDN'T CARE LESS ABOUT ME...

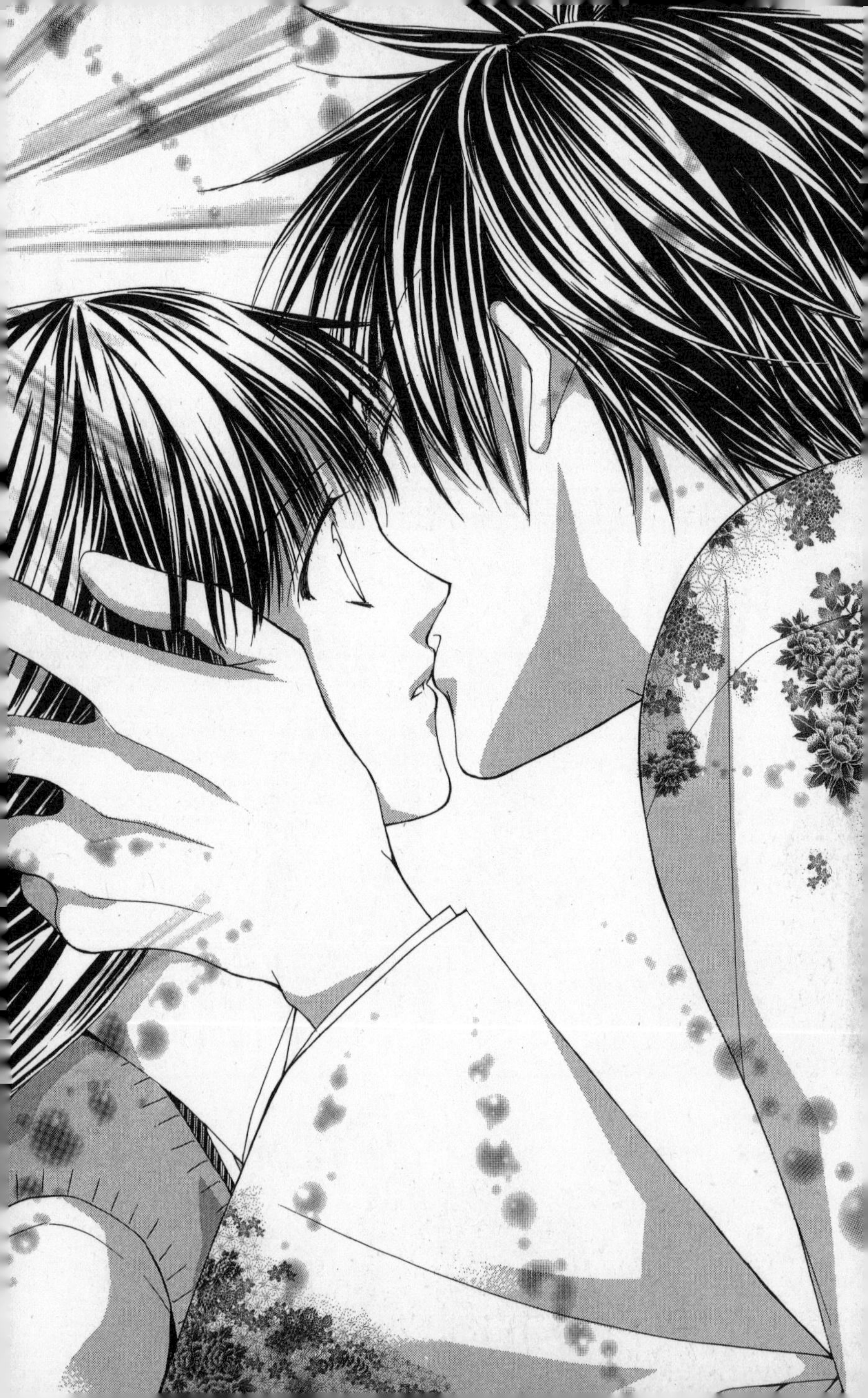

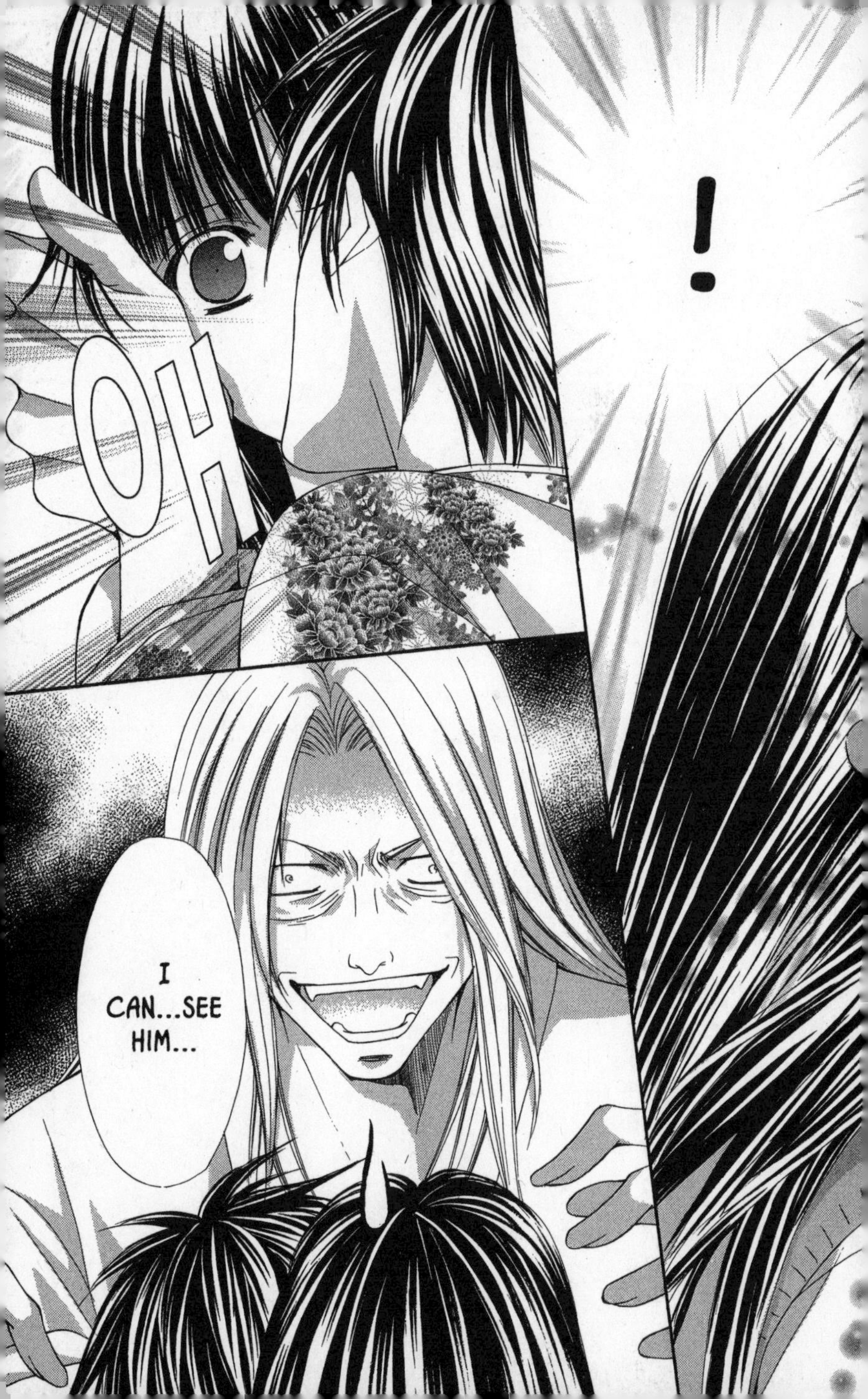
!
OH
I CAN...SEE HIM...

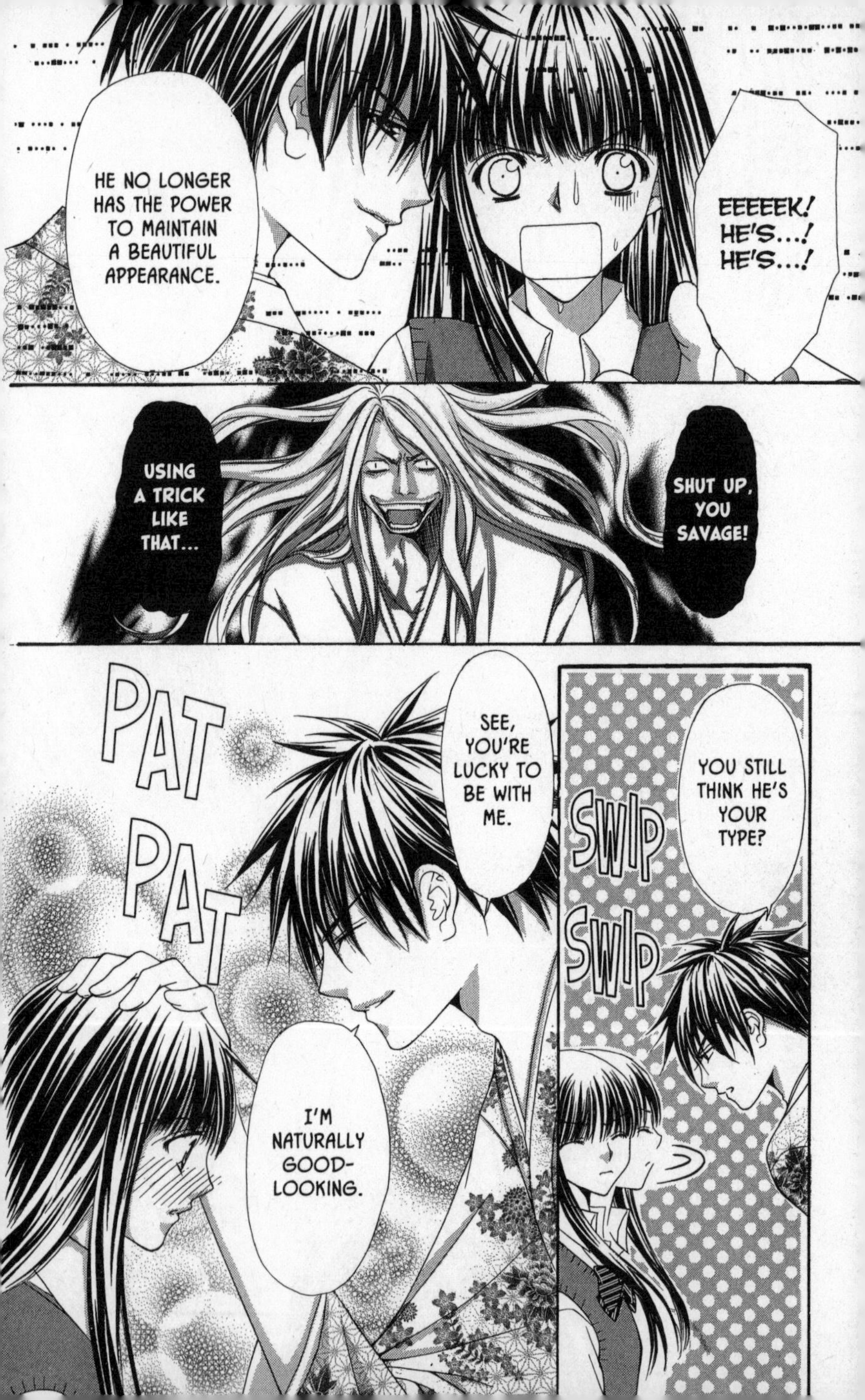
EEEEEK! HE'S...! HE'S...!
HE NO LONGER HAS THE POWER TO MAINTAIN A BEAUTIFUL APPEARANCE.
SHUT UP, YOU SAVAGE!
USING A TRICK LIKE THAT...
YOU STILL THINK HE'S YOUR TYPE?
SWIP SWIP
SEE, YOU'RE LUCKY TO BE WITH ME.
PAT PAT
I'M NATURALLY GOOD-LOOKING.

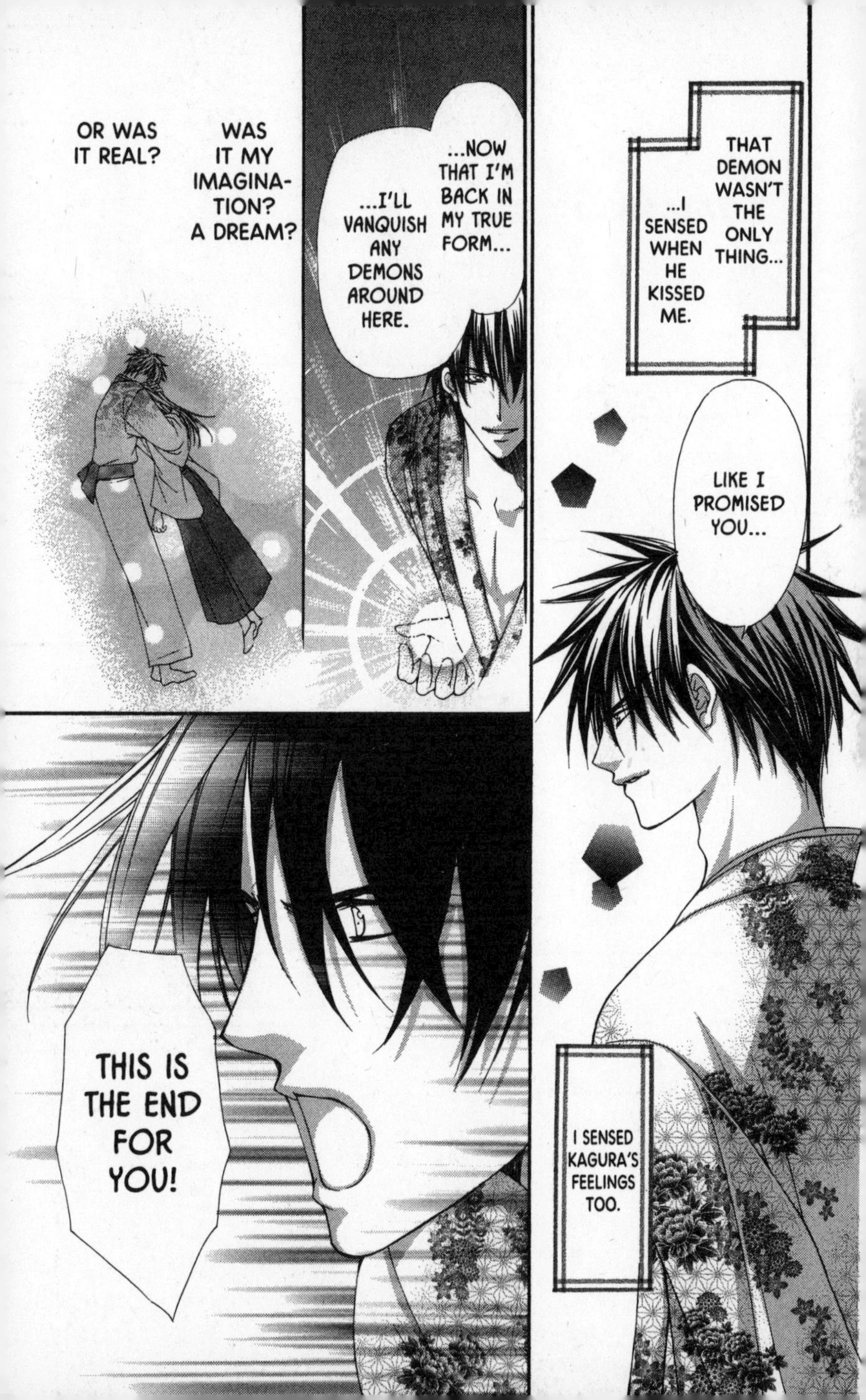
THAT DEMON WASN'T THE ONLY THING...
...I SENSED WHEN HE KISSED ME.
LIKE I PROMISED YOU...
I SENSED KAGURA'S FEELINGS TOO.
...NOW THAT I'M BACK IN MY TRUE FORM...
...I'LL VANQUISH ANY DEMONS AROUND HERE.
WAS IT MY IMAGINATION? A DREAM?
OR WAS IT REAL?
THIS IS THE END FOR YOU!

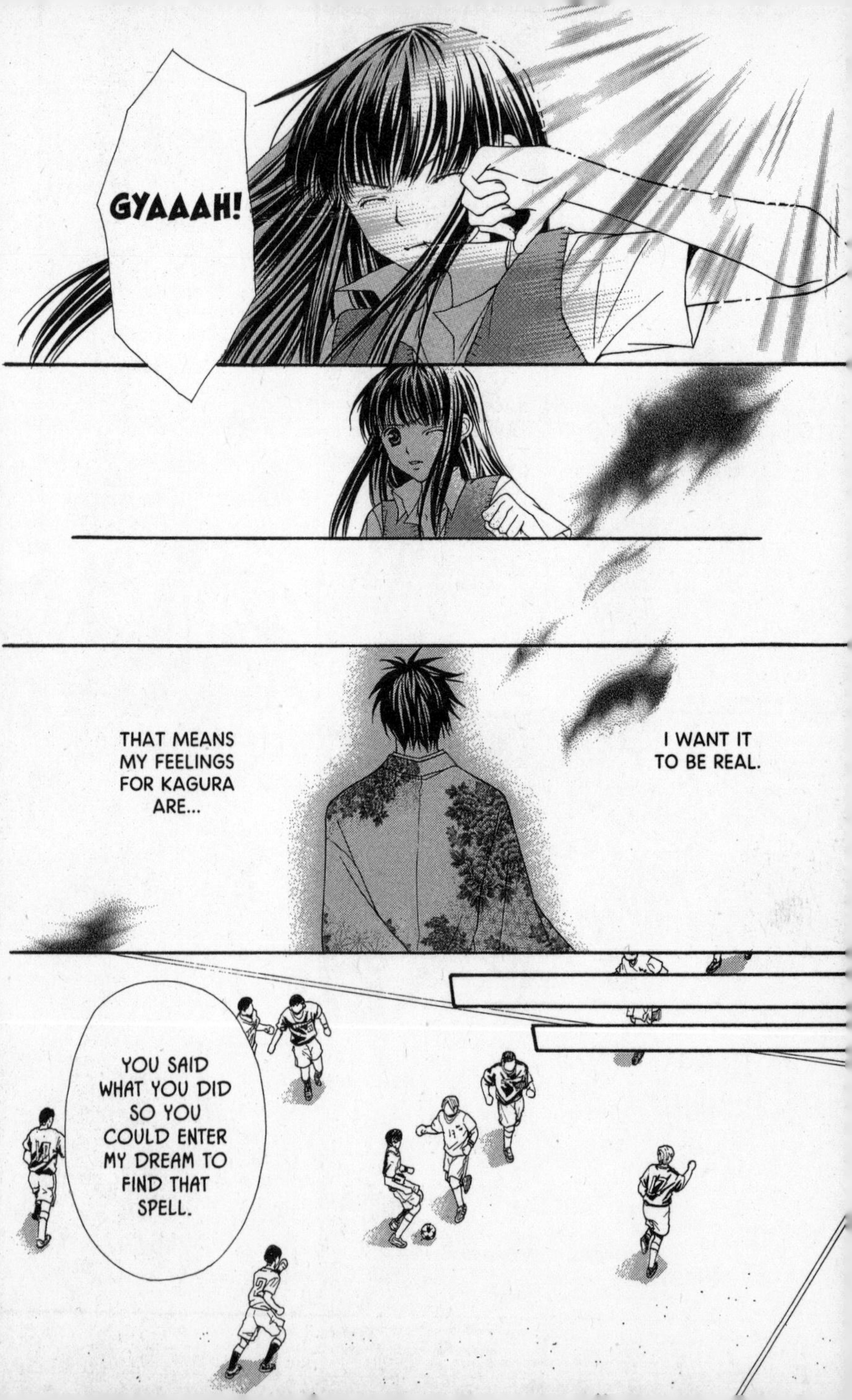
GYAAAH!
I WANT IT TO BE REAL.
THAT MEANS MY FEELINGS FOR KAGURA ARE...
YOU SAID WHAT YOU DID SO YOU COULD ENTER MY DREAM TO FIND THAT SPELL.

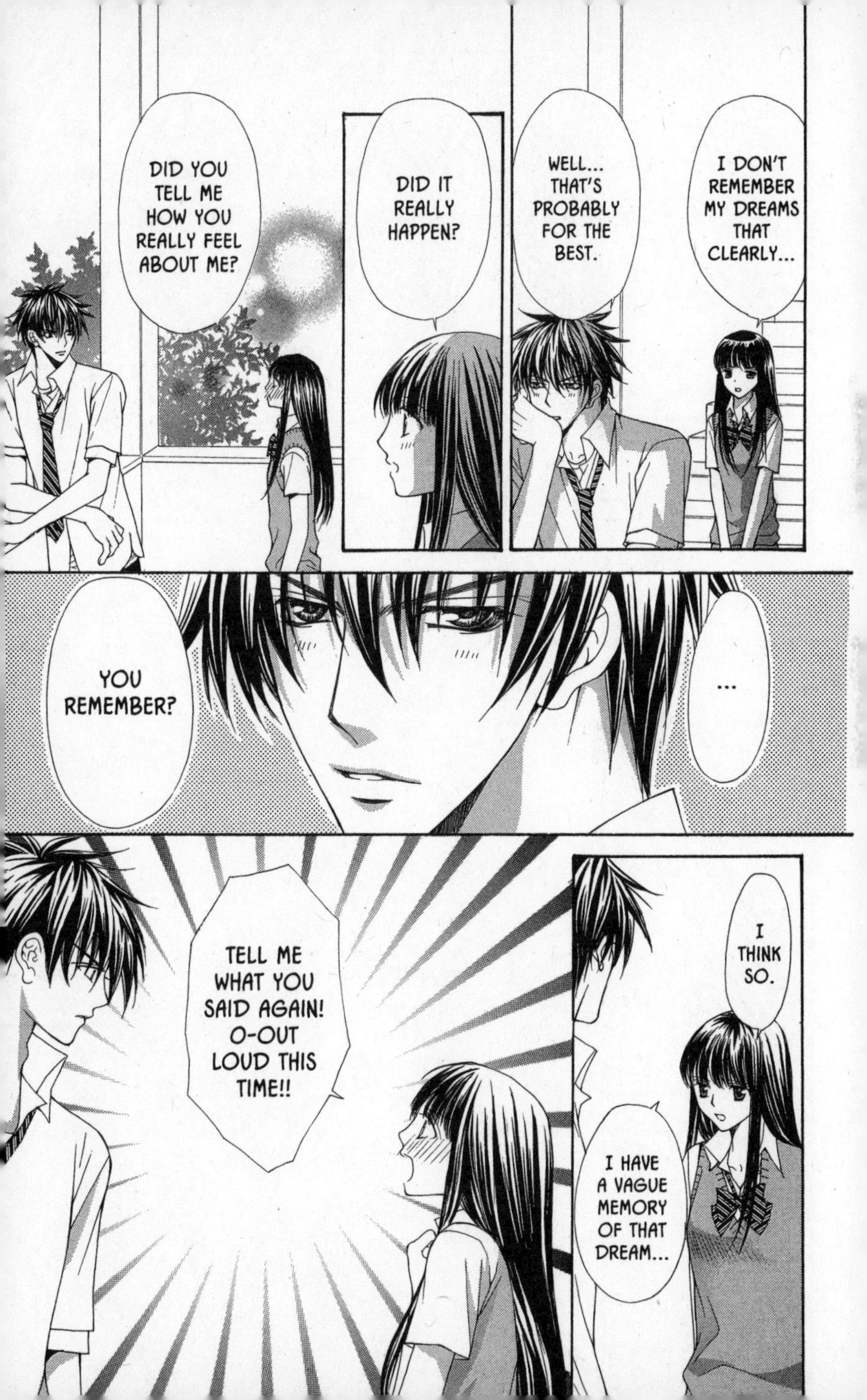
I DON'T REMEMBER MY DREAMS THAT CLEARLY...
WELL... THAT'S PROBABLY FOR THE BEST.
DID IT REALLY HAPPEN?
DID YOU TELL ME HOW YOU REALLY FEEL ABOUT ME?
...
YOU REMEMBER?
I THINK SO.
I HAVE A VAGUE MEMORY OF THAT DREAM...
TELL ME WHAT YOU SAID AGAIN! O-OUT LOUD THIS TIME!!

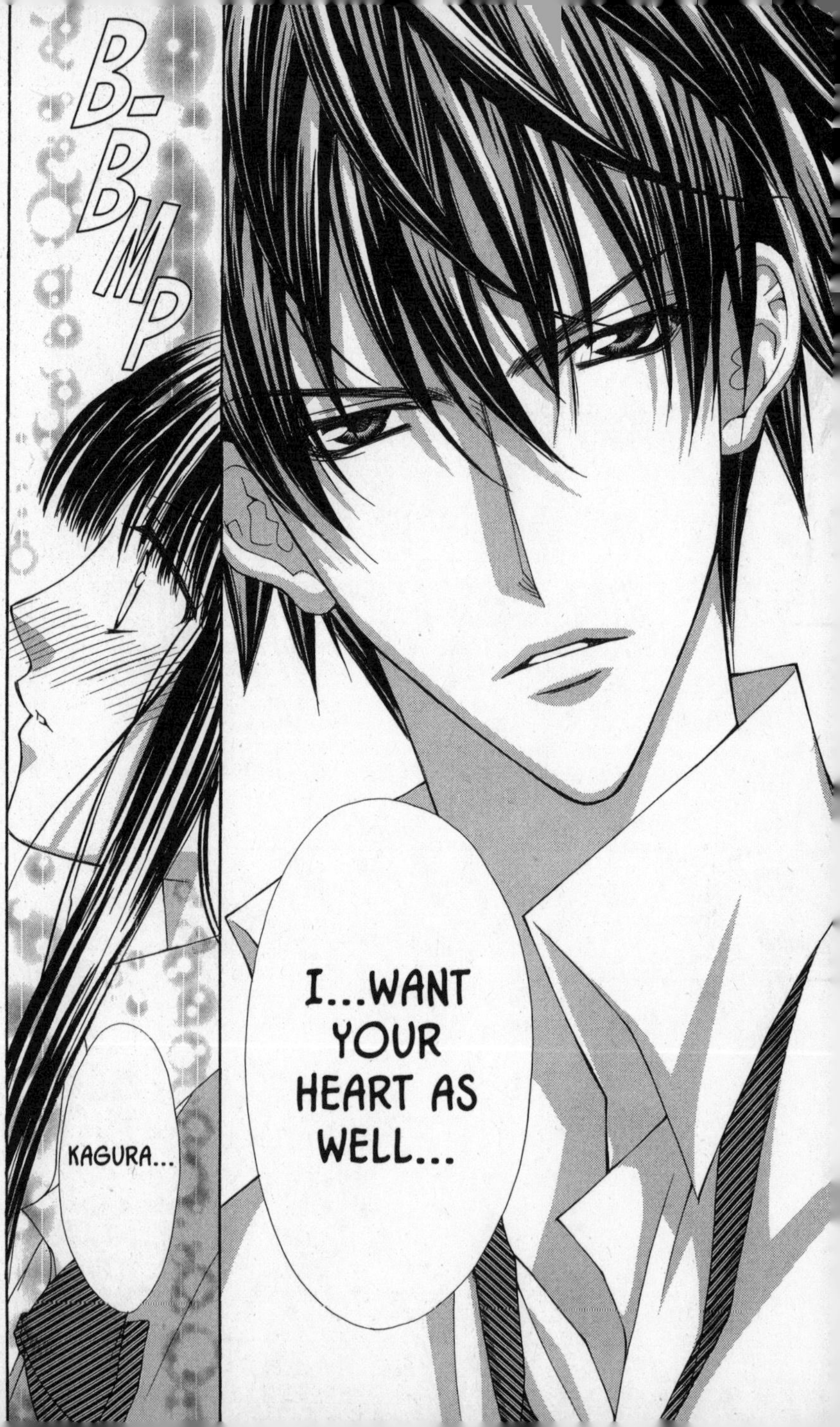
B-BMP
I...WANT YOUR HEART AS WELL...
KAGURA...

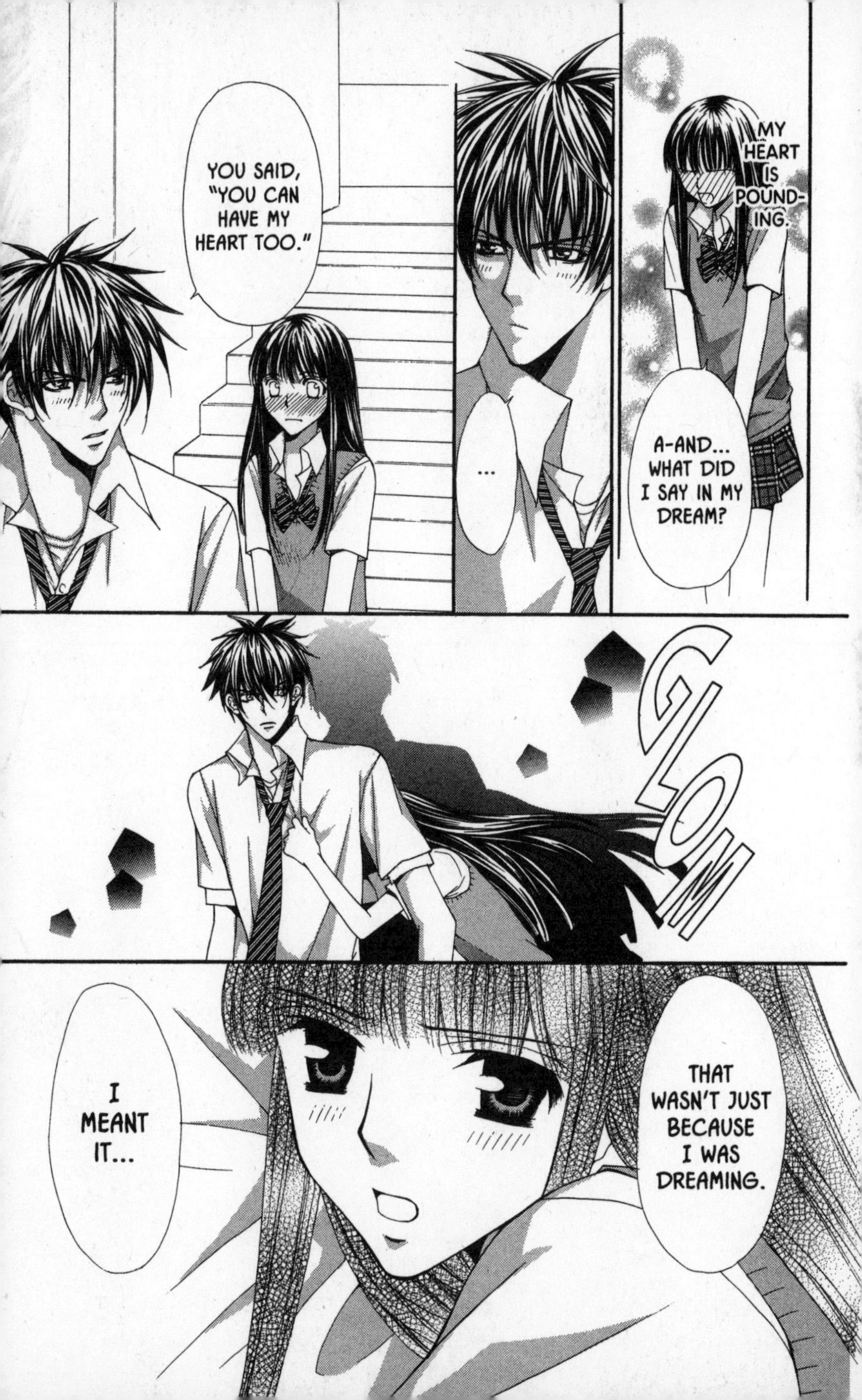
MY HEART IS POUNDING.
A-AND... WHAT DID I SAY IN MY DREAM?
...
YOU SAID, "YOU CAN HAVE MY HEART TOO."
GLOM
THAT WASN'T JUST BECAUSE I WAS DREAMING.
I MEANT IT...

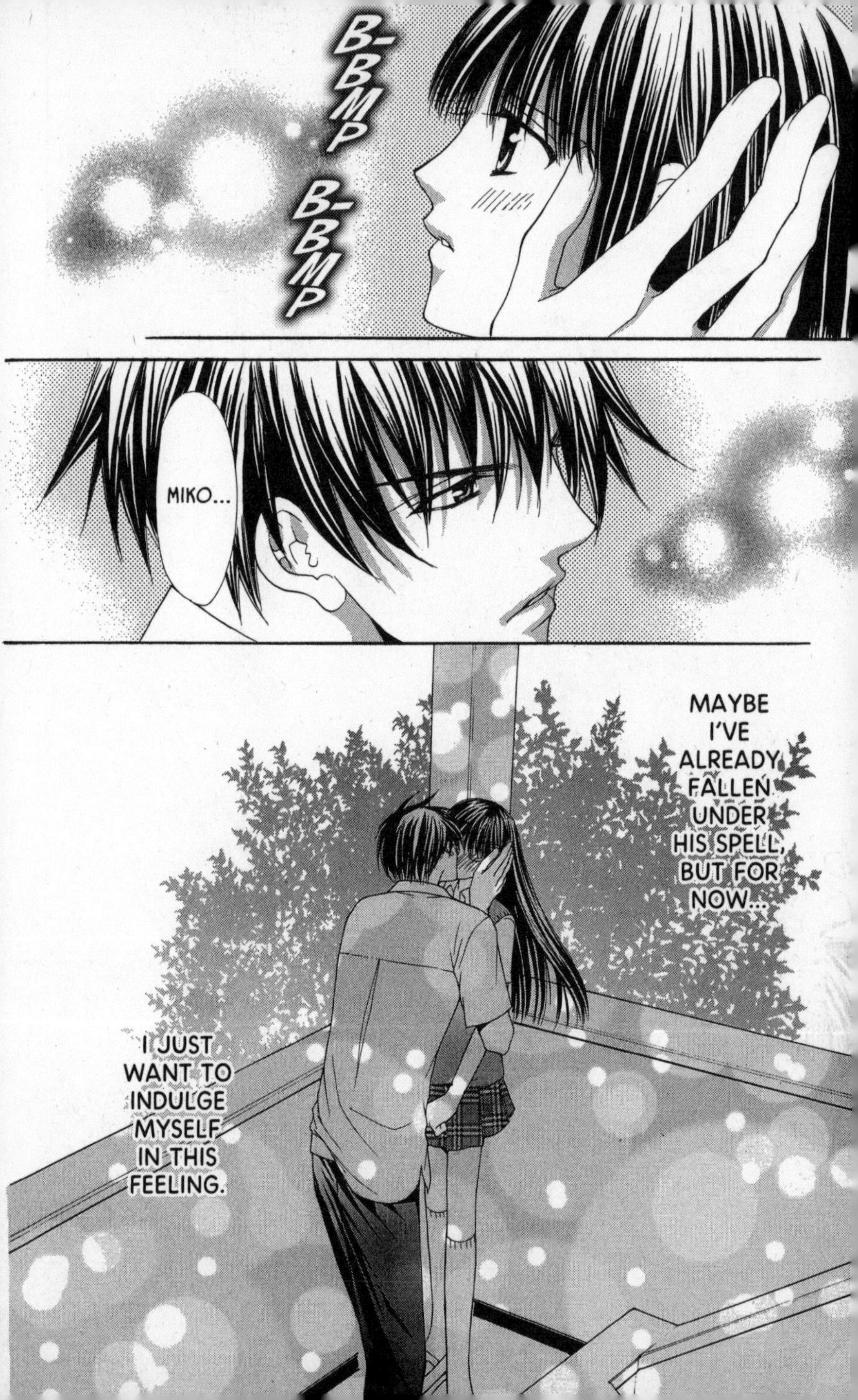
B-BMP B-BMP
MIKO...
MAYBE I'VE ALREADY FALLEN UNDER HIS SPELL, BUT FOR NOW...
I JUST WANT TO INDULGE MYSELF IN THIS FEELING.

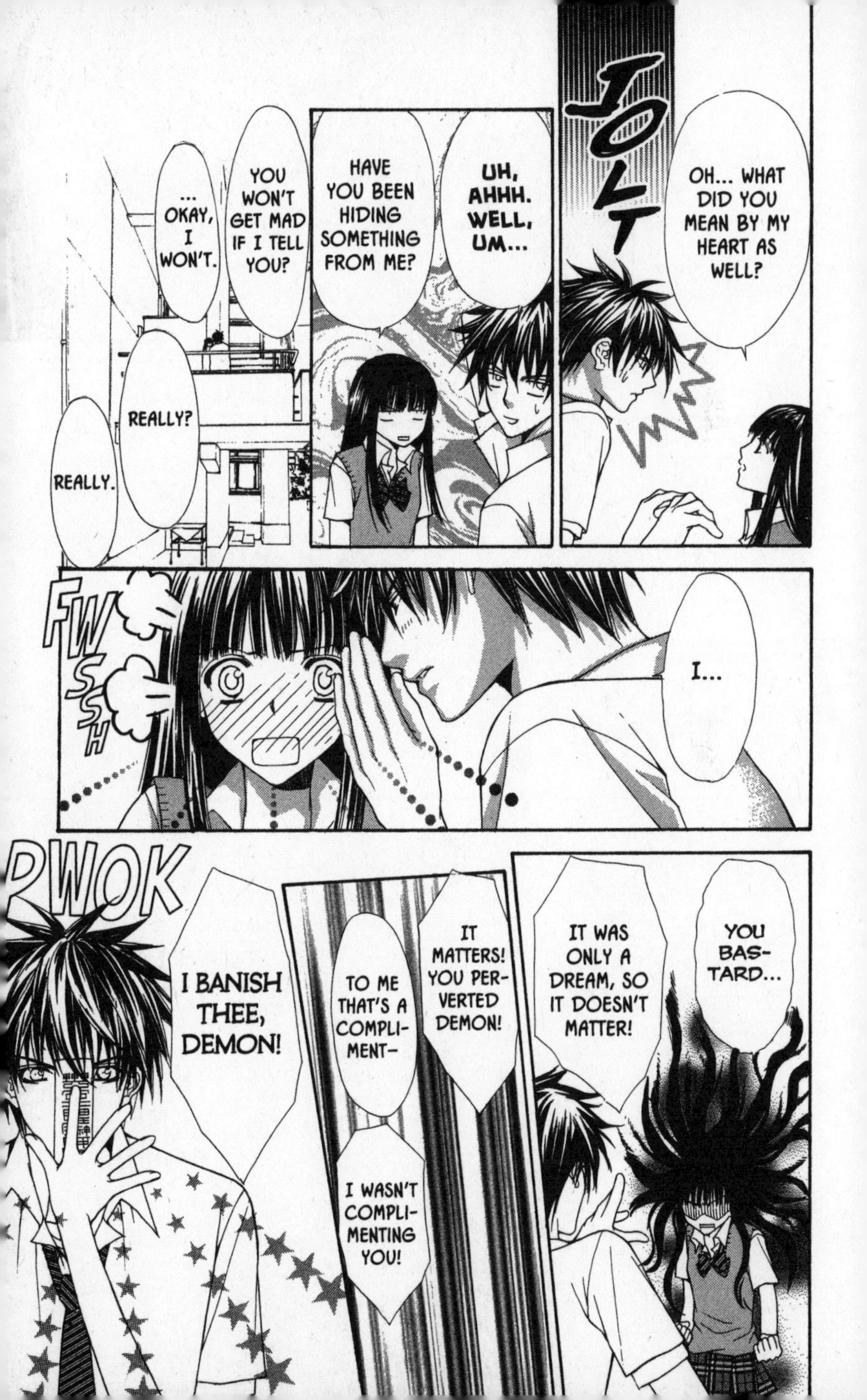
JOLT
OH... WHAT DID YOU MEAN BY MY HEART AS WELL?
UH, AHHH. WELL, UM...
HAVE YOU BEEN HIDING SOMETHING FROM ME?
YOU WON'T GET MAD IF I TELL YOU?
... OKAY, I WON'T.
REALLY?
REALLY.
I...
FWSSH
YOU BASTARD...
IT WAS ONLY A DREAM, SO IT DOESN'T MATTER!
IT MATTERS! YOU PERVERTED DEMON!
TO ME THAT'S A COMPLIMENT-
I WASN'T COMPLIMENTING YOU!
I BANISH THEE, DEMON!
RWOK

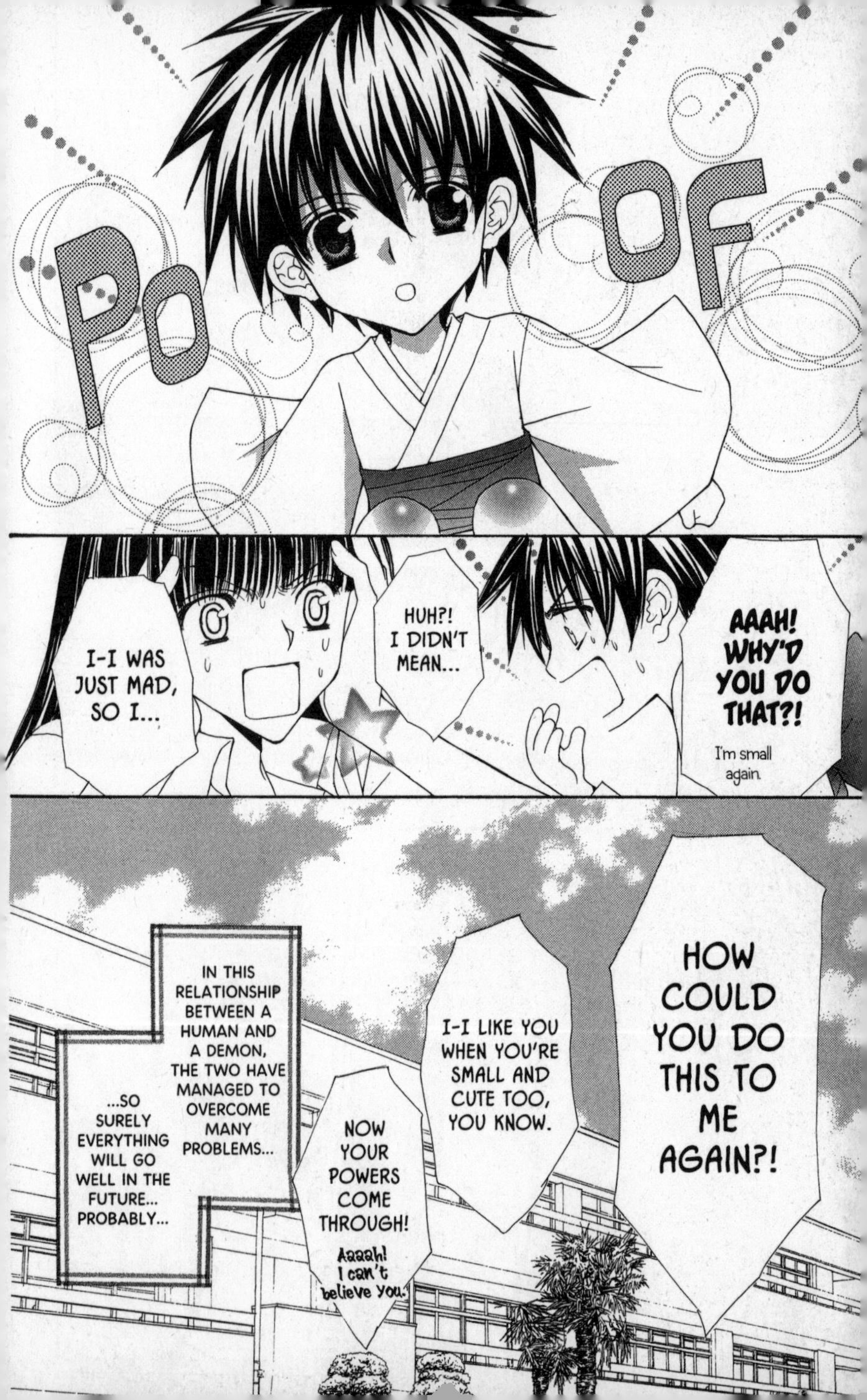
POOF
AAAH! WHY'D YOU DO THAT?!
I'm small again.
HUH?! I DIDN'T MEAN...
I-I WAS JUST MAD, SO I...
HOW COULD YOU DO THIS TO ME AGAIN?!
I-I LIKE YOU WHEN YOU'RE SMALL AND CUTE TOO, YOU KNOW.
NOW YOUR POWERS COME THROUGH!
Aaaah! I can't believe you.
IN THIS RELATIONSHIP BETWEEN A HUMAN AND A DEMON, THE TWO HAVE MANAGED TO OVERCOME MANY PROBLEMS...
...SO SURELY EVERYTHING WILL GO WELL IN THE FUTURE... PROBABLY...

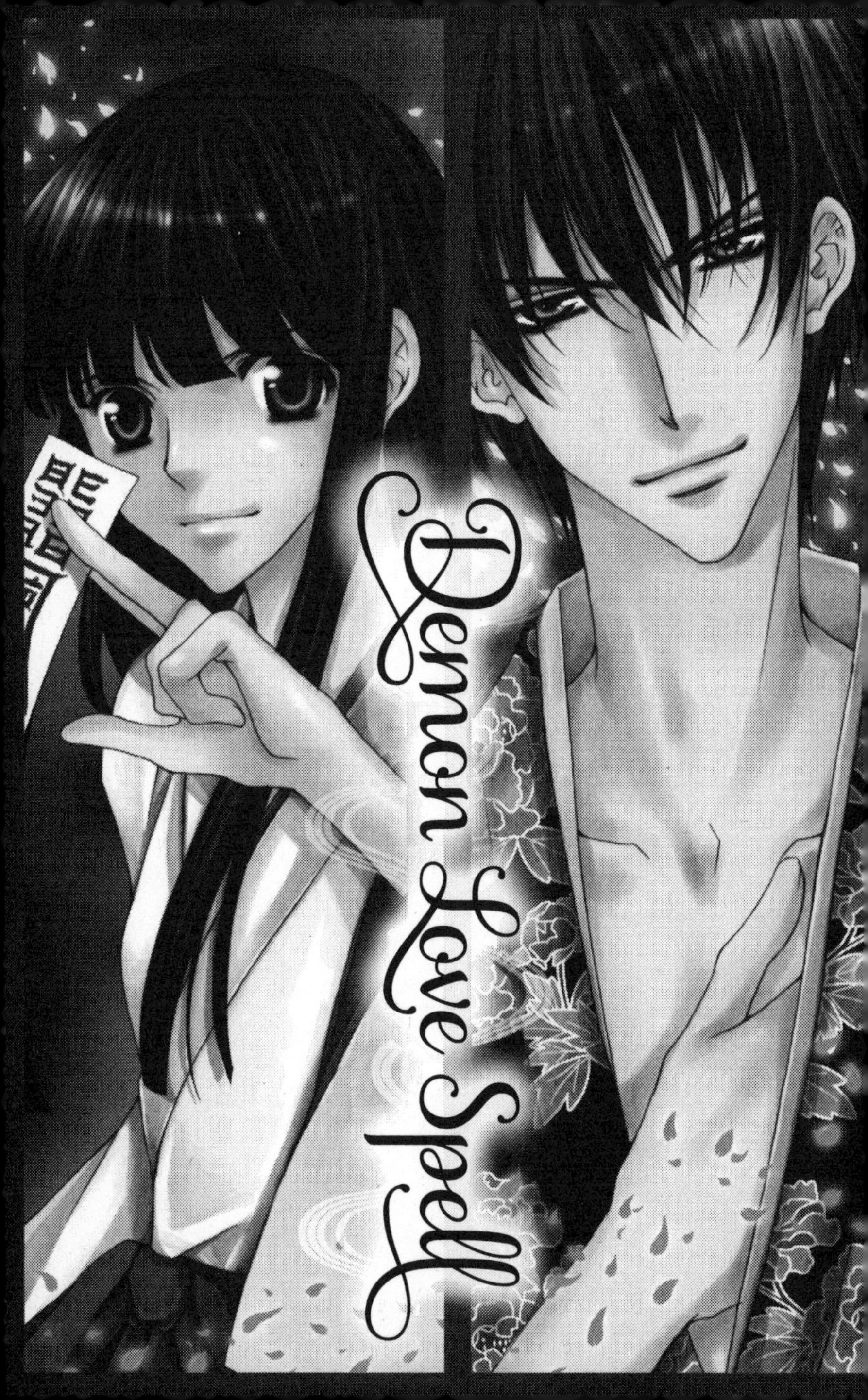
Demon Love Spell

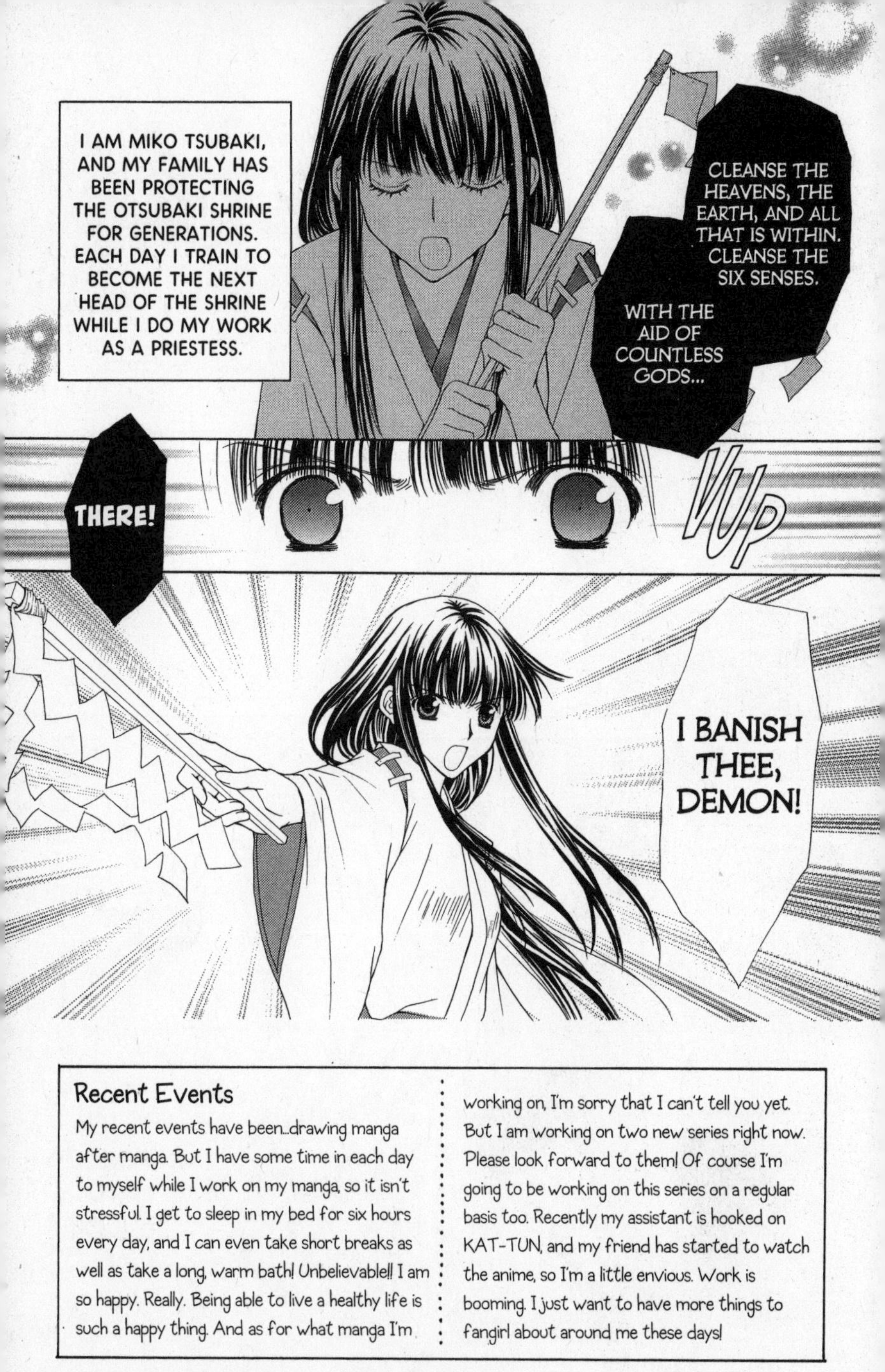
CLEANSE THE HEAVENS, THE EARTH, AND ALL THAT IS WITHIN. CLEANSE THE SIX SENSES.
WITH THE AID OF COUNTLESS GODS...
I AM MIKO TSUBAKI, AND MY FAMILY HAS BEEN PROTECTING THE OTSUBAKI SHRINE FOR GENERATIONS. EACH DAY I TRAIN TO BECOME THE NEXT HEAD OF THE SHRINE WHILE I DO MY WORK AS A PRIESTESS.
VUP
THERE!
I BANISH THEE, DEMON!

Recent Events

My recent events have been...drawing manga after manga. But I have some time in each day to myself while I work on my manga, so it isn't stressful. I get to sleep in my bed for six hours every day, and I can even take short breaks as well as take a long, warm bath! Unbelievable!! I am so happy. Really. Being able to live a healthy life is such a happy thing. And as for what manga I'm working on, I'm sorry that I can't tell you yet. But I am working on two new series right now. Please look forward to them! Of course I'm going to be working on this series on a regular basis too. Recently my assistant is hooked on KAT-TUN, and my friend has started to watch the anime, so I'm a little envious. Work is booming. I just want to have more things to fangirl about around me these days!

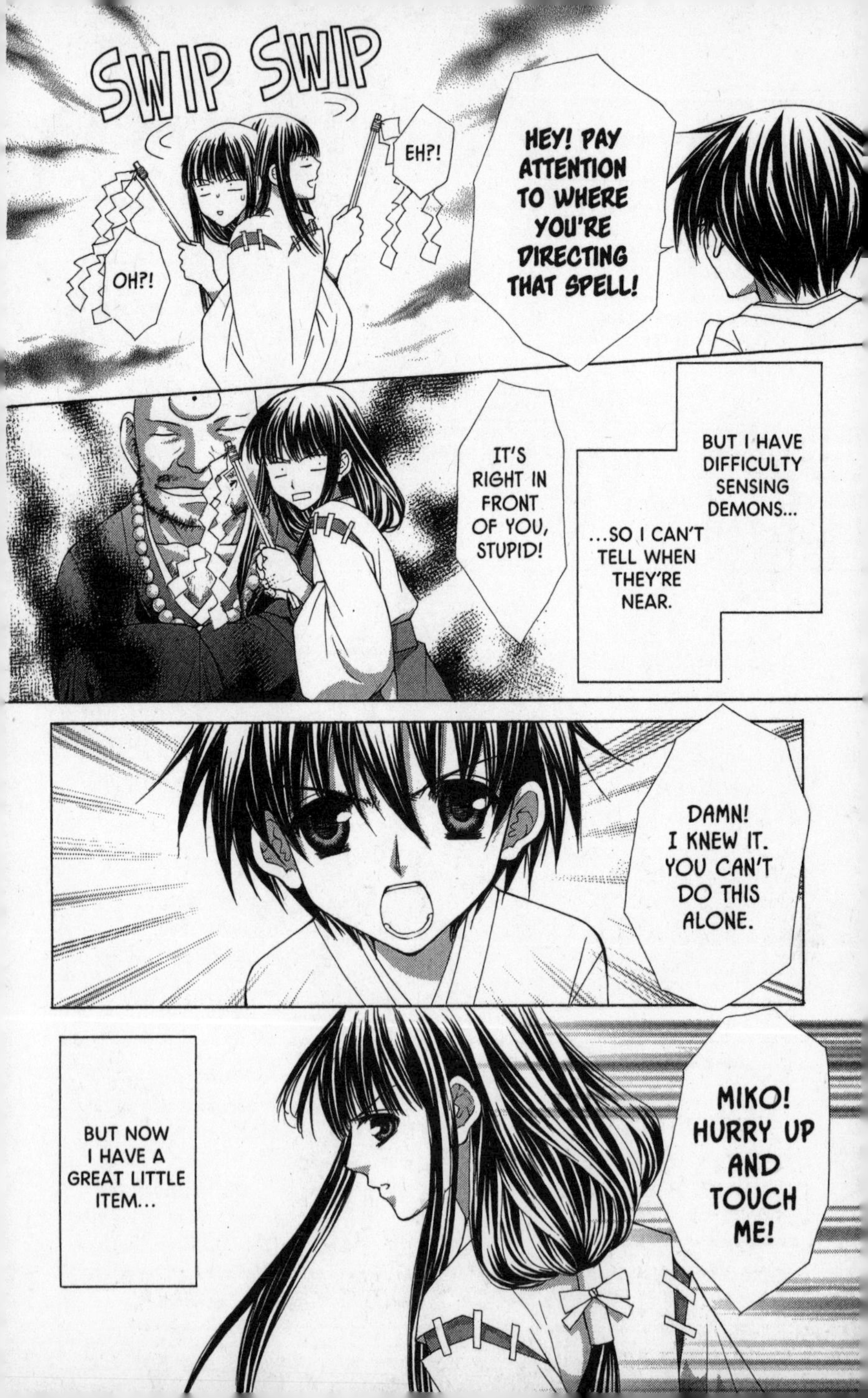
HEY! PAY ATTENTION TO WHERE YOU'RE DIRECTING THAT SPELL!
EH?!
SWIP SWIP
OH?!
BUT I HAVE DIFFICULTY SENSING DEMONS...
...SO I CAN'T TELL WHEN THEY'RE NEAR.
IT'S RIGHT IN FRONT OF YOU, STUPID!
DAMN! I KNEW IT. YOU CAN'T DO THIS ALONE.
MIKO! HURRY UP AND TOUCH ME!
BUT NOW I HAVE A GREAT LITTLE ITEM...

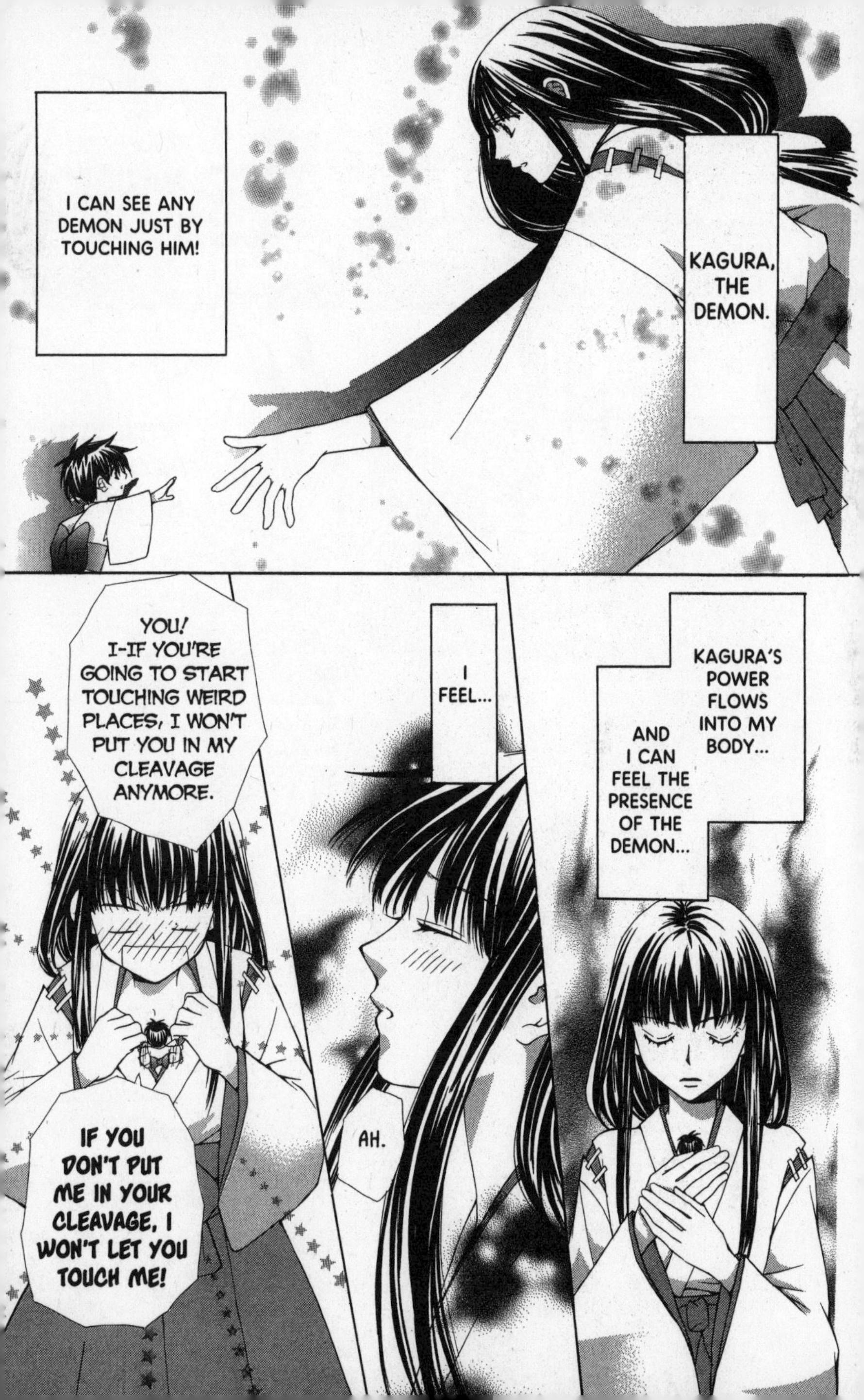
KAGURA, THE DEMON.
I CAN SEE ANY DEMON JUST BY TOUCHING HIM!
KAGURA'S POWER FLOWS INTO MY BODY...
AND I CAN FEEL THE PRESENCE OF THE DEMON...
I FEEL...
AH.
YOU! I-IF YOU'RE GOING TO START TOUCHING WEIRD PLACES, I WON'T PUT YOU IN MY CLEAVAGE ANYMORE.
IF YOU DON'T PUT ME IN YOUR CLEAVAGE, I WON'T LET YOU TOUCH ME!

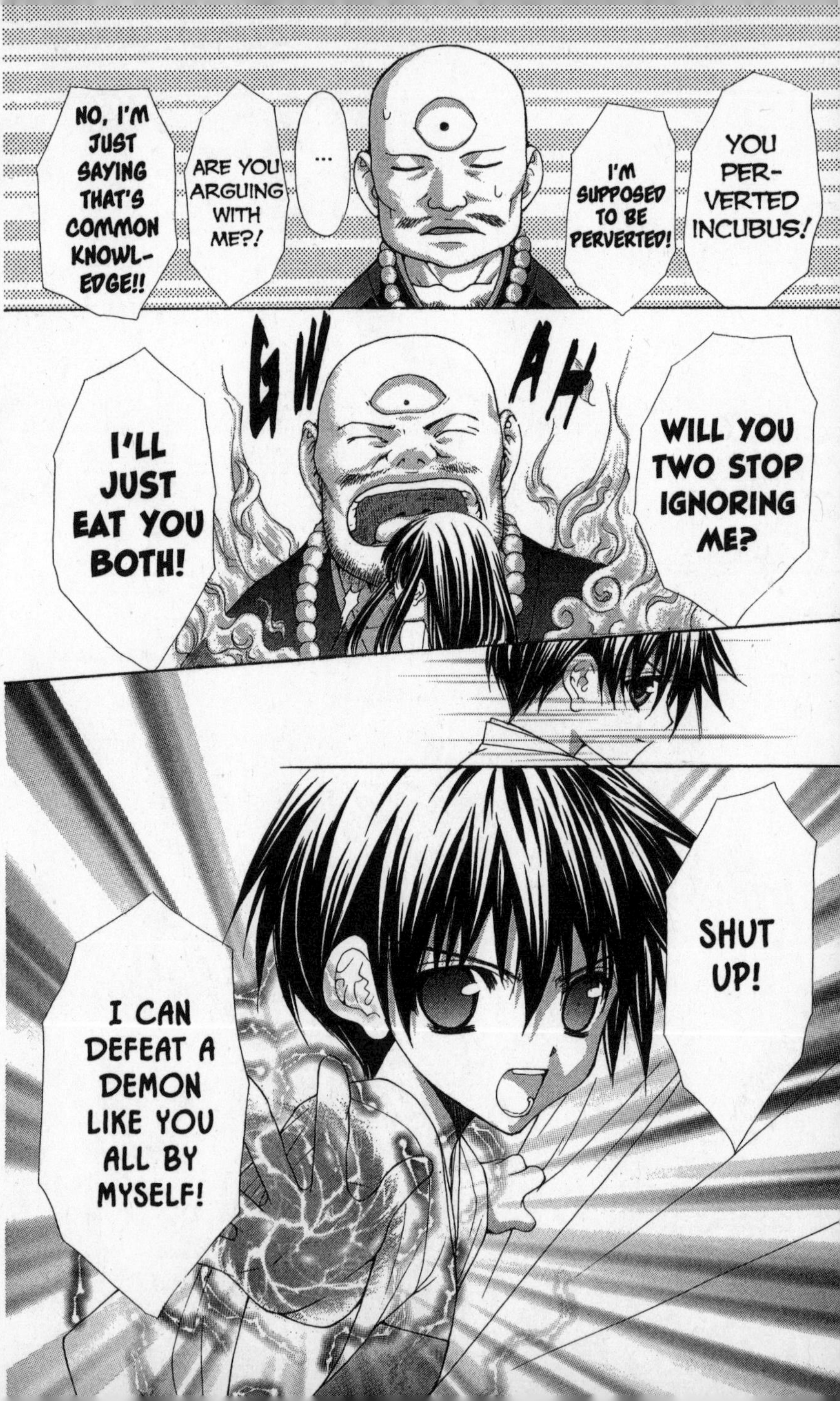
YOU PERVERTED INCUBUS!
I'M SUPPOSED TO BE PERVERTED!
...
ARE YOU ARGUING WITH ME?!
NO, I'M JUST SAYING THAT'S COMMON KNOWLEDGE!!
GWAH
WILL YOU TWO STOP IGNORING ME?
I'LL JUST EAT YOU BOTH!
SHUT UP!
I CAN DEFEAT A DEMON LIKE YOU ALL BY MYSELF!

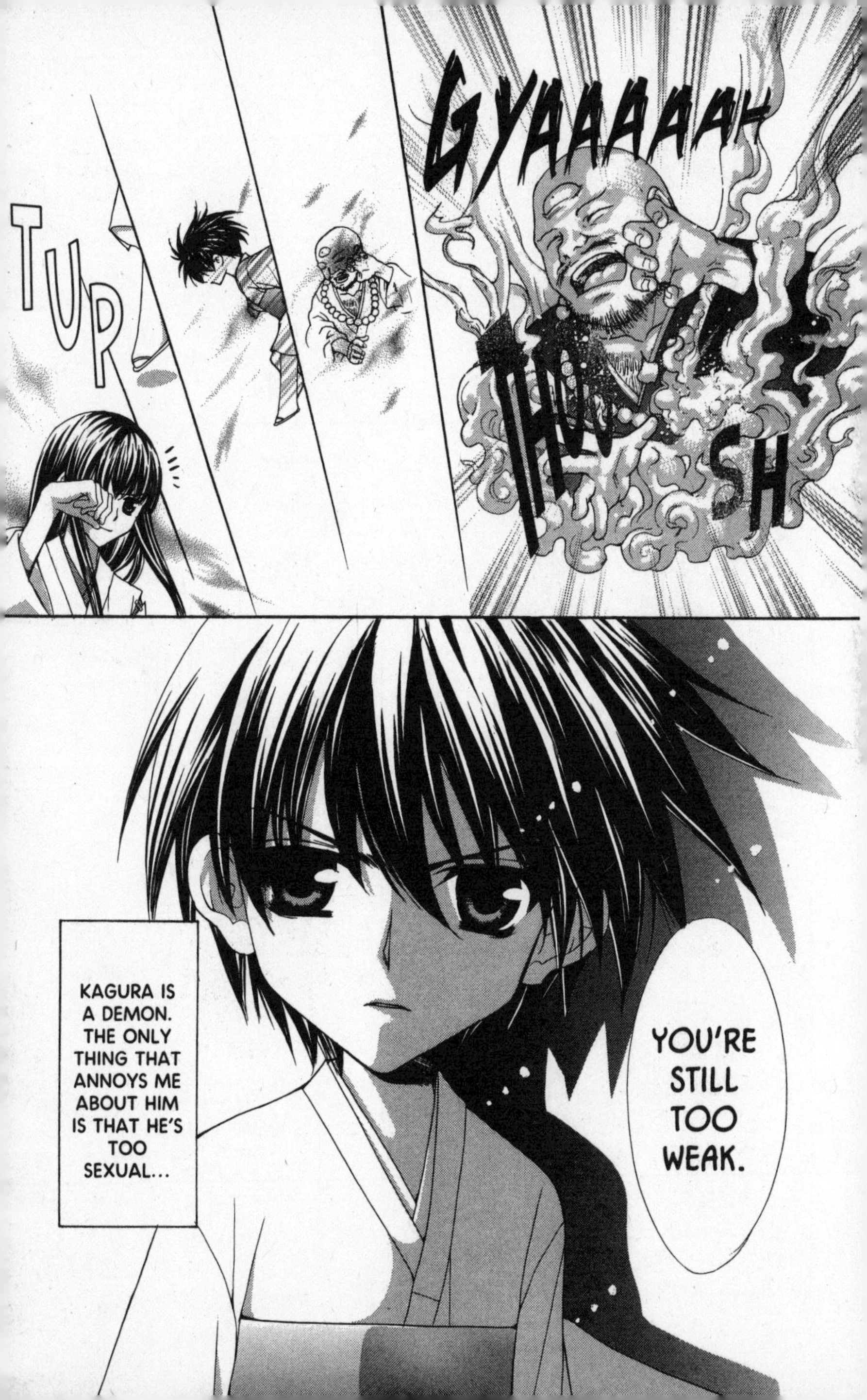
GYAAAAAAH
TUP
YOU'RE STILL TOO WEAK.
KAGURA IS A DEMON. THE ONLY THING THAT ANNOYS ME ABOUT HIM IS THAT HE'S TOO SEXUAL...

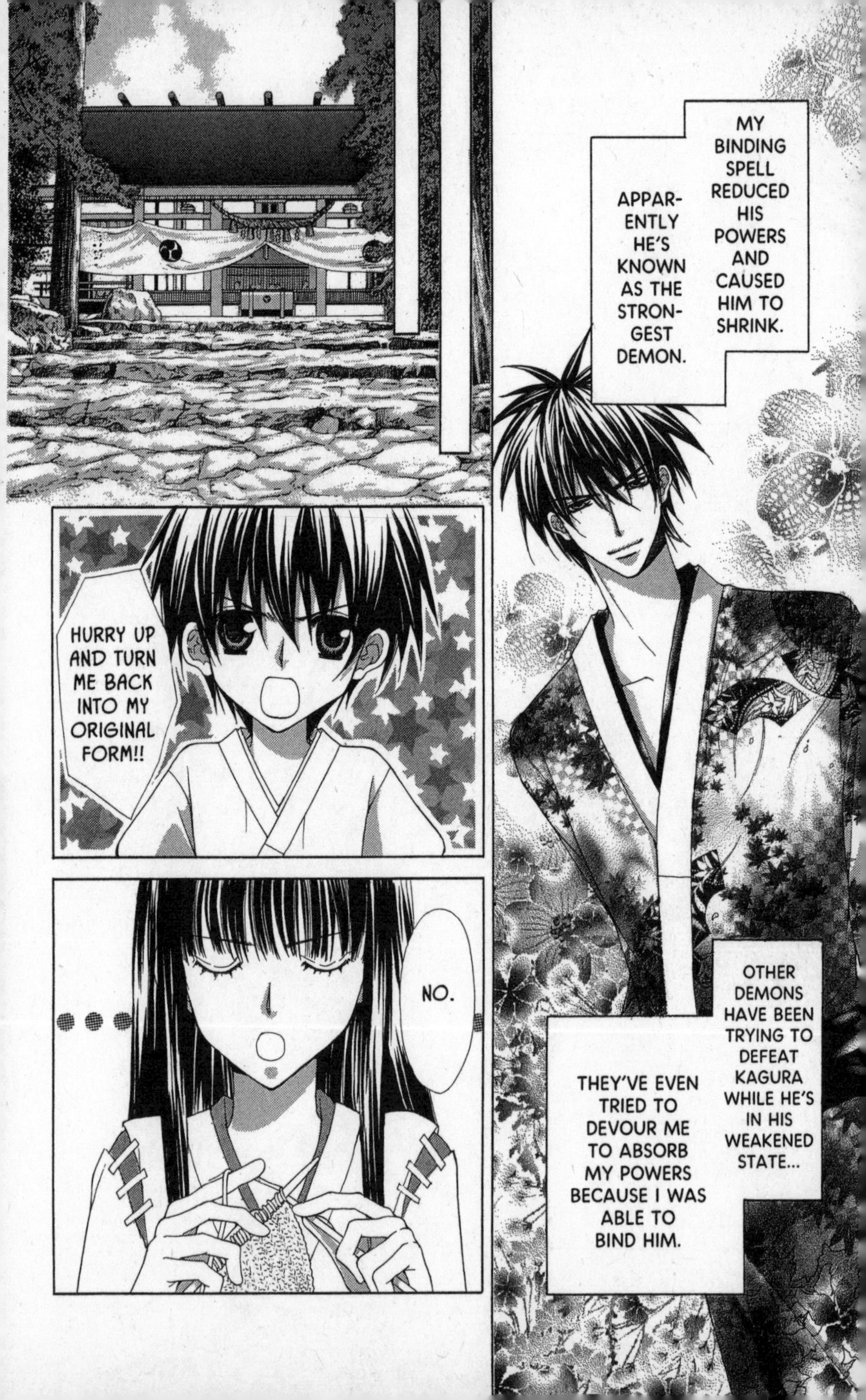
MY BINDING SPELL REDUCED HIS POWERS AND CAUSED HIM TO SHRINK.
APPAR-ENTLY HE'S KNOWN AS THE STRON-GEST DEMON.
OTHER DEMONS HAVE BEEN TRYING TO DEFEAT KAGURA WHILE HE'S IN HIS WEAKENED STATE...
THEY'VE EVEN TRIED TO DEVOUR ME TO ABSORB MY POWERS BECAUSE I WAS ABLE TO BIND HIM.
HURRY UP AND TURN ME BACK INTO MY ORIGINAL FORM!!
NO.

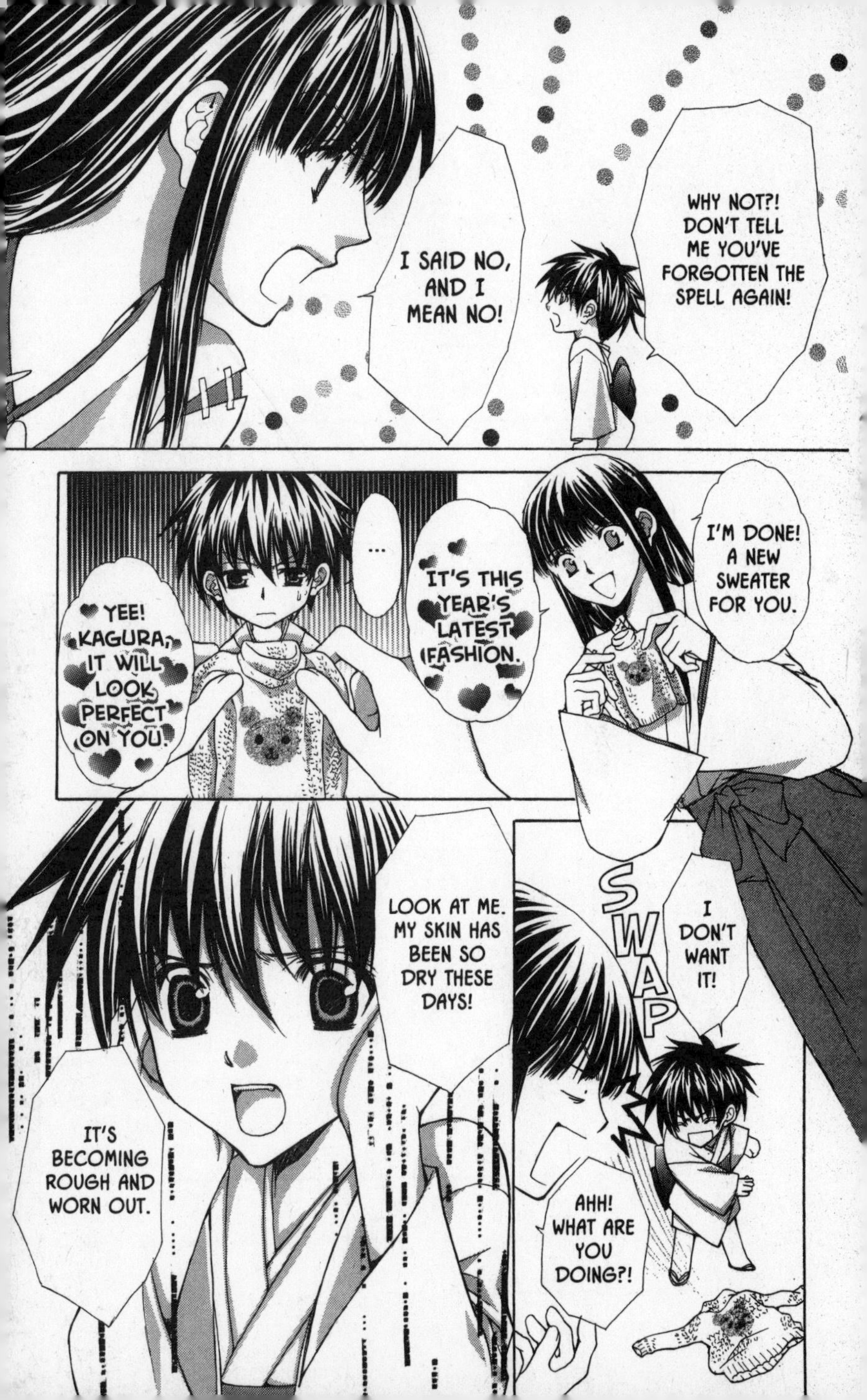
WHY NOT?! DON'T TELL ME YOU'VE FORGOTTEN THE SPELL AGAIN!
I SAID NO, AND I MEAN NO!
I'M DONE! A NEW SWEATER FOR YOU.
IT'S THIS YEAR'S LATEST FASHION.
...
YEE! KAGURA, IT WILL LOOK PERFECT ON YOU.
SWAP
I DON'T WANT IT!
AHH! WHAT ARE YOU DOING?!
LOOK AT ME. MY SKIN HAS BEEN SO DRY THESE DAYS!
IT'S BECOMING ROUGH AND WORN OUT.

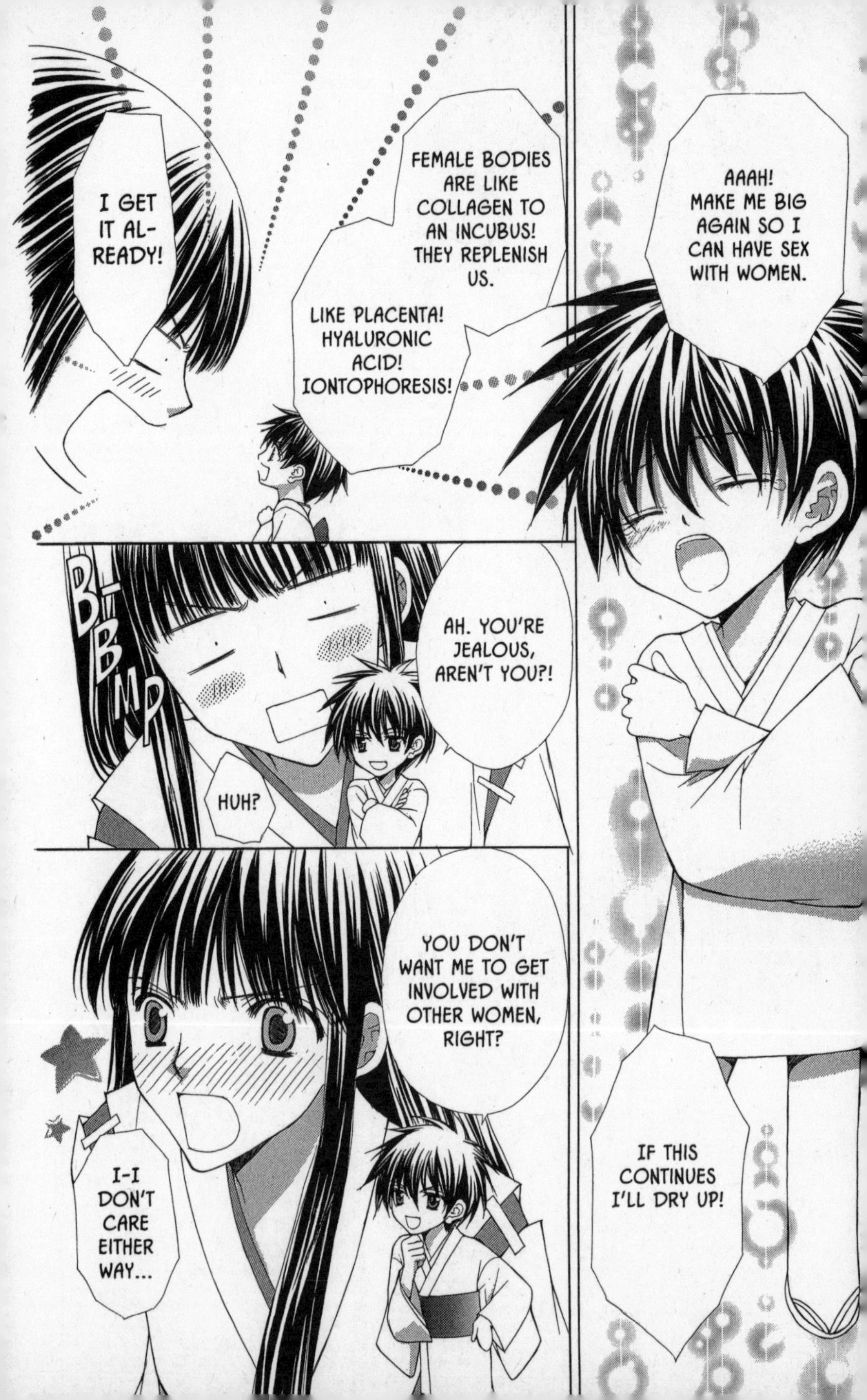
AAAH! MAKE ME BIG AGAIN SO I CAN HAVE SEX WITH WOMEN.
IF THIS CONTINUES I'LL DRY UP!
FEMALE BODIES ARE LIKE COLLAGEN TO AN INCUBUS! THEY REPLENISH US.
LIKE PLACENTA! HYALURONIC ACID! IONTOPHORESIS!
I GET IT AL-READY!
AH. YOU'RE JEALOUS, AREN'T YOU?!
HUH?
B-BMP
YOU DON'T WANT ME TO GET INVOLVED WITH OTHER WOMEN, RIGHT?
I-I DON'T CARE EITHER WAY...

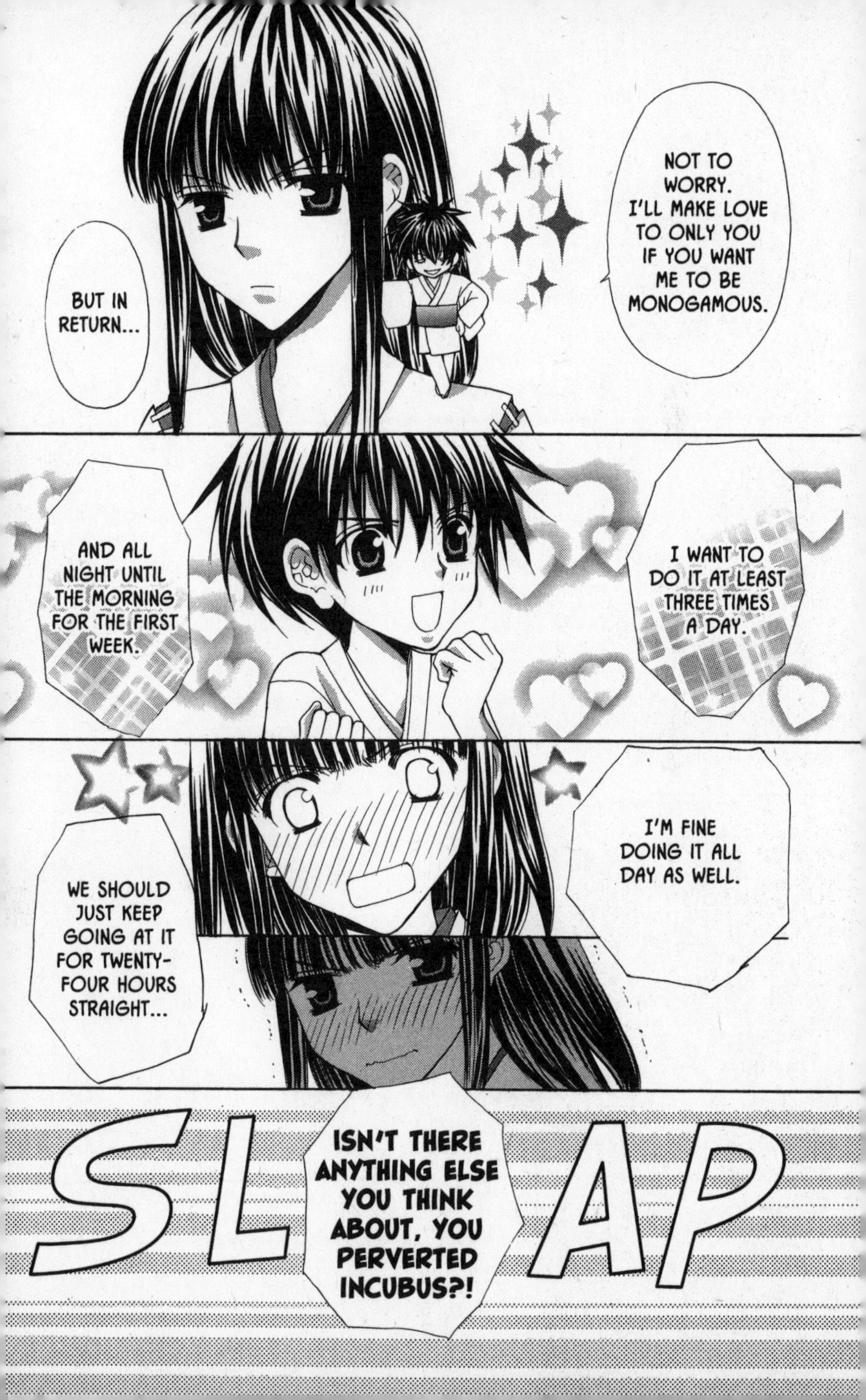
NOT TO WORRY. I'LL MAKE LOVE TO ONLY YOU IF YOU WANT ME TO BE MONOGAMOUS.
BUT IN RETURN...
I WANT TO DO IT AT LEAST THREE TIMES A DAY.
AND ALL NIGHT UNTIL THE MORNING FOR THE FIRST WEEK.
I'M FINE DOING IT ALL DAY AS WELL.
WE SHOULD JUST KEEP GOING AT IT FOR TWENTY-FOUR HOURS STRAIGHT...
SLAP
ISN'T THERE ANYTHING ELSE YOU THINK ABOUT, YOU PERVERTED INCUBUS?!

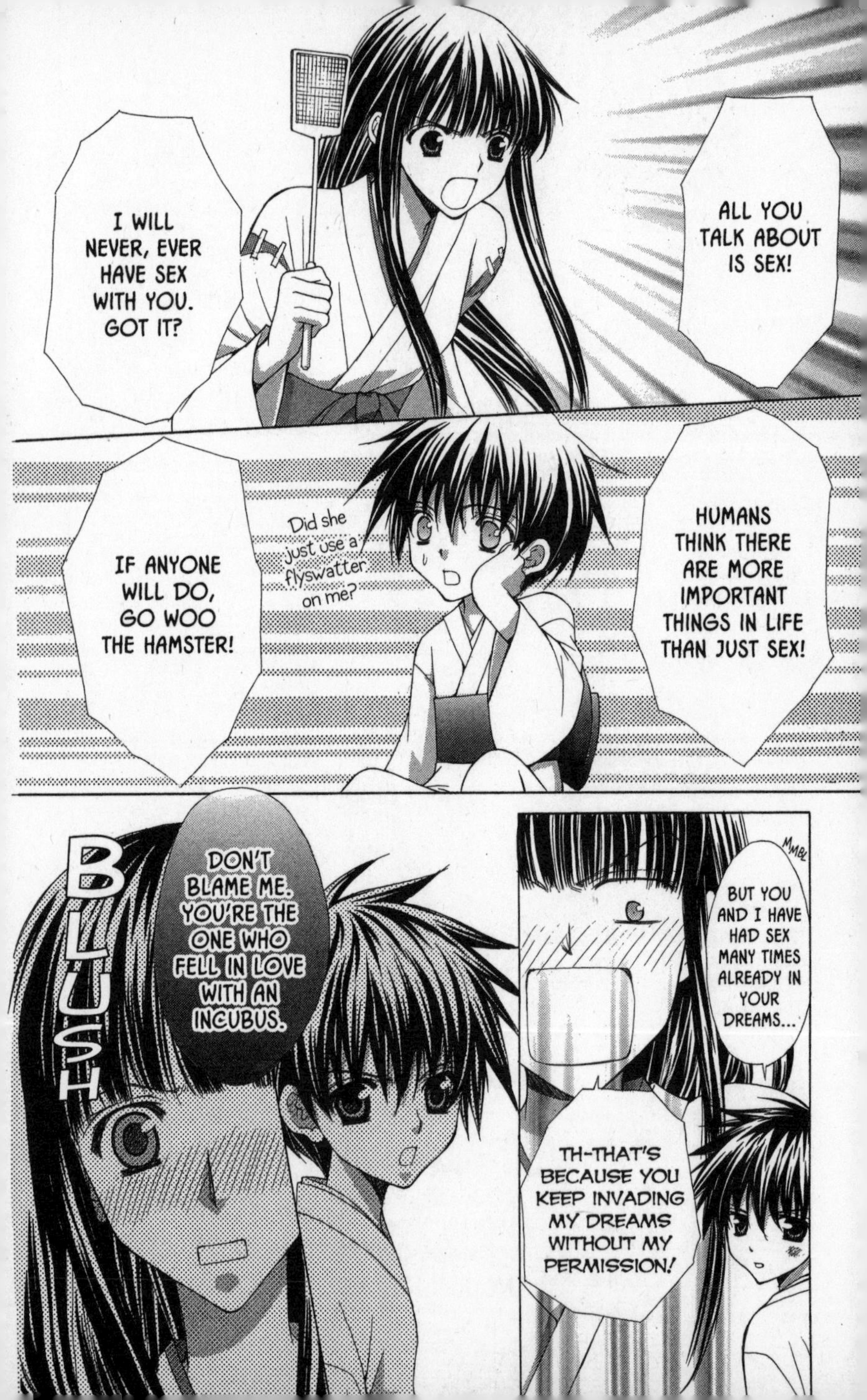
ALL YOU TALK ABOUT IS SEX!
I WILL NEVER, EVER HAVE SEX WITH YOU. GOT IT?
HUMANS THINK THERE ARE MORE IMPORTANT THINGS IN LIFE THAN JUST SEX!
Did she just use a flyswatter on me?
IF ANYONE WILL DO, GO WOO THE HAMSTER!
MMBL
BUT YOU AND I HAVE HAD SEX MANY TIMES ALREADY IN YOUR DREAMS...
TH-THAT'S BECAUSE YOU KEEP INVADING MY DREAMS WITHOUT MY PERMISSION!
BLUSH
DON'T BLAME ME. YOU'RE THE ONE WHO FELL IN LOVE WITH AN INCUBUS.

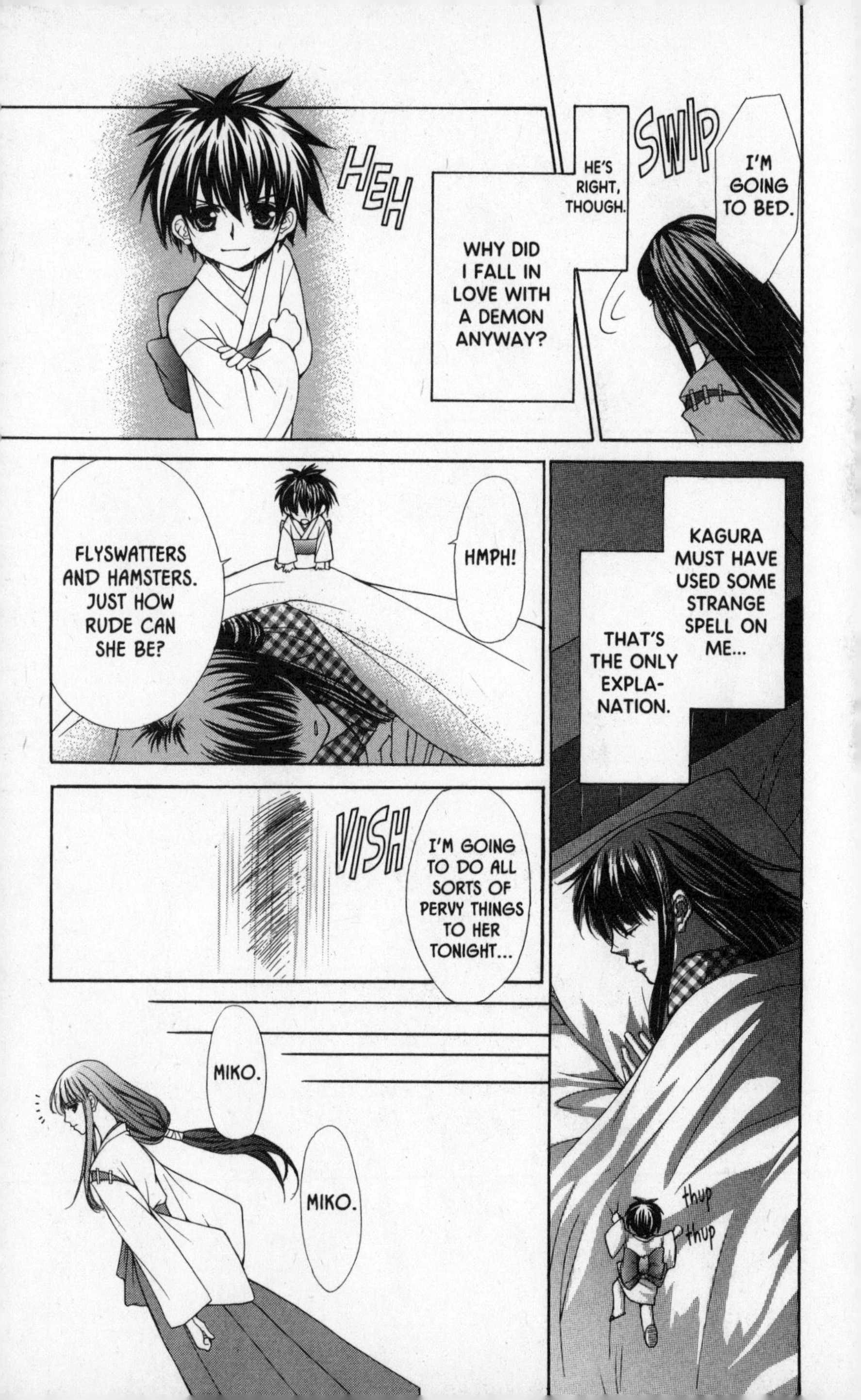
I'M GOING TO BED.
SWIP
HE'S RIGHT, THOUGH.
WHY DID I FALL IN LOVE WITH A DEMON ANYWAY?
HEH
KAGURA MUST HAVE USED SOME STRANGE SPELL ON ME...
THAT'S THE ONLY EXPLANATION.
thup thup
HMPH!
FLYSWATTERS AND HAMSTERS. JUST HOW RUDE CAN SHE BE?
I'M GOING TO DO ALL SORTS OF PERVY THINGS TO HER TONIGHT...
VISH
MIKO.
MIKO.

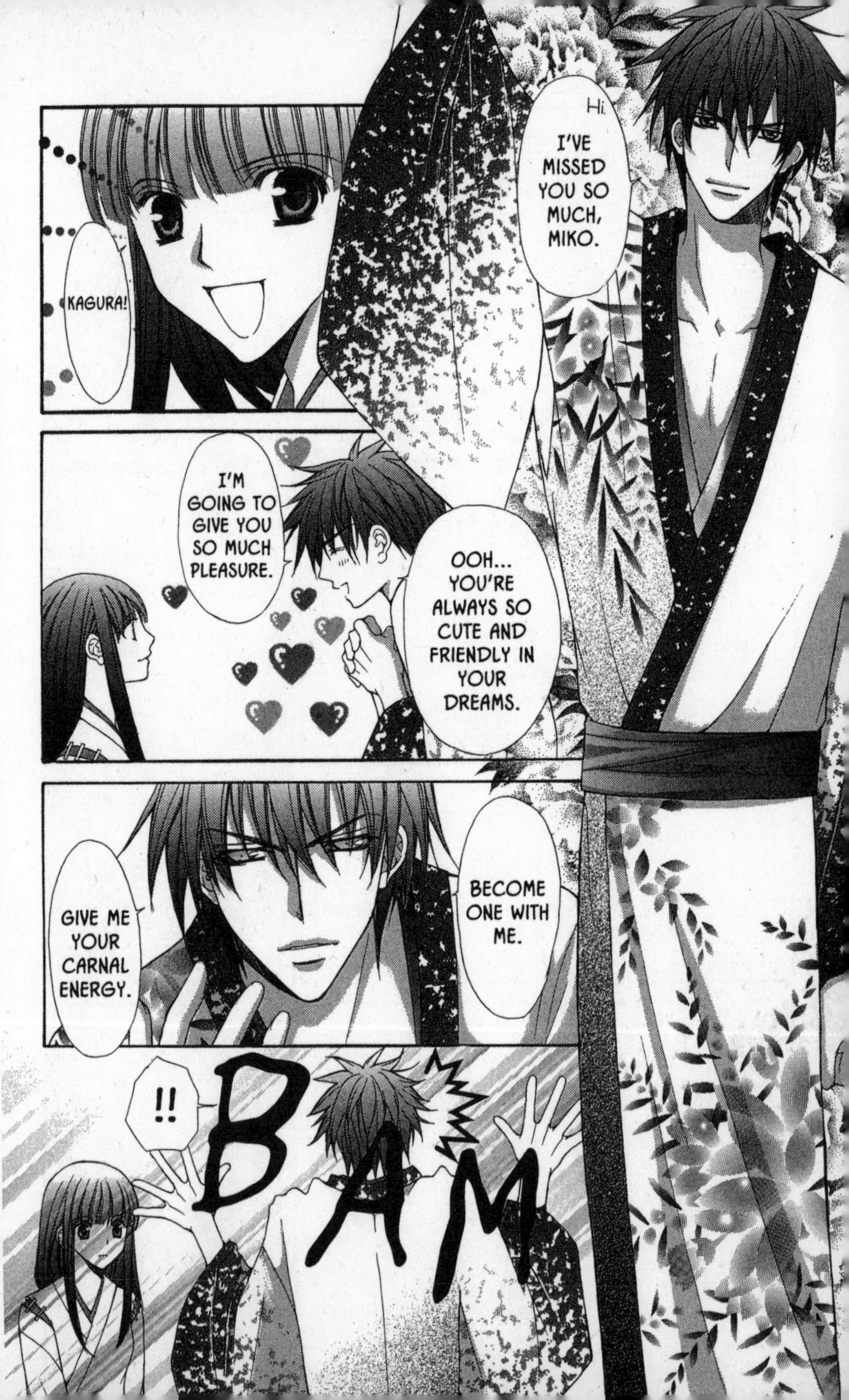
Hi.
I'VE MISSED YOU SO MUCH, MIKO.
KAGURA!
I'M GOING TO GIVE YOU SO MUCH PLEASURE.
OOH... YOU'RE ALWAYS SO CUTE AND FRIENDLY IN YOUR DREAMS.
BECOME ONE WITH ME.
GIVE ME YOUR CARNAL ENERGY.
BAM
!!

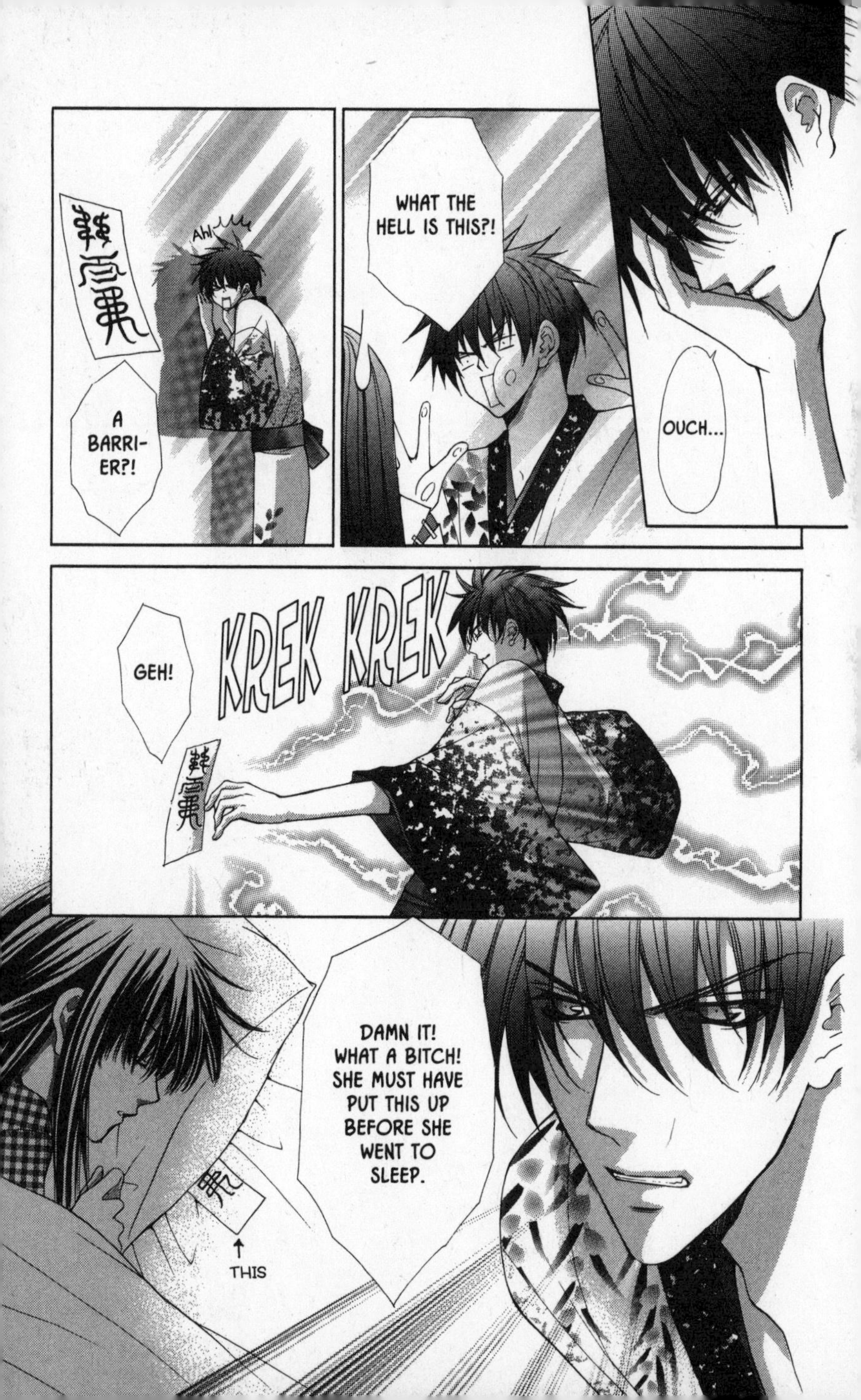
OUCH...
WHAT THE HELL IS THIS?!
AH!
A BARRIER?!
KREK KREK
GEH!
DAMN IT! WHAT A BITCH! SHE MUST HAVE PUT THIS UP BEFORE SHE WENT TO SLEEP.
THIS

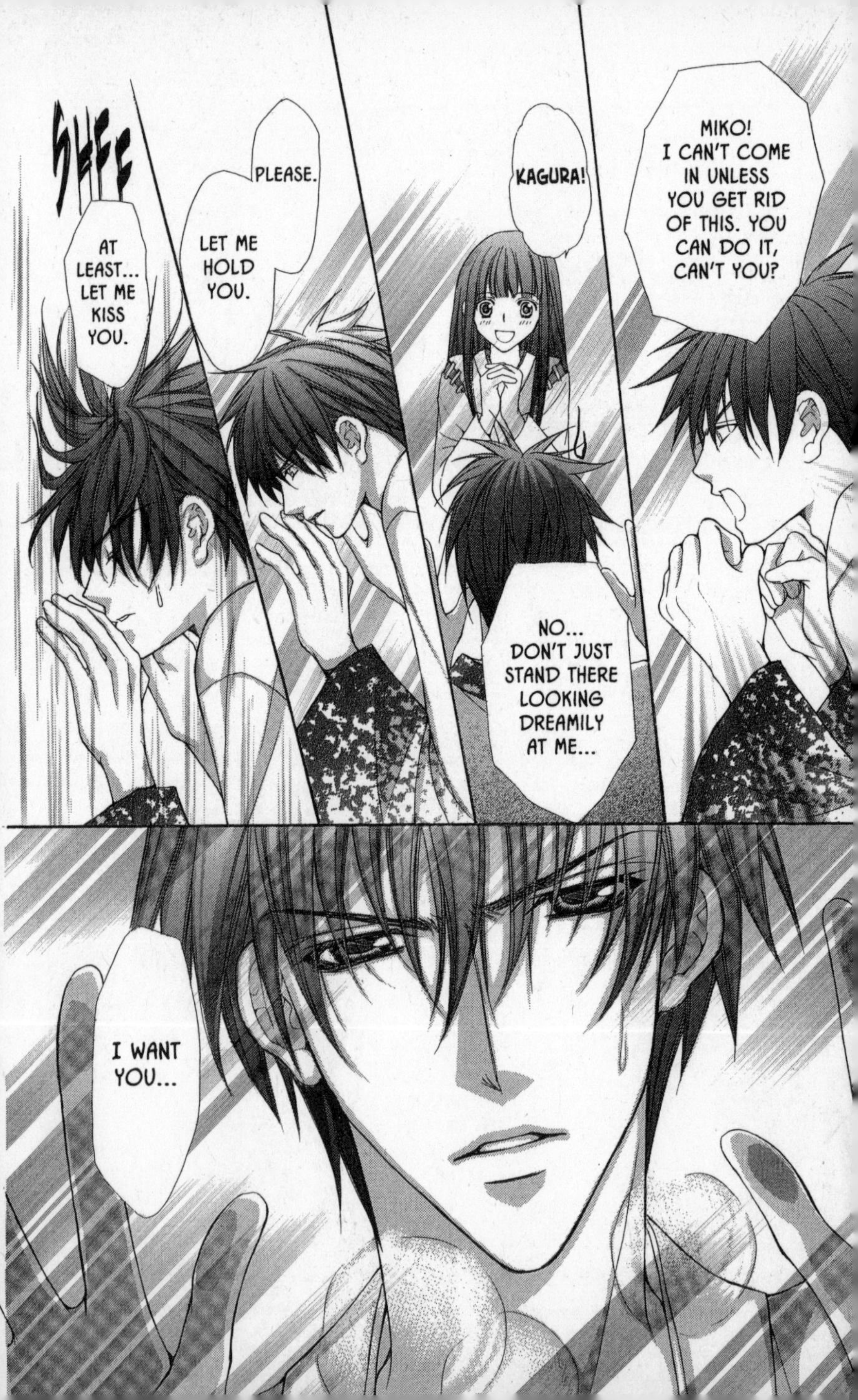
MIKO! I CAN'T COME IN UNLESS YOU GET RID OF THIS. YOU CAN DO IT, CAN'T YOU?
KAGURA!
NO... DON'T JUST STAND THERE LOOKING DREAMILY AT ME...
PLEASE.
LET ME HOLD YOU.
SHFF
AT LEAST... LET ME KISS YOU.
I WANT YOU...

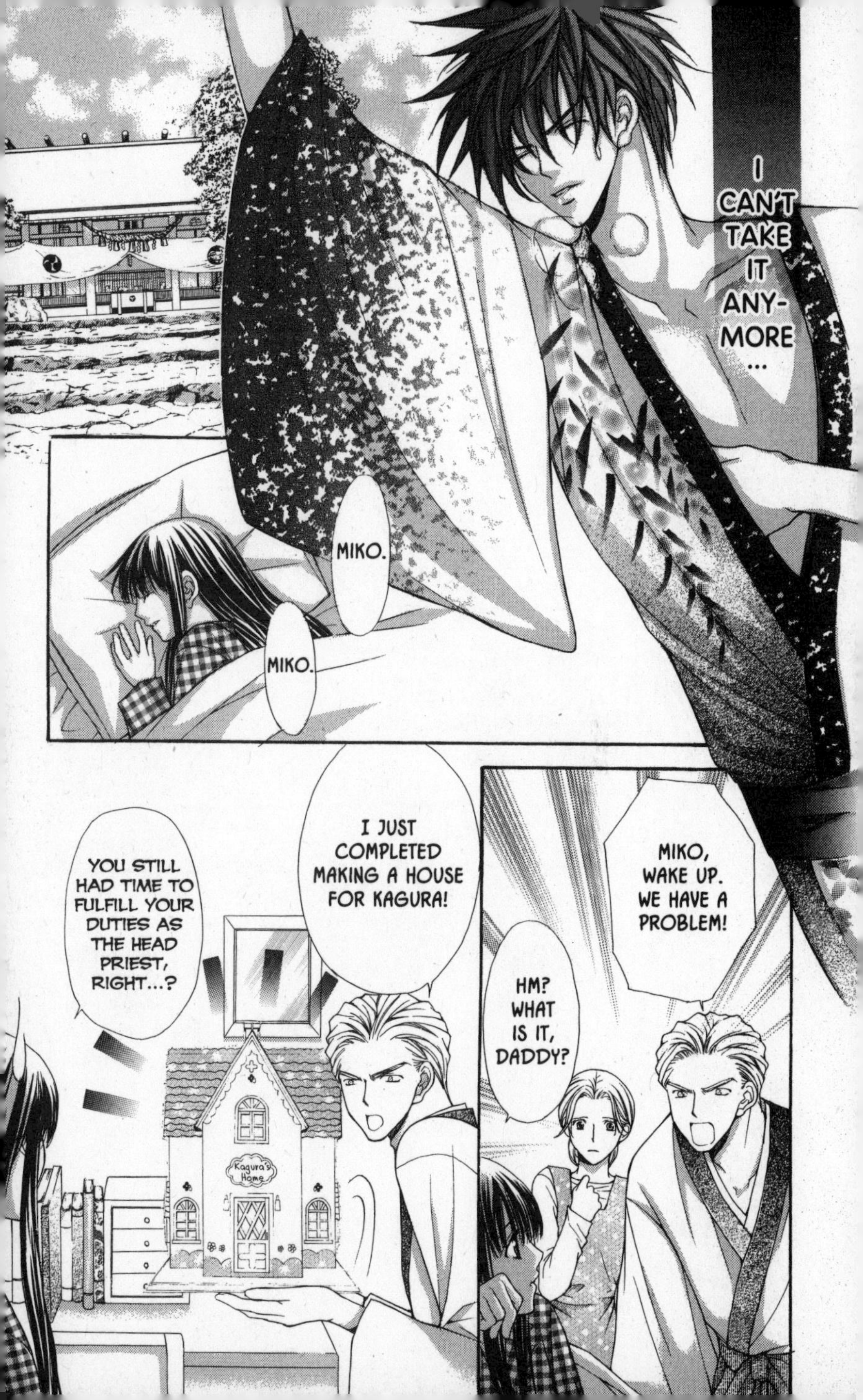
I CAN'T TAKE IT ANY-MORE...
MIKO.
MIKO.
MIKO, WAKE UP. WE HAVE A PROBLEM!
HM? WHAT IS IT, DADDY?
I JUST COMPLETED MAKING A HOUSE FOR KAGURA!
Kagura's Home
YOU STILL HAD TIME TO FULFILL YOUR DUTIES AS THE HEAD PRIEST, RIGHT...?

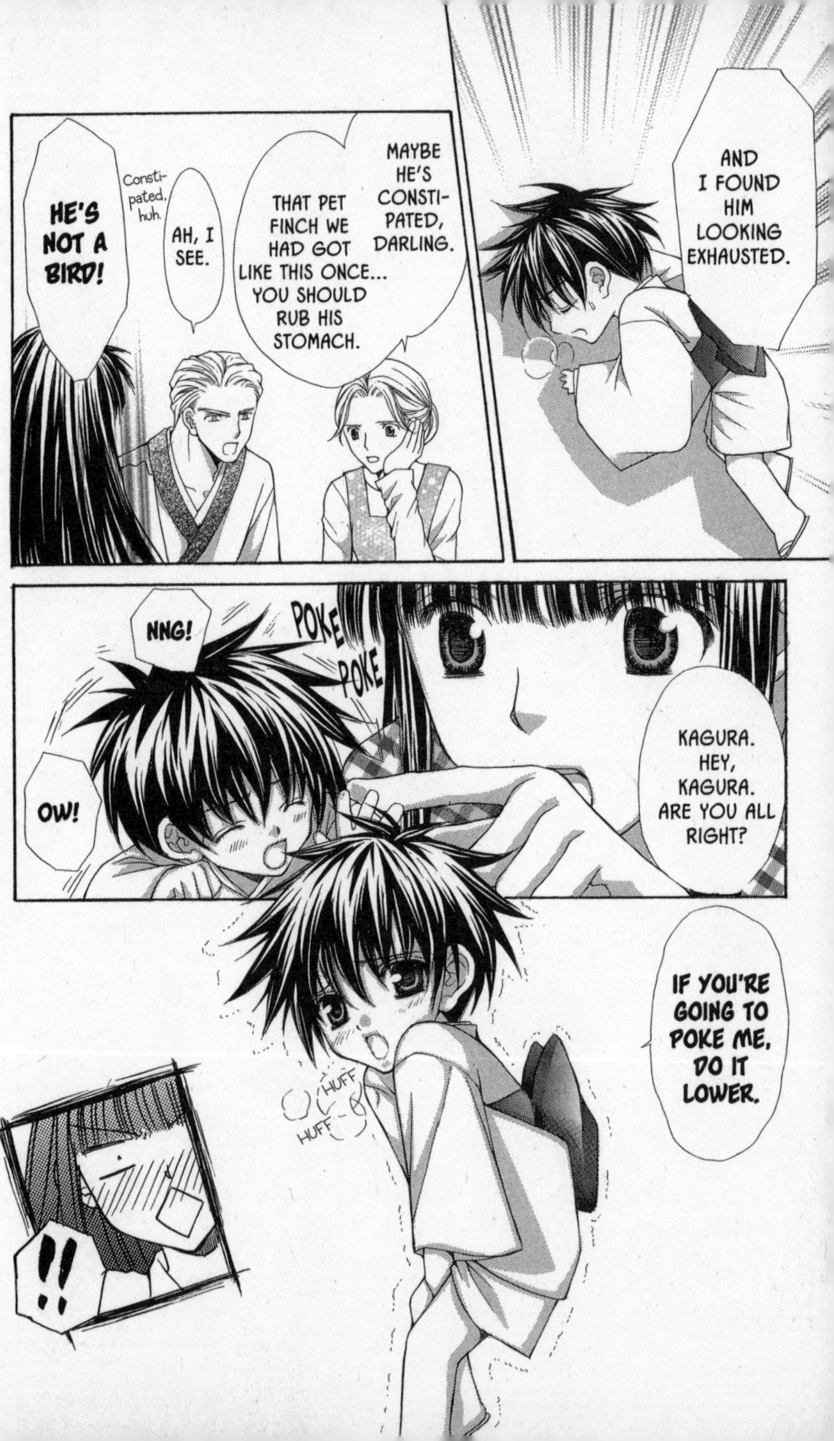
AND I FOUND HIM LOOKING EXHAUSTED.
MAYBE HE'S CONSTIPATED, DARLING.
THAT PET FINCH WE HAD GOT LIKE THIS ONCE... YOU SHOULD RUB HIS STOMACH.
AH, I SEE.
Constipated, huh.
HE'S NOT A BIRD!
KAGURA. HEY, KAGURA. ARE YOU ALL RIGHT?
POKE
POKE
NNG!
OW!
IF YOU'RE GOING TO POKE ME, DO IT LOWER.
HUFF
HUFF
!!

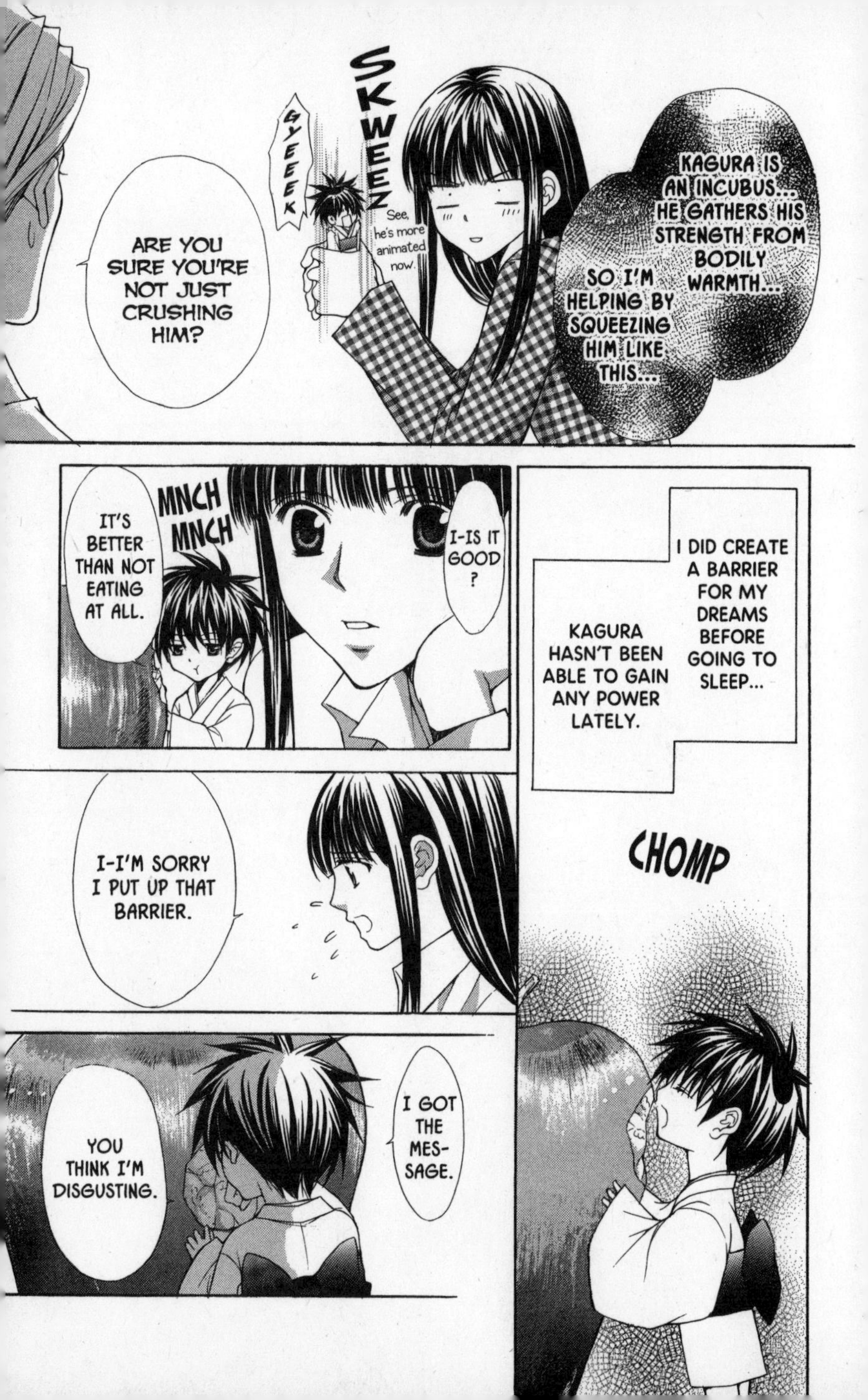
KAGURA IS AN INCUBUS... HE GATHERS HIS STRENGTH FROM BODILY WARMTH...
SO I'M HELPING BY SQUEEZING HIM LIKE THIS...
SKWEEZ
GYEEEK
See, he's more animated now.
ARE YOU SURE YOU'RE NOT JUST CRUSHING HIM?
I DID CREATE A BARRIER FOR MY DREAMS BEFORE GOING TO SLEEP...
KAGURA HASN'T BEEN ABLE TO GAIN ANY POWER LATELY.
CHOMP
I-IS IT GOOD?
MNCH MNCH
IT'S BETTER THAN NOT EATING AT ALL.
I-I'M SORRY I PUT UP THAT BARRIER.
I GOT THE MES-SAGE.
YOU THINK I'M DISGUSTING.

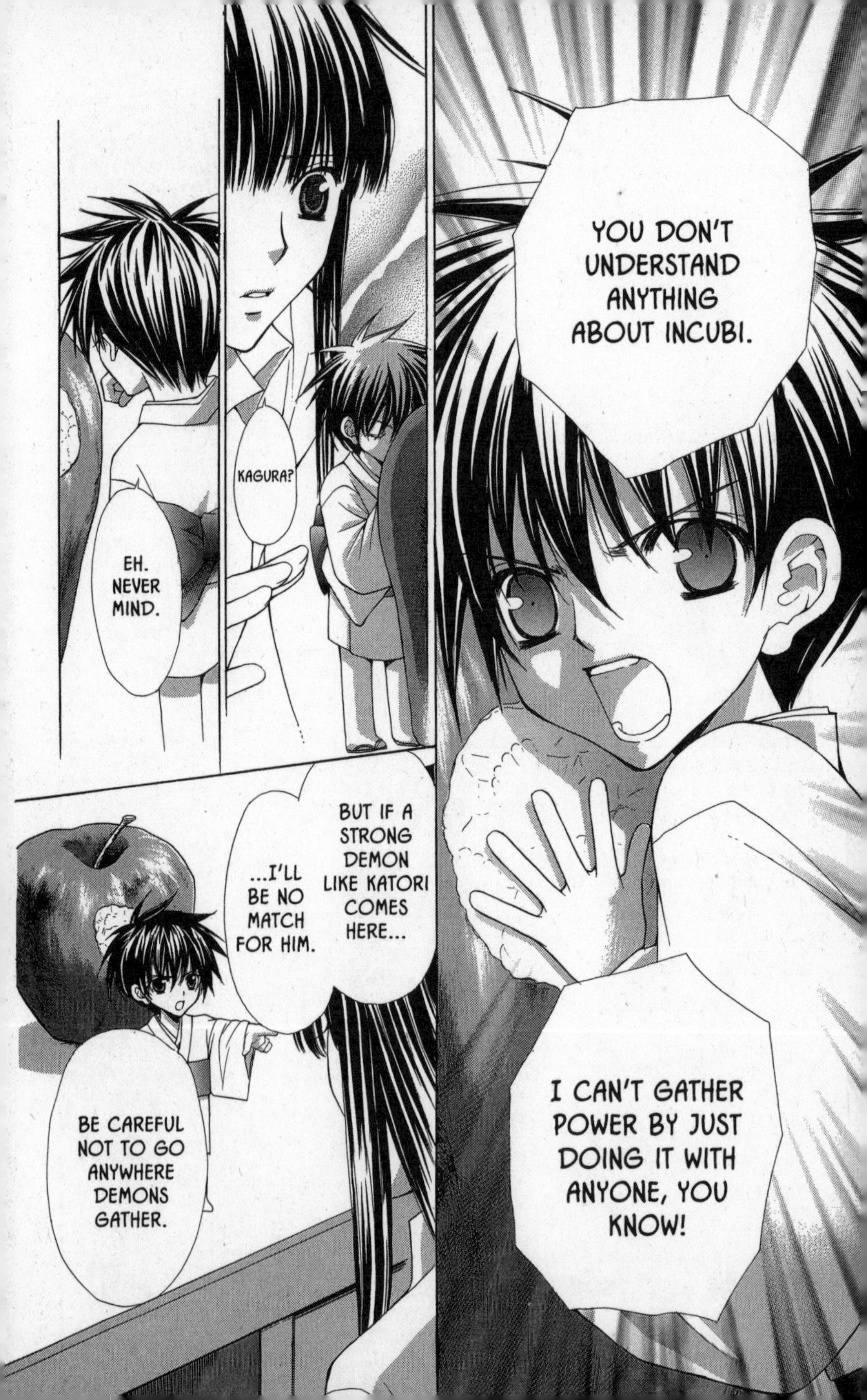
YOU DON'T UNDERSTAND ANYTHING ABOUT INCUBI.
I CAN'T GATHER POWER BY JUST DOING IT WITH ANYONE, YOU KNOW!
KAGURA?
EH. NEVER MIND.
BUT IF A STRONG DEMON LIKE KATORI COMES HERE...
...I'LL BE NO MATCH FOR HIM.
BE CAREFUL NOT TO GO ANYWHERE DEMONS GATHER.

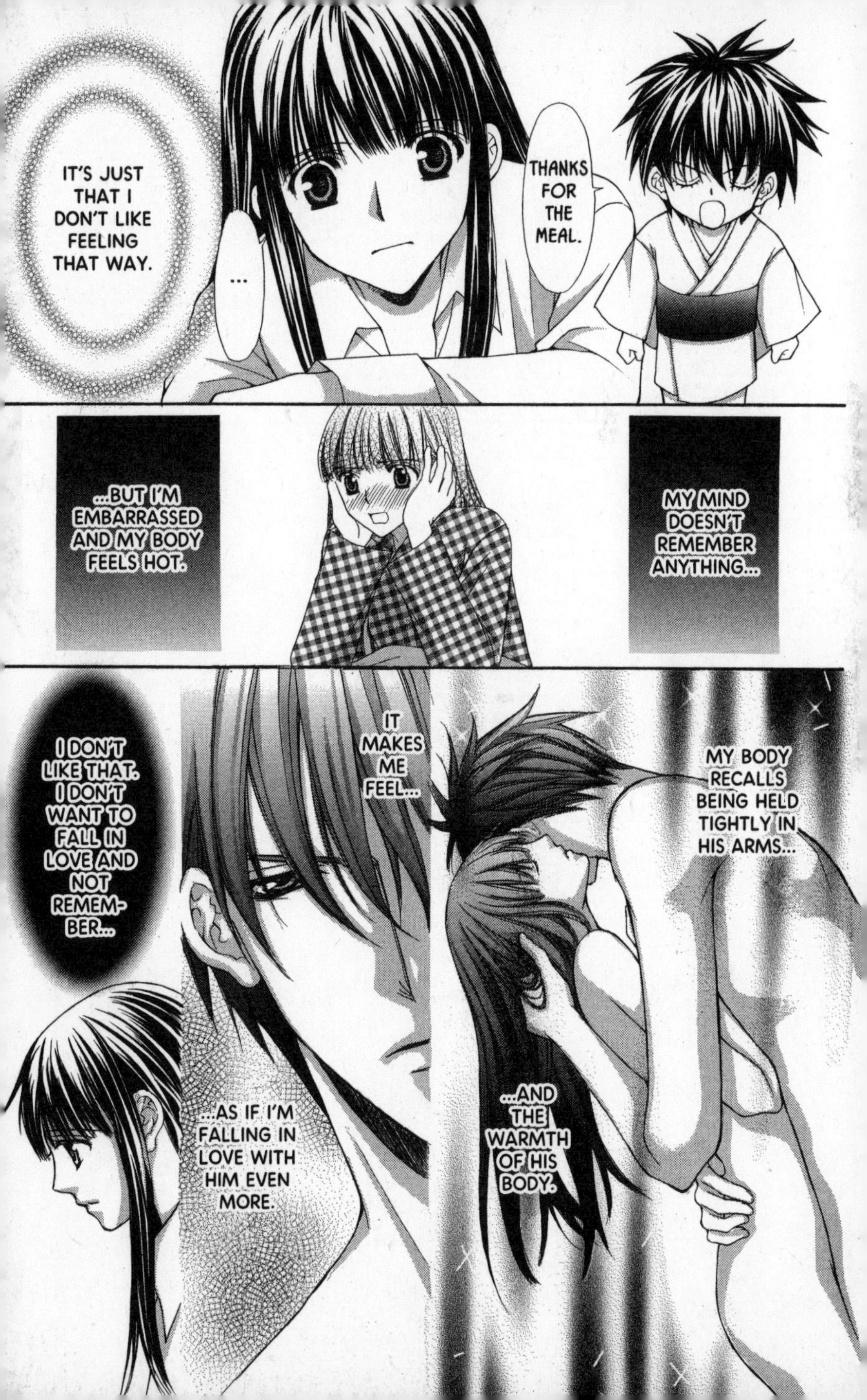
THANKS FOR THE MEAL.
...
IT'S JUST THAT I DON'T LIKE FEELING THAT WAY.
MY MIND DOESN'T REMEMBER ANYTHING...
...BUT I'M EMBARRASSED AND MY BODY FEELS HOT.
MY BODY RECALLS BEING HELD TIGHTLY IN HIS ARMS...
...AND THE WARMTH OF HIS BODY.
IT MAKES ME FEEL...
...AS IF I'M FALLING IN LOVE WITH HIM EVEN MORE.
I DON'T LIKE THAT. I DON'T WANT TO FALL IN LOVE AND NOT REMEM-BER...

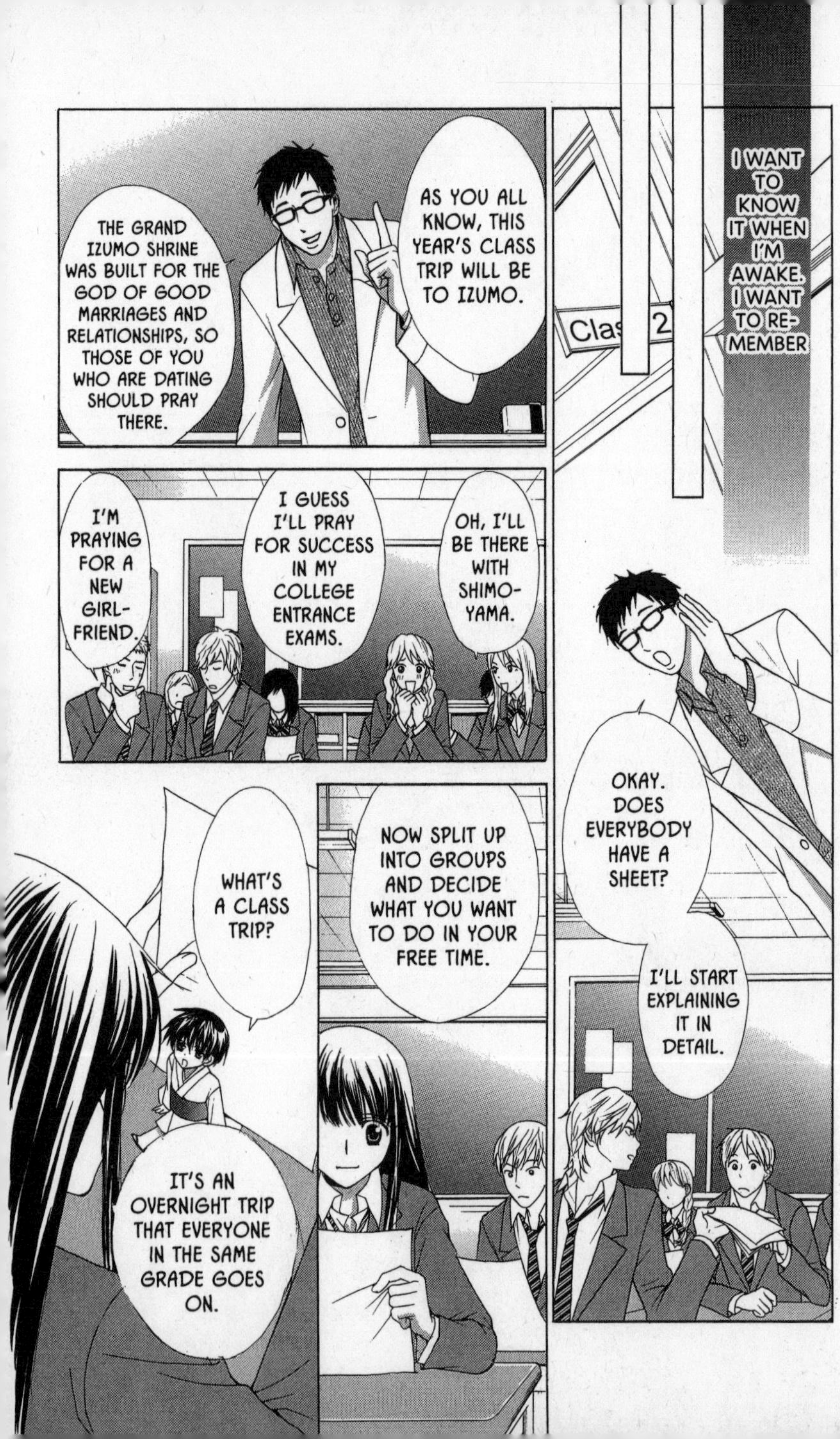
I WANT TO KNOW IT WHEN I'M AWAKE. I WANT TO REMEMBER
Clas 2
AS YOU ALL KNOW, THIS YEAR'S CLASS TRIP WILL BE TO IZUMO.
THE GRAND IZUMO SHRINE WAS BUILT FOR THE GOD OF GOOD MARRIAGES AND RELATIONSHIPS, SO THOSE OF YOU WHO ARE DATING SHOULD PRAY THERE.
OH, I'LL BE THERE WITH SHIMOYAMA.
I GUESS I'LL PRAY FOR SUCCESS IN MY COLLEGE ENTRANCE EXAMS.
I'M PRAYING FOR A NEW GIRLFRIEND.
OKAY. DOES EVERYBODY HAVE A SHEET?
I'LL START EXPLAINING IT IN DETAIL.
NOW SPLIT UP INTO GROUPS AND DECIDE WHAT YOU WANT TO DO IN YOUR FREE TIME.
WHAT'S A CLASS TRIP?
IT'S AN OVERNIGHT TRIP THAT EVERYONE IN THE SAME GRADE GOES ON.

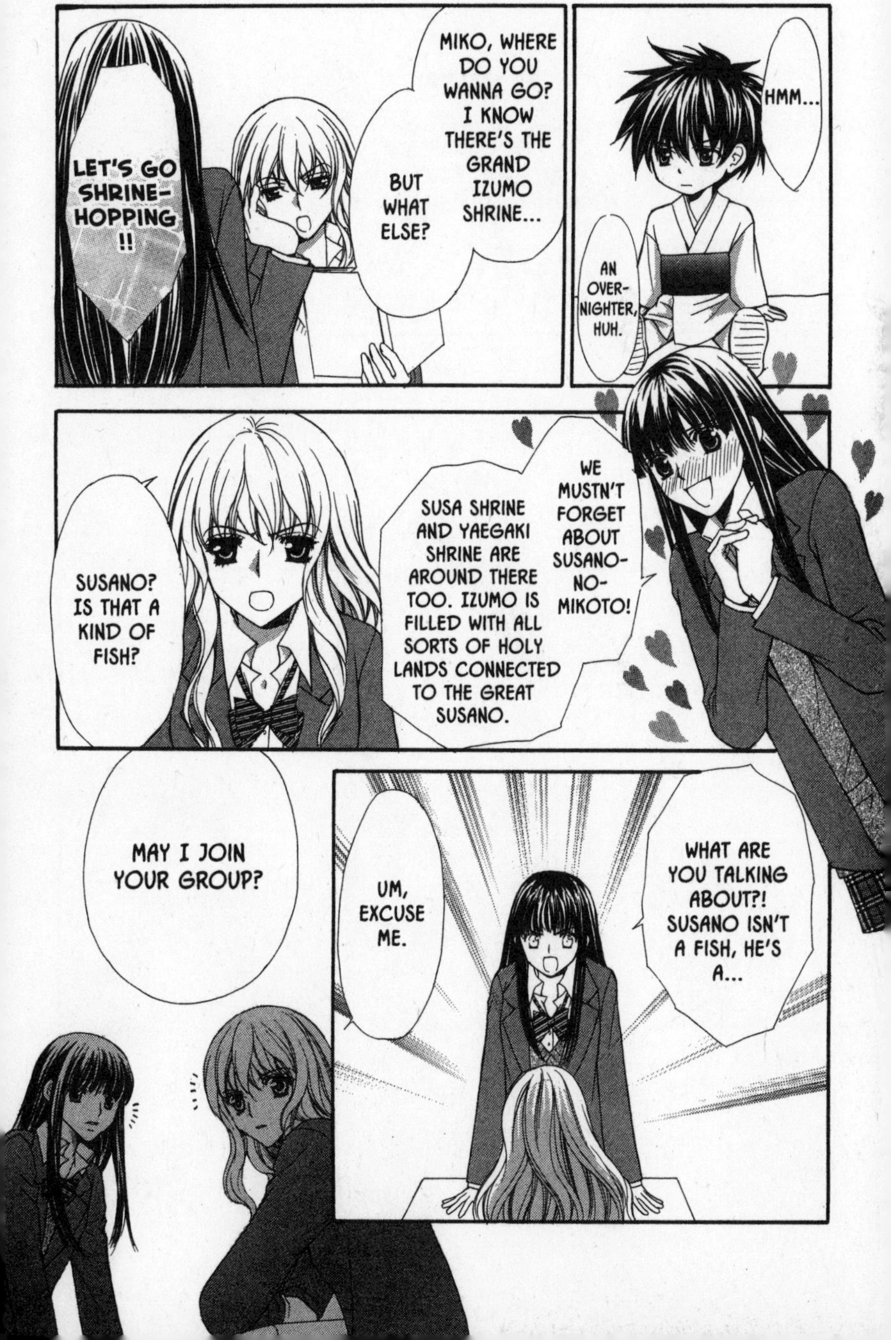
HMM...
AN OVER-NIGHTER, HUH.
MIKO, WHERE DO YOU WANNA GO? I KNOW THERE'S THE GRAND IZUMO SHRINE...
BUT WHAT ELSE?
LET'S GO SHRINE-HOPPING!!
WE MUSTN'T FORGET ABOUT SUSANO-NO-MIKOTO!
SUSA SHRINE AND YAEGAKI SHRINE ARE AROUND THERE TOO. IZUMO IS FILLED WITH ALL SORTS OF HOLY LANDS CONNECTED TO THE GREAT SUSANO.
SUSANO? IS THAT A KIND OF FISH?
WHAT ARE YOU TALKING ABOUT?! SUSANO ISN'T A FISH, HE'S A...
UM, EXCUSE ME.
MAY I JOIN YOUR GROUP?

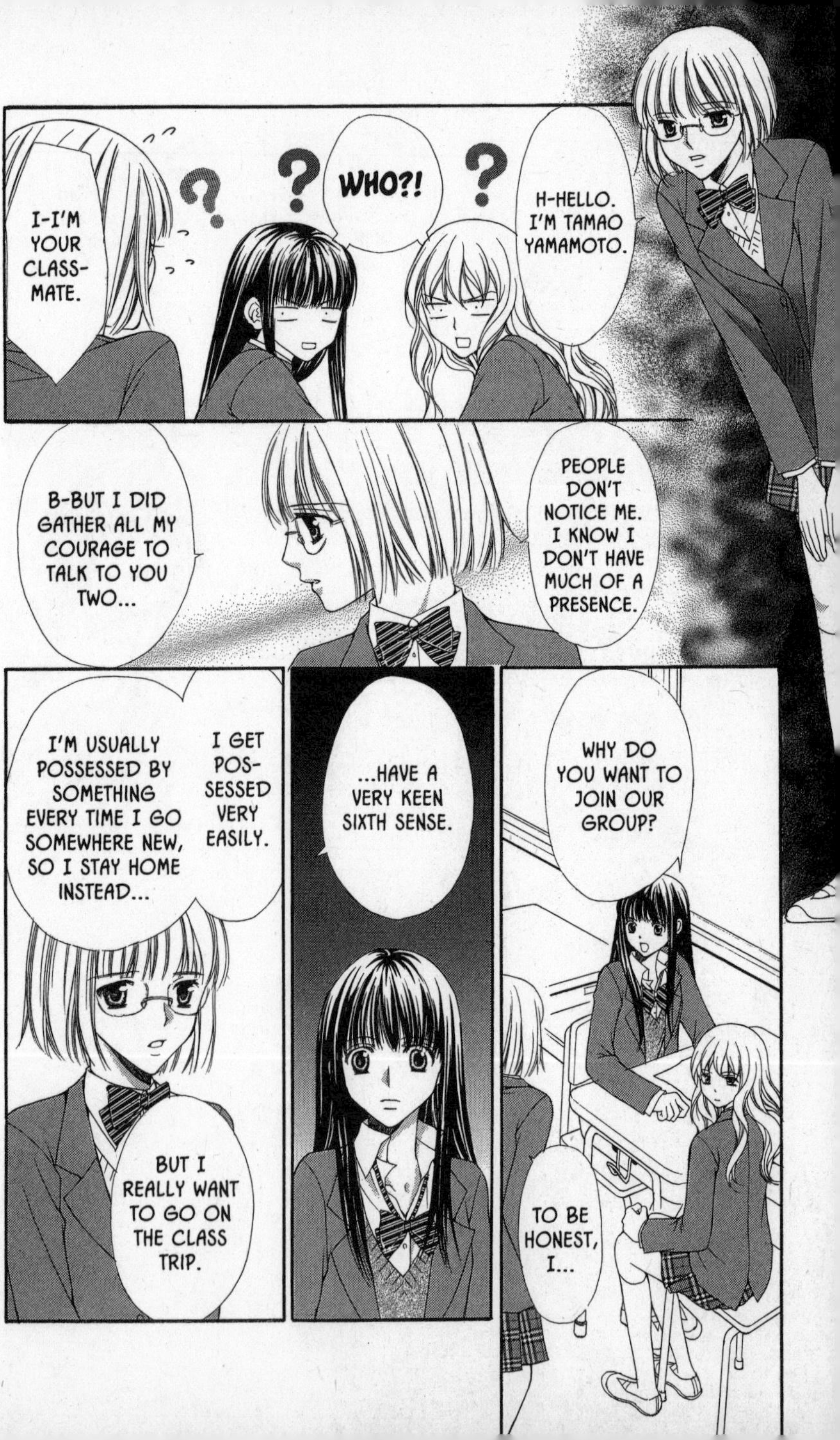
H-HELLO. I'M TAMAO YAMAMOTO.
WHO?!
I-I'M YOUR CLASS-MATE.
PEOPLE DON'T NOTICE ME. I KNOW I DON'T HAVE MUCH OF A PRESENCE.
B-BUT I DID GATHER ALL MY COURAGE TO TALK TO YOU TWO...
WHY DO YOU WANT TO JOIN OUR GROUP?
TO BE HONEST, I...
...HAVE A VERY KEEN SIXTH SENSE.
I GET POS-SESSED VERY EASILY.
I'M USUALLY POSSESSED BY SOMETHING EVERY TIME I GO SOMEWHERE NEW, SO I STAY HOME INSTEAD...
BUT I REALLY WANT TO GO ON THE CLASS TRIP.

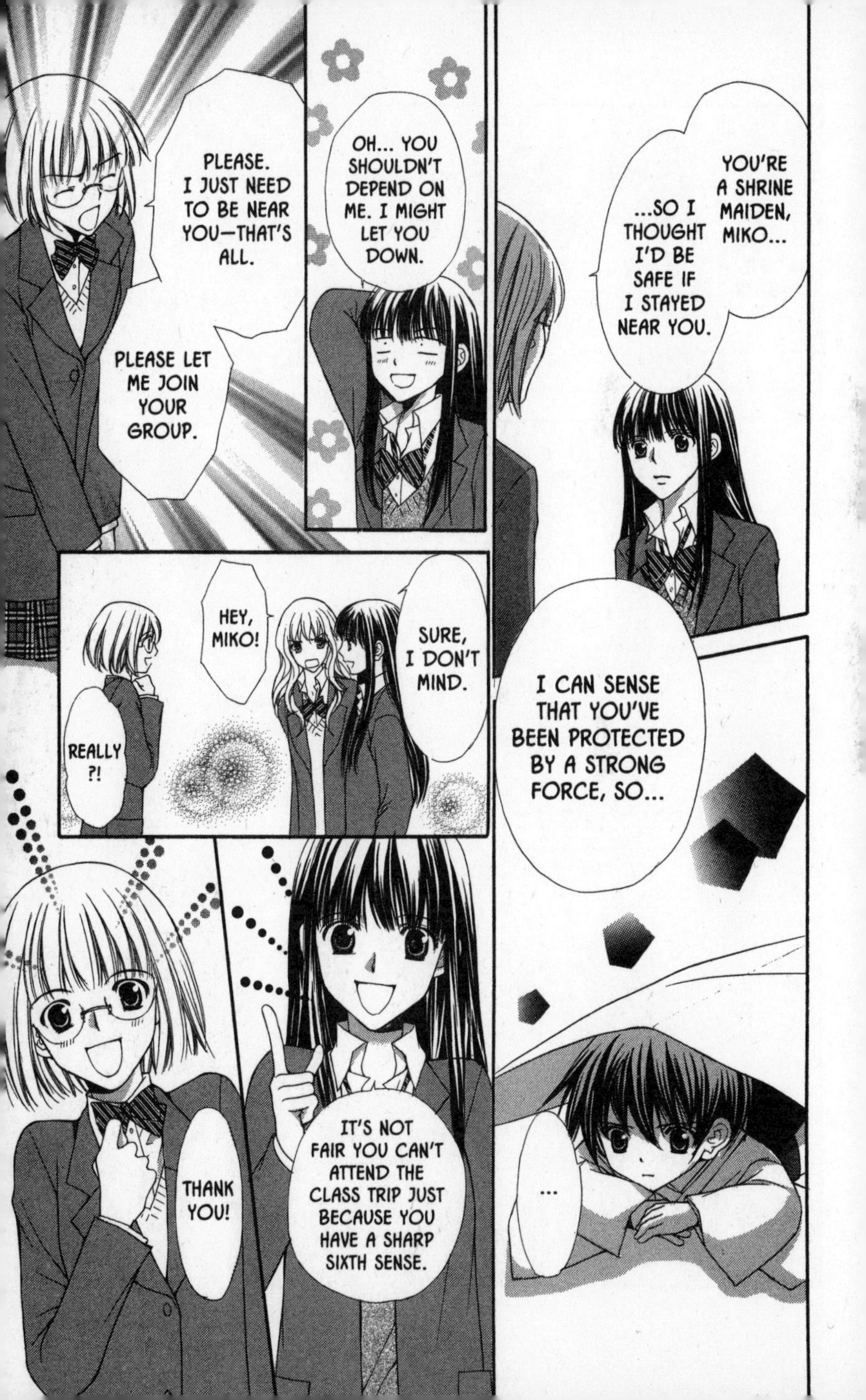
YOU'RE A SHRINE MAIDEN, MIKO...
...SO I THOUGHT I'D BE SAFE IF I STAYED NEAR YOU.
I CAN SENSE THAT YOU'VE BEEN PROTECTED BY A STRONG FORCE, SO...
...
OH... YOU SHOULDN'T DEPEND ON ME. I MIGHT LET YOU DOWN.
PLEASE. I JUST NEED TO BE NEAR YOU—THAT'S ALL.
PLEASE LET ME JOIN YOUR GROUP.
SURE, I DON'T MIND.
HEY, MIKO!
REALLY?!
IT'S NOT FAIR YOU CAN'T ATTEND THE CLASS TRIP JUST BECAUSE YOU HAVE A SHARP SIXTH SENSE.
THANK YOU!

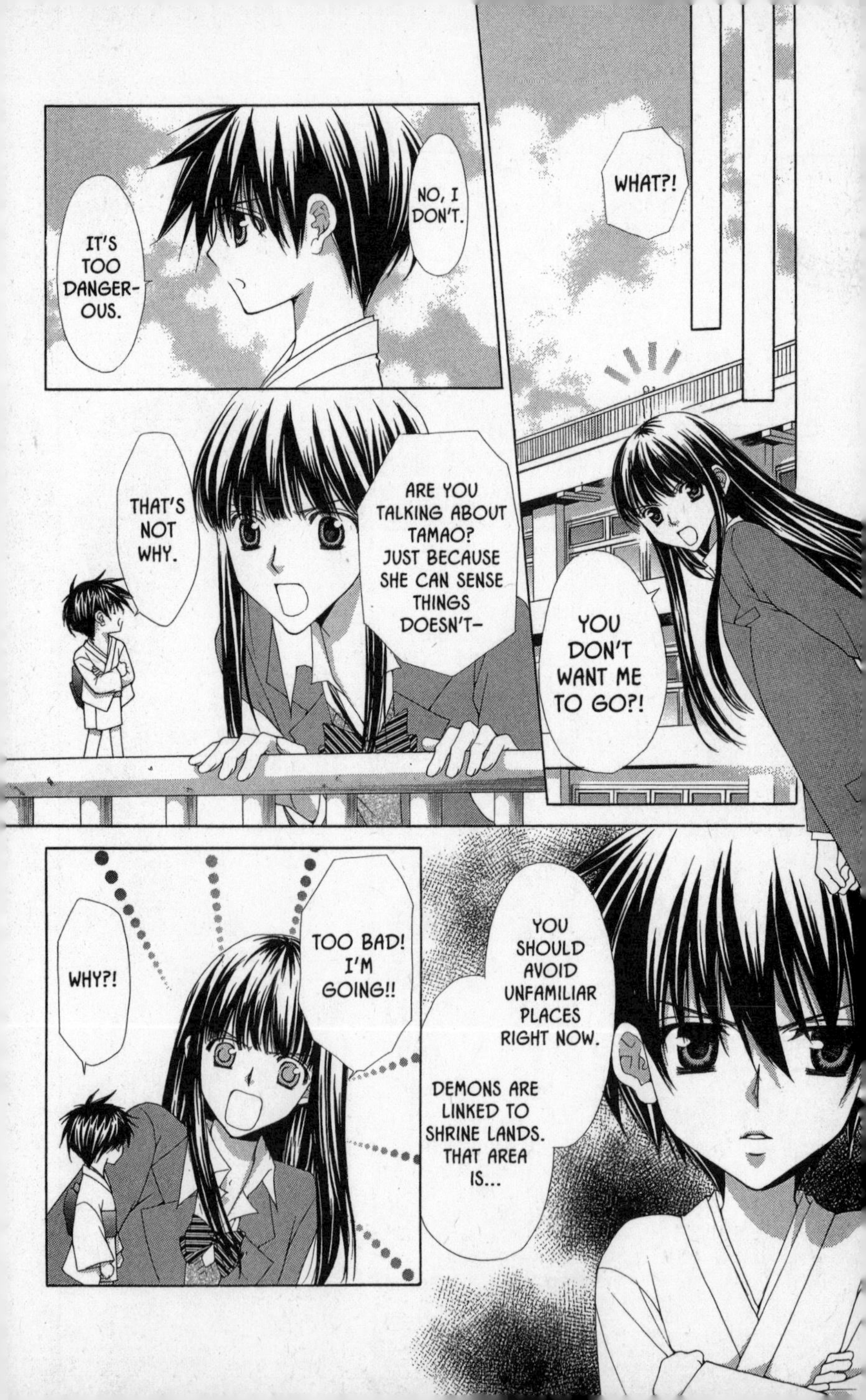

WHAT?!
YOU DON'T WANT ME TO GO?!
NO, I DON'T.
IT'S TOO DANGER-OUS.
ARE YOU TALKING ABOUT TAMAO? JUST BECAUSE SHE CAN SENSE THINGS DOESN'T–
THAT'S NOT WHY.
YOU SHOULD AVOID UNFAMILIAR PLACES RIGHT NOW.
DEMONS ARE LINKED TO SHRINE LANDS. THAT AREA IS...
TOO BAD! I'M GOING!!
WHY?!

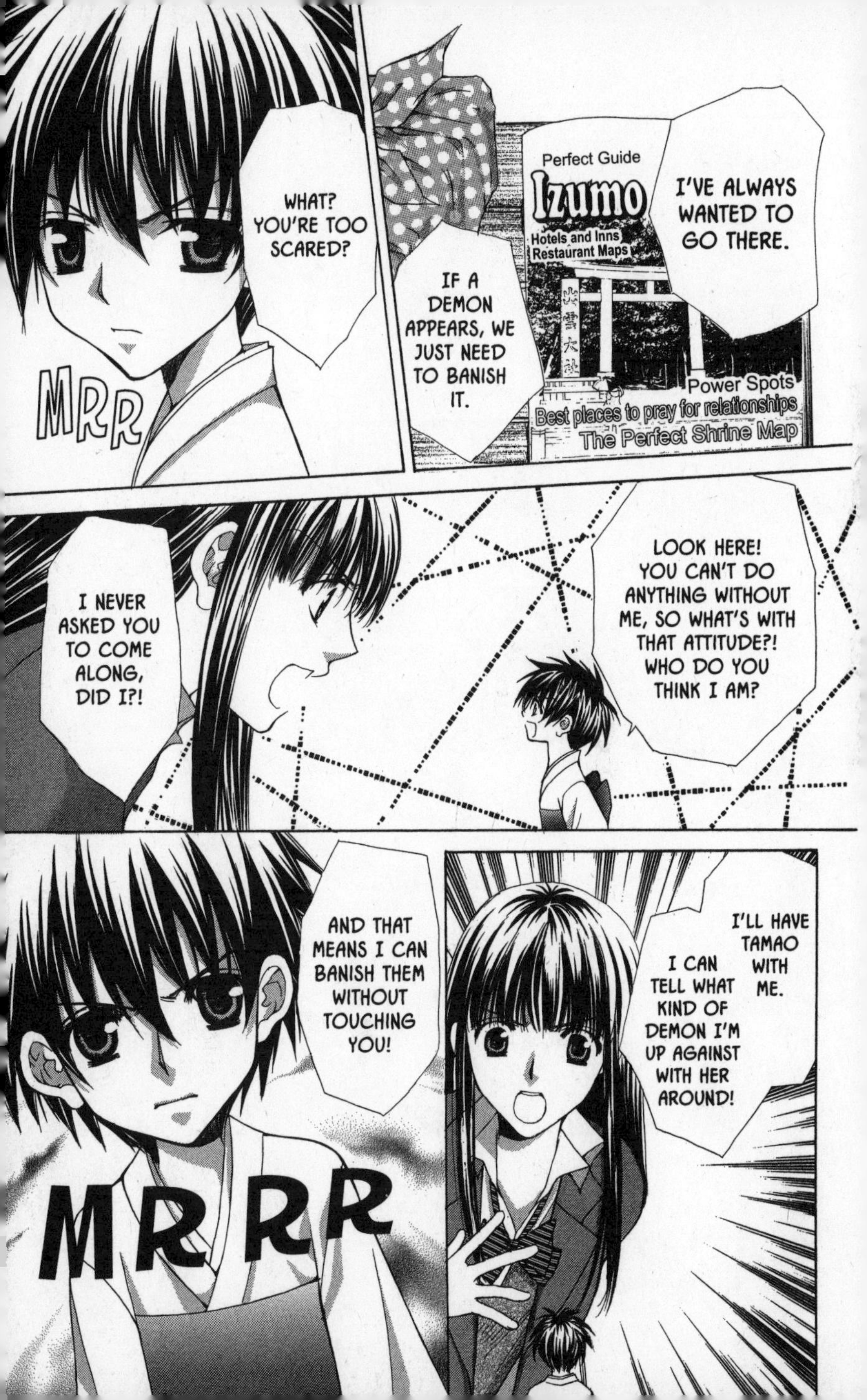
I'VE ALWAYS WANTED TO GO THERE.
Perfect Guide
Izumo
Hotels and Inns
Restaurant Maps
Power Spots
Best places to pray for relationships
The Perfect Shrine Map
IF A DEMON APPEARS, WE JUST NEED TO BANISH IT.
WHAT? YOU'RE TOO SCARED?
MRR
LOOK HERE! YOU CAN'T DO ANYTHING WITHOUT ME, SO WHAT'S WITH THAT ATTITUDE?! WHO DO YOU THINK I AM?
I NEVER ASKED YOU TO COME ALONG, DID I?!
I'LL HAVE TAMAO WITH ME.
I CAN TELL WHAT KIND OF DEMON I'M UP AGAINST WITH HER AROUND!
AND THAT MEANS I CAN BANISH THEM WITHOUT TOUCHING YOU!
MRRR

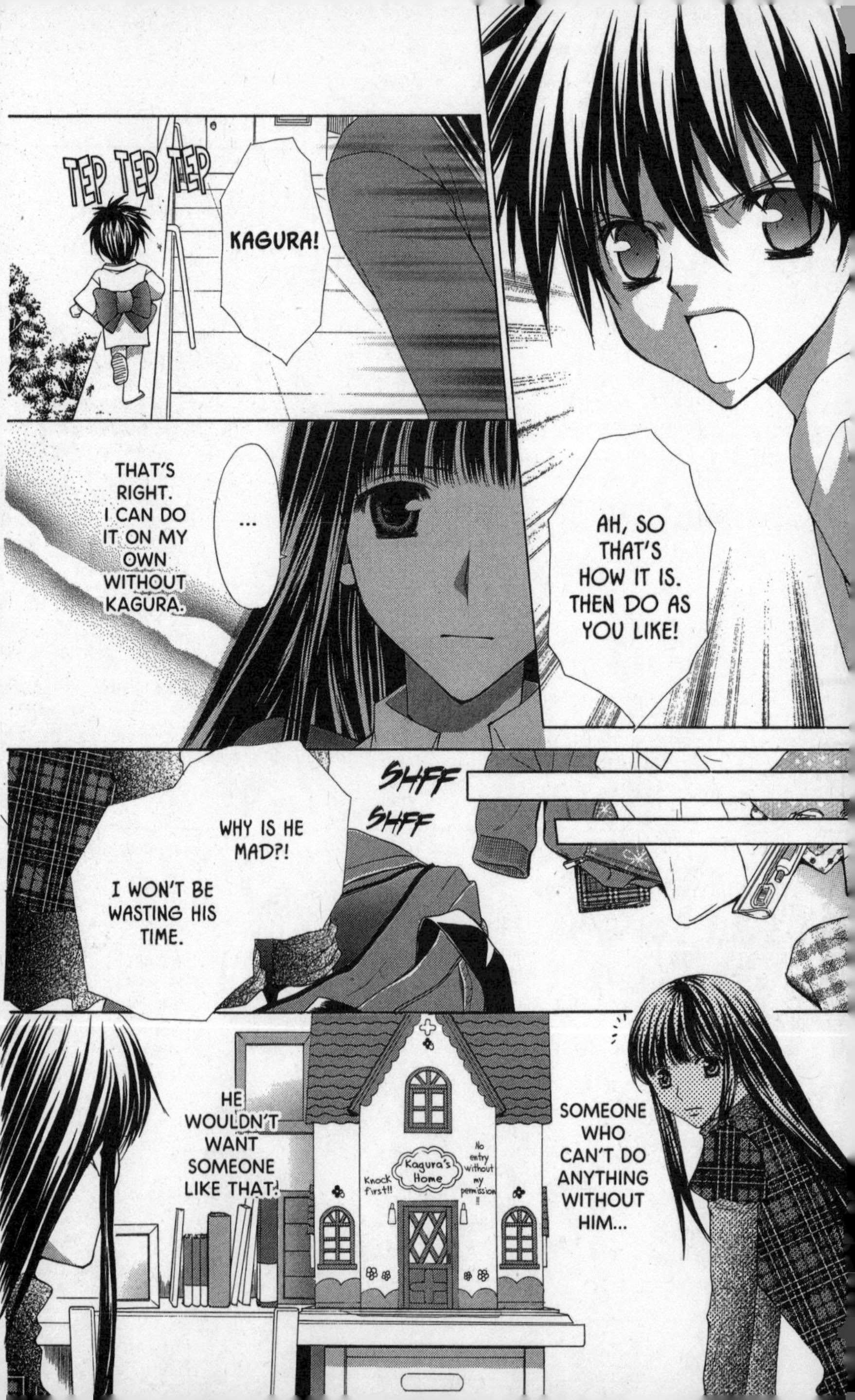
AH, SO THAT'S HOW IT IS. THEN DO AS YOU LIKE!
TEP TEP TEP
KAGURA!
...
THAT'S RIGHT. I CAN DO IT ON MY OWN WITHOUT KAGURA.
SHFF
SHFF
WHY IS HE MAD?!
I WON'T BE WASTING HIS TIME.
SOMEONE WHO CAN'T DO ANYTHING WITHOUT HIM...
No entry without my permission!!
Kagura's Home
Knock first!!
HE WOULDN'T WANT SOMEONE LIKE THAT!

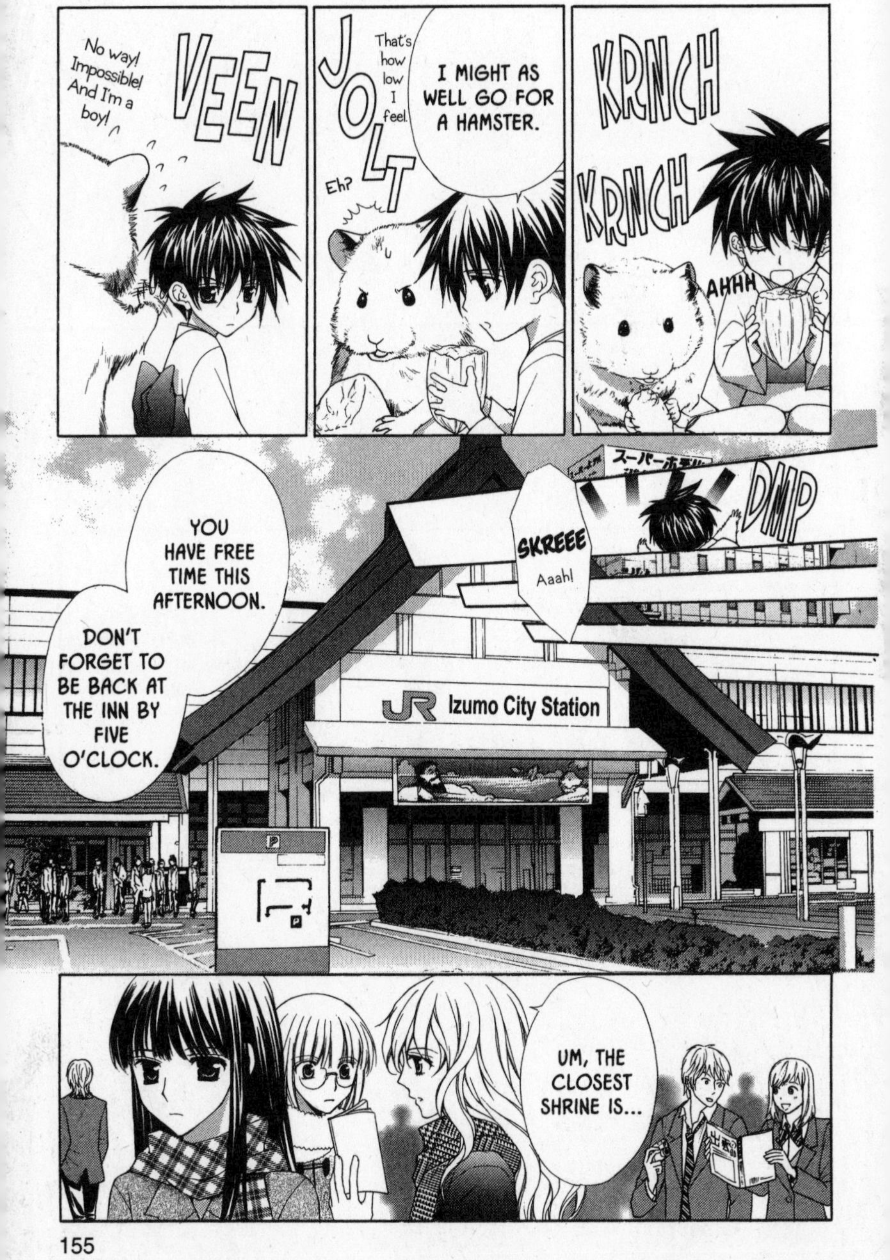
KRNCH
KRNCH
AHHH
I MIGHT AS WELL GO FOR A HAMSTER.
That's how low I feel.
JOLT
Eh?
VEEN
No way! Impossible! And I'm a boy!
DMP
SKREEE
Aaah!
YOU HAVE FREE TIME THIS AFTERNOON.
DON'T FORGET TO BE BACK AT THE INN BY FIVE O'CLOCK.
JR Izumo City Station
UM, THE CLOSEST SHRINE IS...

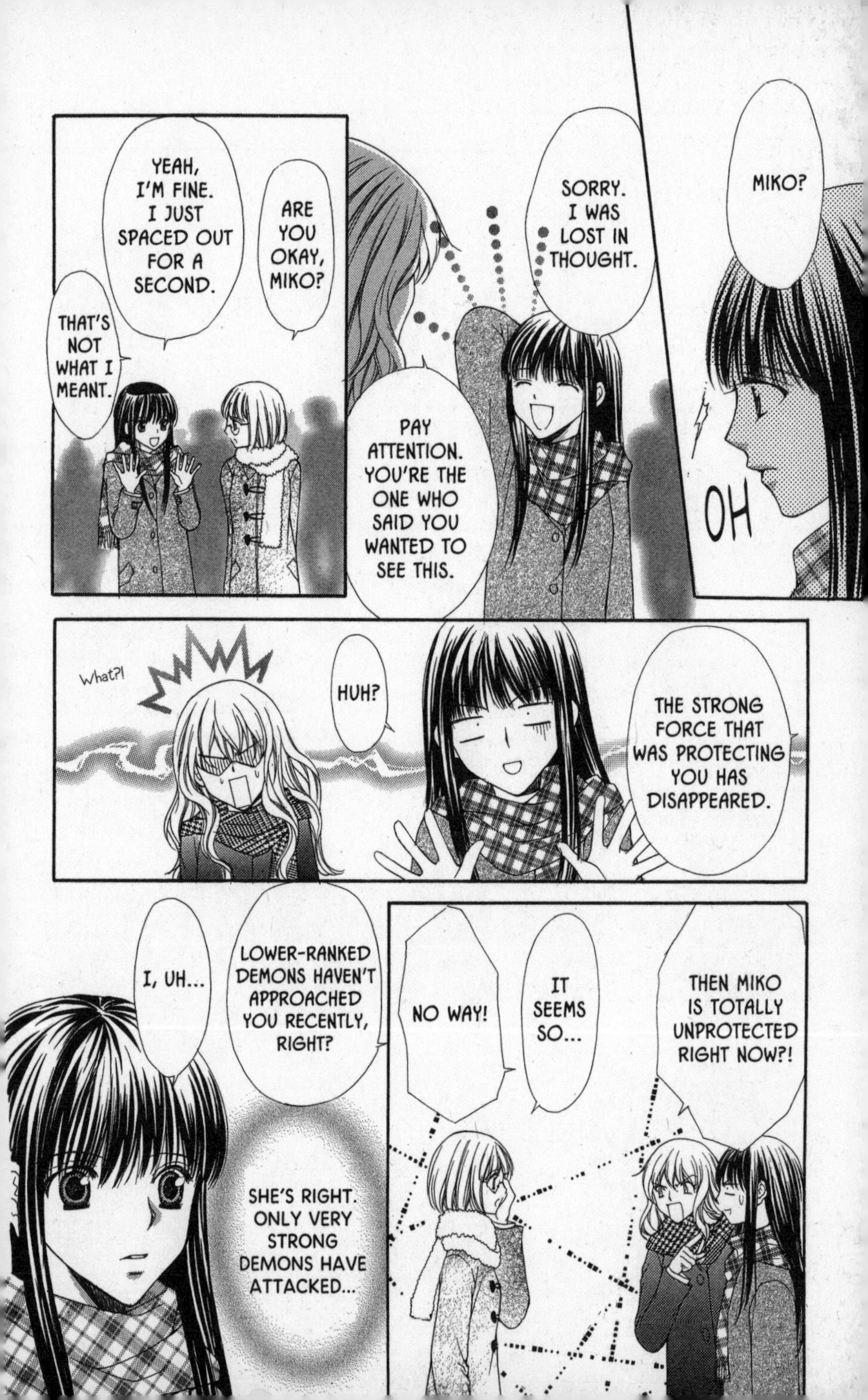
MIKO?
OH
SORRY. I WAS LOST IN THOUGHT.
PAY ATTENTION. YOU'RE THE ONE WHO SAID YOU WANTED TO SEE THIS.
ARE YOU OKAY, MIKO?
YEAH, I'M FINE. I JUST SPACED OUT FOR A SECOND.
THAT'S NOT WHAT I MEANT.
THE STRONG FORCE THAT WAS PROTECTING YOU HAS DISAPPEARED.
HUH?
What?!
THEN MIKO IS TOTALLY UNPROTECTED RIGHT NOW?!
IT SEEMS SO...
NO WAY!
LOWER-RANKED DEMONS HAVEN'T APPROACHED YOU RECENTLY, RIGHT?
I, UH...
SHE'S RIGHT. ONLY VERY STRONG DEMONS HAVE ATTACKED...

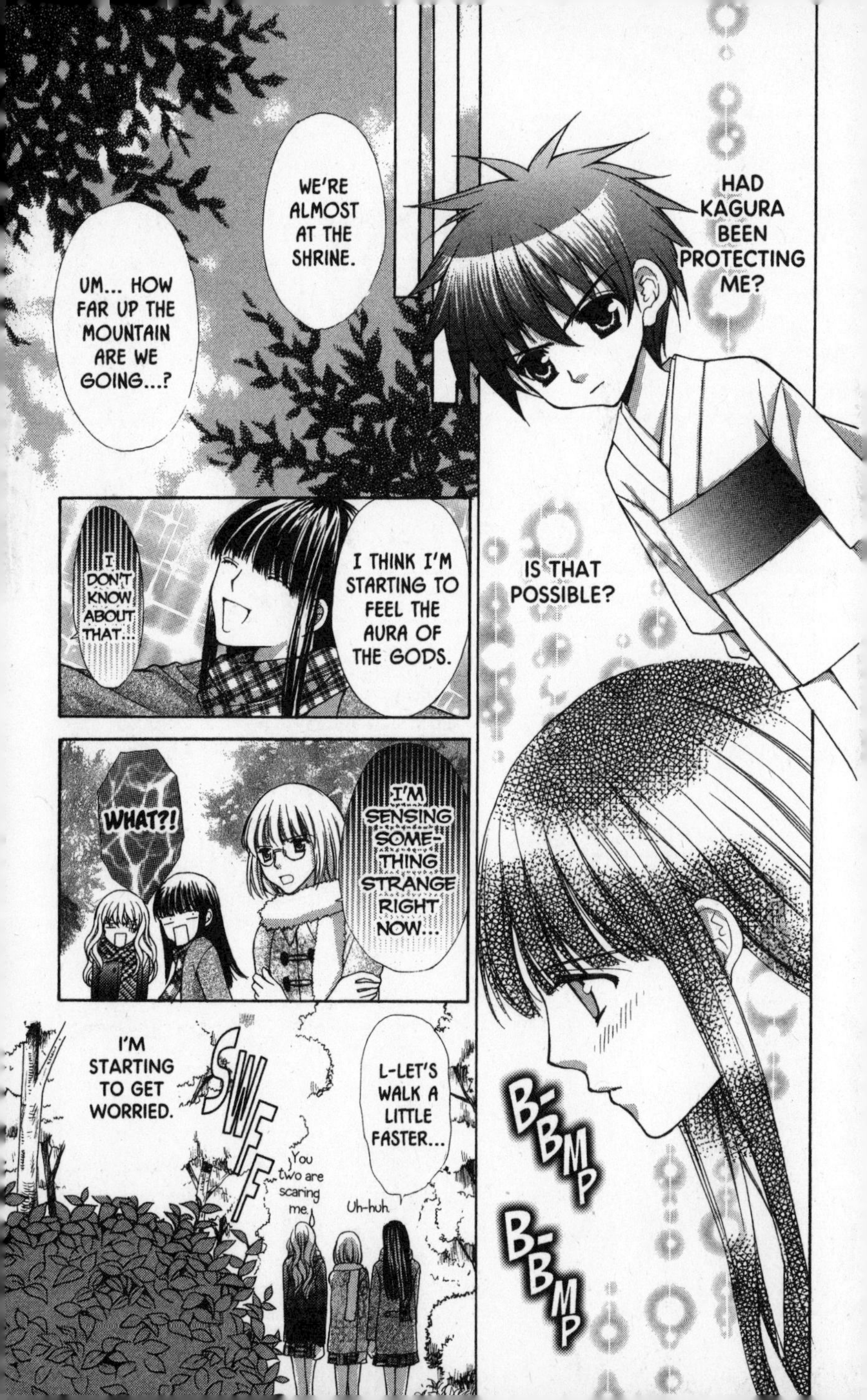
HAD KAGURA BEEN PROTECTING ME?
IS THAT POSSIBLE?
B-BMP
B-BMP
WE'RE ALMOST AT THE SHRINE.
UM... HOW FAR UP THE MOUNTAIN ARE WE GOING...?
I THINK I'M STARTING TO FEEL THE AURA OF THE GODS.
I DON'T KNOW ABOUT THAT...
I'M SENSING SOME-THING STRANGE RIGHT NOW...
WHAT?!
L-LET'S WALK A LITTLE FASTER...
Uh-huh.
You two are scaring me.
SWFF
I'M STARTING TO GET WORRIED.

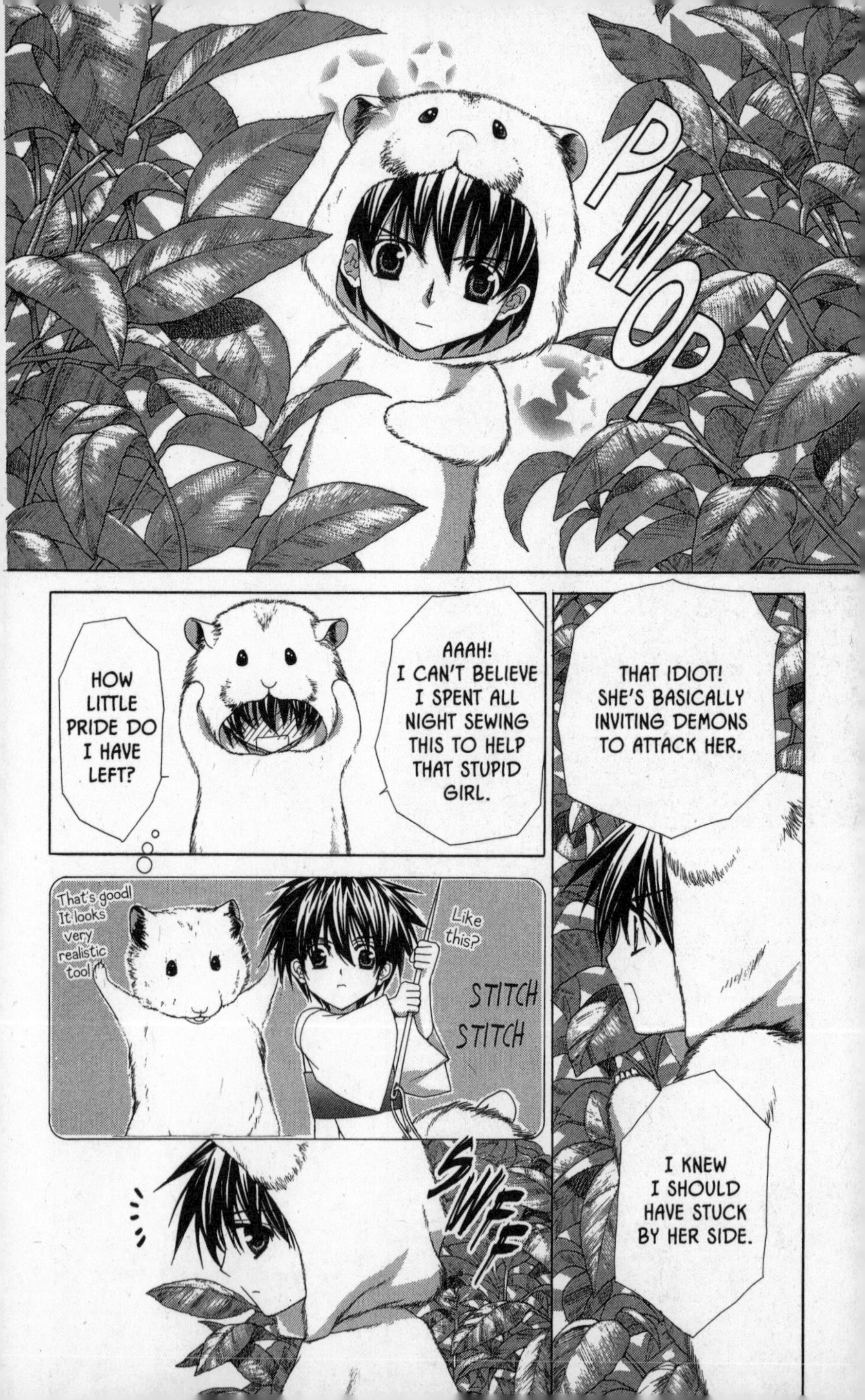
PWOP
THAT IDIOT! SHE'S BASICALLY INVITING DEMONS TO ATTACK HER.
I KNEW I SHOULD HAVE STUCK BY HER SIDE.
AAAH! I CAN'T BELIEVE I SPENT ALL NIGHT SEWING THIS TO HELP THAT STUPID GIRL.
HOW LITTLE PRIDE DO I HAVE LEFT?
Like this?
STITCH STITCH
That's good! It looks very realistic too!
SNIFF

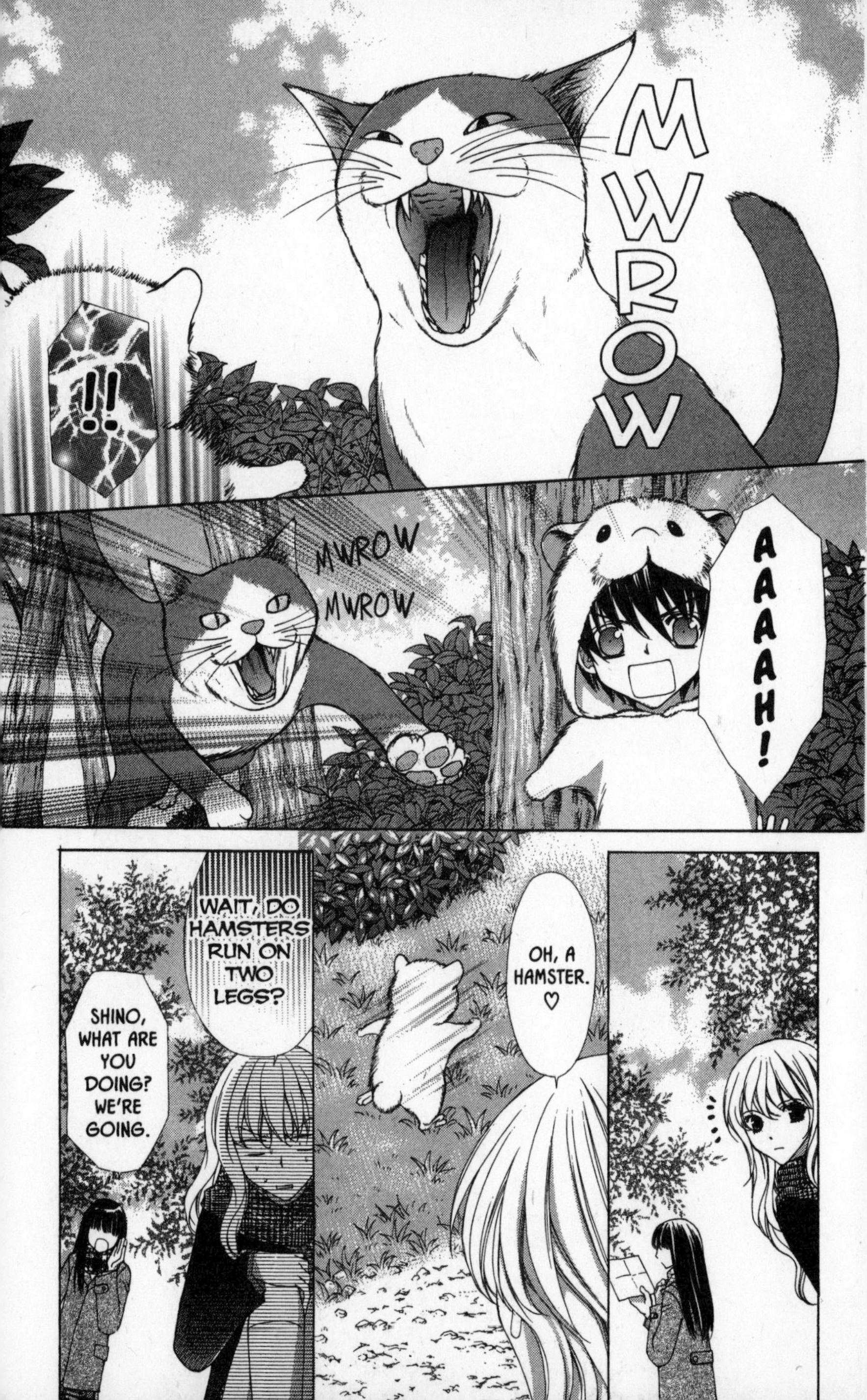
MWROW
!!
AAAAAH!
MWROW
MWROW
OH, A HAMSTER. ♡
WAIT, DO HAMSTERS RUN ON TWO LEGS?
SHINO, WHAT ARE YOU DOING? WE'RE GOING.

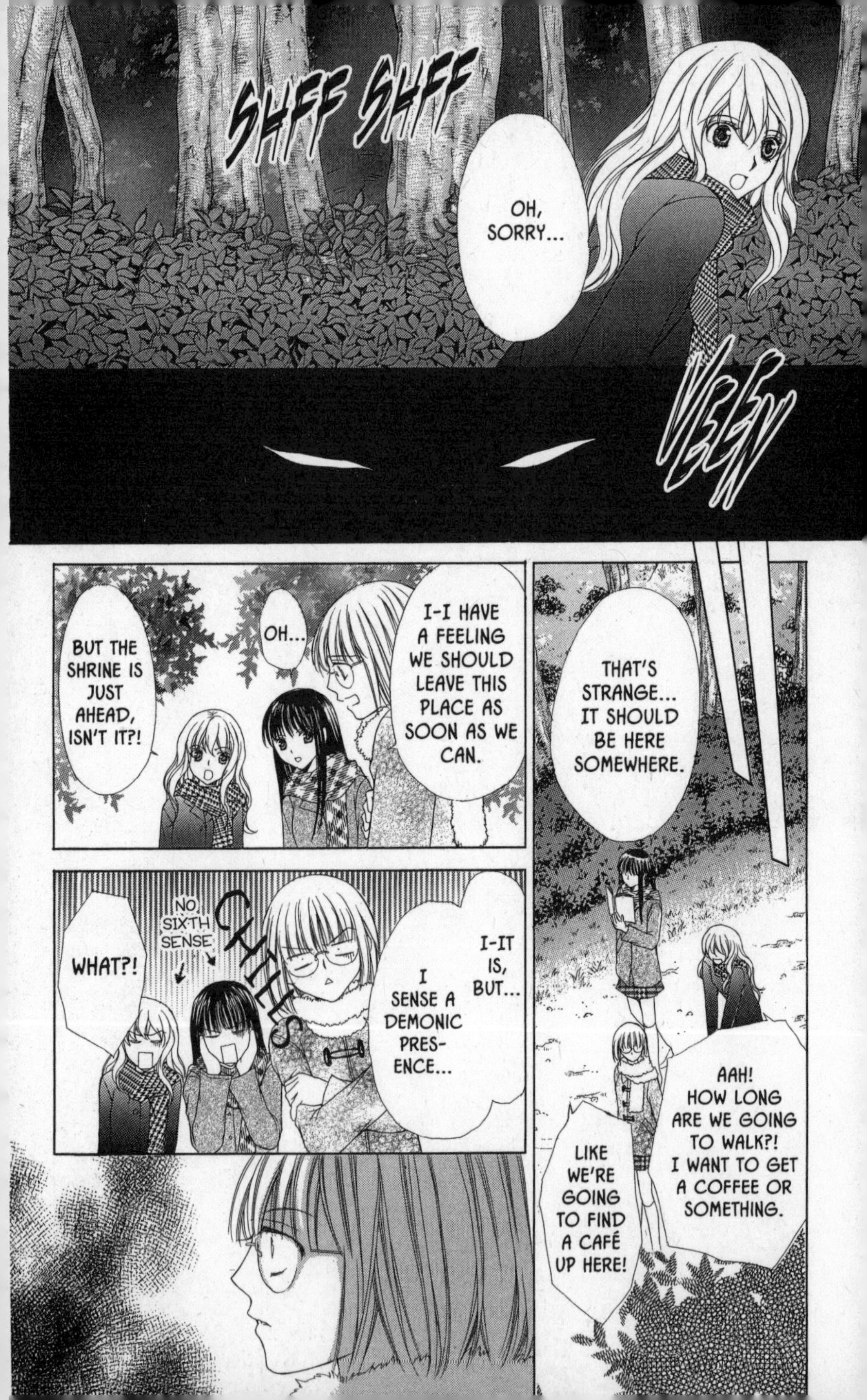
SHFF SHFF
OH, SORRY...
THAT'S STRANGE... IT SHOULD BE HERE SOMEWHERE.
AAH! HOW LONG ARE WE GOING TO WALK?! I WANT TO GET A COFFEE OR SOMETHING.
LIKE WE'RE GOING TO FIND A CAFÉ UP HERE!
I-I HAVE A FEELING WE SHOULD LEAVE THIS PLACE AS SOON AS WE CAN.
OH...
BUT THE SHRINE IS JUST AHEAD, ISN'T IT?!
I-IT IS, BUT...
I SENSE A DEMONIC PRES-ENCE...
CHILLS
NO SIXTH SENSE
WHAT?!

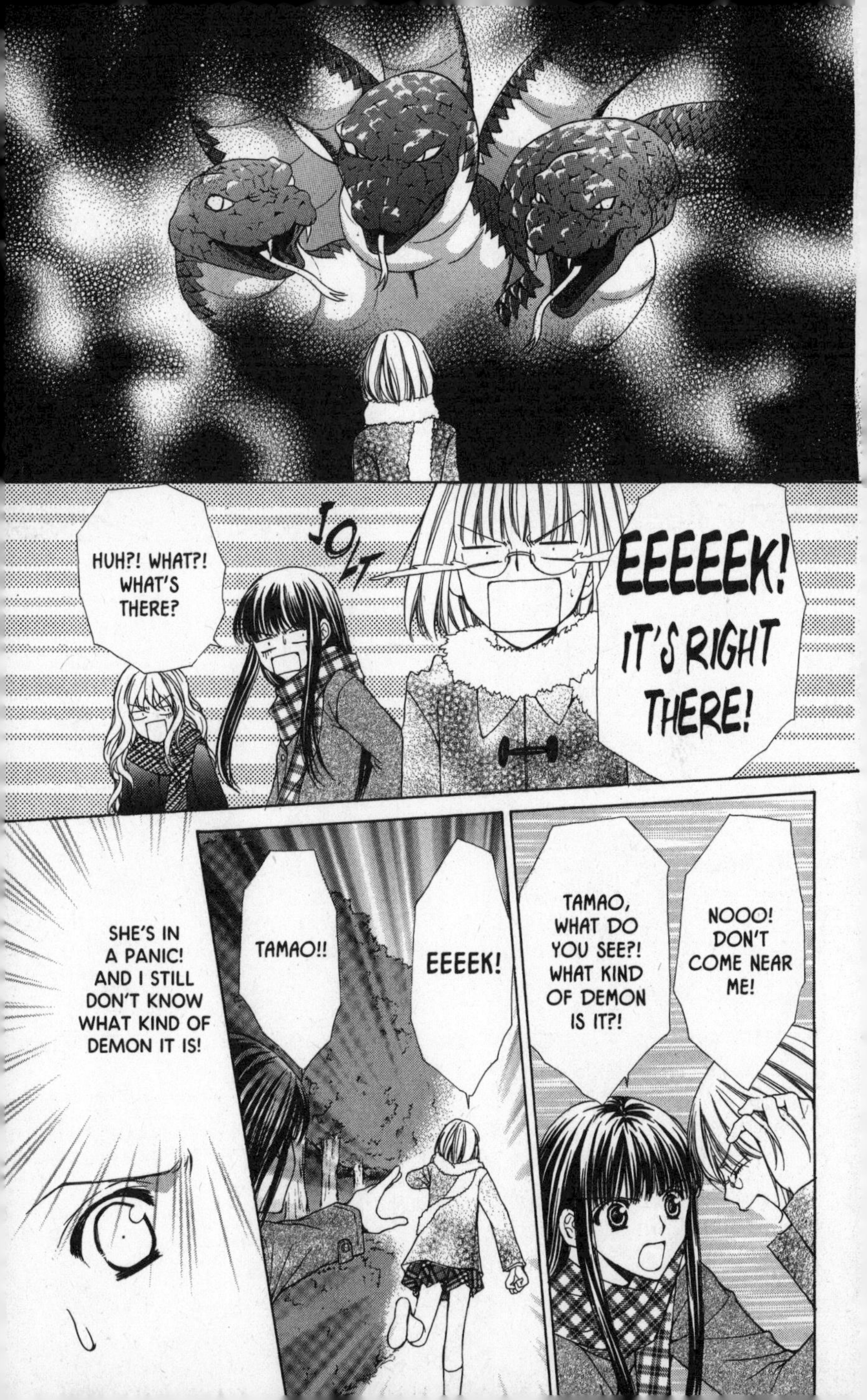
EEEEEK! IT'S RIGHT THERE!
JOLT
HUH?! WHAT?! WHAT'S THERE?
NOOO! DON'T COME NEAR ME!
TAMAO, WHAT DO YOU SEE?! WHAT KIND OF DEMON IS IT?!
EEEEK!
TAMAO!!
SHE'S IN A PANIC! AND I STILL DON'T KNOW WHAT KIND OF DEMON IT IS!

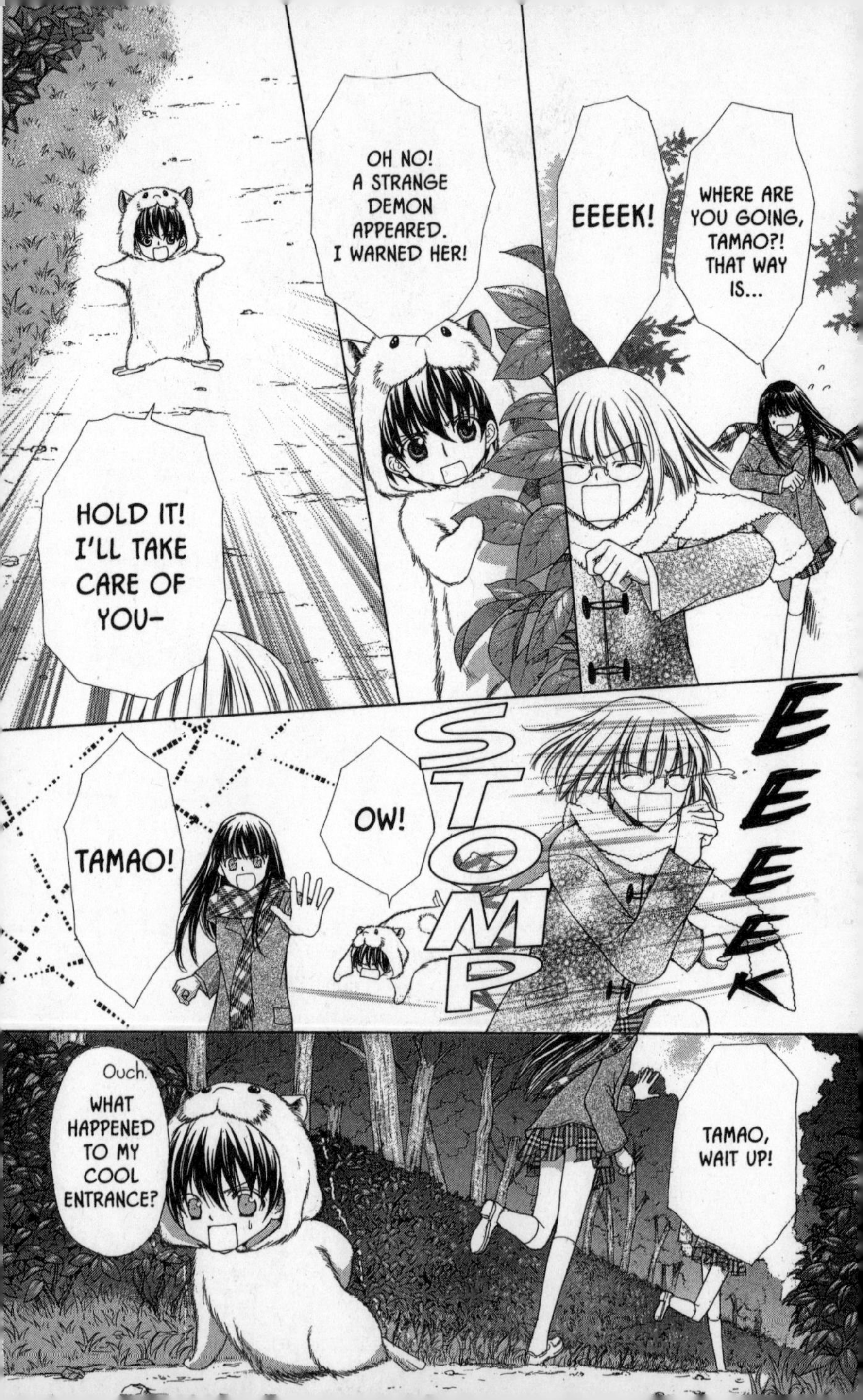
WHERE ARE YOU GOING, TAMAO?! THAT WAY IS...
EEEEK!
OH NO! A STRANGE DEMON APPEARED. I WARNED HER!
HOLD IT! I'LL TAKE CARE OF YOU–
EEEEEEK
STOMP
OW!
TAMAO!
TAMAO, WAIT UP!
Ouch.
WHAT HAPPENED TO MY COOL ENTRANCE?

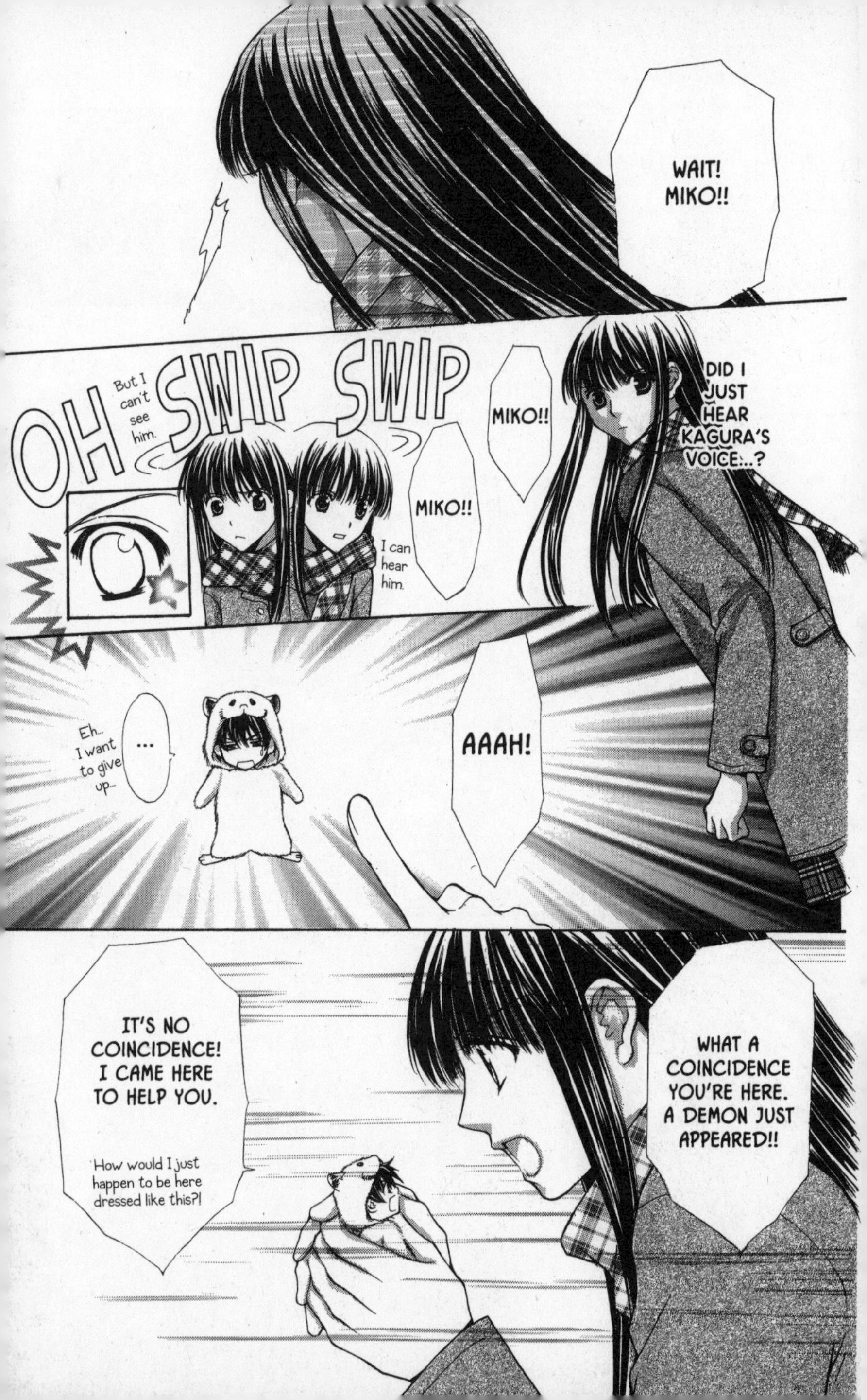
WAIT! MIKO!!
DID I JUST HEAR KAGURA'S VOICE...?
MIKO!!
MIKO!!
I can hear him.
SWIP SWIP
But I can't see him.
OH
AAAH!
...
Eh... I want to give up...
WHAT A COINCIDENCE YOU'RE HERE. A DEMON JUST APPEARED!!
IT'S NO COINCIDENCE! I CAME HERE TO HELP YOU.
How would I just happen to be here dressed like this?!

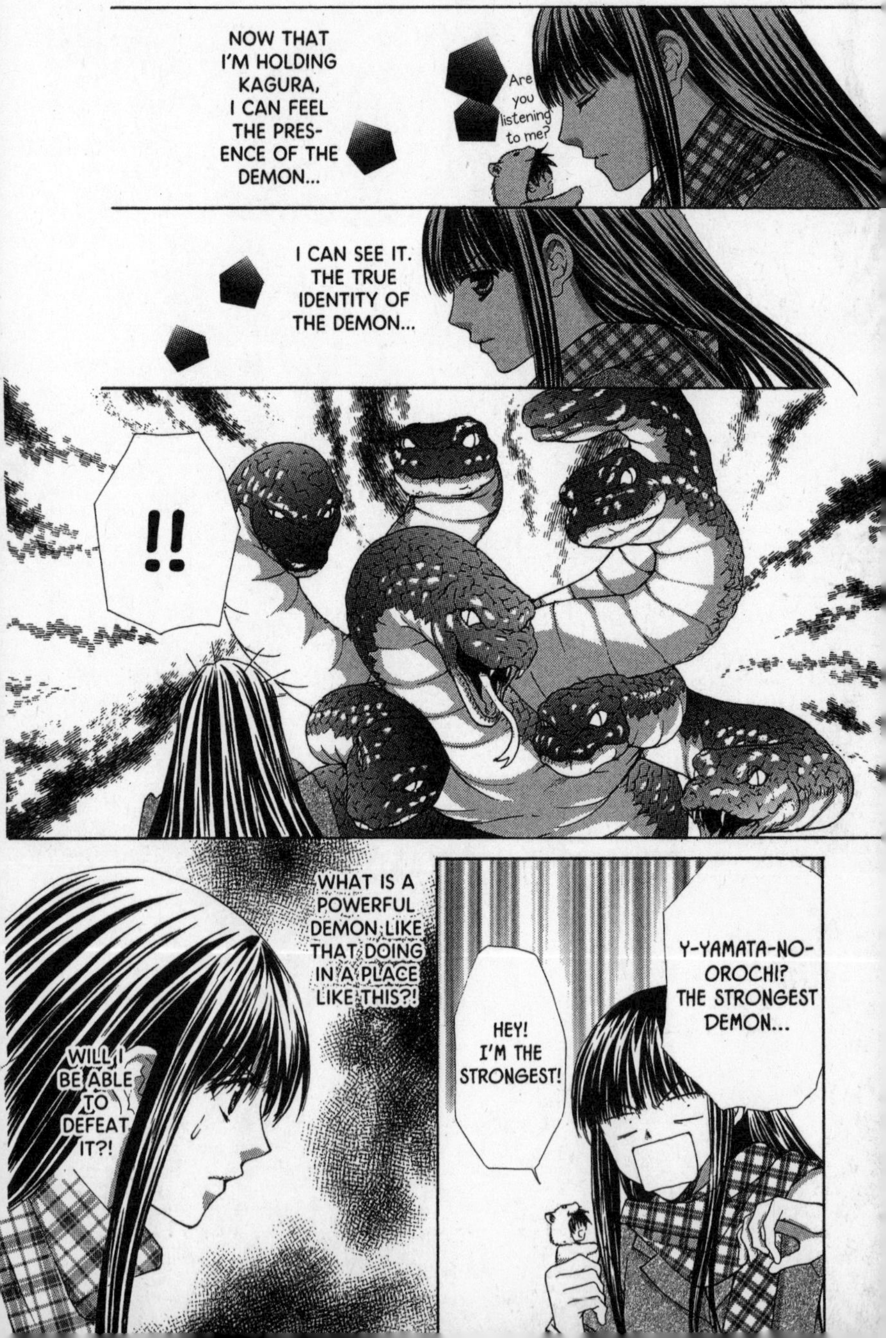
NOW THAT I'M HOLDING KAGURA, I CAN FEEL THE PRES-ENCE OF THE DEMON...
Are you listening to me?
I CAN SEE IT. THE TRUE IDENTITY OF THE DEMON...
!!
Y-YAMATA-NO-OROCHI? THE STRONGEST DEMON...
HEY! I'M THE STRONGEST!
WHAT IS A POWERFUL DEMON LIKE THAT DOING IN A PLACE LIKE THIS?!
WILL I BE ABLE TO DEFEAT IT?!

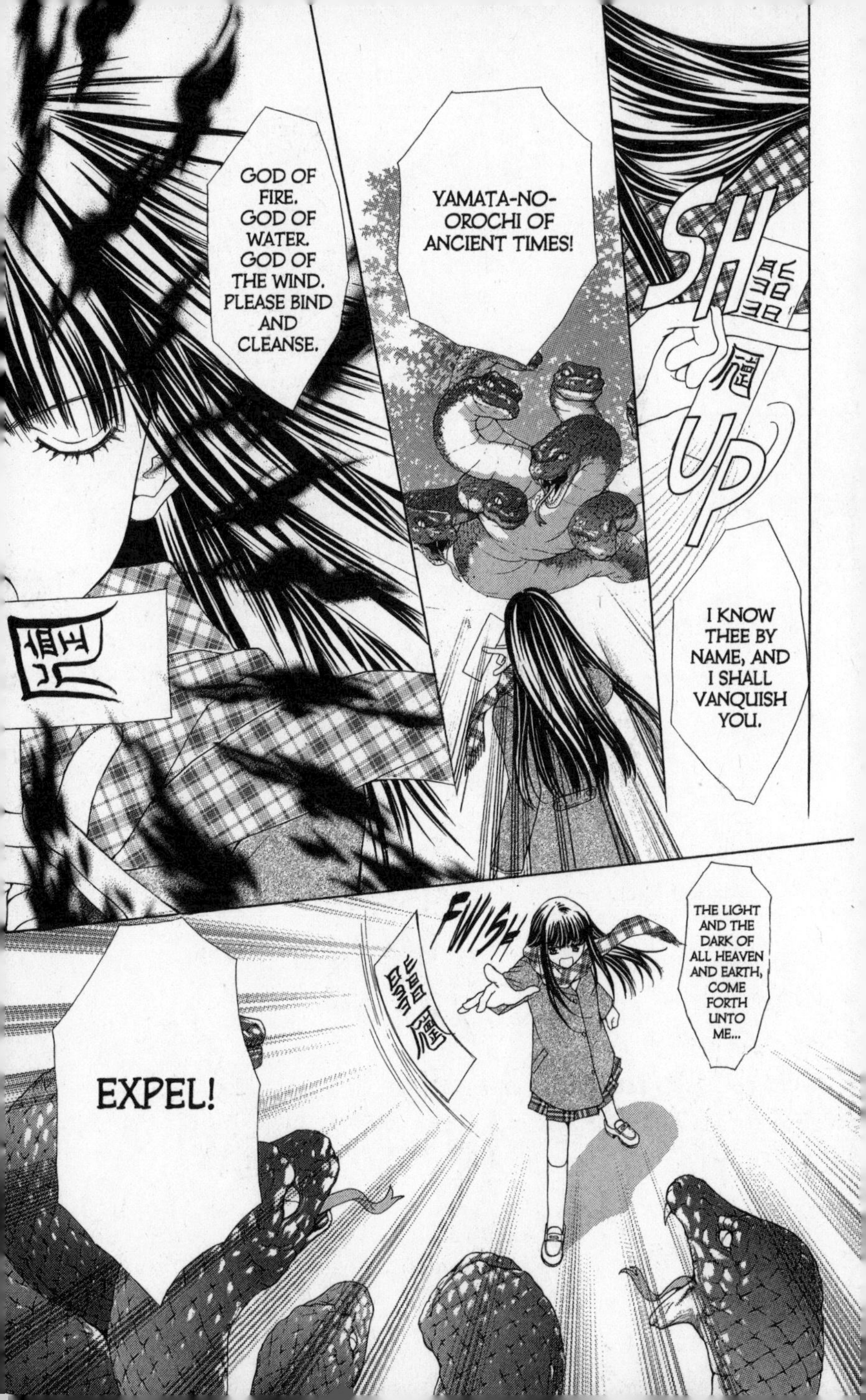
SHUP
I KNOW THEE BY NAME, AND I SHALL VANQUISH YOU.
YAMATA-NO-OROCHI OF ANCIENT TIMES!
GOD OF FIRE. GOD OF WATER. GOD OF THE WIND. PLEASE BIND AND CLEANSE.
THE LIGHT AND THE DARK OF ALL HEAVEN AND EARTH, COME FORTH UNTO ME...
FWISH
EXPEL!

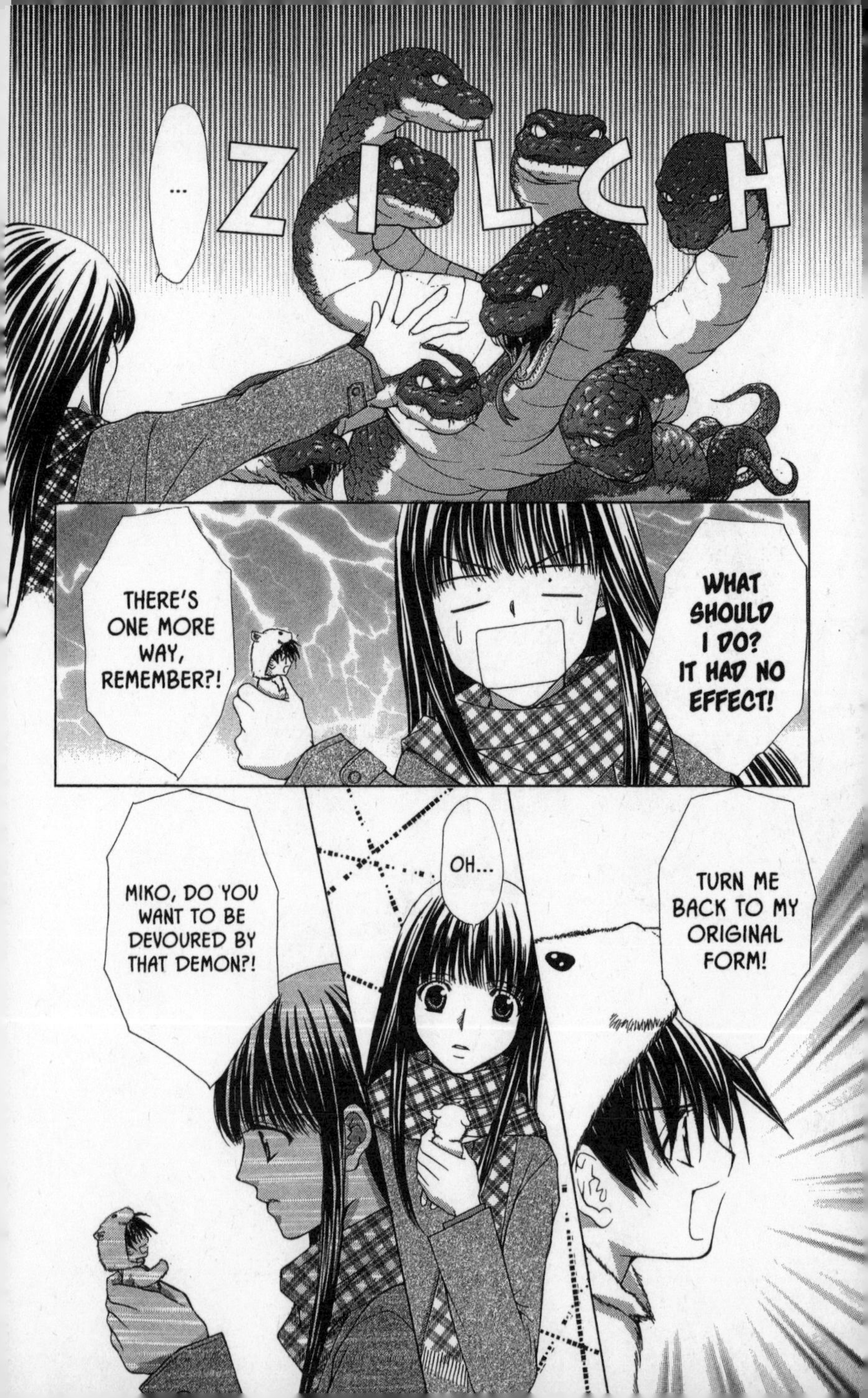

ZILCH
...
WHAT SHOULD I DO? IT HAD NO EFFECT!
THERE'S ONE MORE WAY, REMEMBER?!
TURN ME BACK TO MY ORIGINAL FORM!
OH...
MIKO, DO YOU WANT TO BE DEVOURED BY THAT DEMON?!

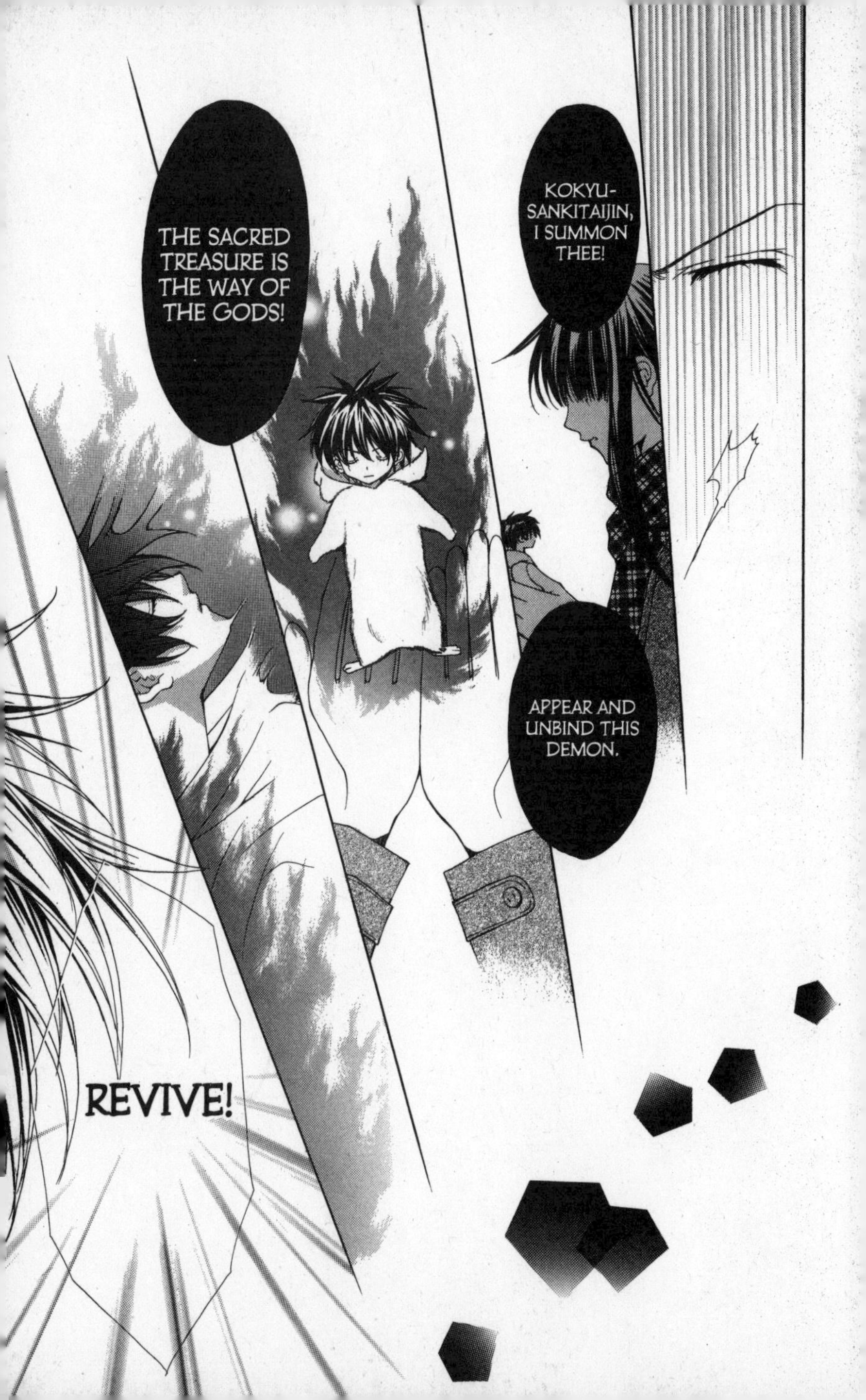
KOKYU-SANKITAIJIN, I SUMMON THEE!
APPEAR AND UNBIND THIS DEMON.
THE SACRED TREASURE IS THE WAY OF THE GODS!
REVIVE!

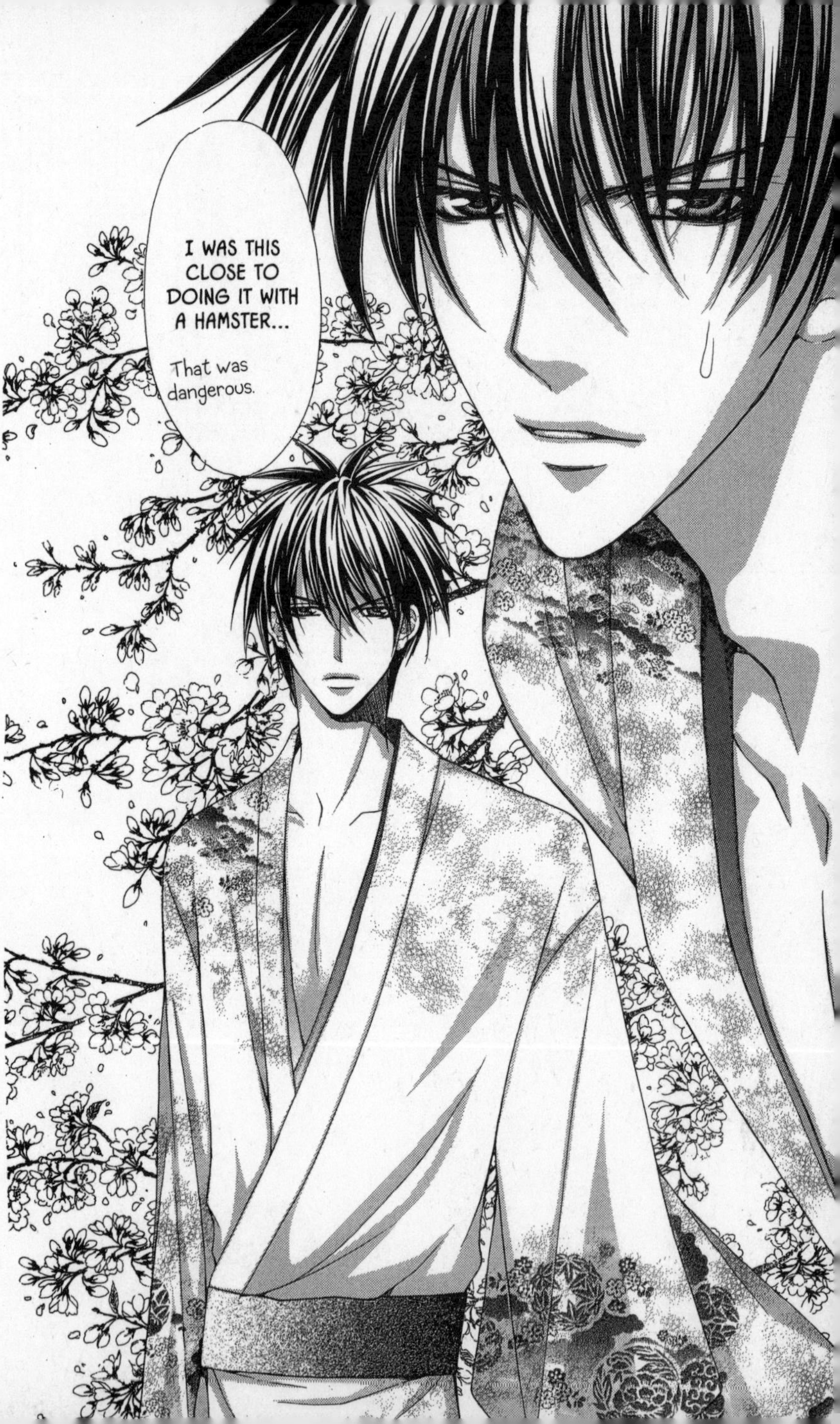
I WAS THIS CLOSE TO DOING IT WITH A HAMSTER...
That was dangerous.

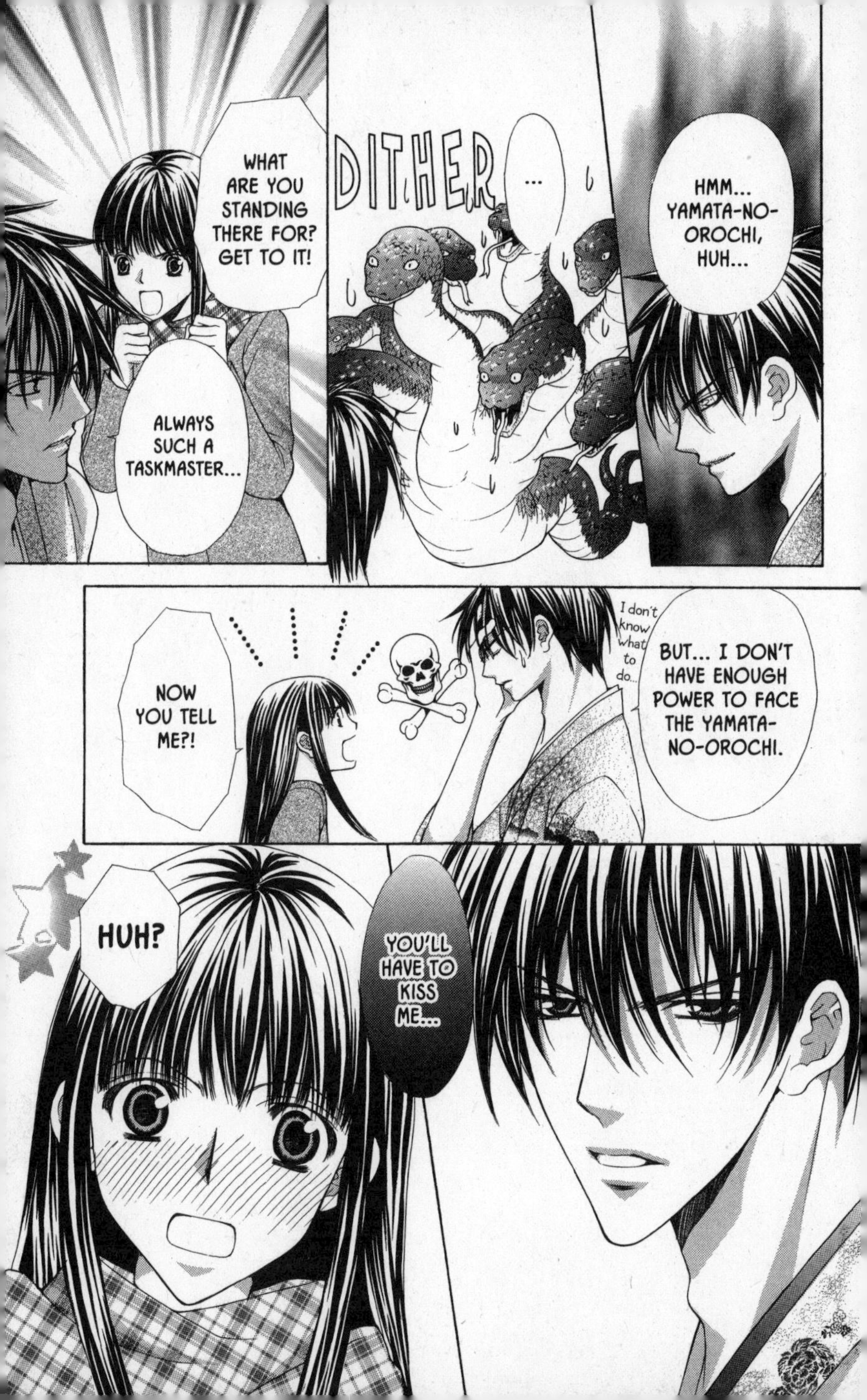
HMM... YAMATA-NO-OROCHI, HUH...
DITHER
...
WHAT ARE YOU STANDING THERE FOR? GET TO IT!
ALWAYS SUCH A TASKMASTER...
BUT... I DON'T HAVE ENOUGH POWER TO FACE THE YAMATA-NO-OROCHI.
I don't know what to do...
NOW YOU TELL ME?!
YOU'LL HAVE TO KISS ME...
HUH?

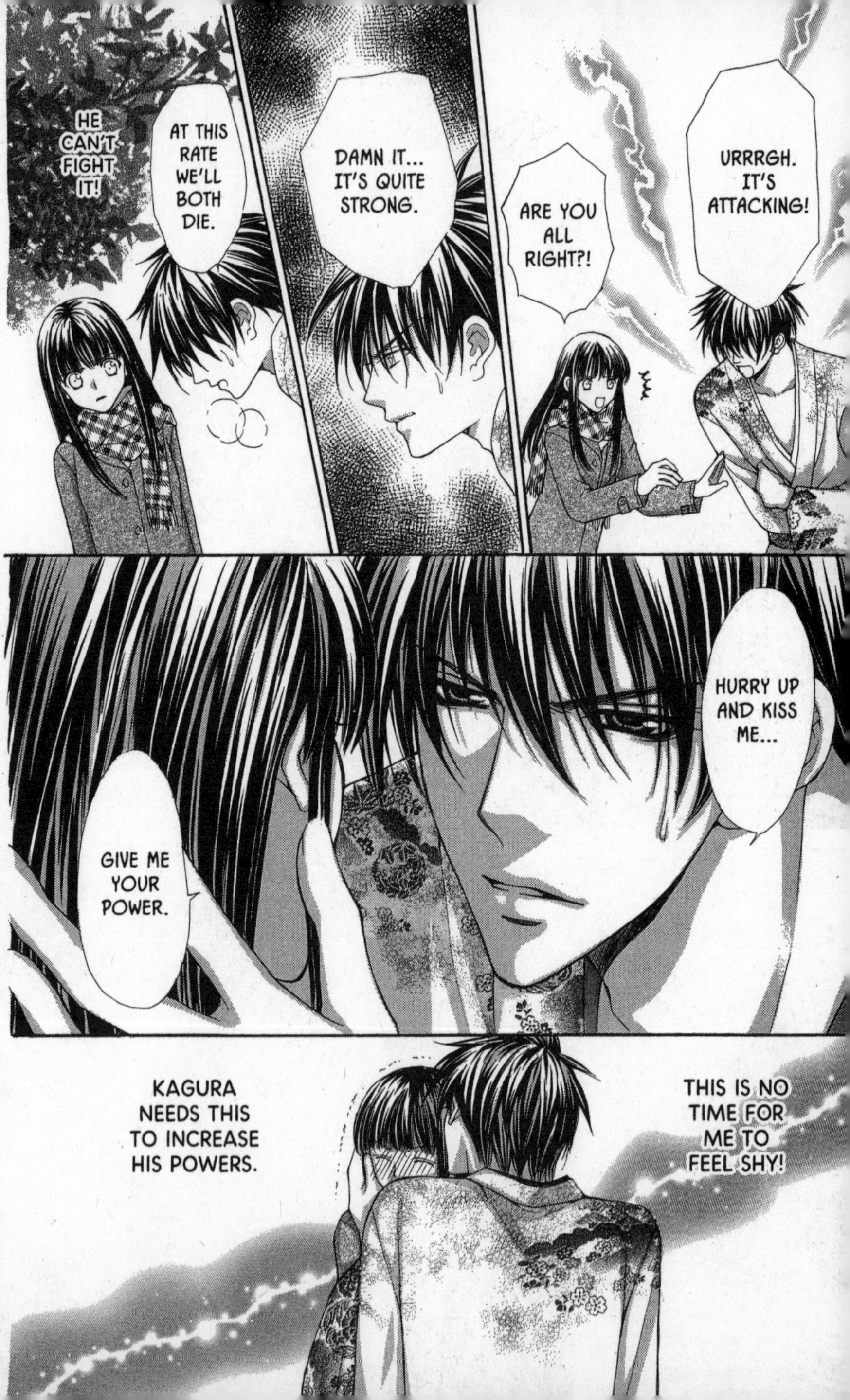
URRRGH. IT'S ATTACKING!
ARE YOU ALL RIGHT?!
DAMN IT... IT'S QUITE STRONG.
AT THIS RATE WE'LL BOTH DIE.
HE CAN'T FIGHT IT!
HURRY UP AND KISS ME...
GIVE ME YOUR POWER.
THIS IS NO TIME FOR ME TO FEEL SHY!
KAGURA NEEDS THIS TO INCREASE HIS POWERS.

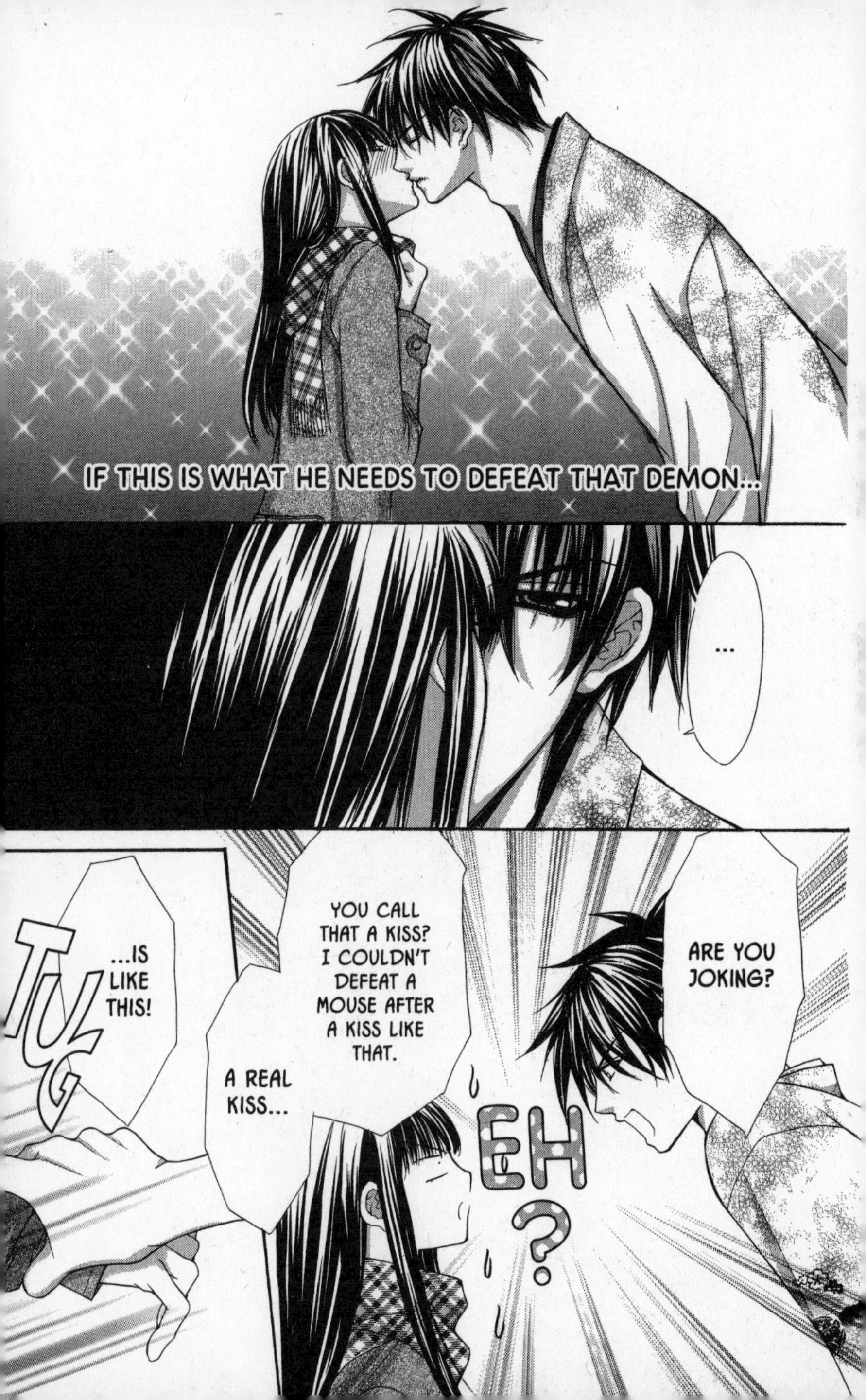
IF THIS IS WHAT HE NEEDS TO DEFEAT THAT DEMON...
...
ARE YOU JOKING?
YOU CALL THAT A KISS? I COULDN'T DEFEAT A MOUSE AFTER A KISS LIKE THAT.
EH?
A REAL KISS...
...IS LIKE THIS!
TUG

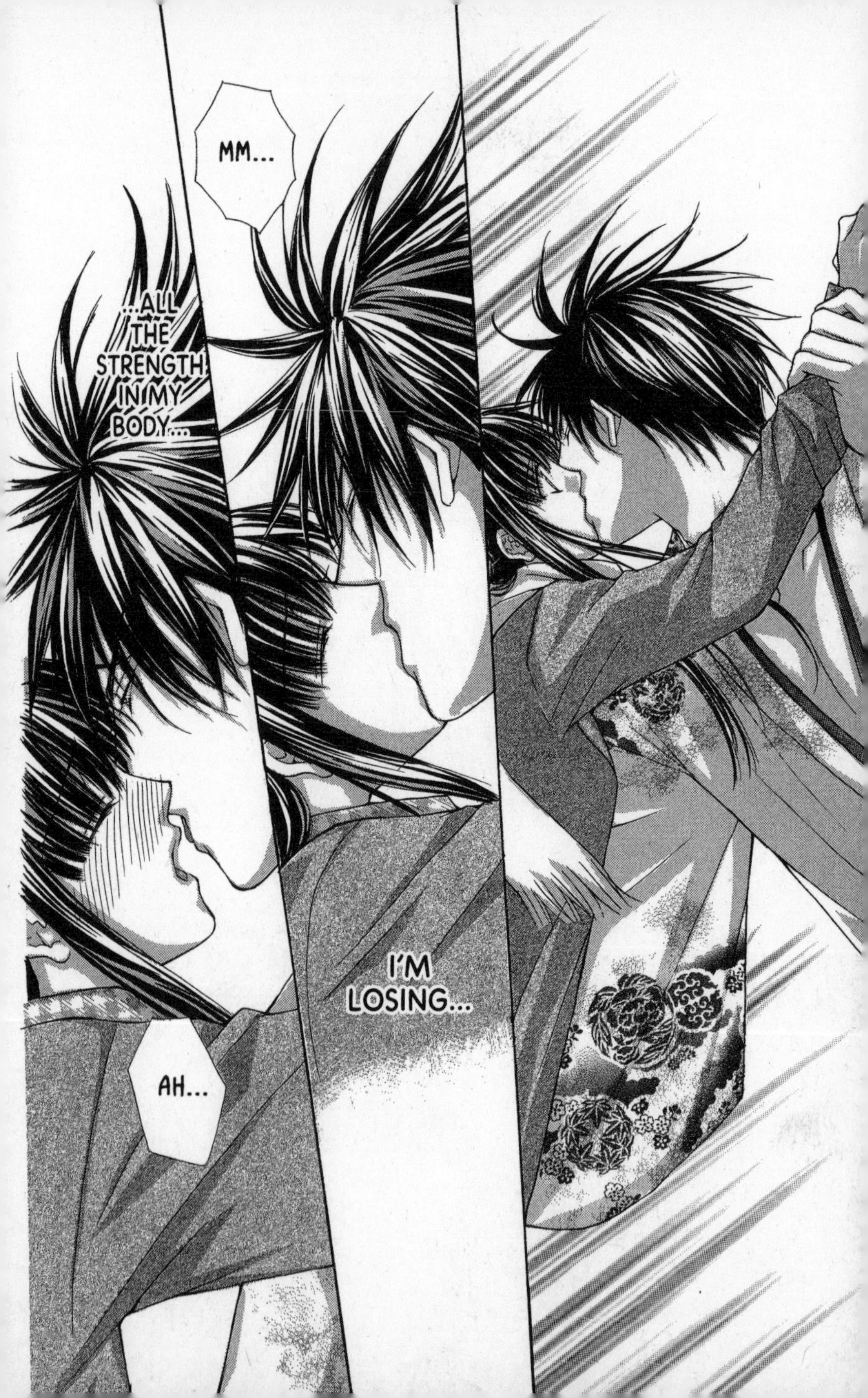
MM...
I'M LOSING...
...ALL THE STRENGTH IN MY BODY...
AH...

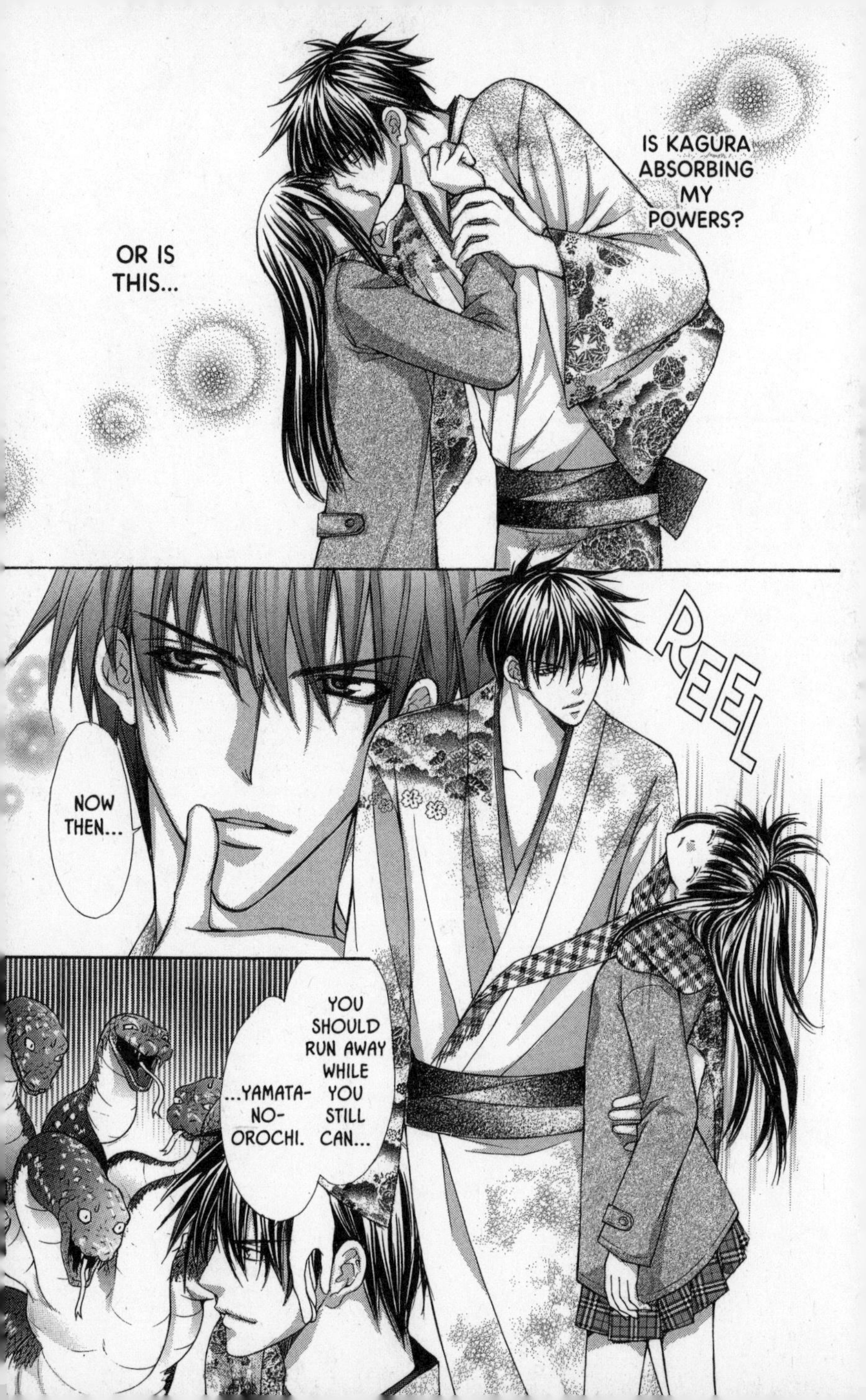
IS KAGURA ABSORBING MY POWERS?
OR IS THIS...
REEL
NOW THEN...
YOU SHOULD RUN AWAY WHILE YOU STILL CAN...
...YAMATA-NO-OROCHI.

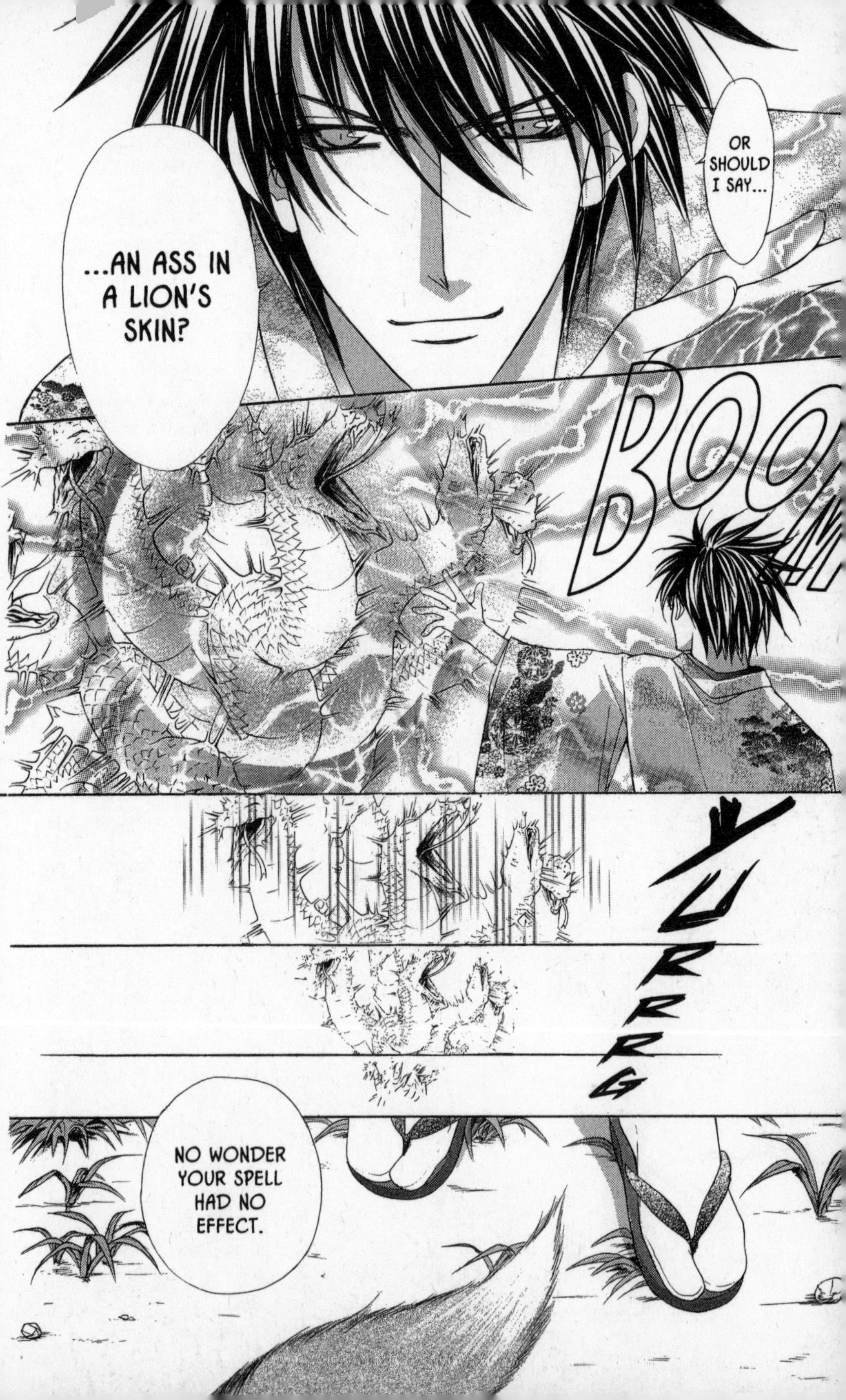
OR SHOULD I SAY...
...AN ASS IN A LION'S SKIN?
BOOM
YURRRRG
NO WONDER YOUR SPELL HAD NO EFFECT.

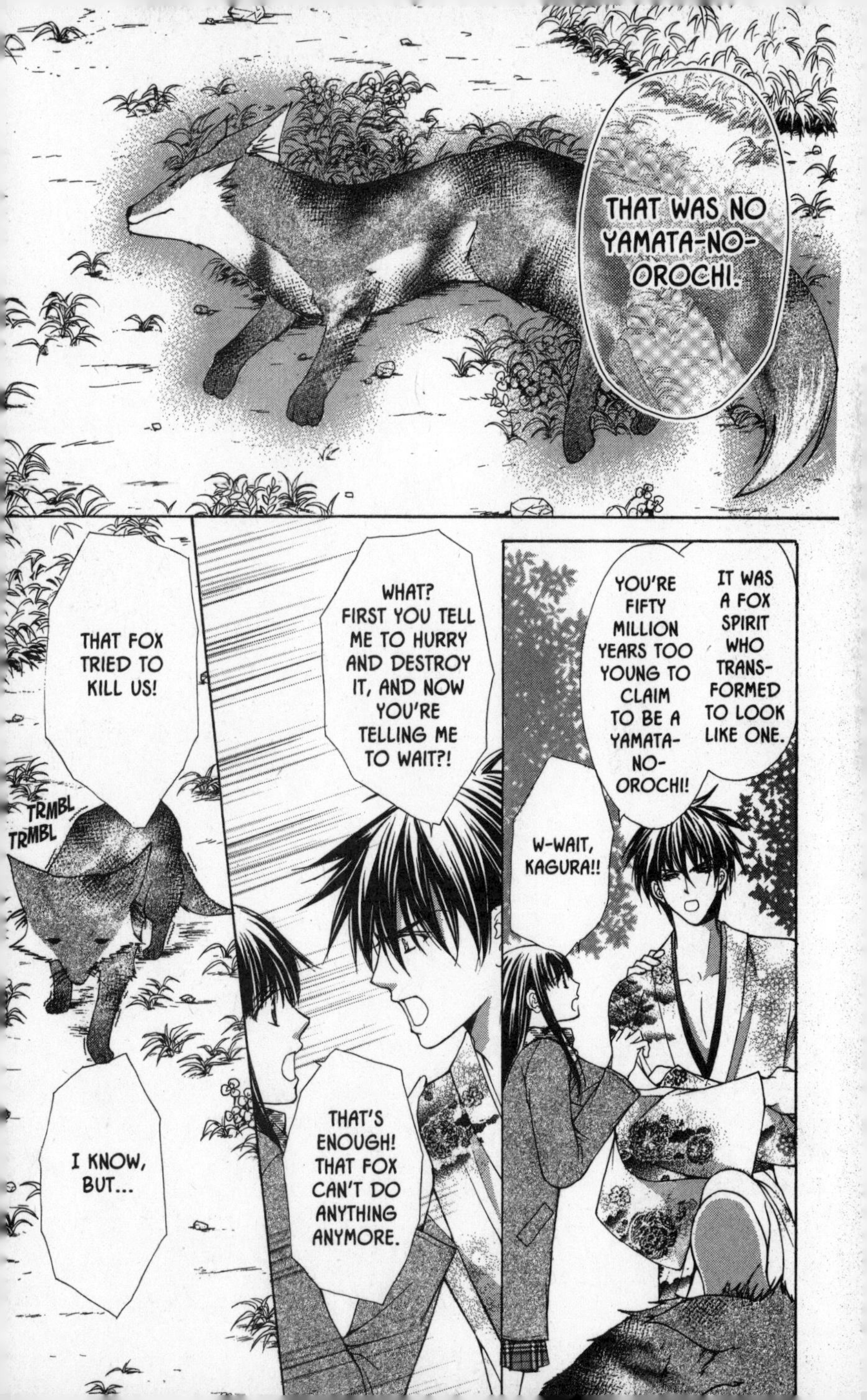
THAT WAS NO YAMATA-NO-OROCHI.
IT WAS A FOX SPIRIT WHO TRANSFORMED TO LOOK LIKE ONE.
YOU'RE FIFTY MILLION YEARS TOO YOUNG TO CLAIM TO BE A YAMATA-NO-OROCHI!
W-WAIT, KAGURA!!
WHAT? FIRST YOU TELL ME TO HURRY AND DESTROY IT, AND NOW YOU'RE TELLING ME TO WAIT?!
THAT'S ENOUGH! THAT FOX CAN'T DO ANYTHING ANYMORE.
THAT FOX TRIED TO KILL US!
TRMBL TRMBL
I KNOW, BUT...

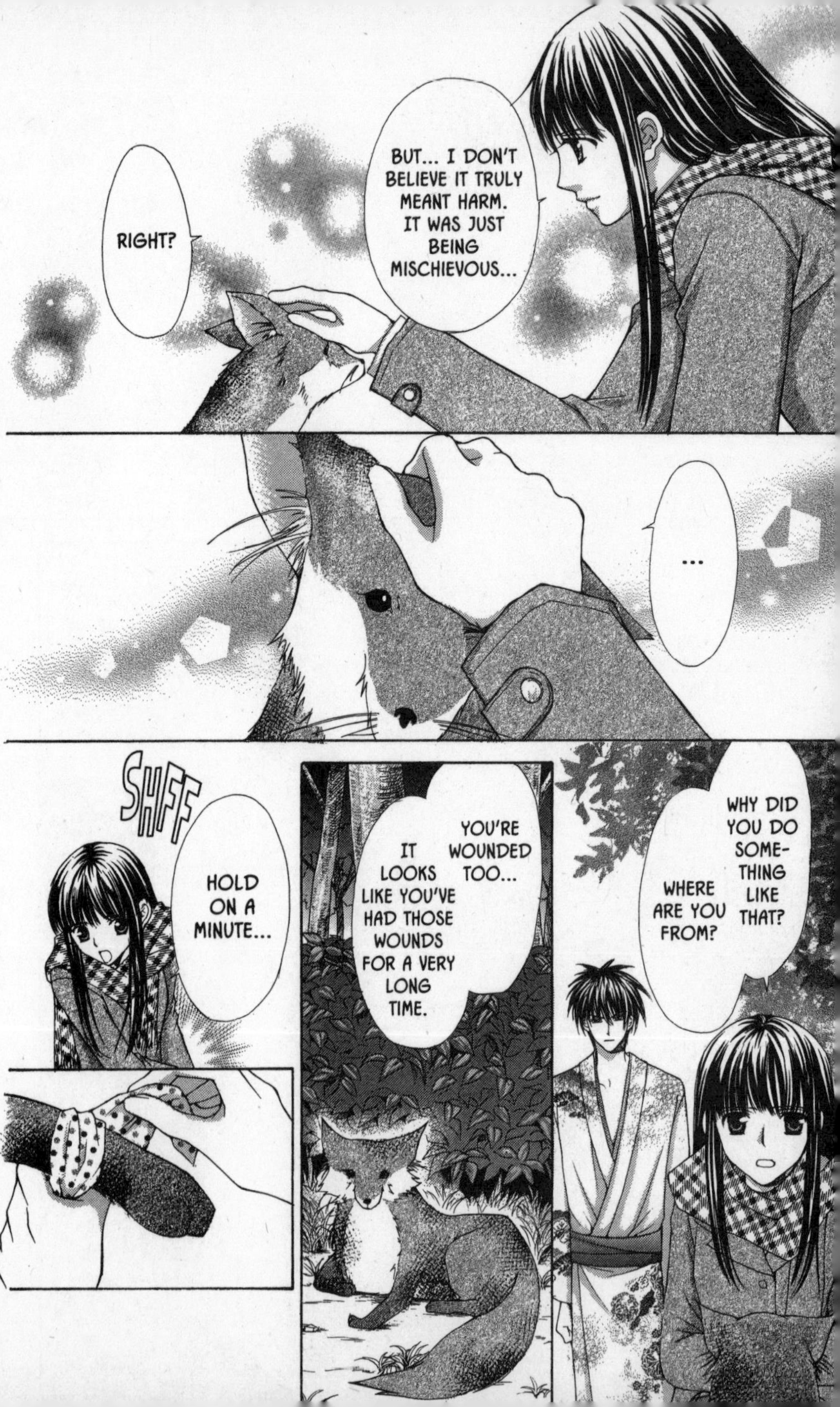
BUT... I DON'T BELIEVE IT TRULY MEANT HARM. IT WAS JUST BEING MISCHIEVOUS...
RIGHT?
...
WHY DID YOU DO SOME-THING LIKE THAT?
WHERE ARE YOU FROM?
YOU'RE WOUNDED TOO...
IT LOOKS LIKE YOU'VE HAD THOSE WOUNDS FOR A VERY LONG TIME.
SHFF
HOLD ON A MINUTE...

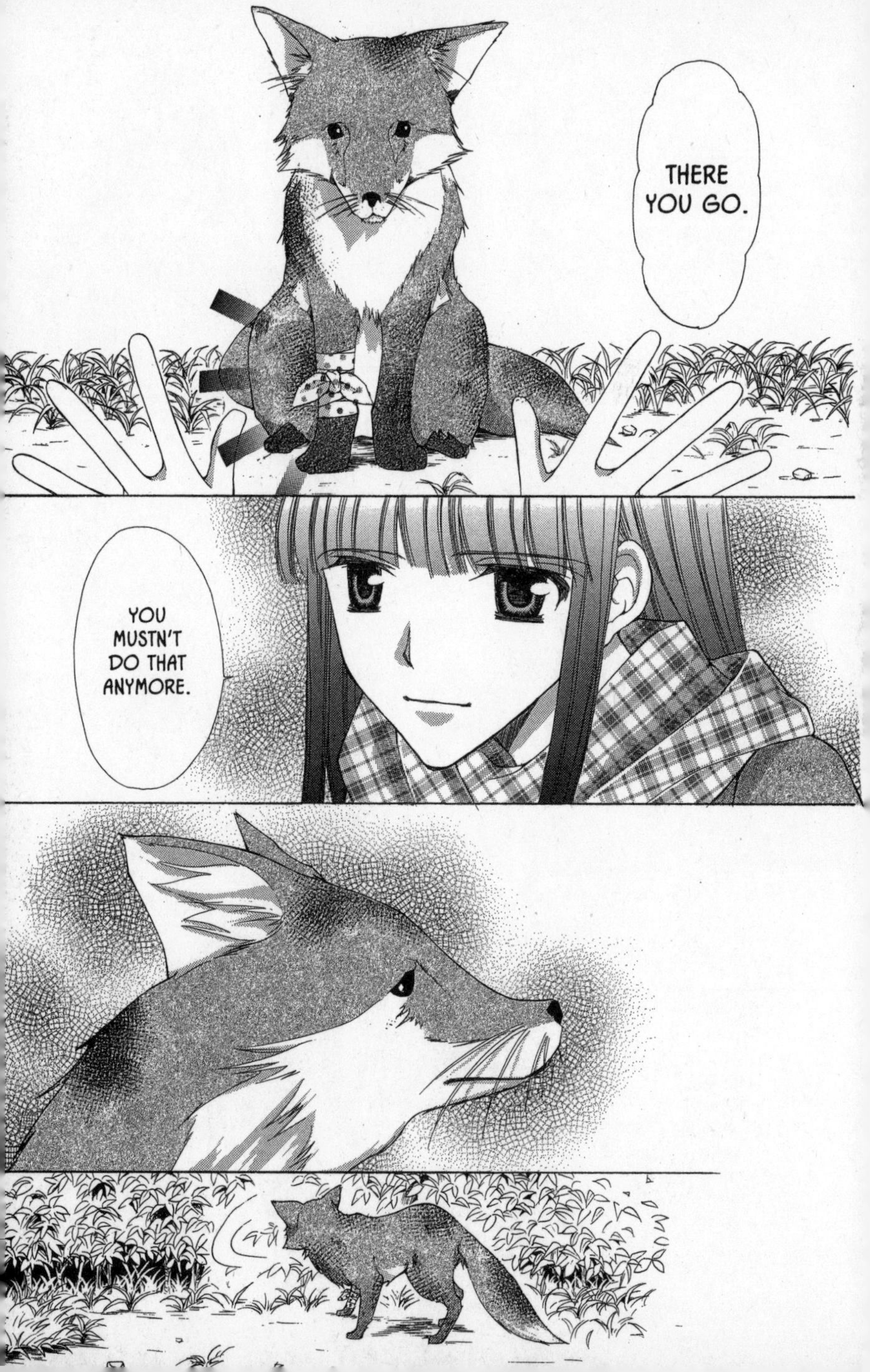
THERE YOU GO.
YOU MUSTN'T DO THAT ANYMORE.

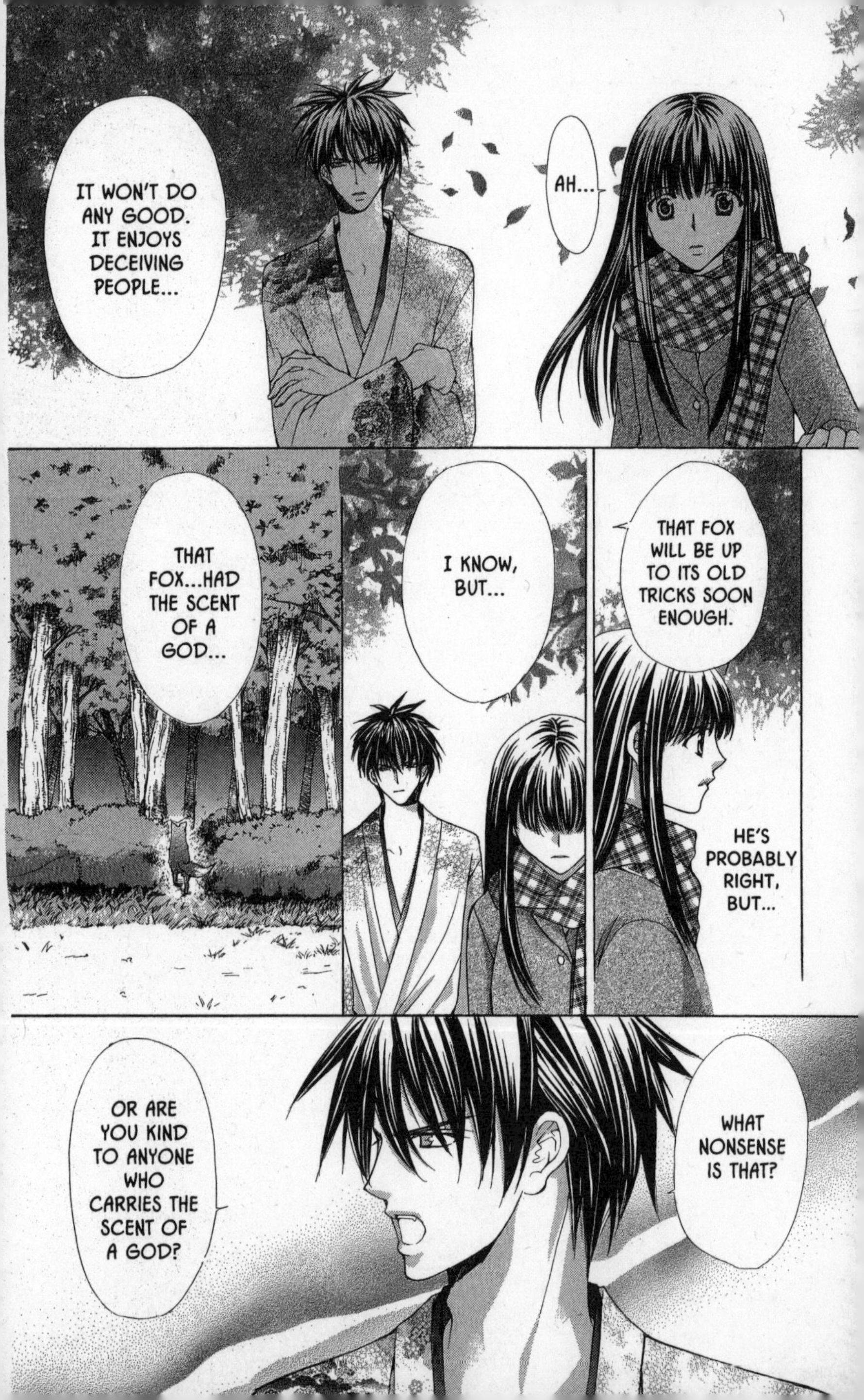
AH...
IT WON'T DO ANY GOOD. IT ENJOYS DECEIVING PEOPLE...
THAT FOX WILL BE UP TO ITS OLD TRICKS SOON ENOUGH.
HE'S PROBABLY RIGHT, BUT...
I KNOW, BUT...
THAT FOX...HAD THE SCENT OF A GOD...
WHAT NONSENSE IS THAT?
OR ARE YOU KIND TO ANYONE WHO CARRIES THE SCENT OF A GOD?

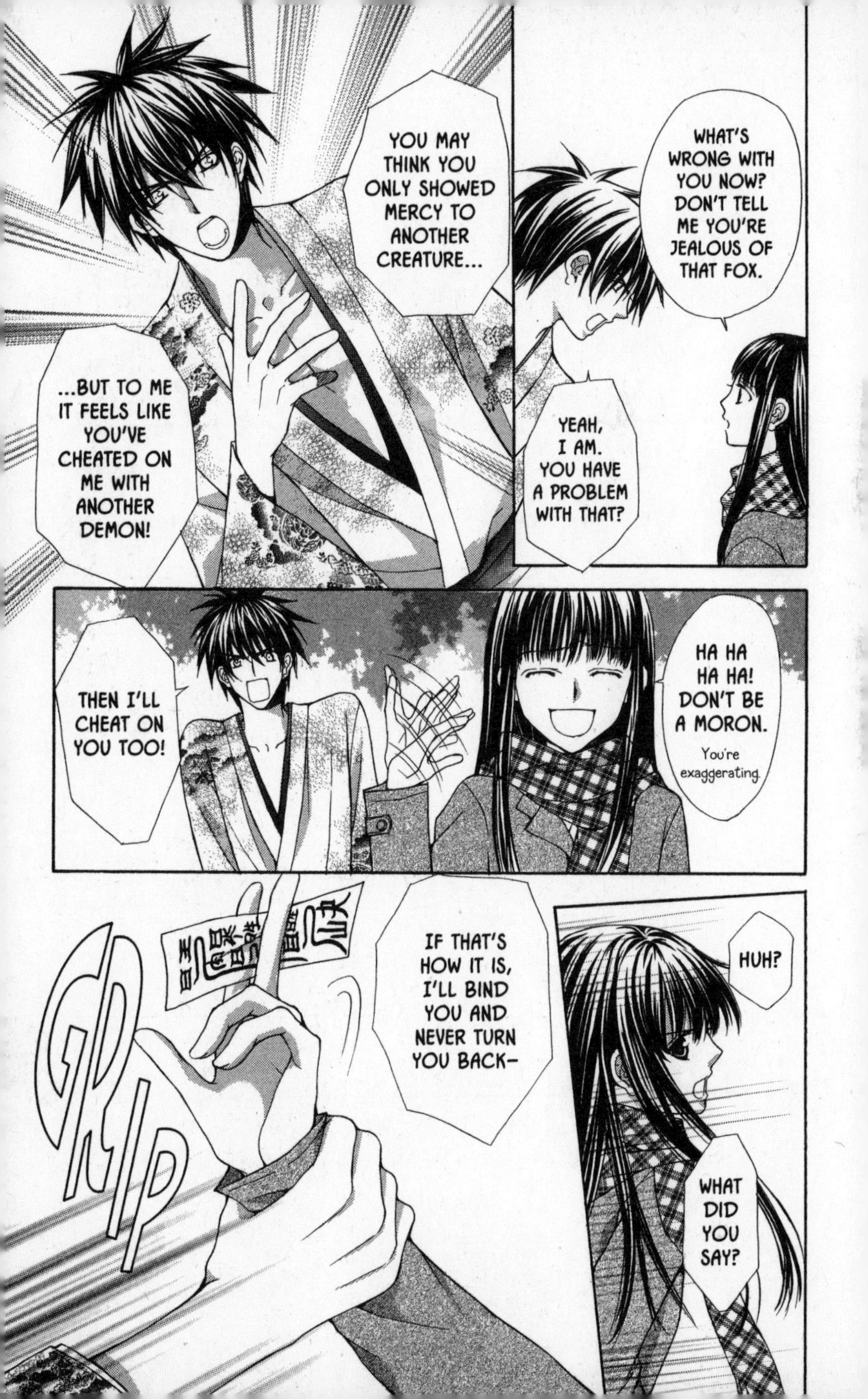
WHAT'S WRONG WITH YOU NOW? DON'T TELL ME YOU'RE JEALOUS OF THAT FOX.
YEAH, I AM. YOU HAVE A PROBLEM WITH THAT?
YOU MAY THINK YOU ONLY SHOWED MERCY TO ANOTHER CREATURE...
...BUT TO ME IT FEELS LIKE YOU'VE CHEATED ON ME WITH ANOTHER DEMON!
HA HA HA HA! DON'T BE A MORON.
You're exaggerating.
THEN I'LL CHEAT ON YOU TOO!
HUH?
WHAT DID YOU SAY?
IF THAT'S HOW IT IS, I'LL BIND YOU AND NEVER TURN YOU BACK-
GRIP

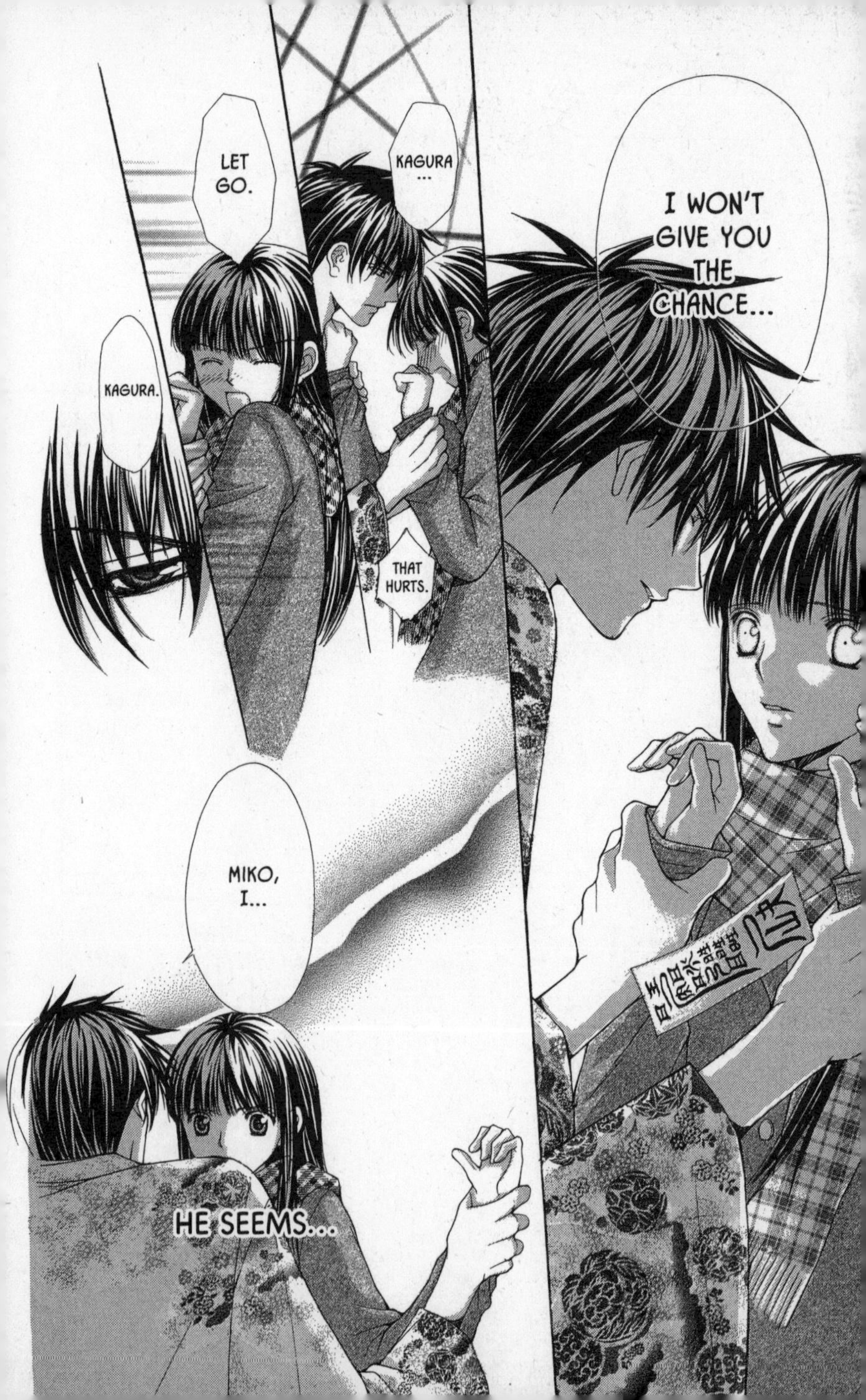
I WON'T GIVE YOU THE CHANCE...
KAGURA ...
THAT HURTS.
LET GO.
KAGURA.
MIKO, I...
HE SEEMS...

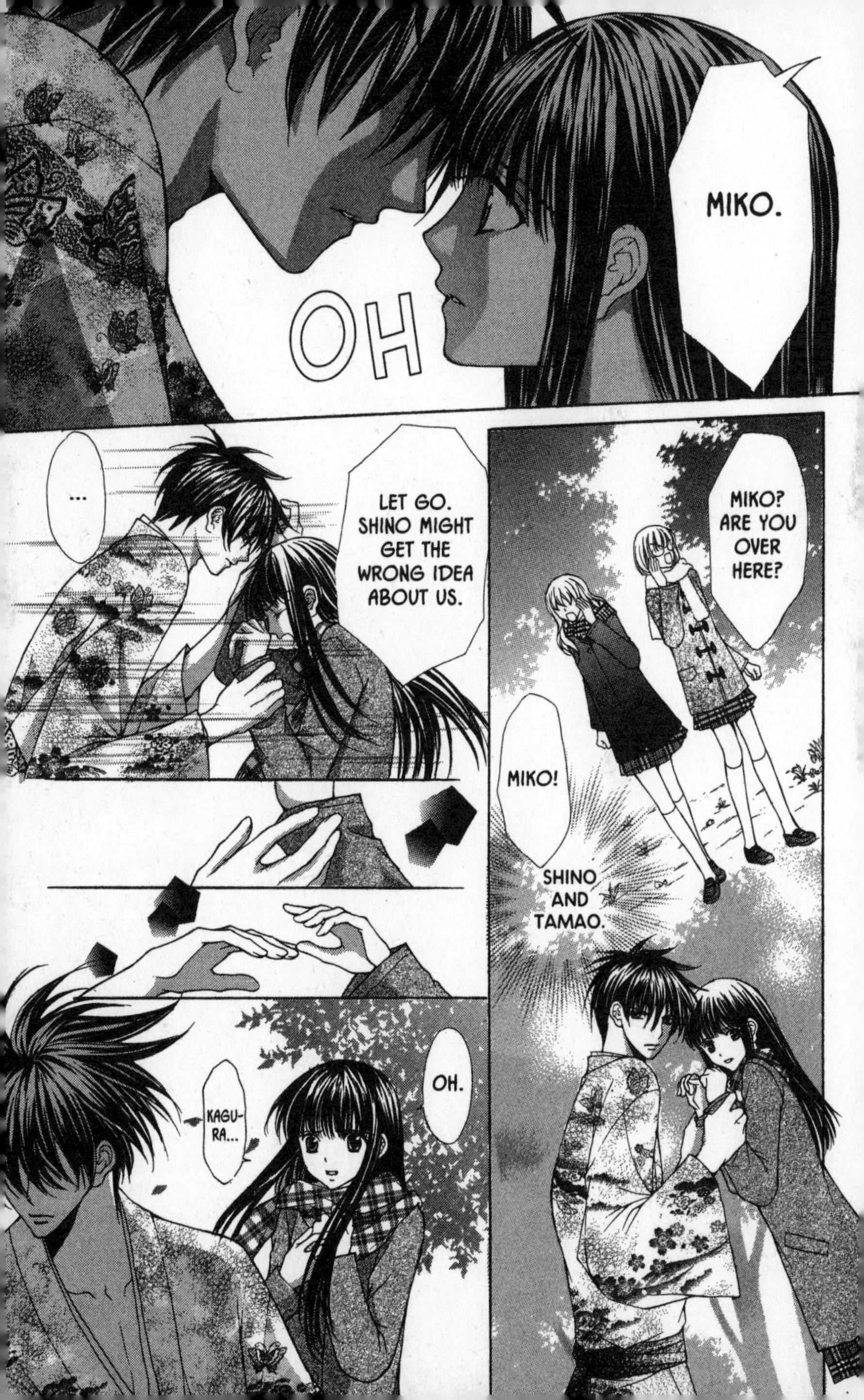

MIKO.
OH
MIKO? ARE YOU OVER HERE?
MIKO!
SHINO AND TAMAO.
LET GO. SHINO MIGHT GET THE WRONG IDEA ABOUT US.
...
OH.
KAGU-RA...

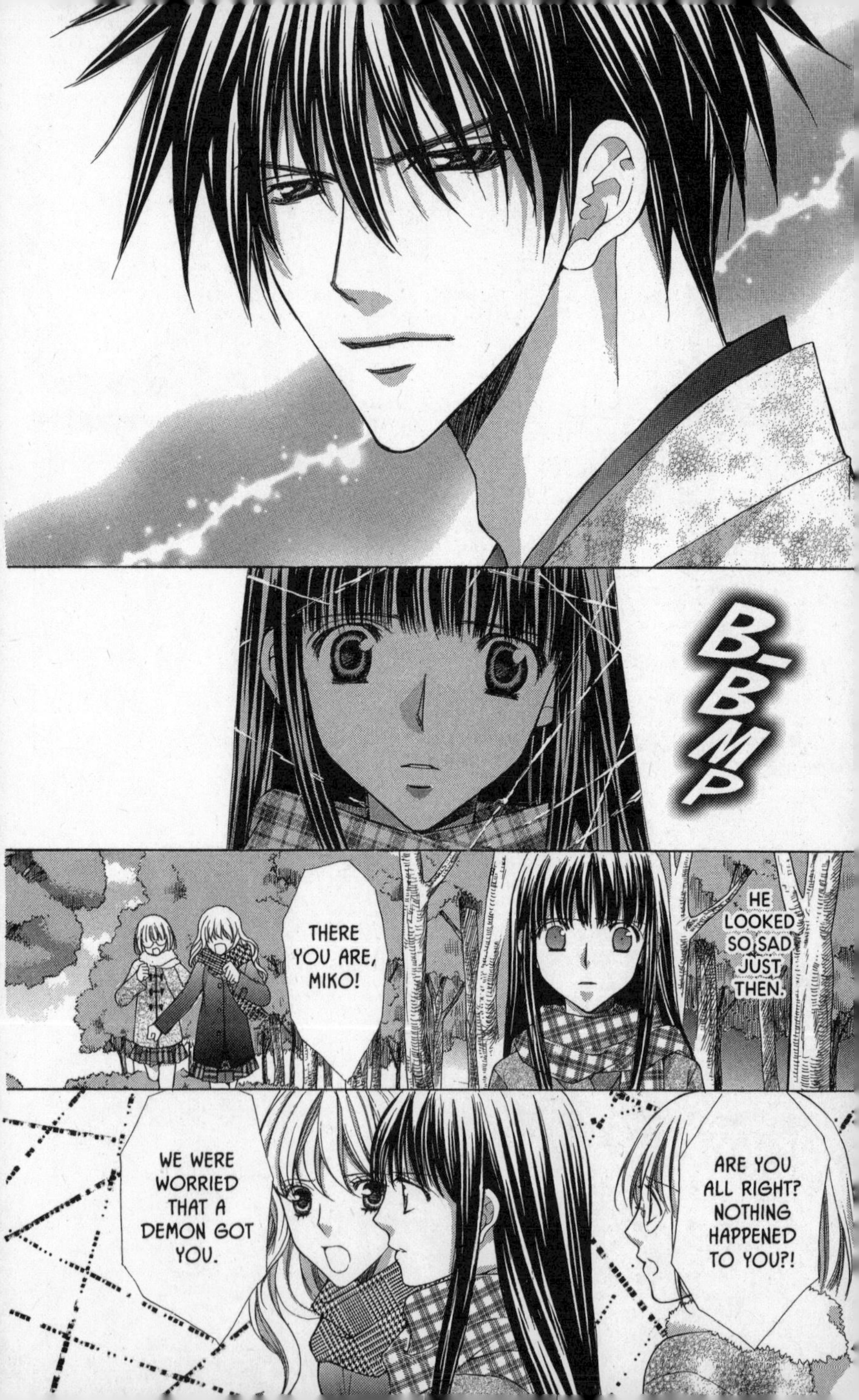
B-BMP
HE LOOKED SO SAD JUST THEN.
THERE YOU ARE, MIKO!
ARE YOU ALL RIGHT? NOTHING HAPPENED TO YOU?!
WE WERE WORRIED THAT A DEMON GOT YOU.

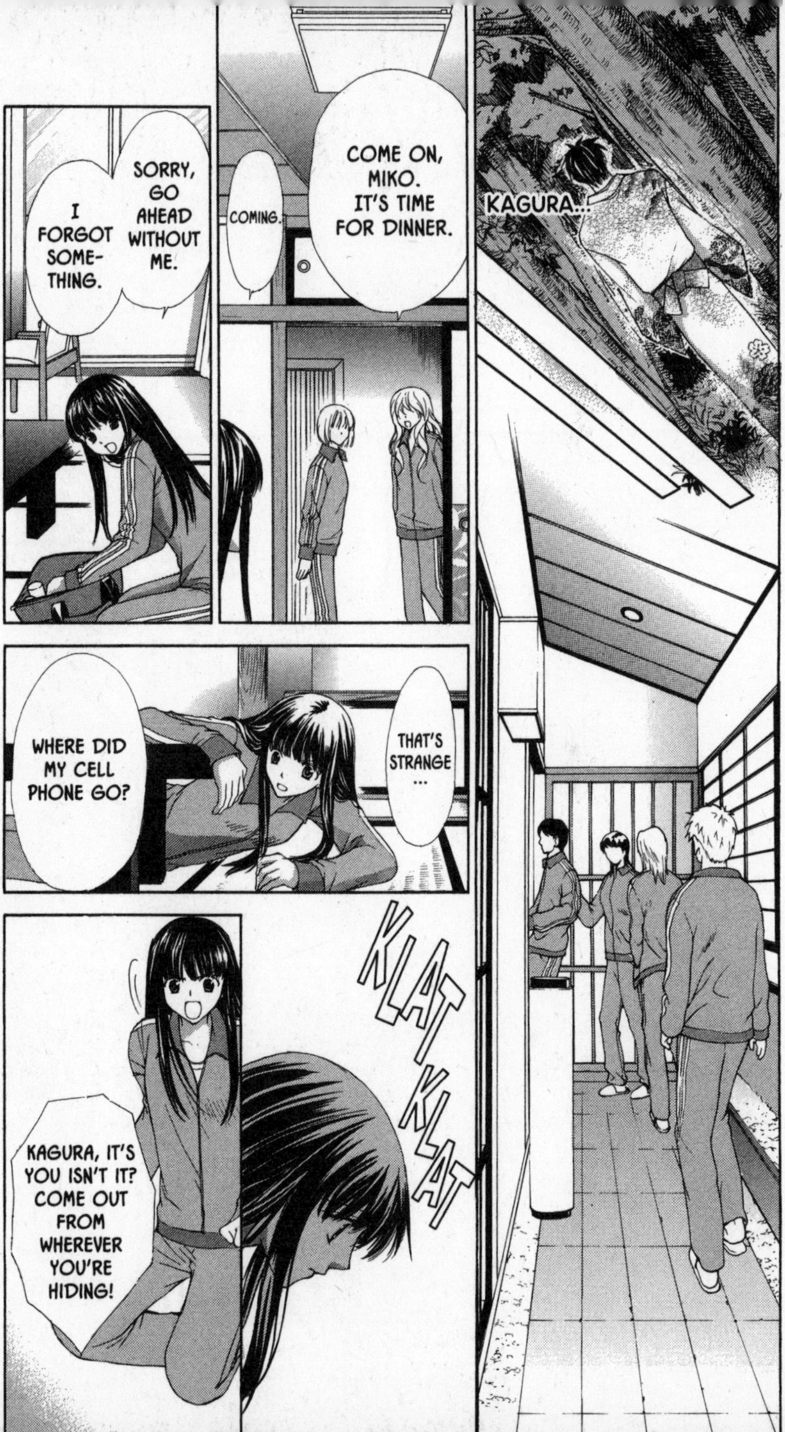
KAGURA...
KLAT KLAT KLAT
COME ON, MIKO. IT'S TIME FOR DINNER.
COMING.
SORRY, GO AHEAD WITHOUT ME.
I FORGOT SOME-THING.
THAT'S STRANGE...
WHERE DID MY CELL PHONE GO?
KAGURA, IT'S YOU ISN'T IT? COME OUT FROM WHEREVER YOU'RE HIDING!

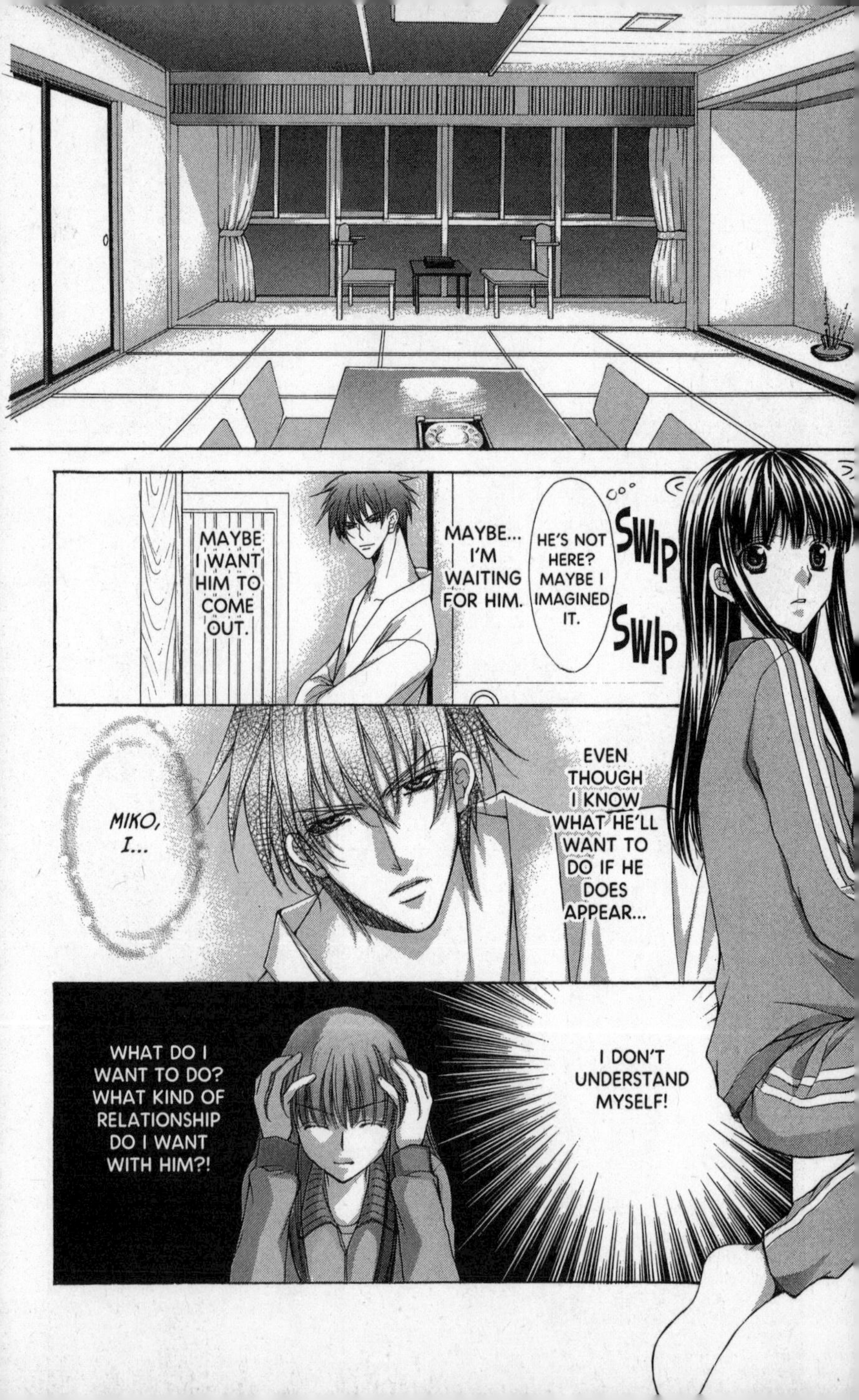
SWIP
SWIP
HE'S NOT HERE? MAYBE I IMAGINED IT.
MAYBE... I'M WAITING FOR HIM.
MAYBE I WANT HIM TO COME OUT.
EVEN THOUGH I KNOW WHAT HE'LL WANT TO DO IF HE DOES APPEAR...
MIKO, I...
I DON'T UNDERSTAND MYSELF!
WHAT DO I WANT TO DO? WHAT KIND OF RELATIONSHIP DO I WANT WITH HIM?!

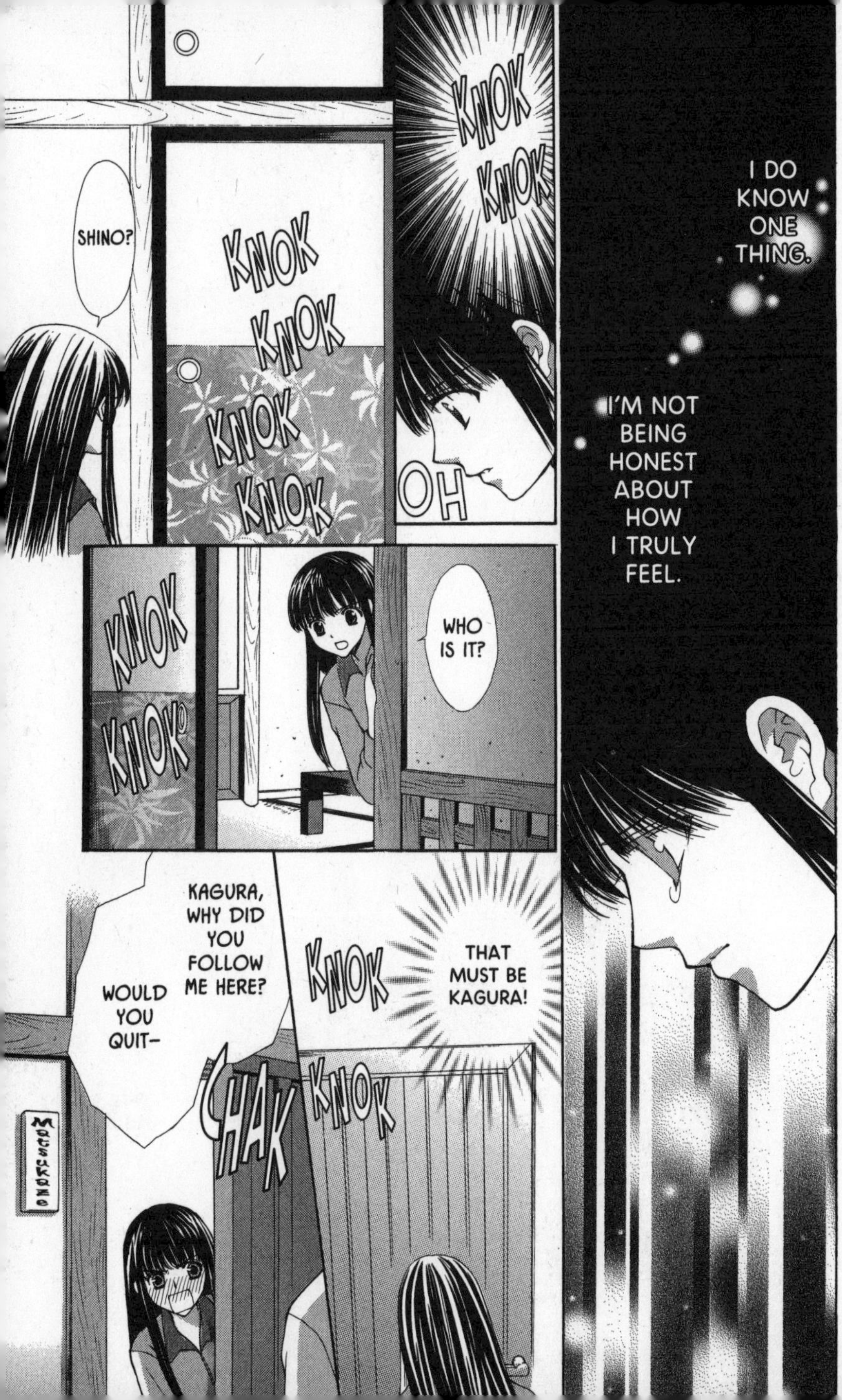
I DO KNOW ONE THING.
I'M NOT BEING HONEST ABOUT HOW I TRULY FEEL.
KNOK KNOK
OH
SHINO?
KNOK KNOK KNOK KNOK
KNOK KNOK
WHO IS IT?
THAT MUST BE KAGURA!
KNOK
KAGURA, WHY DID YOU FOLLOW ME HERE?
WOULD YOU QUIT–
KNOK
CHAK

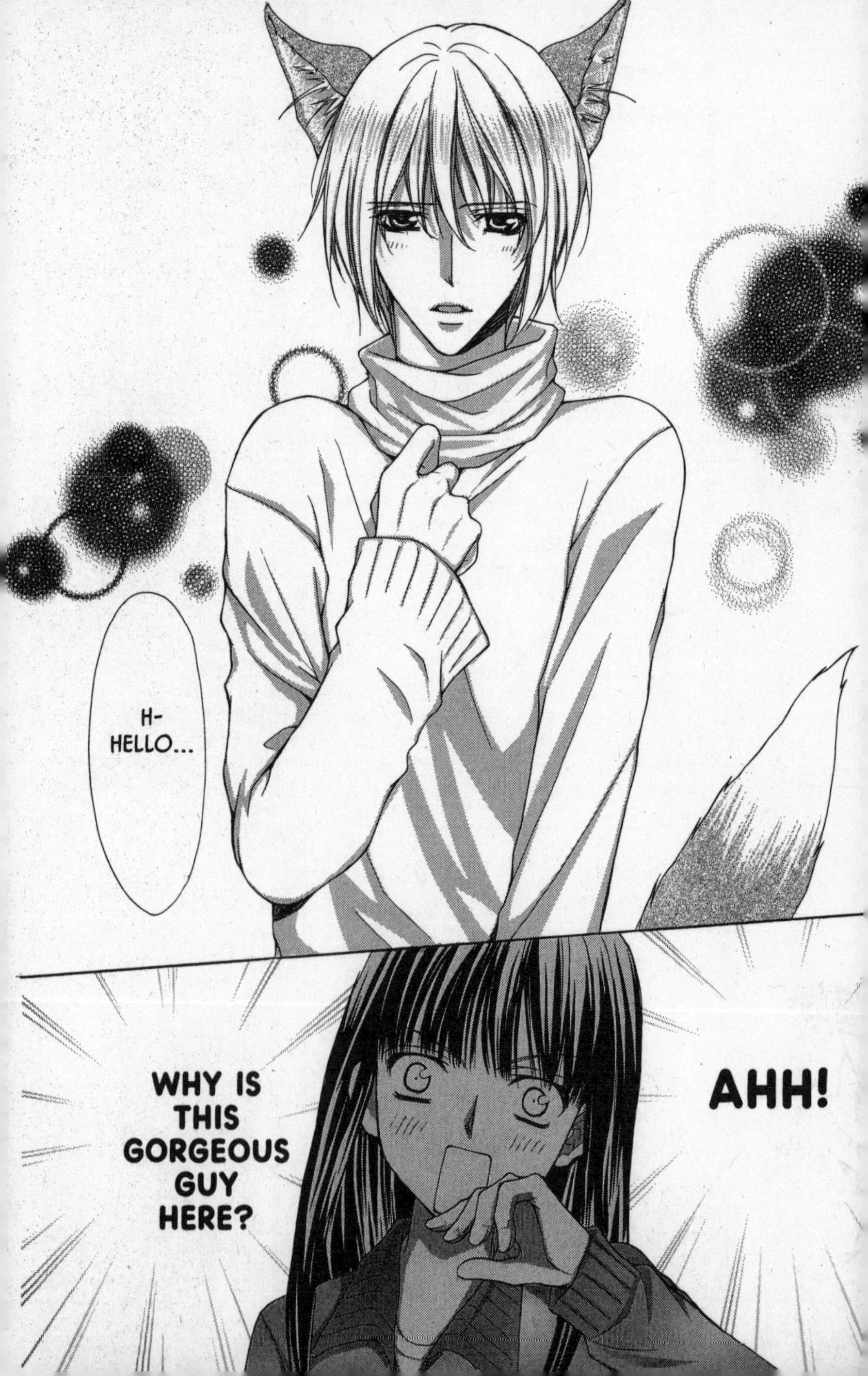
H-
HELLO...
AHH!
WHY IS THIS GORGEOUS GUY HERE?

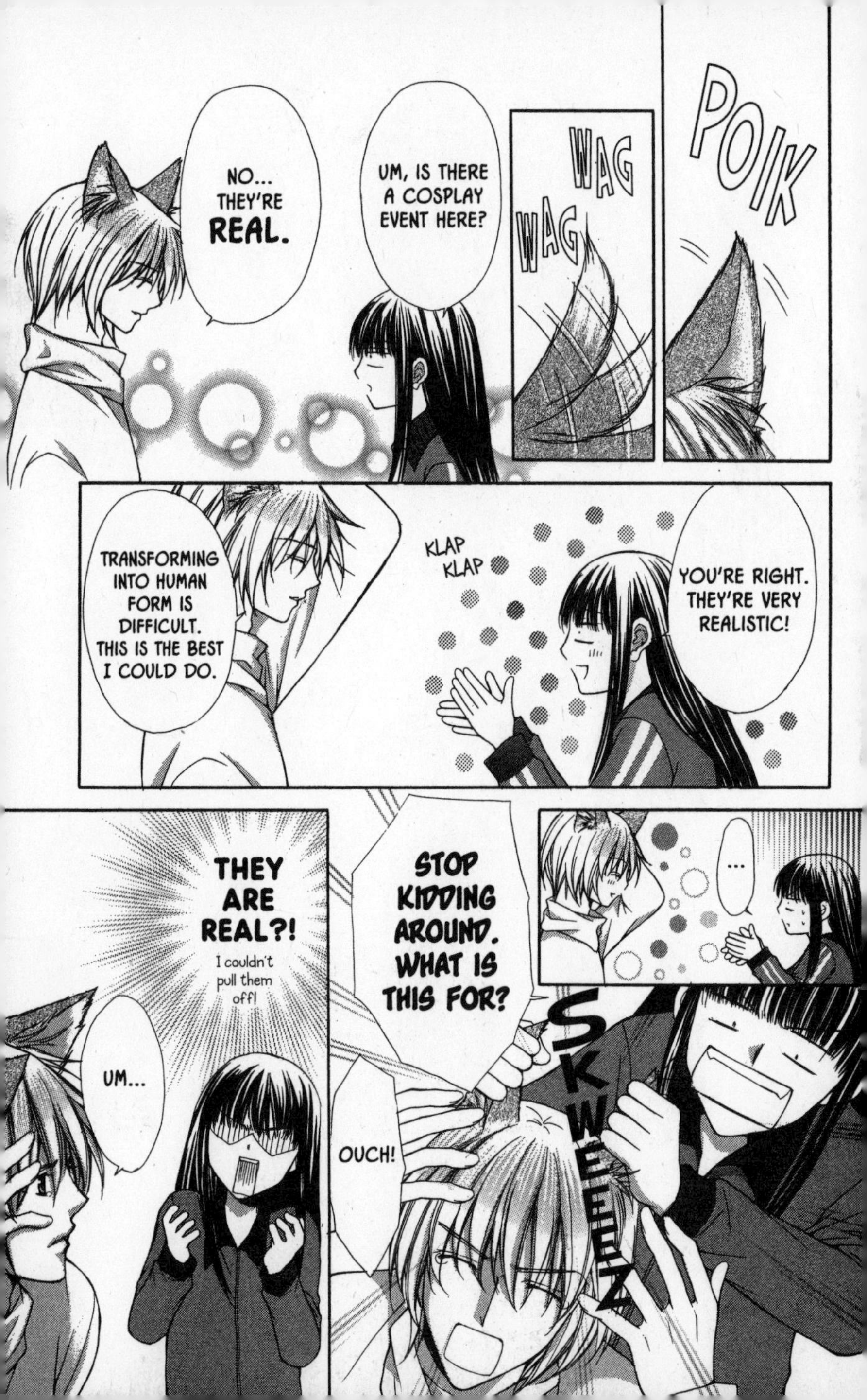
POIK
WAG WAG
UM, IS THERE A COSPLAY EVENT HERE?
NO... THEY'RE **REAL.**
YOU'RE RIGHT. THEY'RE VERY REALISTIC!
KLAP KLAP
TRANSFORMING INTO HUMAN FORM IS DIFFICULT. THIS IS THE BEST I COULD DO.
...
SKWEEEZ
STOP KIDDING AROUND. WHAT IS THIS FOR?
OUCH!
THEY ARE REAL?!
I couldn't pull them off!
UM...

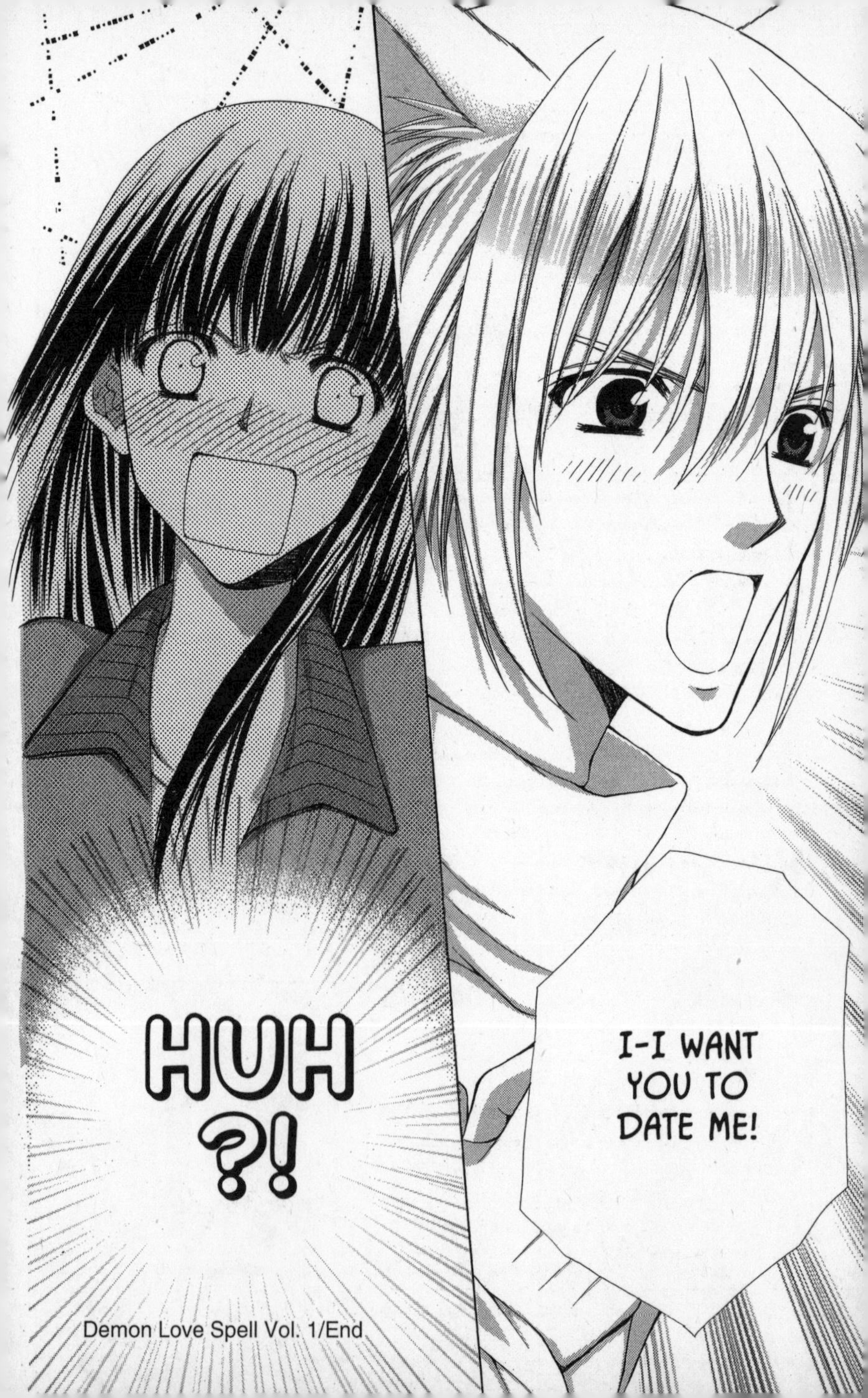
I-I WANT YOU TO DATE ME!
HUH ?!
Demon Love Spell Vol. 1/End

VOMIC RECORDING REPORT!!

The recording session for the Vomic of *Demon Love Spell* was held on a certain day in April at a certain place in Tokyo! Vomic stands for "Voice Comic" and voice actors dub their voices while panels of manga are displayed. You can take a look at chapters 1 through 3 at the Shueisha homepage.

Here ↓

http://www.s-cast.net/

Here is the cast!

Miko: Saori Hayami

Kagura: Kazuya Nakai

Mini-Kagura: Koki Miyata

And so, I would like to do a quick report of that recording session.

Kazuya Nakai, playing the role of Kagura, is known for other roles like Zolo in *One Piece*, Hijikata in *Gin Tama*, Masamune in *Sengoku Basara*, and other characters that girls adore. Koki Miyata, in the role of chibi Kagura, is famous for Murata in *Kyo Kara Maoh!*, Hanataro in *Bleach*, Nataku in *Hoshin Engi*, and he has played other cute and cool characters using his miraculous voice. He also received an award at the first Seiyu Awards ceremony for Best Supporting Actor. To be honest, I couldn't have thought of a better cast for Kagura than these two. I would like to show my gratitude to the people who brought this wonderful cast together! I've written about the recording session on my blog so please read about the details there... I would like to secretly (I guess I'm not doing it very secretly...) tell you about our conversations. After the recording, I had the opportunity to talk to them. I am a huge fan of Nakai and Miyata and have all the drama CDs they have taken part in. To be more exact, I have all of their character songs as well, and I love to hear Miyata sing. So I told them, "I can't sing Nakai's songs unless I raise the pitch by four notches." Miyata then asked me, "Which songs?" When I mentioned song likes "Eyes of Zolo," Nakai responded with an "Aaaaaah" and seemed unsettled. I quickly added, "And the character songs for Switch, which made it into the karaoke machine recently..." He started fidgeting like he was embarrassed and moaned "Ooooh!" H-How cute of him... (laugh) I wonder if I would have been able to make both Miyata and Nakai squirm in embarrassment if I had asked, "Will the song you two were singing in the school entrance ceremony of Pink Kitten ever come out on CD?" Eh... I'm sorry for the very otaku subject matter. I also told them I can sing Miyata's songs without raising the pitch. Miyata asked me, "Which song do you sing?" I replied, "I can sing all your songs because I have them all, but I especially like 'Mille-Feuille Dream'." He simply replied "Ah!!" and didn't seem embarrassed, as if he understood what I meant. They were both very nice people, and I was touched at how caring they were because I was so nervous about meeting them. I'm going to work hard so I can meet them again!!

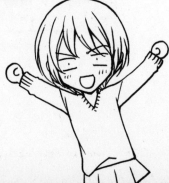

This started as a two-chapter story for the magazine. The *Margaret* editorial office asked me if I wanted to make it into a series, and I immediately accepted. But now that I'm working on it, I'm having a hard time coming up with ideas for the story. But I'll keep at it with all the love and moe I've got!

—Mayu Shinjo

MAYU SHINJO was born on January 26. She is a prolific writer of shojo manga, including the series *Sensual Phrase*. Her current series include *Ai Ore!* and *Demon Love Spell*. Her hobbies are cars, shopping and taking baths. Shinjo likes The Prodigy, Nirvana, U2 and Masaharu Fukuyama.

Demon Love Spell

Vol. 1
Shojo Beat Edition

STORY AND ART BY *Mayu Shinjo*

Translation & Adaptation
Tetsuichiro Miyaki

Touch-up Art & Lettering
Inori Fukuda Trant

Design
Fawn Lau

Editor
Nancy Thistlethwaite

AYAKASHI KOI EMAKI © 2008 by Mayu Shinjo
All rights reserved.
First published in Japan in 2008 by SHUEISHA Inc., Tokyo.
English translation rights arranged by SHUEISHA Inc.

Printed in the U.S.A.

Published by VIZ Media, LLC
P.O. Box 77010
San Francisco, CA 94107

10 9 8 7 6 5 4
First printing, December 2012
Fourth printing, December 2017

www.viz.com

www.shojobeat.com

You may be reading the wrong way!

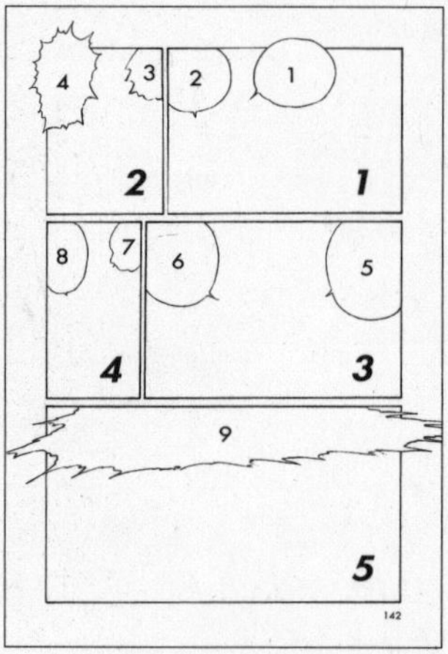

IT'S TRUE: In keeping with the original Japanese comic format, this book reads from right to left—so action, sound effects, and word balloons are completely reversed. This preserves the orientation of the original artwork—plus, it's fun! Check out the diagram shown here to get the hang of things, and then turn to the other side of the book to get started!

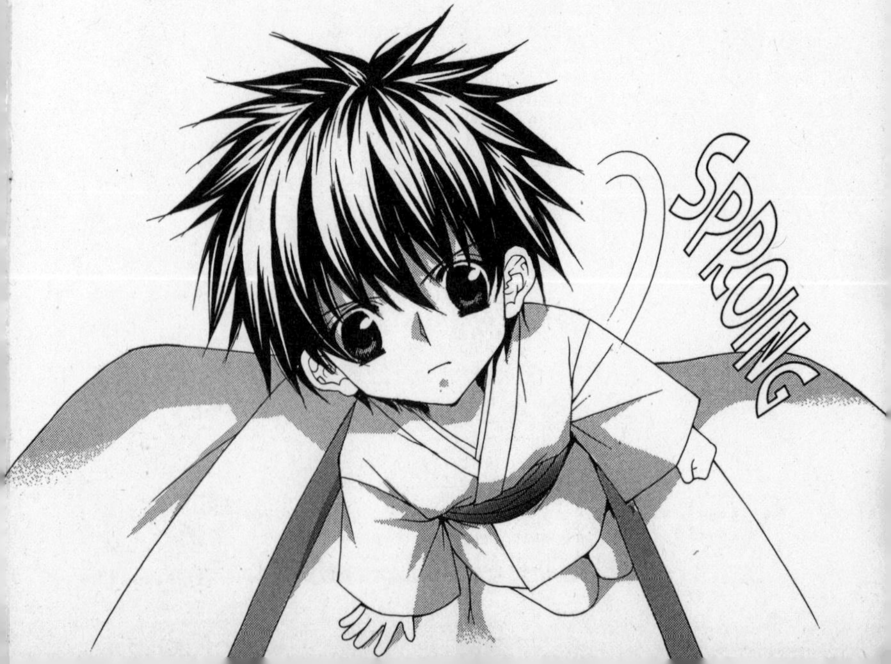
SPROING